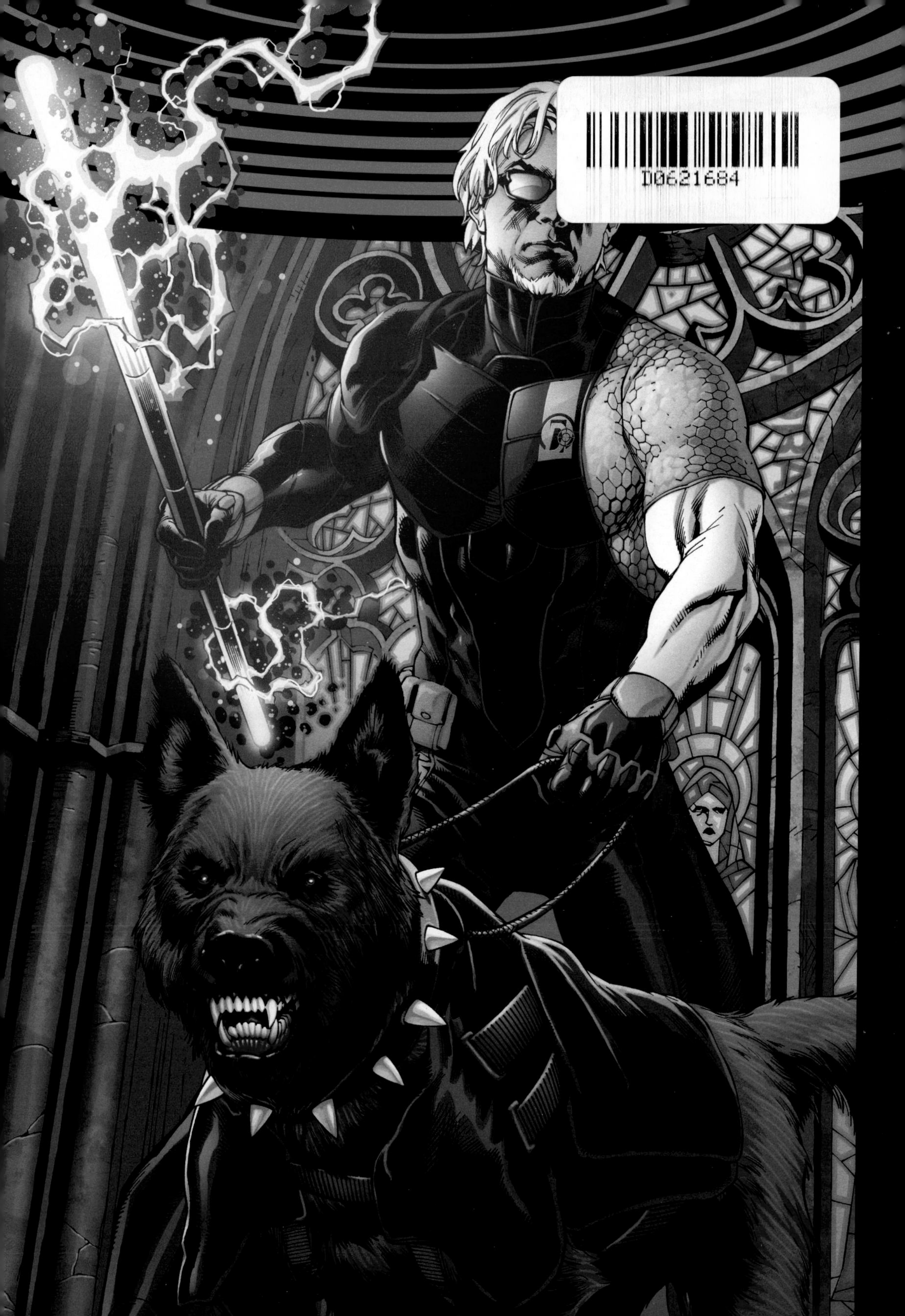



# DEATHSTROKE

## VOL.3 TWILIGHT

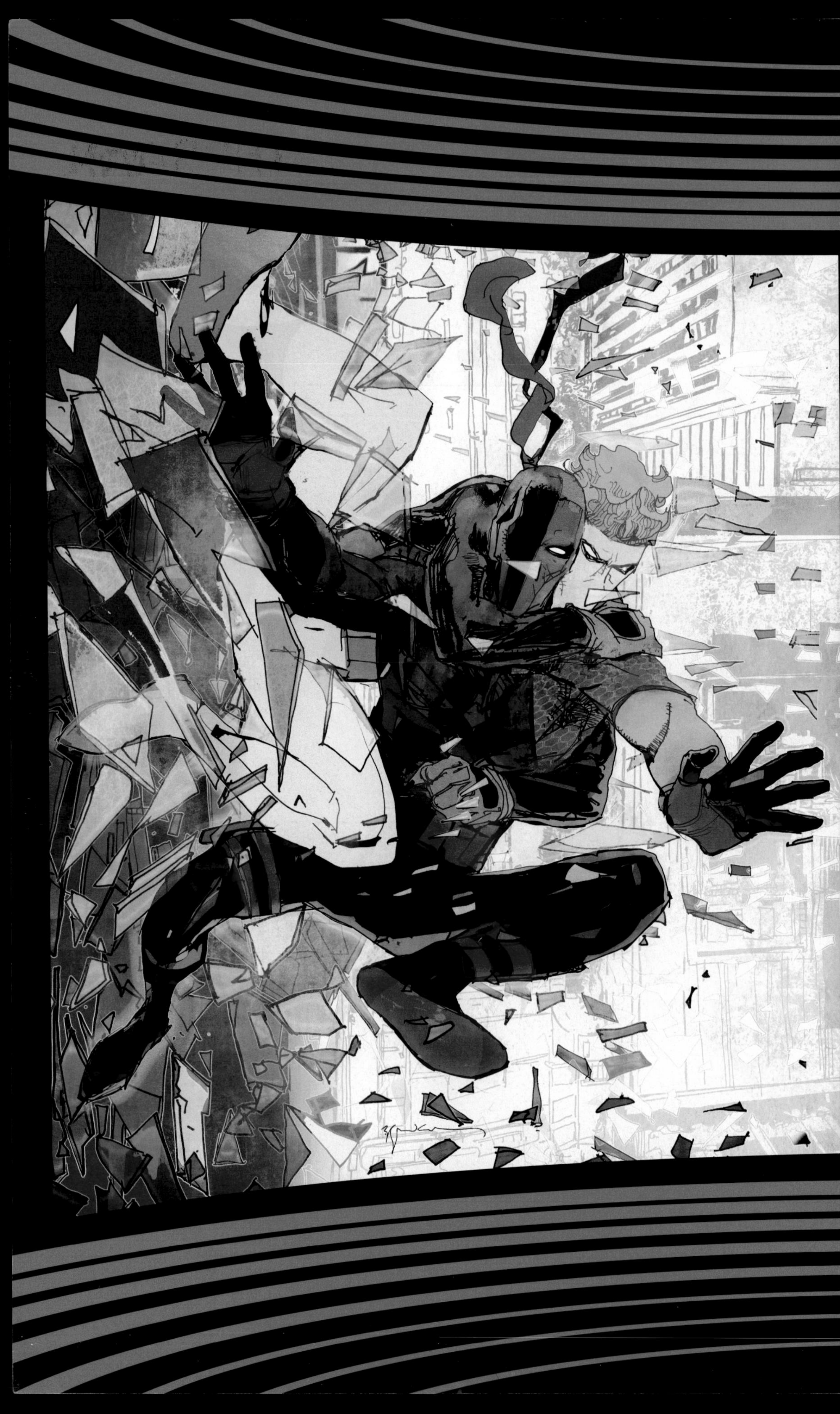

# DEATHSTROKE
## VOL.3 TWILIGHT

**CHRISTOPHER PRIEST**
writer

**LARRY HAMA**
breakdowns

**JOE BENNETT** * **CARLO PAGULAYAN** * **ROBERTO J. VIACAVA**
pencillers

**MARK MORALES** * **NORM RAPMUND**
**JASON PAZ** * **SEAN PARSONS**
inkers

**JEROMY COX**
colorist

**WILLIE SCHUBERT**
letterer

**BILL SIENKIEWICZ**
collection cover artist

DEATHSTROKE created by Marv Wolfman and George Pérez.
JERICHO created by Marv Wolfman and George Pérez.

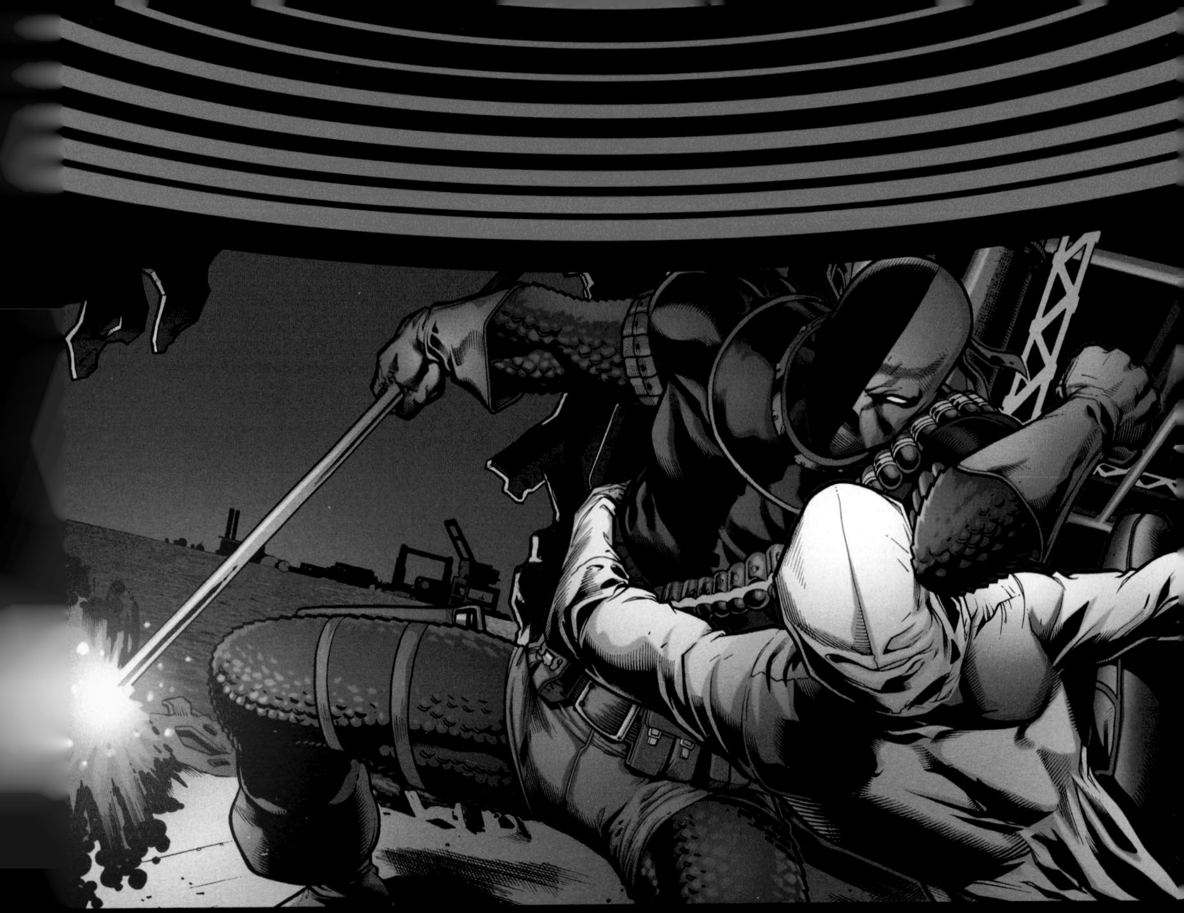

**ALEX ANTONE** Editor - Original Series * **BRITTANY HOLZHERR DIEGO LOPEZ** Assistant Editors - Original Series
**JEB WOODARD** Group Editor - Collected Editions * **LIZ ERICKSON** Editor - Collected Edition
**STEVE COOK** Design Director - Books * **MONIQUE GRUSPE** Publication Design

**BOB HARRAS** Senior VP - Editor-in-Chief, DC Comics

**DIANE NELSON** President * **DAN DiDIO** Publisher * **JIM LEE** Publisher * **GEOFF JOHNS** President & Chief Creative Officer
**AMIT DESAI** Executive VP - Business & Marketing Strategy, Direct to Consumer & Global Franchise Management * **SAM ADES** Senior VP - Direct to Consumer
**BOBBIE CHASE** VP - Talent Development * **MARK CHIARELLO** Senior VP - Art, Design & Collected Editions
**JOHN CUNNINGHAM** Senior VP - Sales & Trade Marketing * **ANNE DePIES** Senior VP - Business Strategy, Finance & Administration
**DON FALLETTI** VP - Manufacturing Operations * **LAWRENCE GANEM** VP - Editorial Administration & Talent Relations
**ALISON GILL** Senior VP - Manufacturing & Operations * **HANK KANALZ** Senior VP - Editorial Strategy & Administration
**JAY KOGAN** VP - Legal Affairs * **THOMAS LOFTUS** VP - Business Affairs
**JACK MAHAN** VP - Business Affairs * **NICK J. NAPOLITANO** VP - Manufacturing Administration
**EDDIE SCANNELL** VP - Consumer Marketing * **COURTNEY SIMMONS** Senior VP - Publicity & Communications
**JIM (SKI) SOKOLOWSKI** VP - Comic Book Specialty Sales & Trade Marketing * **NANCY SPEARS** VP - Mass, Book, Digital Sales & Trade Marketing

**DEATHSTROKE VOL. 3: TWILIGHT**



DC Comics, 2900 West Alameda Ave., Burbank, CA 91505.
Printed by LSC Communications, Kendallville, IN, USA. 9/8/17. First Printing.
ISBN: 978-1-4012-7406-1

Library of Congress Cataloging-in-Publication Data is available.

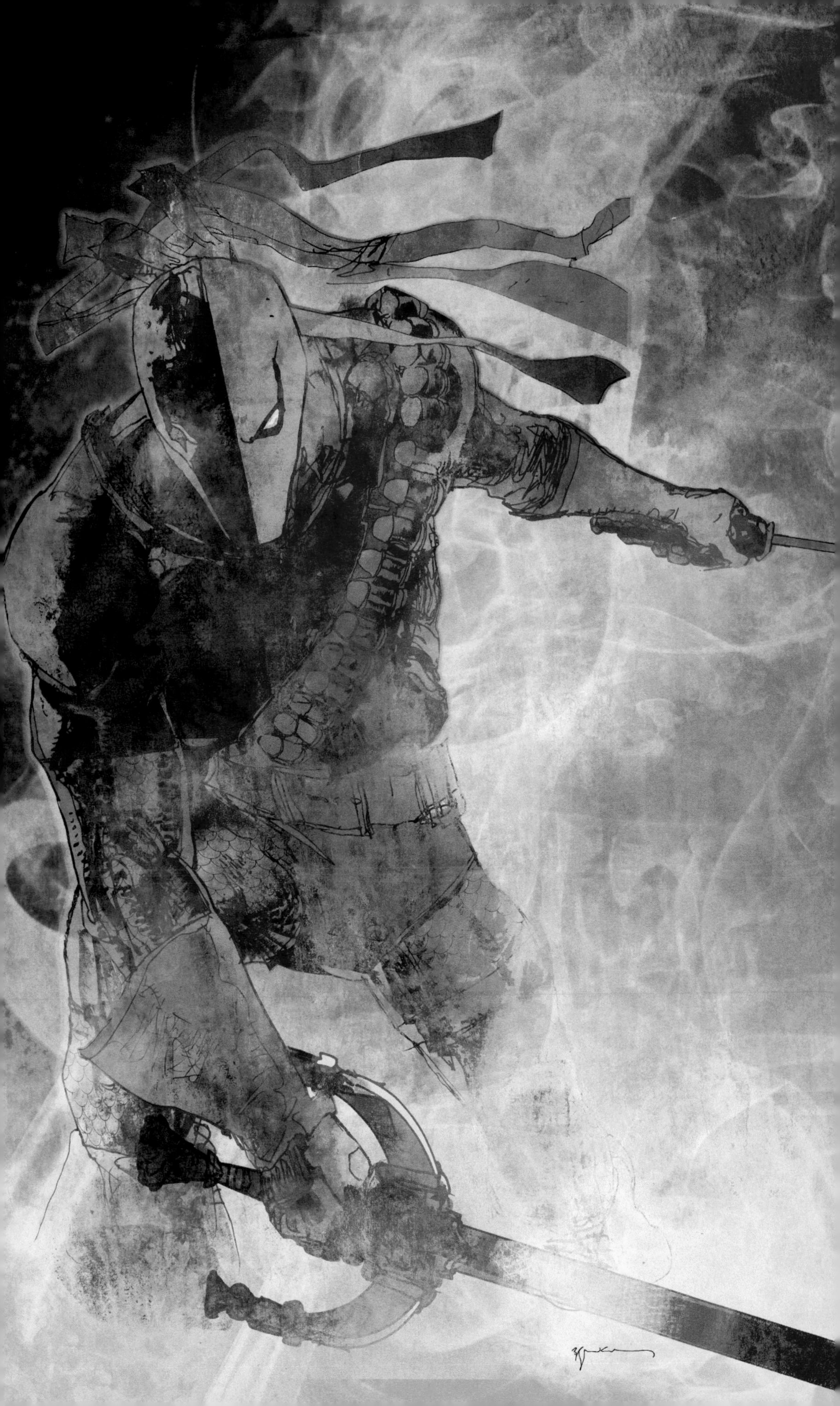

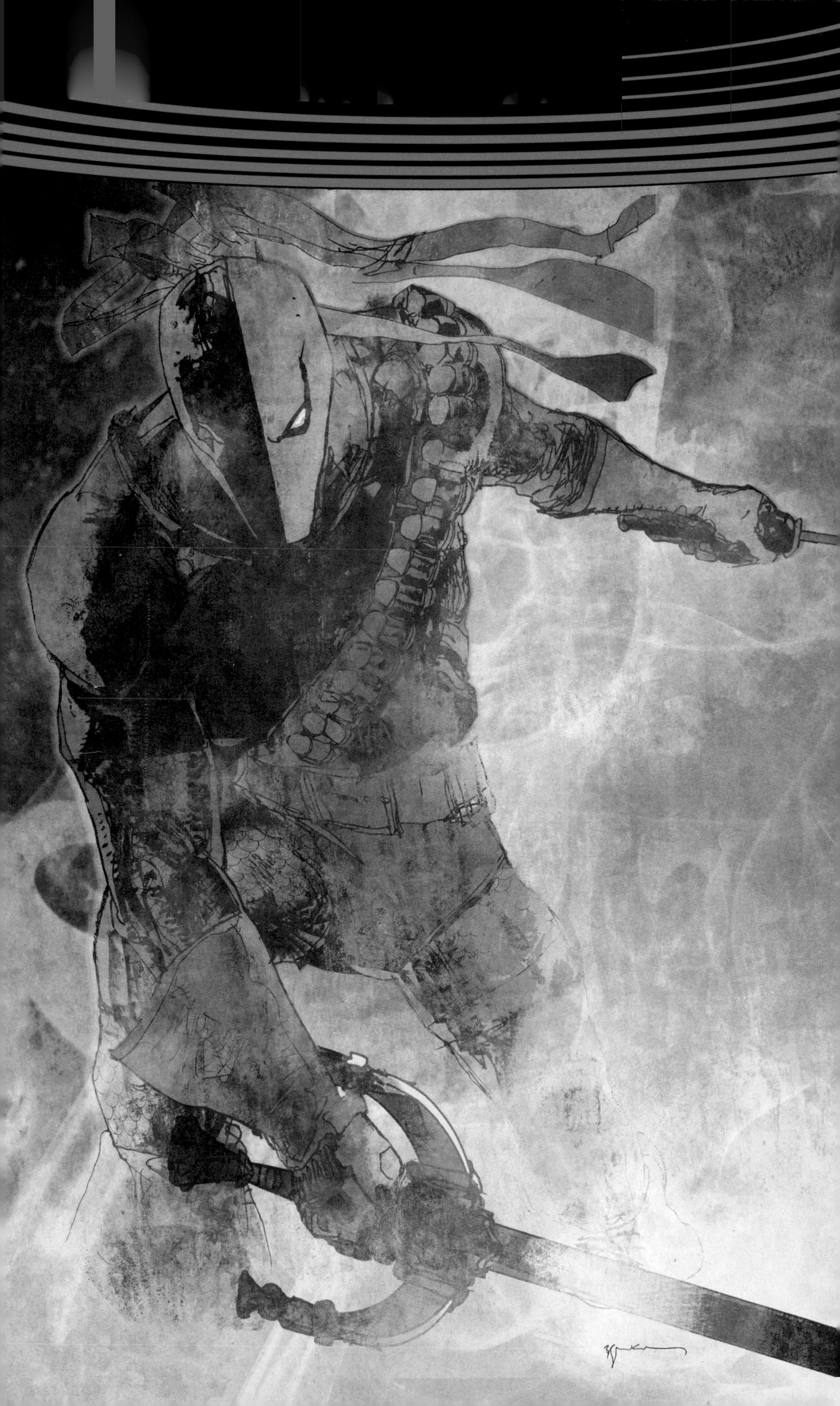

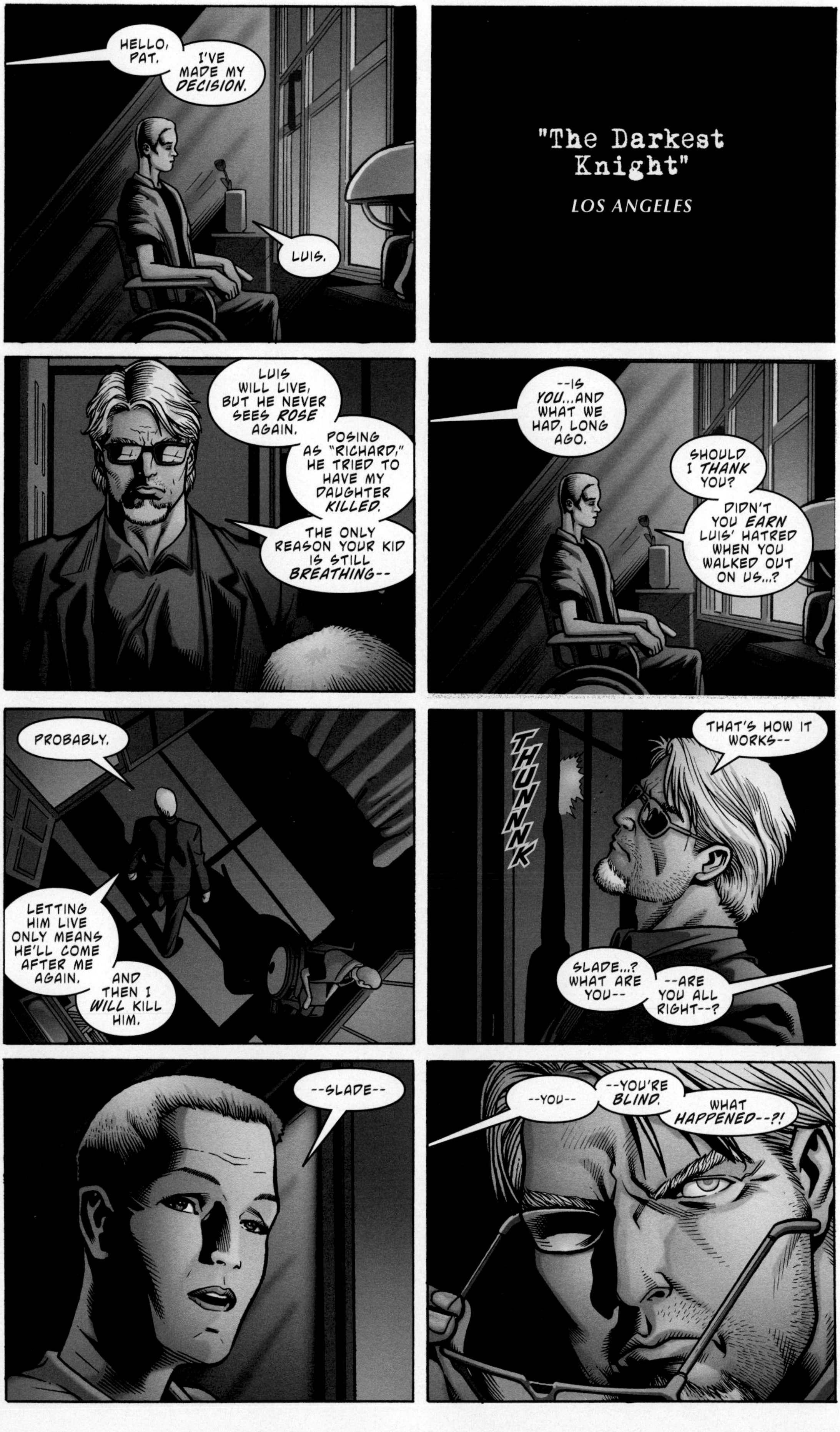
HELLO, PAT.
I'VE MADE MY DECISION.
LUIS.
"The Darkest Knight"
LOS ANGELES
LUIS WILL LIVE, BUT HE NEVER SEES ROSE AGAIN.
POSING AS "RICHARD," HE TRIED TO HAVE MY DAUGHTER KILLED.
THE ONLY REASON YOUR KID IS STILL BREATHING--
--IS YOU...AND WHAT WE HAD, LONG AGO.
SHOULD I THANK YOU?
DIDN'T YOU EARN LUIS' HATRED WHEN YOU WALKED OUT ON US...?
PROBABLY.
LETTING HIM LIVE ONLY MEANS HE'LL COME AFTER ME AGAIN.
AND THEN I WILL KILL HIM.
THUNNNK
THAT'S HOW IT WORKS--
SLADE...? WHAT ARE YOU--
--ARE YOU ALL RIGHT--?
--SLADE--
--YOU--
--YOU'RE BLIND.
WHAT HAPPENED--?!

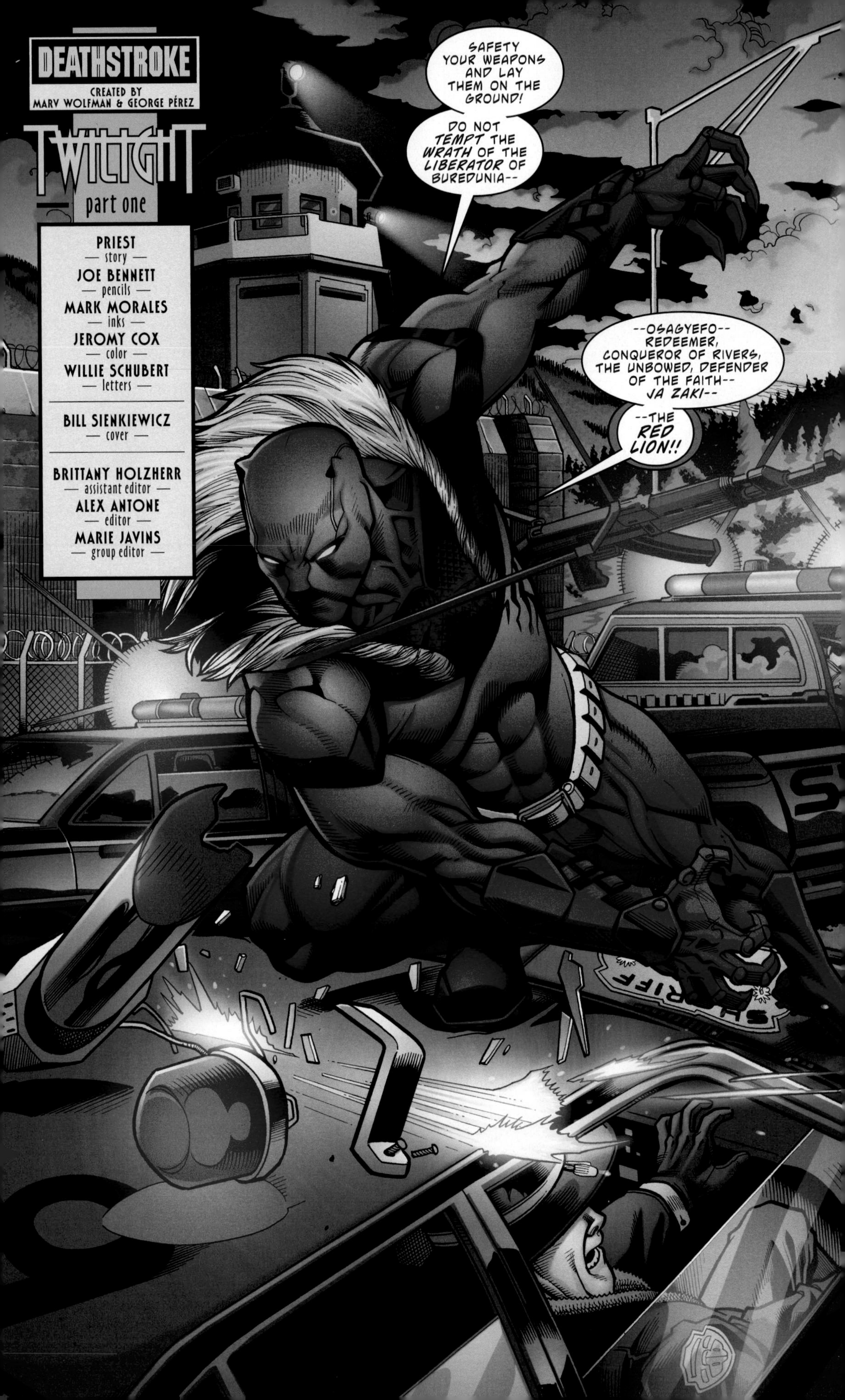
DEATHSTROKE
CREATED BY
MARY WOLFMAN & GEORGE PÉREZ
TWILIGHT
part one
PRIEST
— story —
JOE BENNETT
— pencils —
MARK MORALES
— inks —
JEROMY COX
— color —
WILLIE SCHUBERT
— letters —
BILL SIENKIEWICZ
— cover —
BRITTANY HOLZHERR
— assistant editor —
ALEX ANTONE
— editor —
MARIE JAVINS
— group editor —
SAFETY YOUR WEAPONS AND LAY THEM ON THE GROUND!
DO NOT TEMPT THE WRATH OF THE LIBERATOR OF BUREDUNIA--
--OSAGYEFO-- REDEEMER, CONQUEROR OF RIVERS, THE UNBOWED, DEFENDER OF THE FAITH-- JA ZAKI--
--THE RED LION!!
SHERIFF

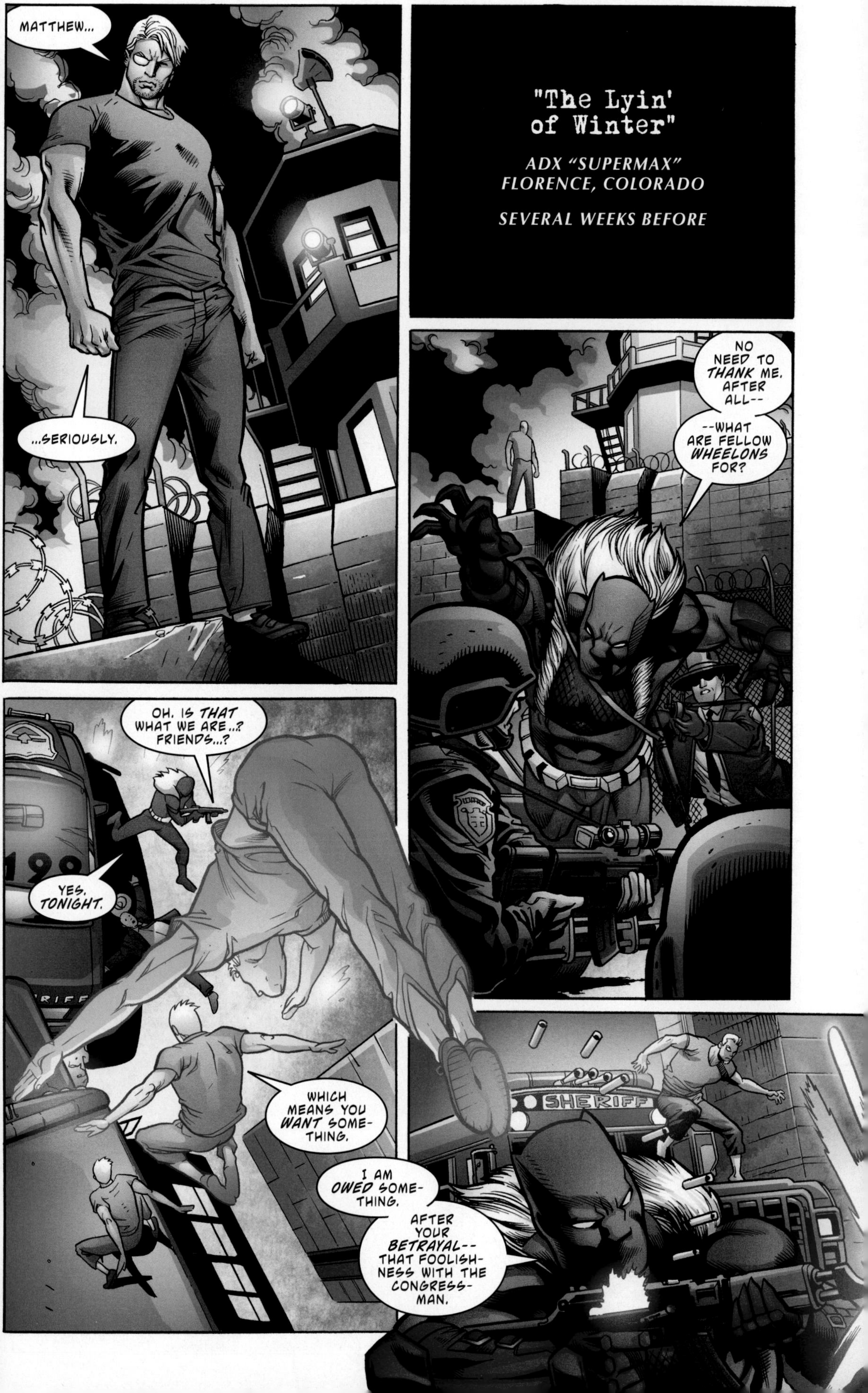
MATTHEW...
...SERIOUSLY.
"The Lyin' of Winter"
ADX "SUPERMAX"
FLORENCE, COLORADO
SEVERAL WEEKS BEFORE
NO NEED TO THANK ME. AFTER ALL--
--WHAT ARE FELLOW WHEELONS FOR?
OH. IS THAT WHAT WE ARE...? FRIENDS...?
YES. TONIGHT.
WHICH MEANS YOU WANT SOMETHING.
I AM OWED SOMETHING.
AFTER YOUR BETRAYAL--THAT FOOLISHNESS WITH THE CONGRESSMAN.
SHERIFF

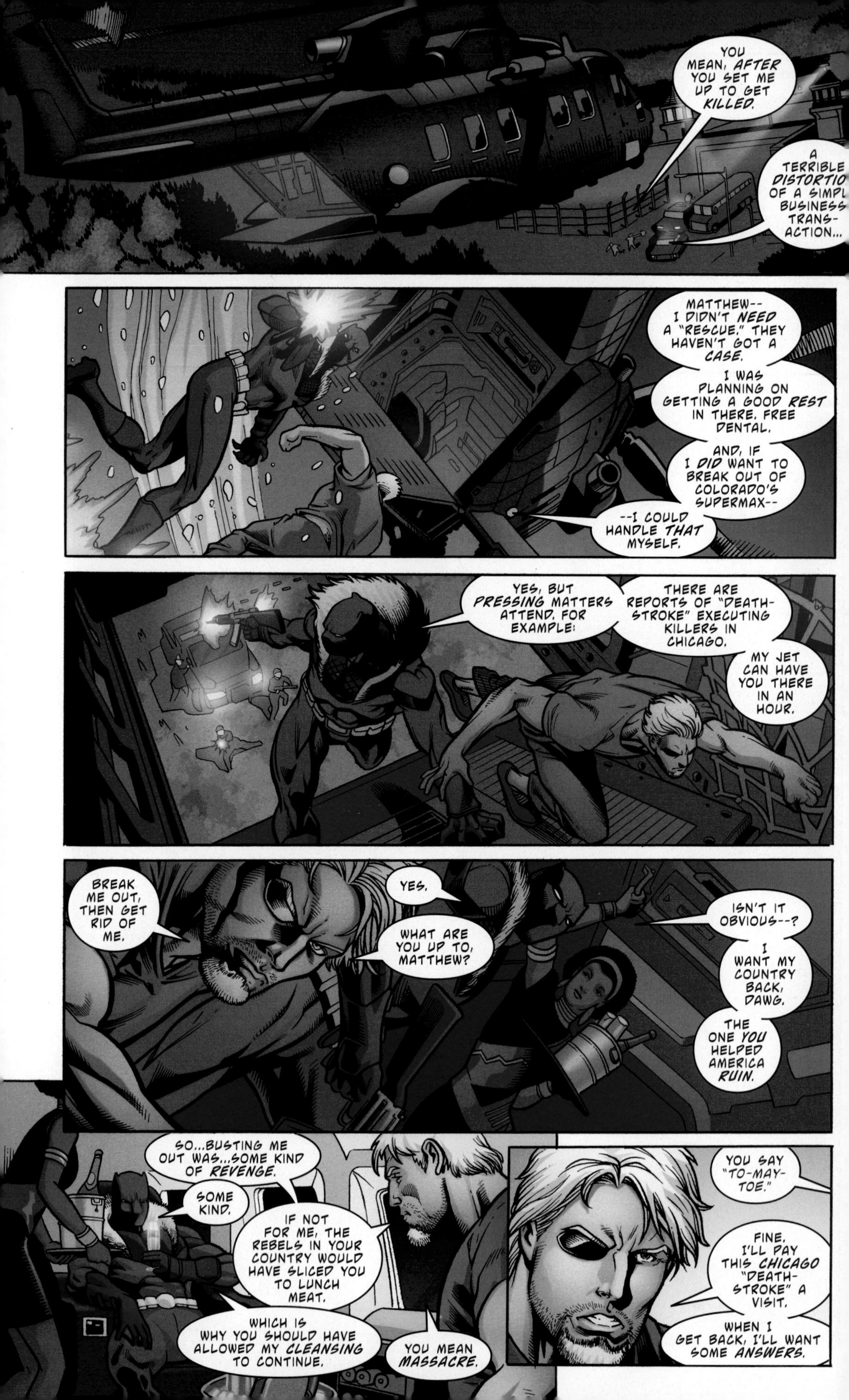

YOU MEAN, *AFTER* YOU SET ME UP TO GET *KILLED*.
A TERRIBLE *DISTORTIO* OF A SIMPL BUSINESS TRANS-ACTION...
MATTHEW-- I DIDN'T *NEED* A "RESCUE." THEY HAVEN'T GOT A *CASE*.
I WAS PLANNING ON GETTING A GOOD *REST* IN THERE. FREE DENTAL.
AND, IF I *DID* WANT TO BREAK OUT OF COLORADO'S SUPERMAX--
--I COULD HANDLE *THAT* MYSELF.
YES, BUT *PRESSING* MATTERS ATTEND. FOR EXAMPLE:
THERE ARE REPORTS OF "DEATH-STROKE" EXECUTING KILLERS IN CHICAGO.
MY JET CAN HAVE YOU THERE IN AN HOUR.
BREAK ME OUT, THEN GET RID OF ME.
YES.
WHAT ARE YOU UP TO, MATTHEW?
ISN'T IT OBVIOUS--?
I WANT MY COUNTRY BACK, DAWG.
THE ONE *YOU* HELPED AMERICA *RUIN*.
SO...BUSTING ME OUT WAS...SOME KIND OF *REVENGE*.
SOME KIND.
IF NOT FOR ME, THE REBELS IN YOUR COUNTRY WOULD HAVE SLICED YOU TO LUNCH MEAT.
WHICH IS WHY YOU SHOULD HAVE ALLOWED MY *CLEANSING* TO CONTINUE.
YOU MEAN *MASSACRE*.
YOU SAY "TO-MAY-TOE."
FINE. I'LL PAY THIS *CHICAGO* "DEATH-STROKE" A VISIT.
WHEN I GET BACK, I'LL WANT SOME *ANSWERS*.

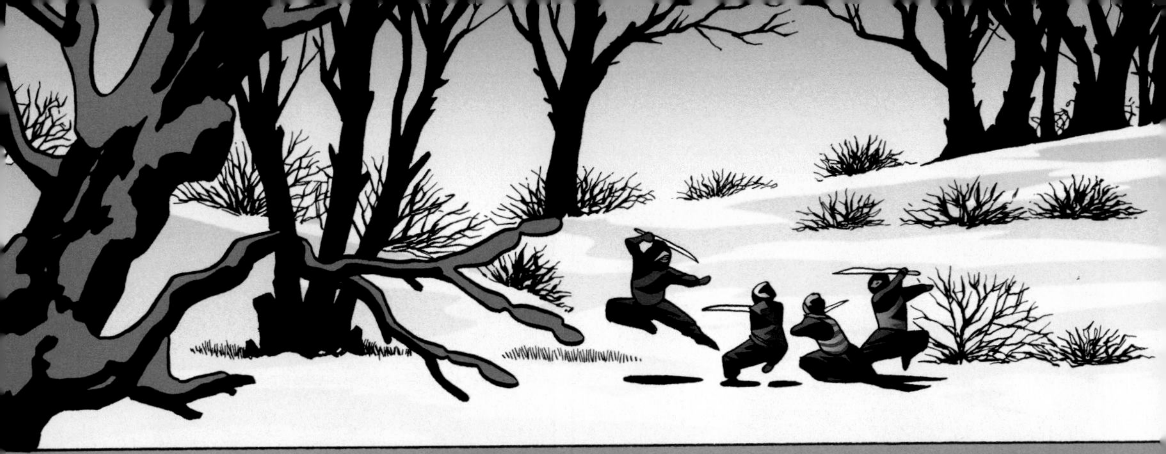

# "Yao Ming"

*MINNEAPOLIS*

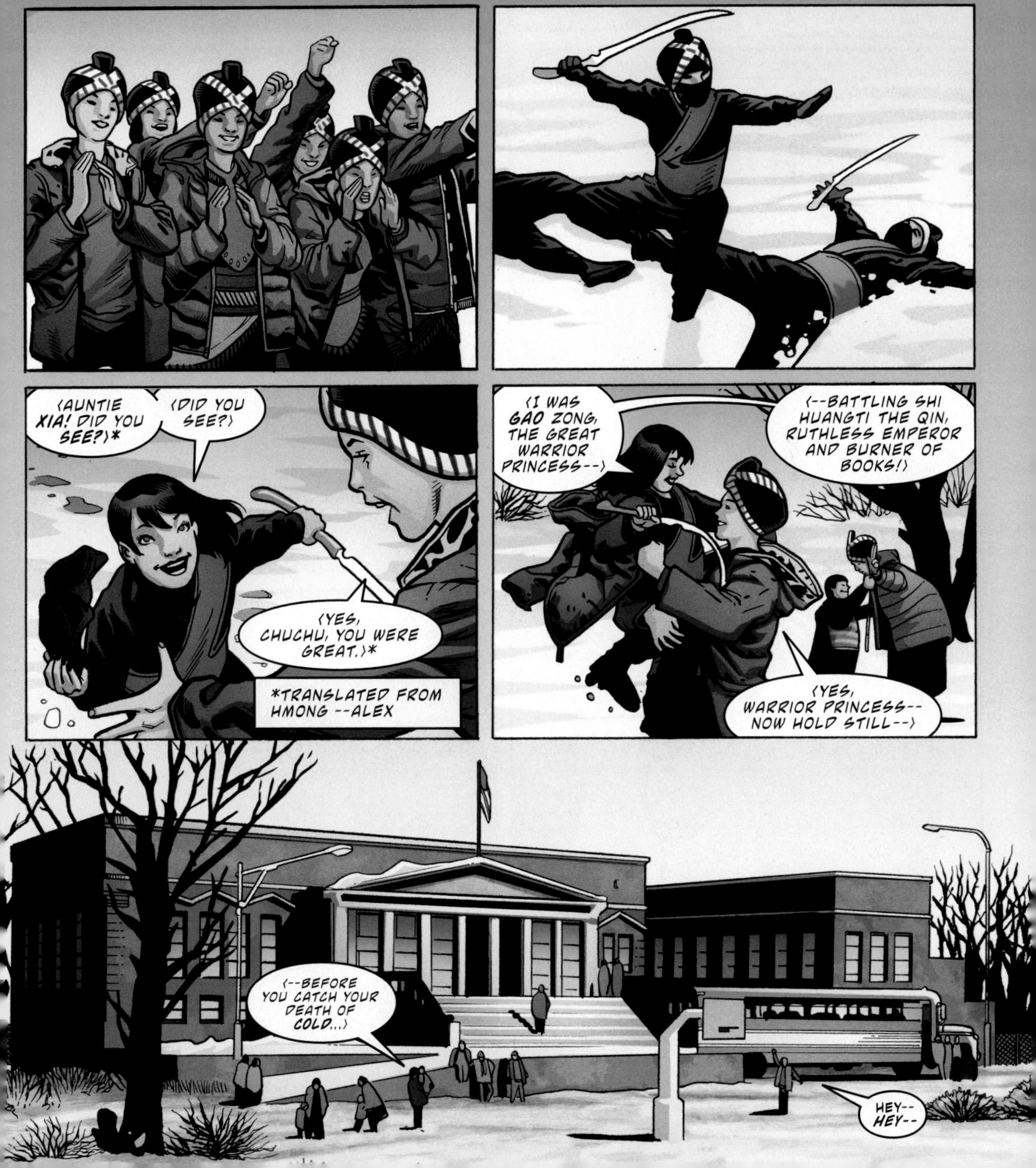

‹AUNTIE XIA! DID YOU SEE?›*
‹DID YOU SEE?›
‹YES, CHUCHU, YOU WERE GREAT.›*
*TRANSLATED FROM HMONG --ALEX
‹I WAS GAO ZONG, THE GREAT WARRIOR PRINCESS--›
‹--BATTLING SHI HUANGTI THE QIN, RUTHLESS EMPEROR AND BURNER OF BOOKS!›
‹YES, WARRIOR PRINCESS-- NOW HOLD STILL--›
‹--BEFORE YOU CATCH YOUR DEATH OF COLD...›
HEY-- HEY--

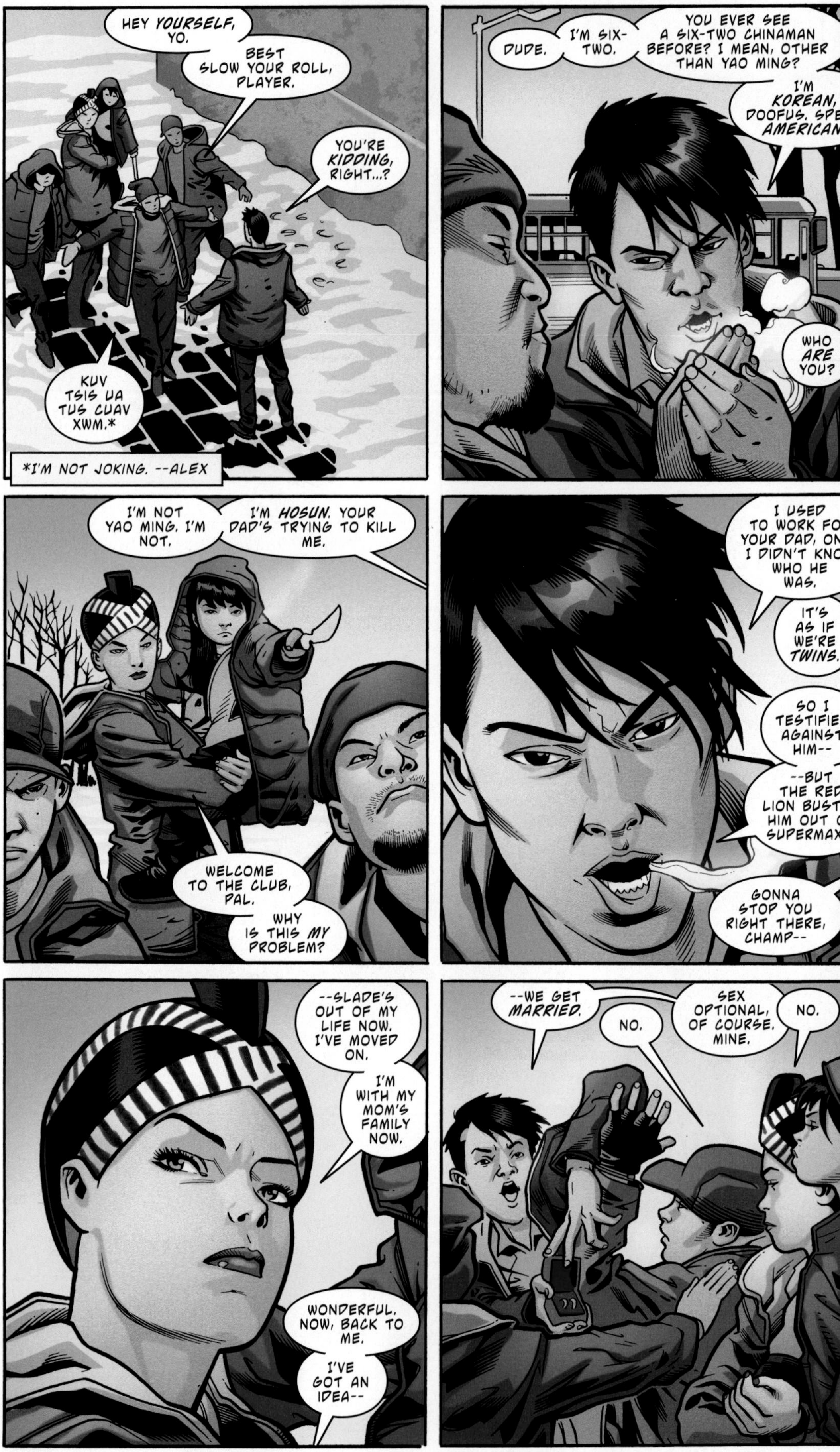
HEY YOURSELF, YO.
BEST SLOW YOUR ROLL, PLAYER.
YOU'RE KIDDING, RIGHT...?
KUV TSIS UA TUS CUAV XWM.*
*I'M NOT JOKING. --ALEX
DUDE.
I'M SIX-TWO.
YOU EVER SEE A SIX-TWO CHINAMAN BEFORE? I MEAN, OTHER THAN YAO MING?
I'M KOREAN, DOOFUS. SPEAK AMERICAN.
WHO ARE YOU?
I'M NOT YAO MING. I'M NOT.
I'M HOSUN. YOUR DAD'S TRYING TO KILL ME.
WELCOME TO THE CLUB, PAL.
WHY IS THIS MY PROBLEM?
I USED TO WORK FOR YOUR DAD, ONLY I DIDN'T KNOW WHO HE WAS.
IT'S AS IF WE'RE TWINS.
SO I TESTIFIED AGAINST HIM--
--BUT THE RED LION BUSTED HIM OUT OF SUPERMAX--
GONNA STOP YOU RIGHT THERE, CHAMP--
--SLADE'S OUT OF MY LIFE NOW. I'VE MOVED ON.
I'M WITH MY MOM'S FAMILY NOW.
WONDERFUL. NOW, BACK TO ME.
I'VE GOT AN IDEA--
--WE GET MARRIED.
NO.
SEX OPTIONAL, OF COURSE. MINE.
NO.

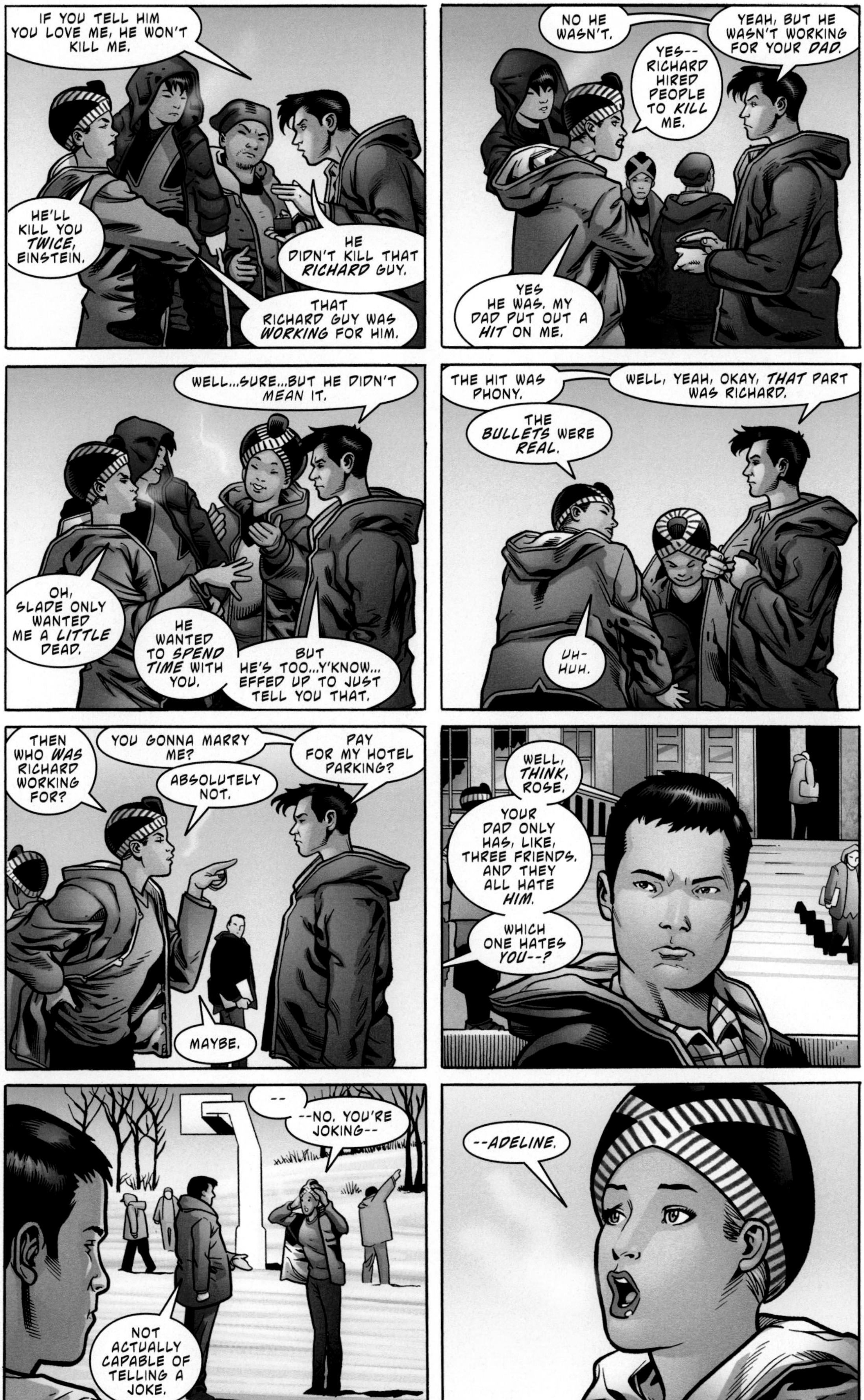
IF YOU TELL HIM YOU LOVE ME, HE WON'T KILL ME.
HE'LL KILL YOU *TWICE*, EINSTEIN.
HE DIDN'T KILL THAT *RICHARD* GUY.
THAT RICHARD GUY WAS *WORKING* FOR HIM.
NO HE WASN'T.
YEAH, BUT HE WASN'T WORKING FOR YOUR *DAD*.
YES-- RICHARD HIRED PEOPLE TO *KILL* ME.
YES HE WAS. MY DAD PUT OUT A *HIT* ON ME.
WELL...SURE...BUT HE DIDN'T MEAN IT.
OH, SLADE ONLY WANTED ME A *LITTLE* DEAD.
HE WANTED TO *SPEND TIME* WITH YOU.
BUT HE'S TOO...Y'KNOW... EFFED UP TO JUST TELL YOU THAT.
THE HIT WAS PHONY.
WELL, YEAH, OKAY, *THAT* PART WAS RICHARD.
THE *BULLETS* WERE *REAL*.
UH-HUH.
THEN WHO *WAS* RICHARD WORKING FOR?
YOU GONNA MARRY ME?
PAY FOR MY HOTEL PARKING?
ABSOLUTELY NOT.
MAYBE.
WELL, *THINK*, ROSE.
YOUR DAD ONLY HAS, LIKE, THREE FRIENDS, AND THEY ALL HATE *HIM*.
WHICH ONE HATES *YOU*--?
--
--NO. YOU'RE JOKING--
NOT ACTUALLY CAPABLE OF TELLING A JOKE.
--*ADELINE*.

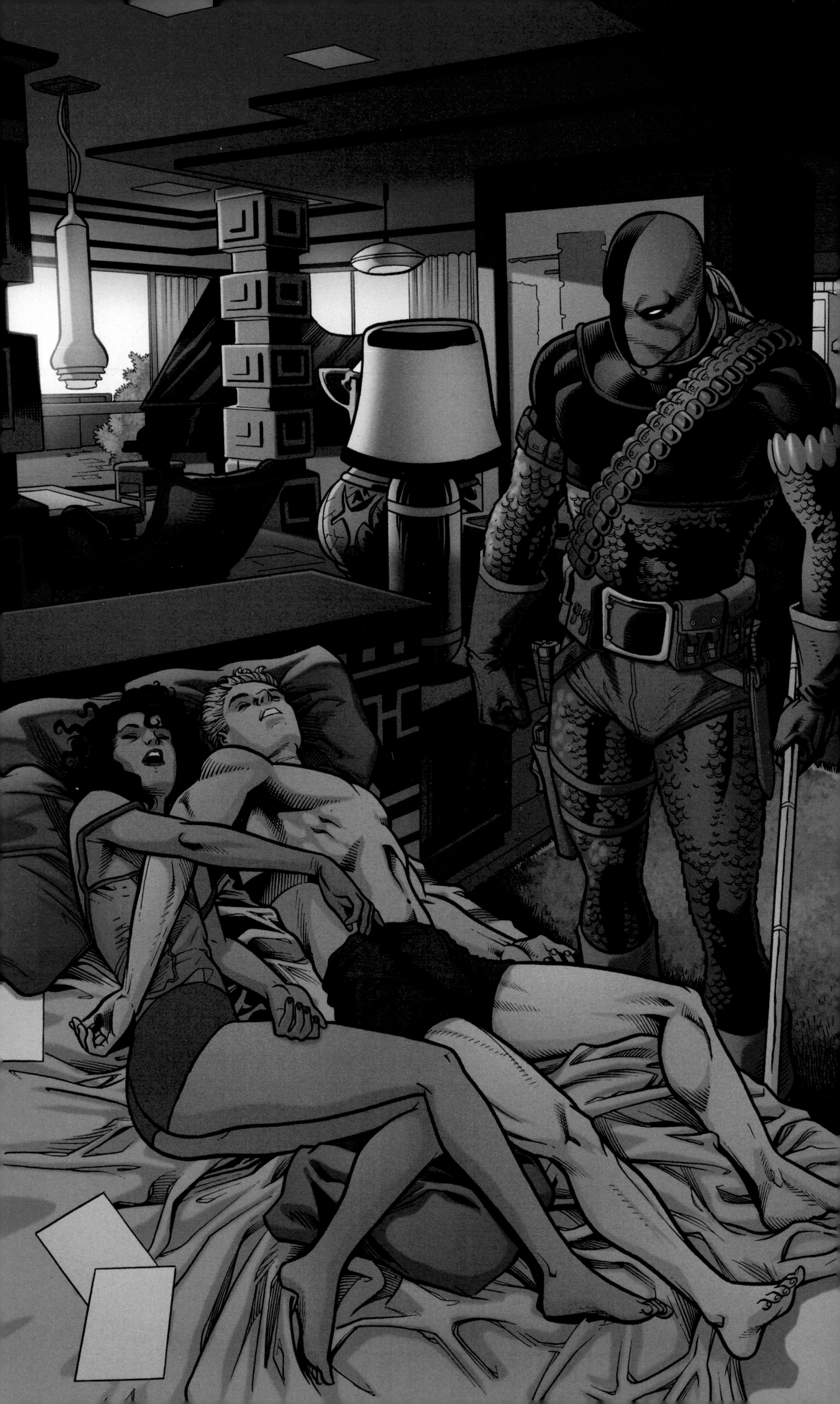

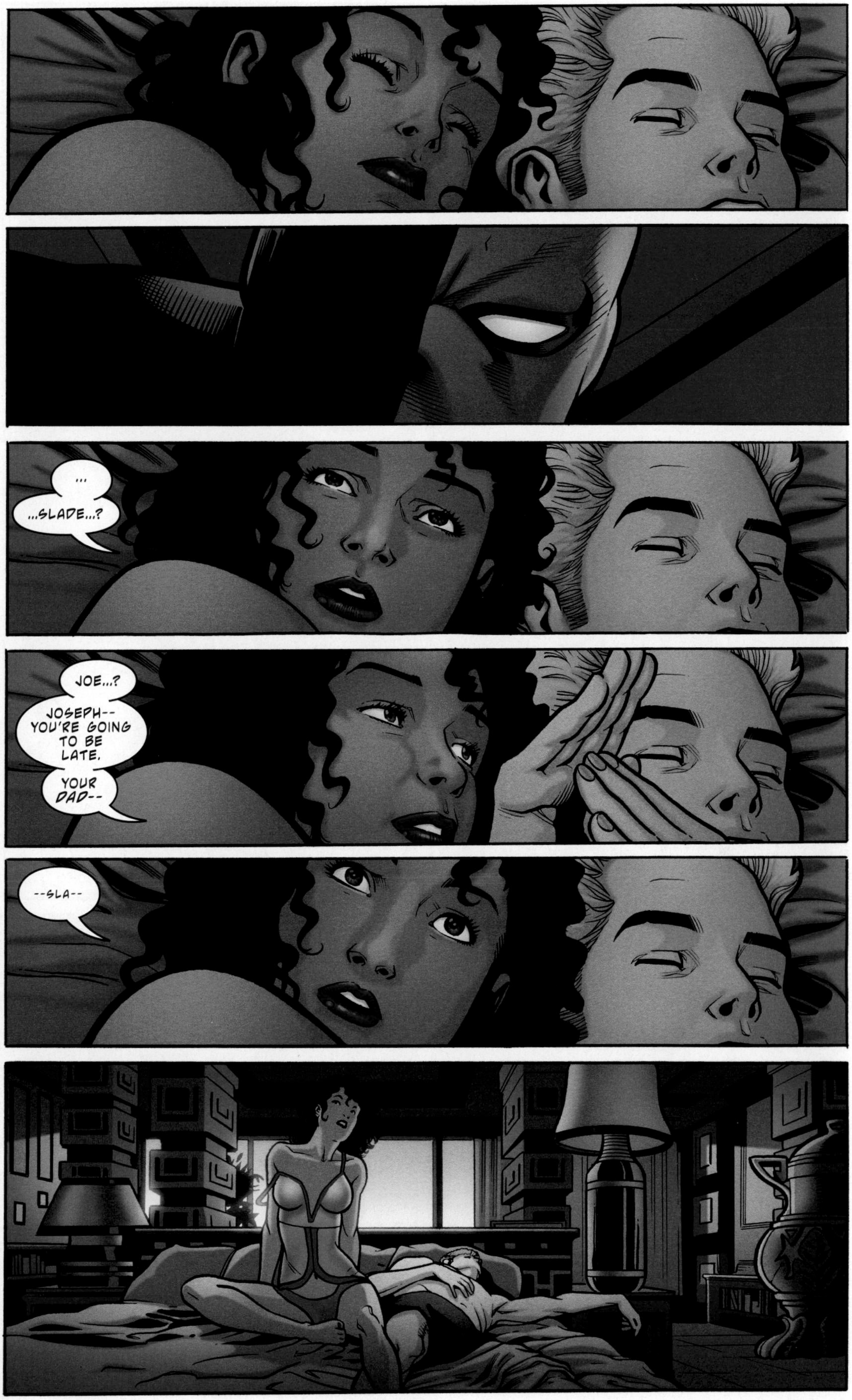
...
...SLADE...?
JOE...?
JOSEPH-- YOU'RE GOING TO BE LATE.
YOUR DAD--
--SLA--

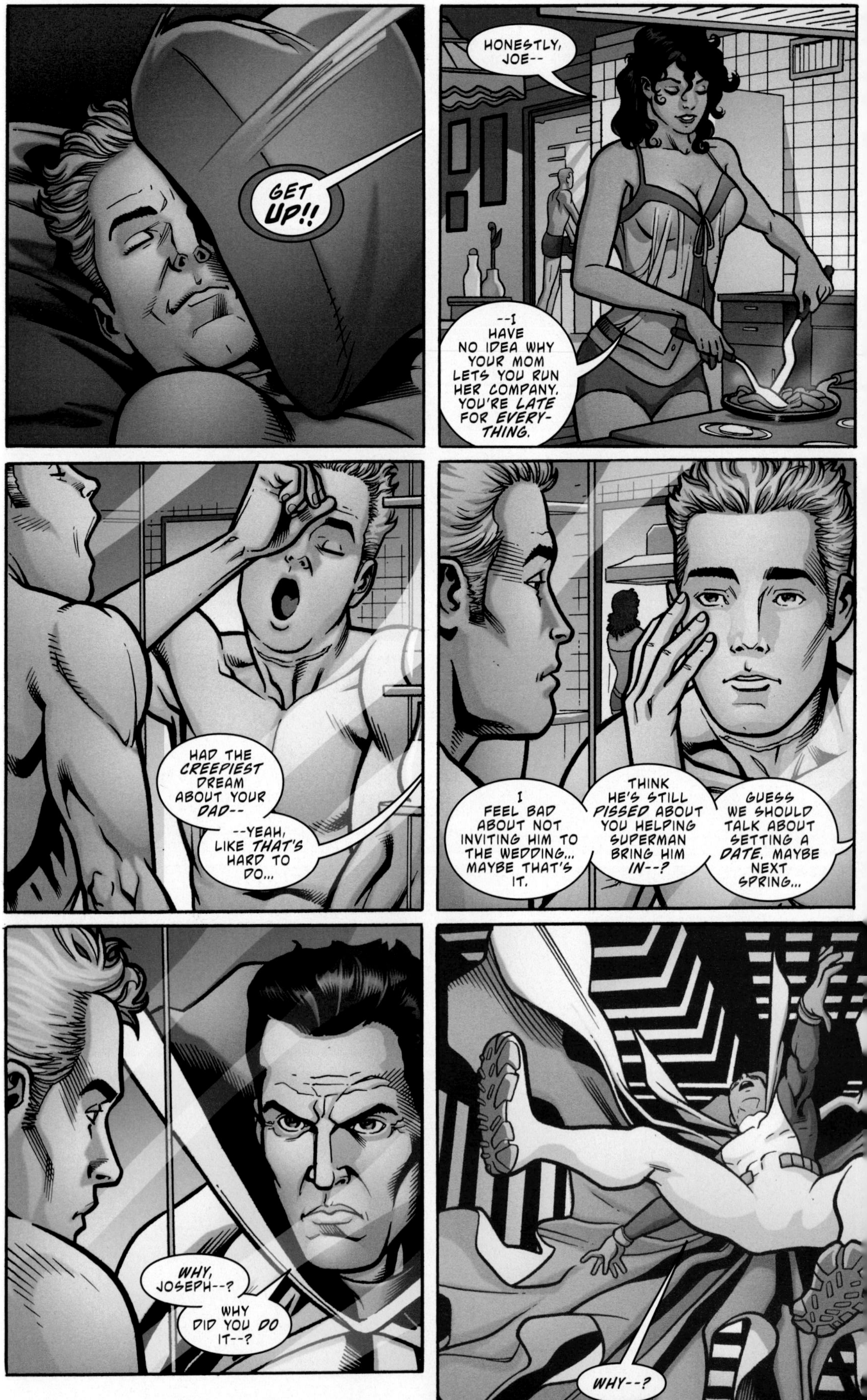
GET UP!!
HONESTLY, JOE--
--I HAVE NO IDEA WHY YOUR MOM LETS YOU RUN HER COMPANY. YOU'RE LATE FOR EVERY-THING.
HAD THE CREEPIEST DREAM ABOUT YOUR DAD--
--YEAH, LIKE THAT'S HARD TO DO...
I FEEL BAD ABOUT NOT INVITING HIM TO THE WEDDING... MAYBE THAT'S IT.
THINK HE'S STILL PISSED ABOUT YOU HELPING SUPERMAN BRING HIM IN--?
GUESS WE SHOULD TALK ABOUT SETTING A DATE. MAYBE NEXT SPRING...
WHY, JOSEPH--?
WHY DID YOU DO IT--?
WHY--?

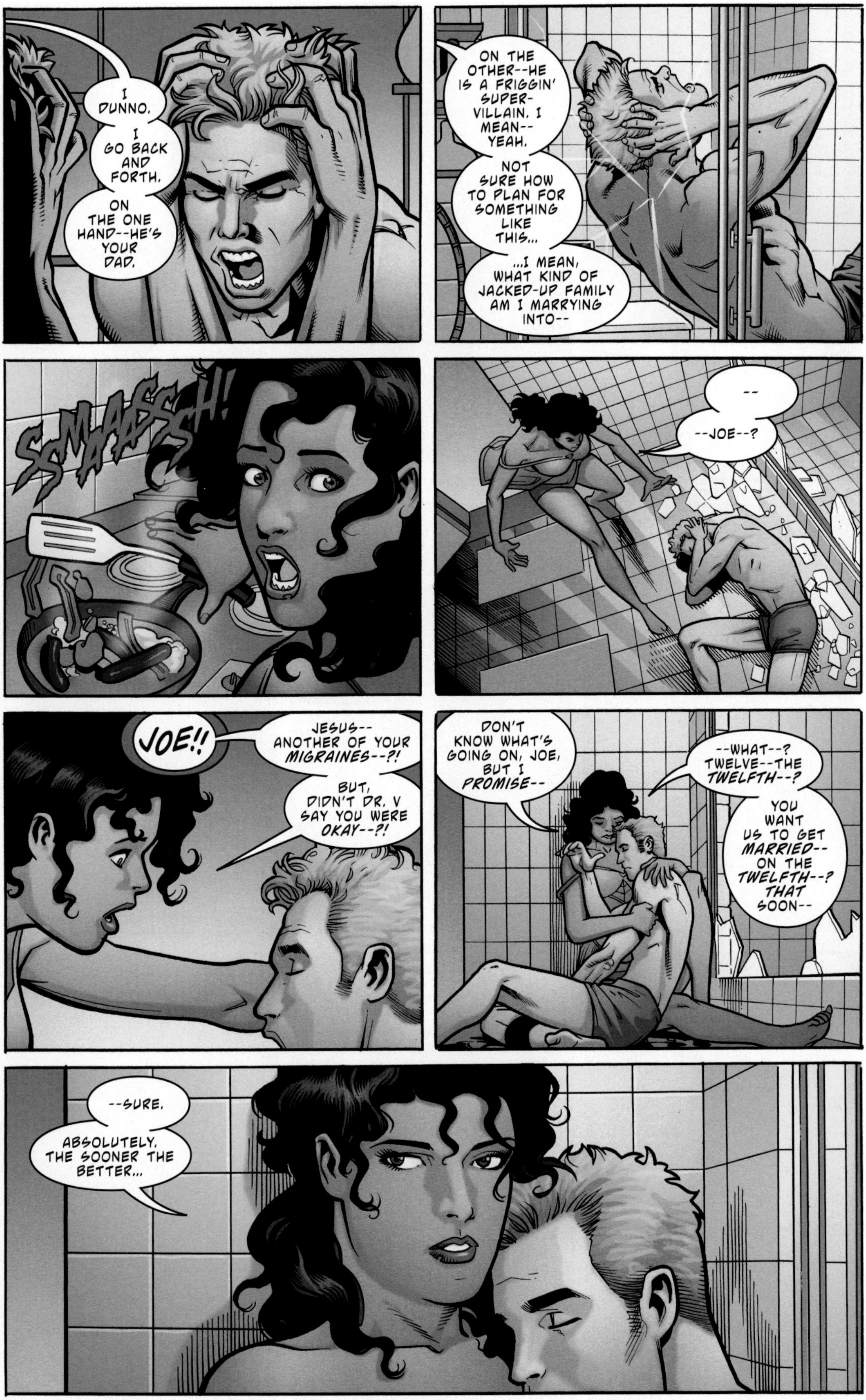
I DUNNO.
I GO BACK AND FORTH.
ON THE ONE HAND--HE'S YOUR DAD.
ON THE OTHER--HE IS A FRIGGIN' SUPER-VILLAIN. I MEAN--YEAH.
NOT SURE HOW TO PLAN FOR SOMETHING LIKE THIS...
...I MEAN, WHAT KIND OF JACKED-UP FAMILY AM I MARRYING INTO--
SSMAASSH!
--
--JOE--?
JOE!!
JESUS--ANOTHER OF YOUR *MIGRAINES*--?!
BUT, DIDN'T DR. V SAY YOU WERE *OKAY*--?!
DON'T KNOW WHAT'S GOING ON, JOE, BUT I *PROMISE*--
--WHAT--? TWELVE--THE *TWELFTH*--?
YOU WANT US TO GET *MARRIED*--ON THE *TWELFTH*--? *THAT* SOON--
--SURE.
ABSOLUTELY. THE SOONER THE BETTER...

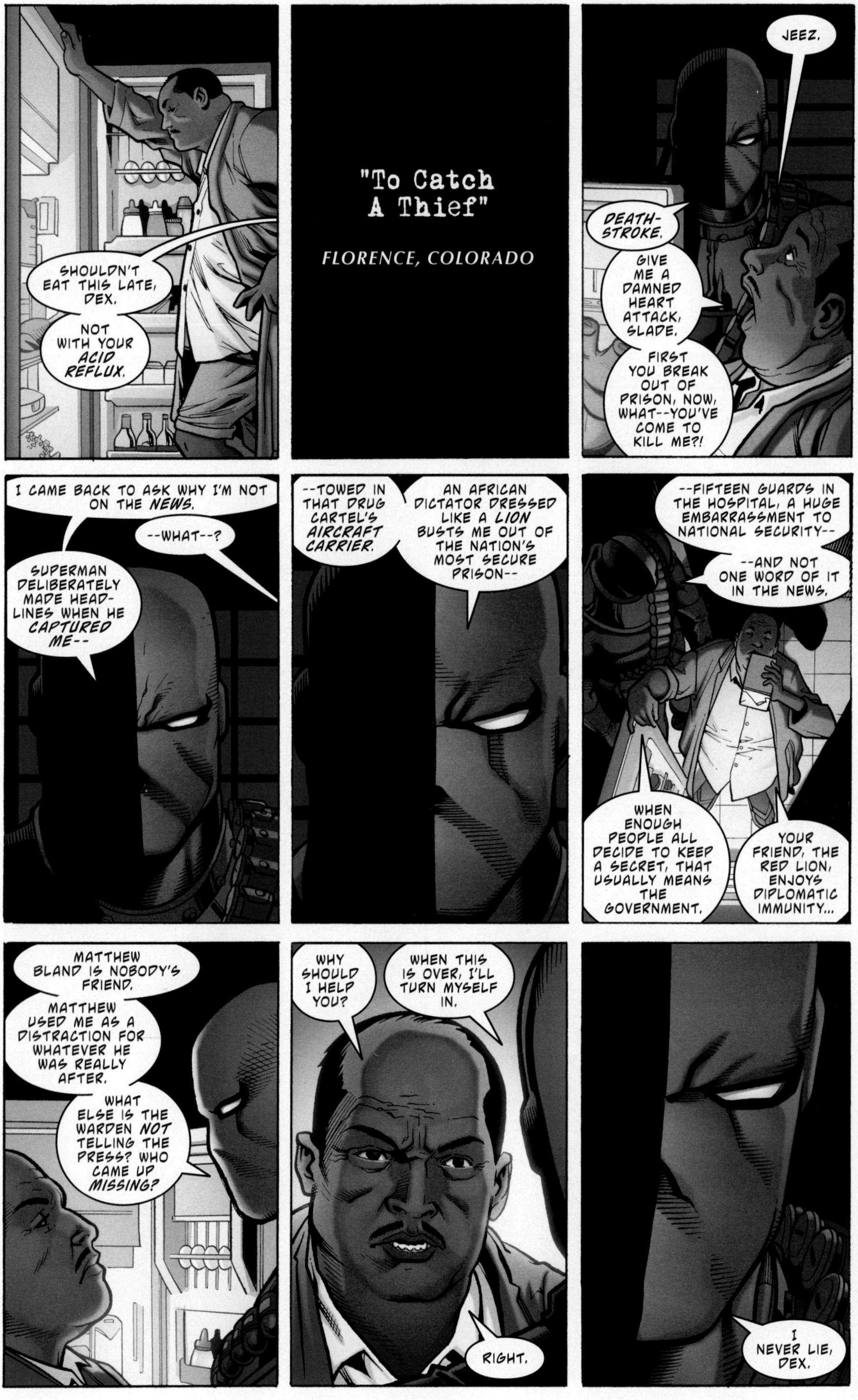
SHOULDN'T EAT THIS LATE, DEX.
NOT WITH YOUR ACID REFLUX.
"To Catch A Thief"
FLORENCE, COLORADO
JEEZ.
DEATH-STROKE.
GIVE ME A DAMNED HEART ATTACK, SLADE.
FIRST YOU BREAK OUT OF PRISON, NOW, WHAT--YOU'VE COME TO KILL ME?!
I CAME BACK TO ASK WHY I'M NOT ON THE NEWS.
--WHAT--?
SUPERMAN DELIBERATELY MADE HEAD-LINES WHEN HE CAPTURED ME--
--TOWED IN THAT DRUG CARTEL'S AIRCRAFT CARRIER.
AN AFRICAN DICTATOR DRESSED LIKE A LION BUSTS ME OUT OF THE NATION'S MOST SECURE PRISON--
--FIFTEEN GUARDS IN THE HOSPITAL, A HUGE EMBARRASSMENT TO NATIONAL SECURITY--
--AND NOT ONE WORD OF IT IN THE NEWS.
WHEN ENOUGH PEOPLE ALL DECIDE TO KEEP A SECRET, THAT USUALLY MEANS THE GOVERNMENT.
YOUR FRIEND, THE RED LION, ENJOYS DIPLOMATIC IMMUNITY...
MATTHEW BLAND IS NOBODY'S FRIEND.
MATTHEW USED ME AS A DISTRACTION FOR WHATEVER HE WAS REALLY AFTER.
WHAT ELSE IS THE WARDEN NOT TELLING THE PRESS? WHO CAME UP MISSING?
WHY SHOULD I HELP YOU?
WHEN THIS IS OVER, I'LL TURN MYSELF IN.
RIGHT.
I NEVER LIE, DEX.

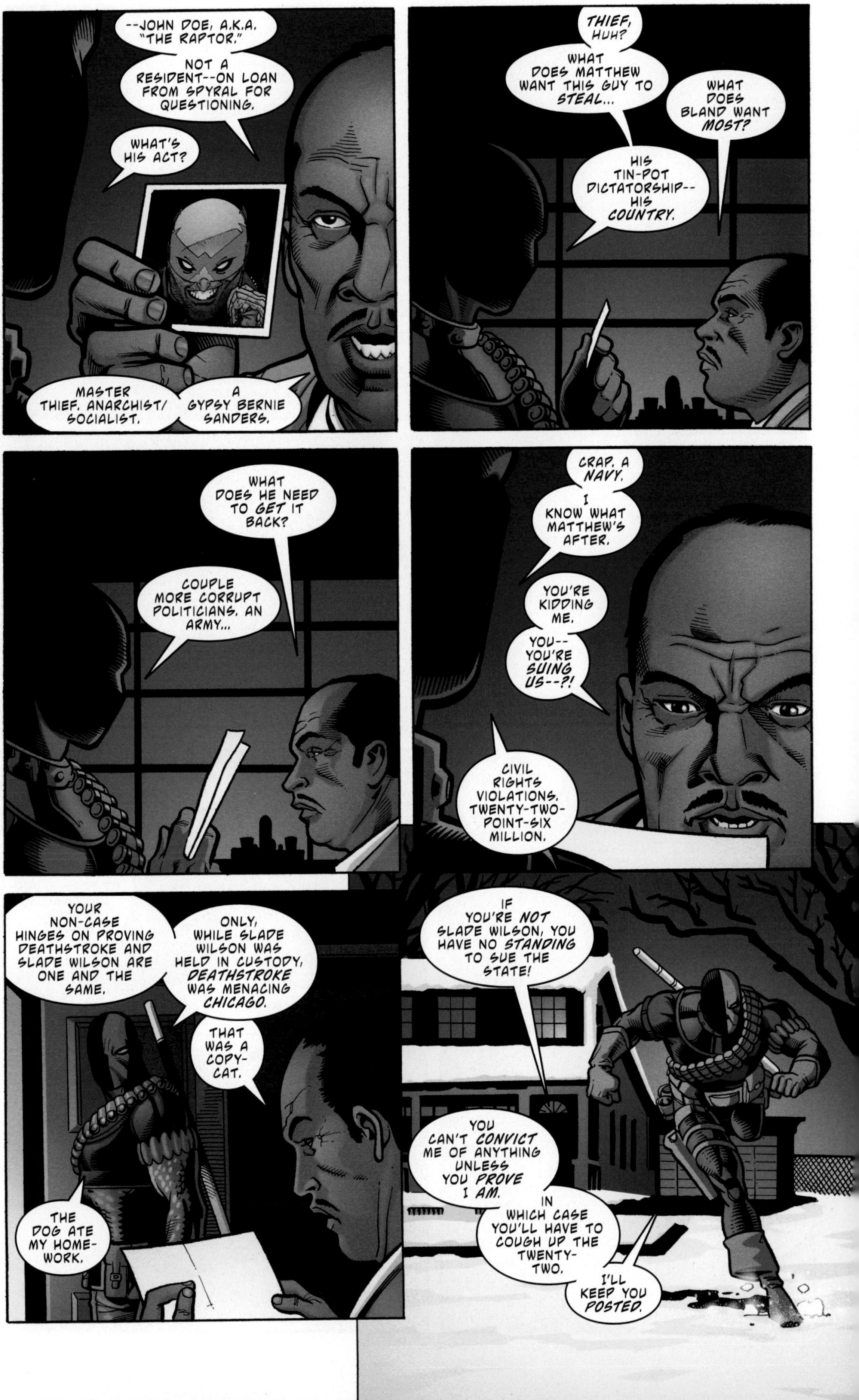
--JOHN DOE, A.K.A. "THE RAPTOR."
NOT A RESIDENT--ON LOAN FROM SPYRAL FOR QUESTIONING.
WHAT'S HIS ACT?
MASTER THIEF. ANARCHIST/ SOCIALIST.
A GYPSY BERNIE SANDERS.
THIEF, HUH?
WHAT DOES MATTHEW WANT THIS GUY TO STEAL...
WHAT DOES BLAND WANT MOST?
HIS TIN-POT DICTATORSHIP--HIS COUNTRY.
WHAT DOES HE NEED TO GET IT BACK?
COUPLE MORE CORRUPT POLITICIANS. AN ARMY...
CRAP. A NAVY.
I KNOW WHAT MATTHEW'S AFTER.
YOU'RE KIDDING ME.
YOU--YOU'RE SUING US--?!
CIVIL RIGHTS VIOLATIONS. TWENTY-TWO-POINT-SIX MILLION.
YOUR NON-CASE HINGES ON PROVING DEATHSTROKE AND SLADE WILSON ARE ONE AND THE SAME.
ONLY, WHILE SLADE WILSON WAS HELD IN CUSTODY, DEATHSTROKE WAS MENACING CHICAGO.
THAT WAS A COPY-CAT.
THE DOG ATE MY HOME-WORK.
IF YOU'RE NOT SLADE WILSON, YOU HAVE NO STANDING TO SUE THE STATE!
YOU CAN'T CONVICT ME OF ANYTHING UNLESS YOU PROVE I AM.
IN WHICH CASE YOU'LL HAVE TO COUGH UP THE TWENTY-TWO.
I'LL KEEP YOU POSTED.

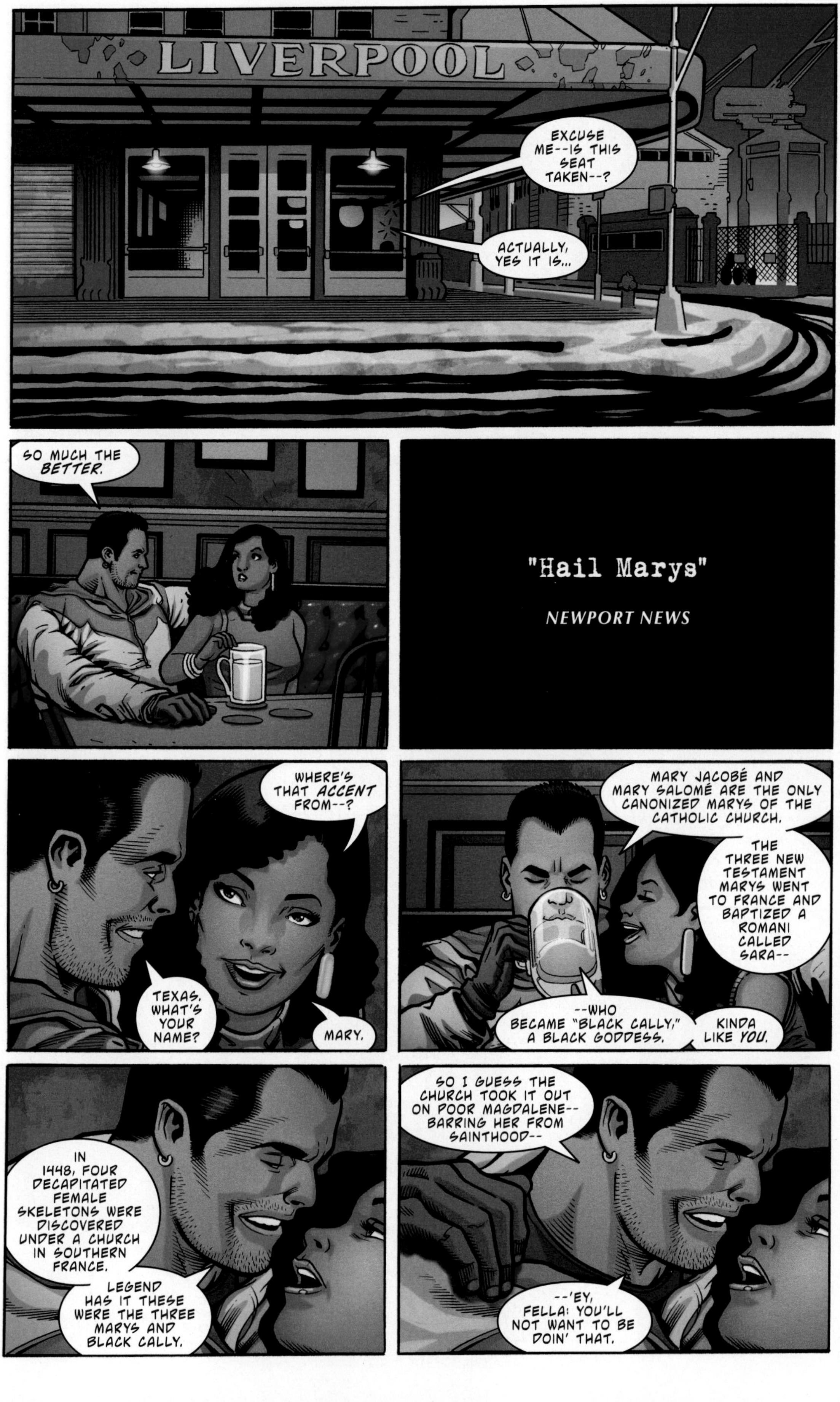
LIVERPOOL
EXCUSE ME--IS THIS SEAT TAKEN--?
ACTUALLY, YES IT IS...
SO MUCH THE BETTER.
"Hail Marys"
NEWPORT NEWS
WHERE'S THAT ACCENT FROM--?
TEXAS. WHAT'S YOUR NAME?
MARY.
MARY JACOBÉ AND MARY SALOMÉ ARE THE ONLY CANONIZED MARYS OF THE CATHOLIC CHURCH.
THE THREE NEW TESTAMENT MARYS WENT TO FRANCE AND BAPTIZED A ROMANI CALLED SARA--
--WHO BECAME "BLACK CALLY," A BLACK GODDESS.
KINDA LIKE YOU.
IN 1448, FOUR DECAPITATED FEMALE SKELETONS WERE DISCOVERED UNDER A CHURCH IN SOUTHERN FRANCE.
LEGEND HAS IT THESE WERE THE THREE MARYS AND BLACK CALLY.
SO I GUESS THE CHURCH TOOK IT OUT ON POOR MAGDALENE-- BARRING HER FROM SAINTHOOD--
--'EY, FELLA: YOU'LL NOT WANT TO BE DOIN' THAT.

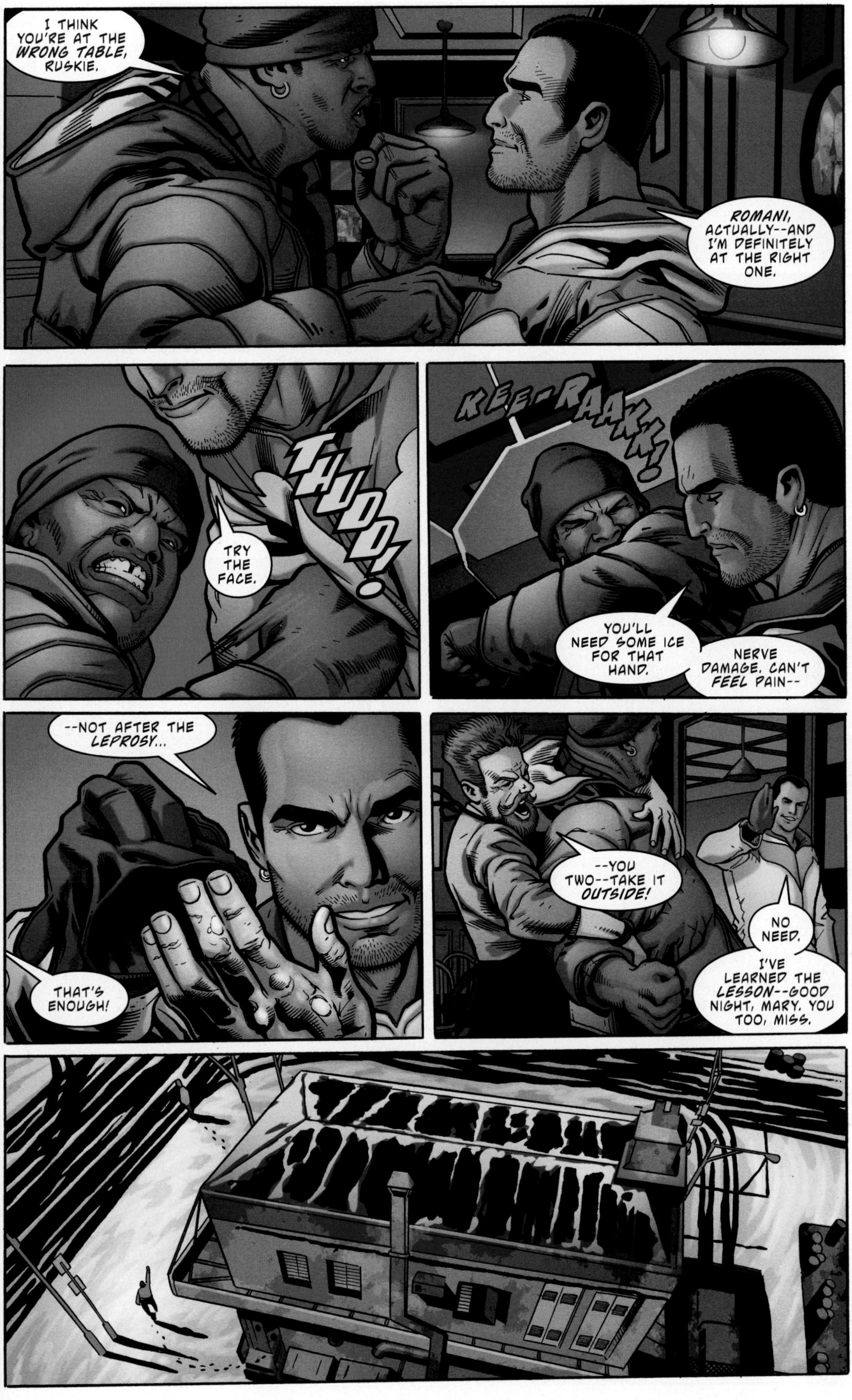
I THINK YOU'RE AT THE WRONG TABLE, RUSKIE.
ROMANI, ACTUALLY--AND I'M DEFINITELY AT THE RIGHT ONE.
THUDD!
TRY THE FACE.
KEE-RAAKK!
YOU'LL NEED SOME ICE FOR THAT HAND.
NERVE DAMAGE. CAN'T FEEL PAIN--
--NOT AFTER THE LEPROSY...
THAT'S ENOUGH!
--YOU TWO--TAKE IT OUTSIDE!
NO NEED.
I'VE LEARNED THE LESSON--GOOD NIGHT, MARY. YOU TOO, MISS.

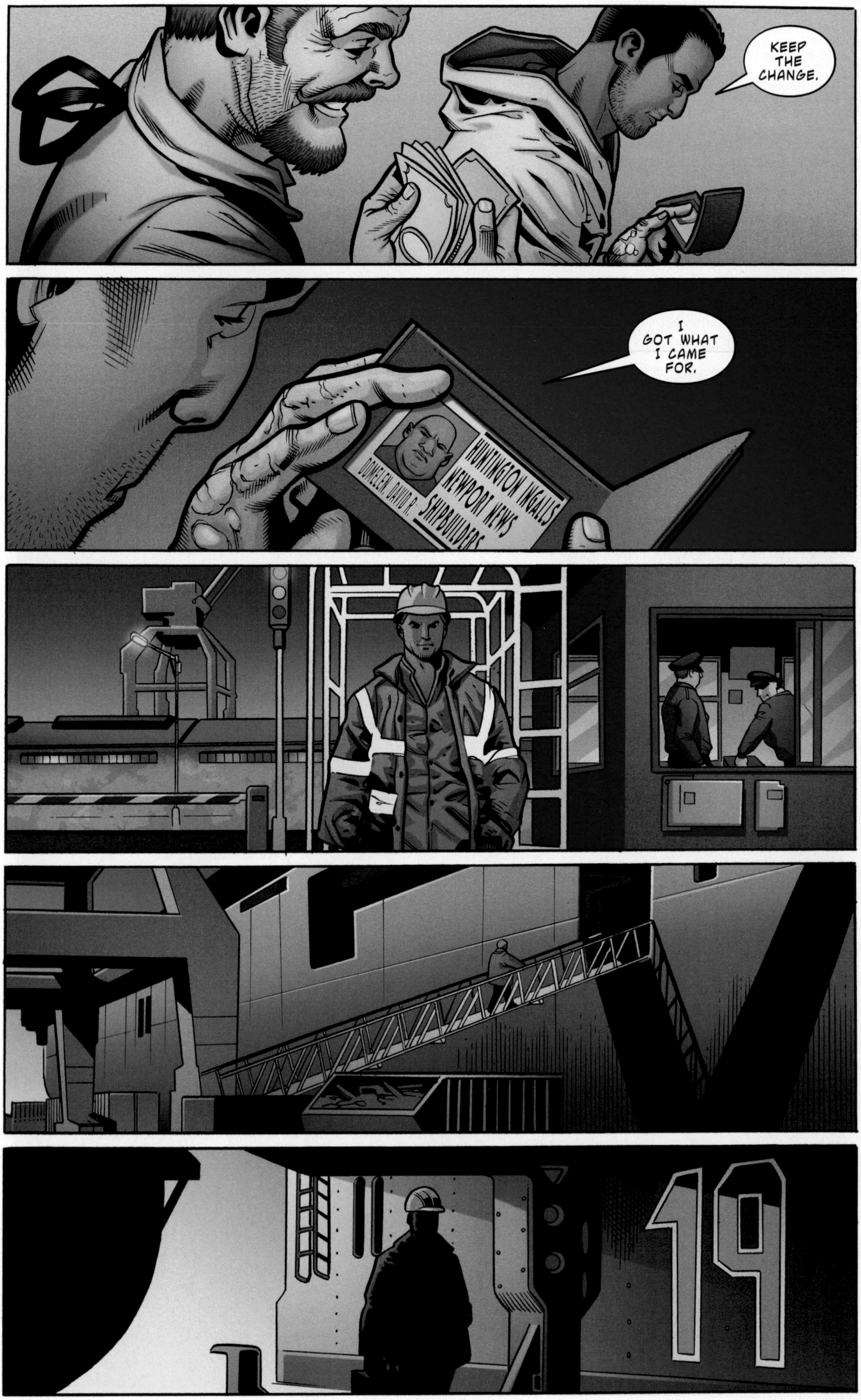

KEEP THE CHANGE.
I GOT WHAT I CAME FOR.
HUNTINGTON INGALLS
NEWPORT NEWS
SHIPBUILDERS
DONELEN, DAVID R.
19

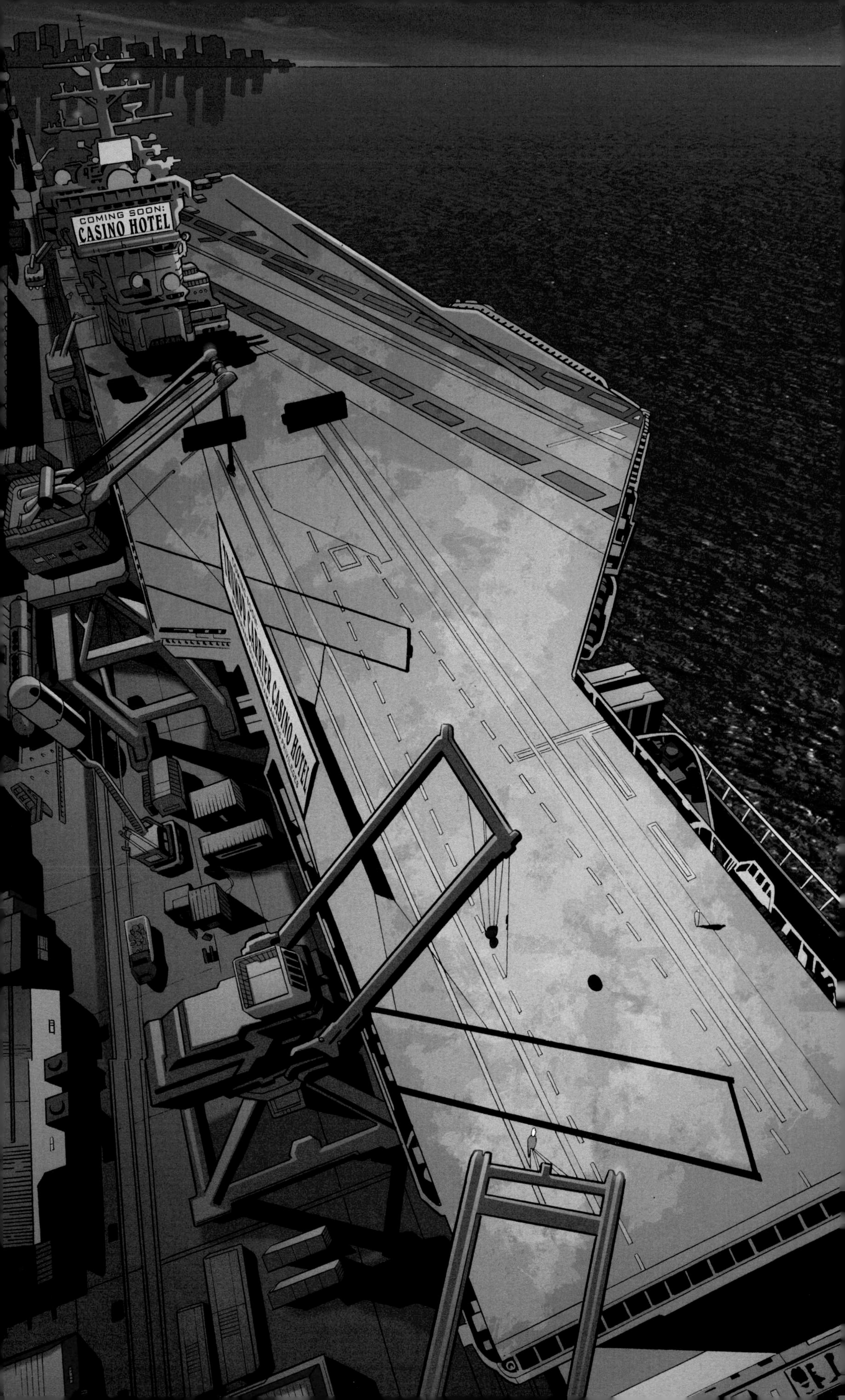
COMING SOON:
CASINO HOTEL
COMING SOON
CARRIER CASINO HOTEL
LANDING PRIVILEGES

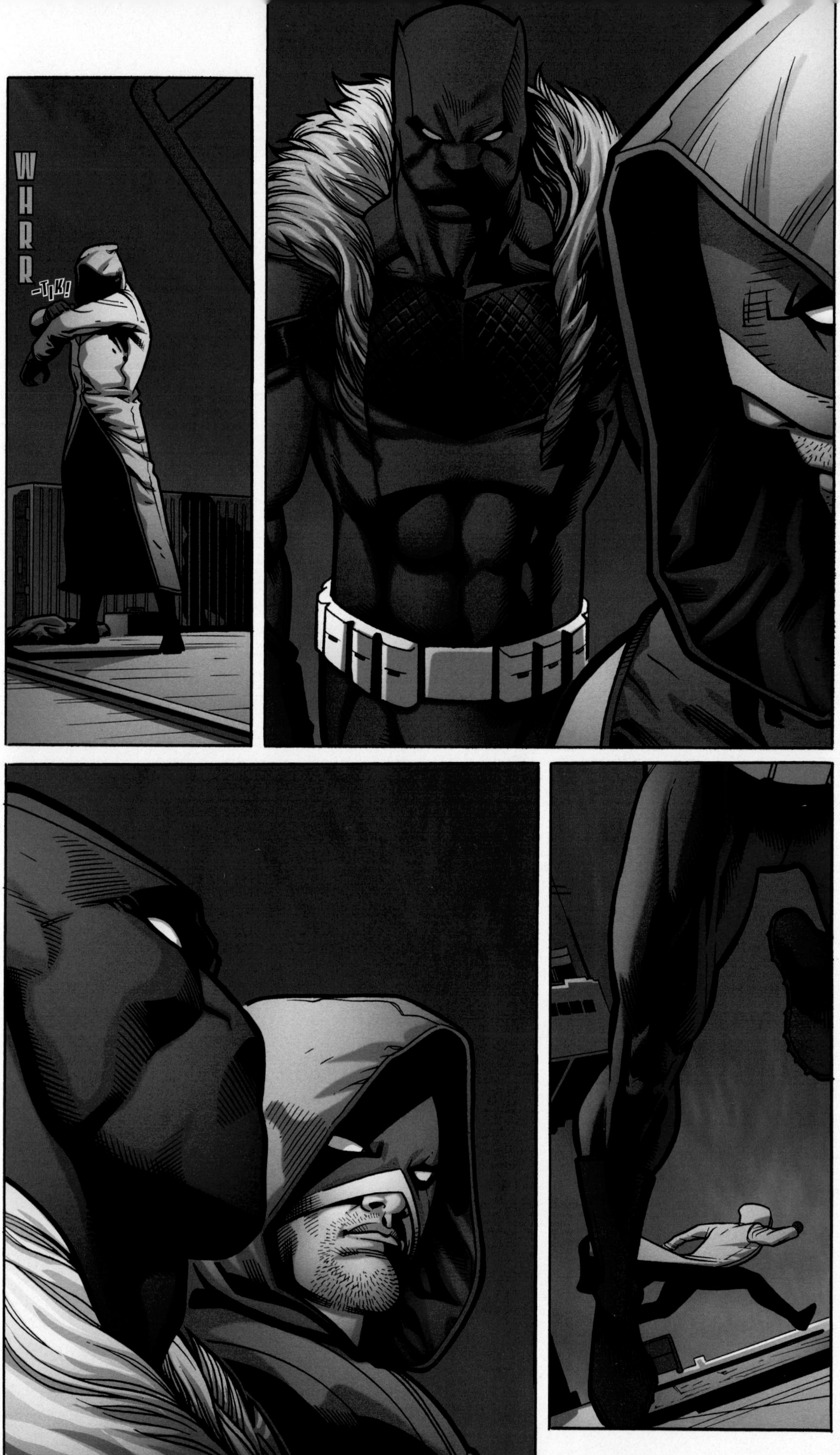
WHRR
-TIK!

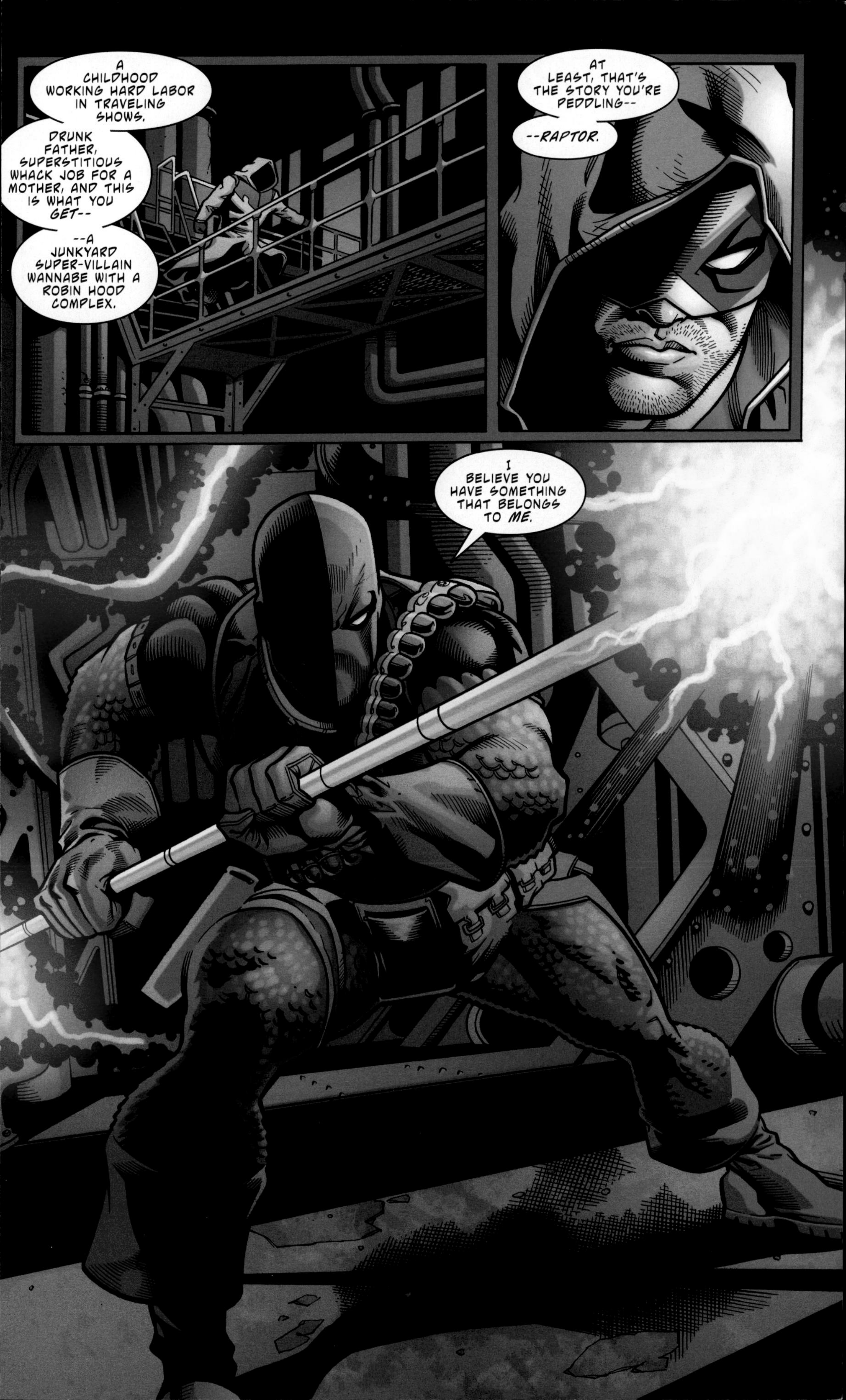
A CHILDHOOD WORKING HARD LABOR IN TRAVELING SHOWS.
DRUNK FATHER, SUPERSTITIOUS WHACK JOB FOR A MOTHER, AND THIS IS WHAT YOU GET--
--A JUNKYARD SUPER-VILLAIN WANNABE WITH A ROBIN HOOD COMPLEX.
AT LEAST, THAT'S THE STORY YOU'RE PEDDLING--
--RAPTOR.
I BELIEVE YOU HAVE SOMETHING THAT BELONGS TO *ME*.

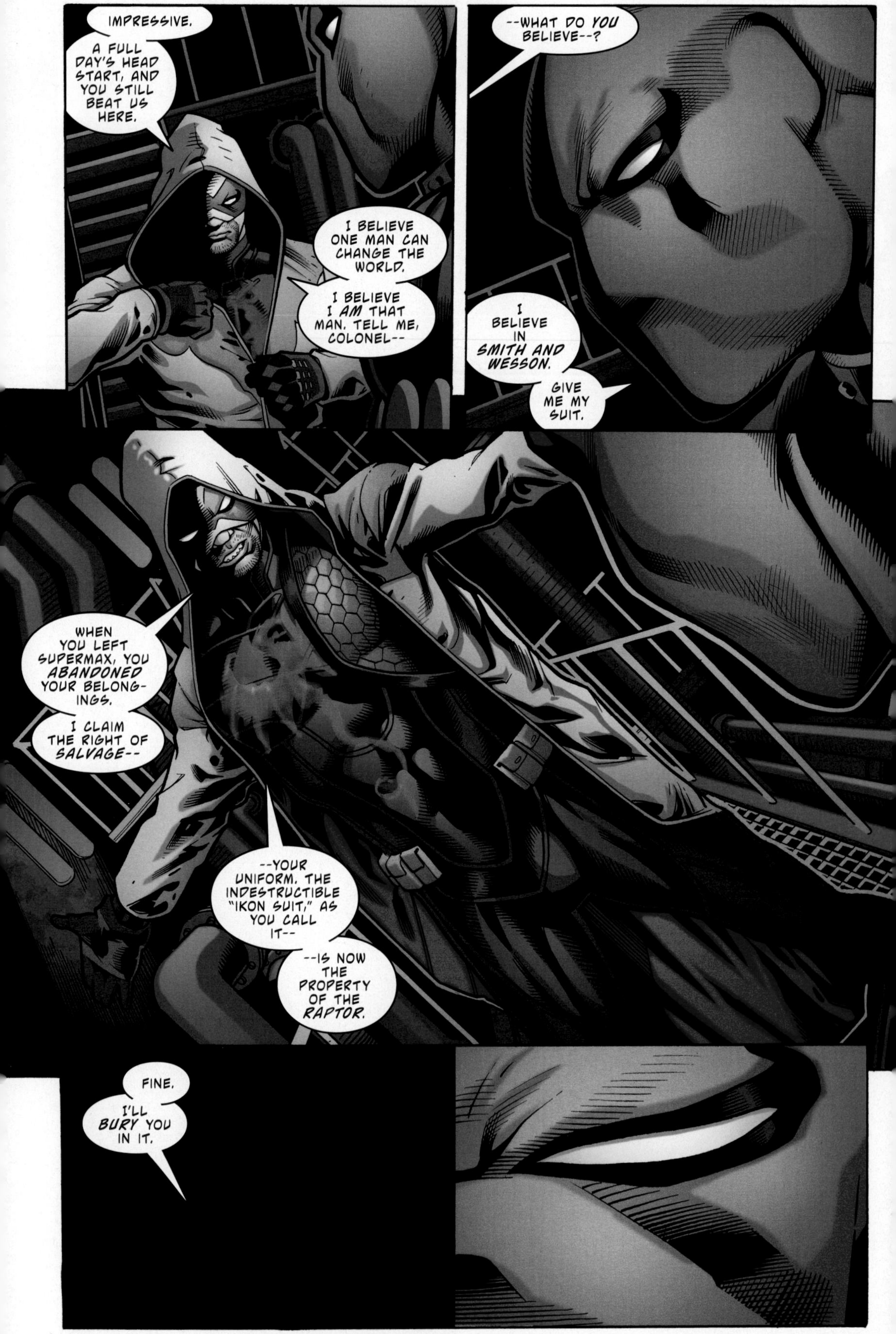
IMPRESSIVE.
A FULL DAY'S HEAD START, AND YOU STILL BEAT US HERE.
I BELIEVE ONE MAN CAN CHANGE THE WORLD.
I BELIEVE I AM THAT MAN. TELL ME, COLONEL--
--WHAT DO YOU BELIEVE--?
I BELIEVE IN SMITH AND WESSON.
GIVE ME MY SUIT.
WHEN YOU LEFT SUPERMAX, YOU ABANDONED YOUR BELONGINGS.
I CLAIM THE RIGHT OF SALVAGE--
--YOUR UNIFORM. THE INDESTRUCTIBLE "IKON SUIT," AS YOU CALL IT--
--IS NOW THE PROPERTY OF THE RAPTOR.
FINE.
I'LL BURY YOU IN IT.

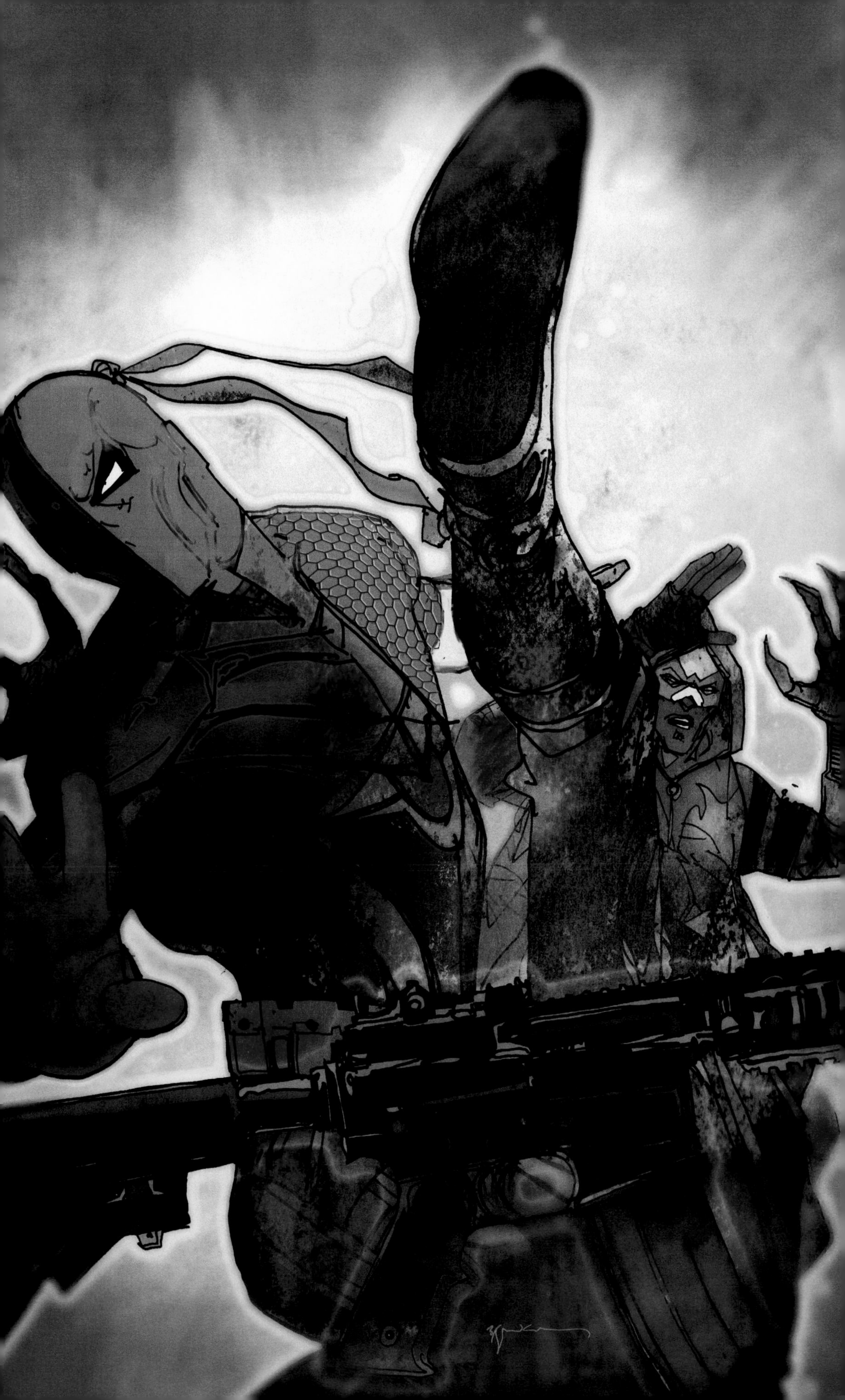

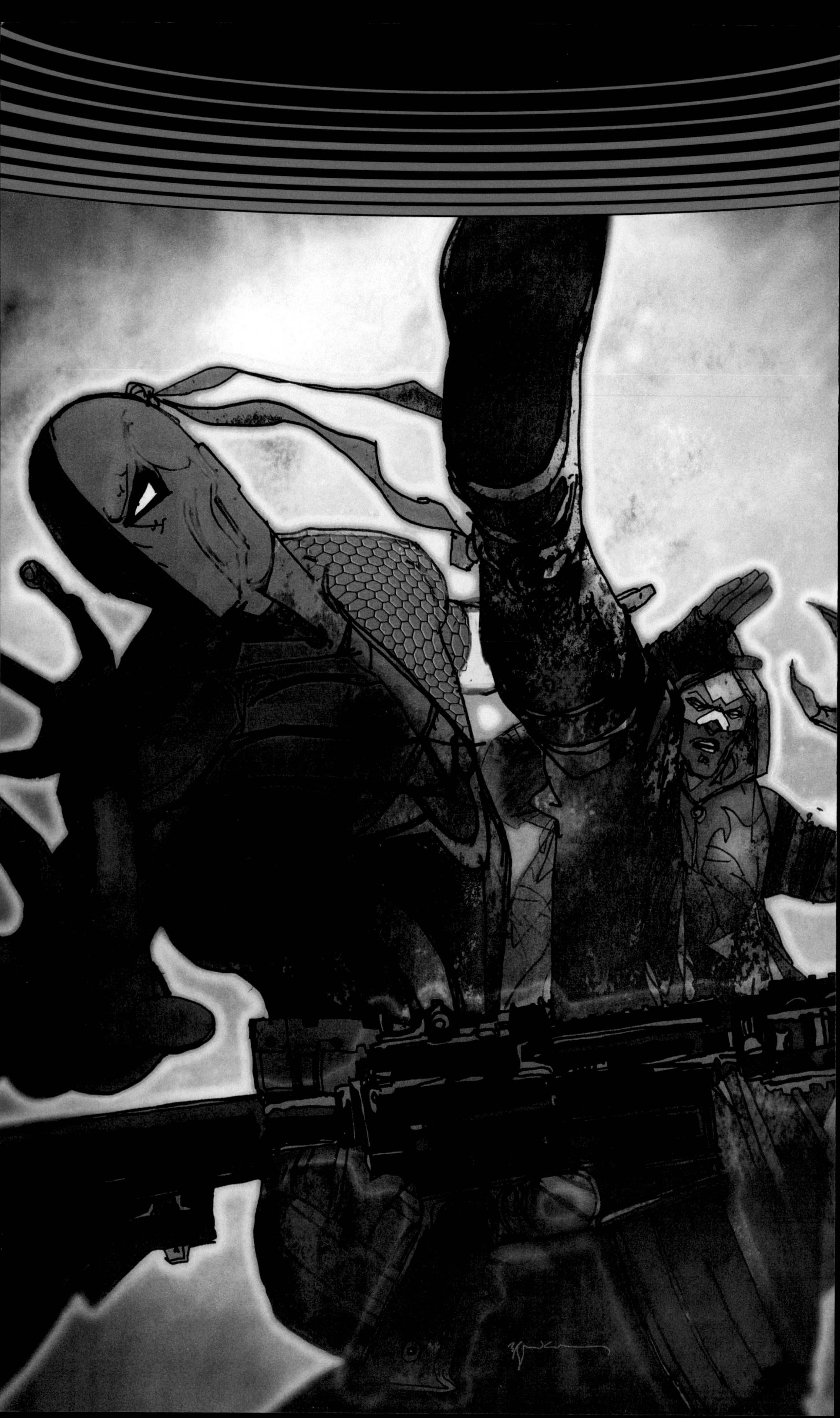

"The 5th"

*LOS ANGELES*

OH GOD.

HE'S SET THE DATE.

THE TWELFTH.

JOE WANTS US TO GET MARRIED IN A WEEK...

BLESS ME, FATHER, FOR I HAVE SINNED.

IT'S BEEN THREE DAYS SINCE MY LAST CONFESSION.

*CCHH HTTT!!*

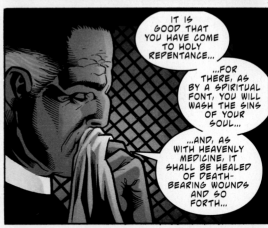

IT IS GOOD THAT YOU HAVE COME TO HOLY REPENTANCE...

...FOR THERE, AS BY A SPIRITUAL FONT, YOU WILL WASH THE SINS OF YOUR SOUL...

...AND, AS WITH HEAVENLY MEDICINE, IT SHALL BE HEALED OF DEATH-BEARING WOUNDS AND SO FORTH...

I BETRAYED MY FATHER... DISHONORED MY MOTHER...

...BETRAYED SOMEONE WHO LOVED ME...

...DESTROYED A *LIFE*, FATHER...

DON'T GIVE UP HOPE.

THERE'S NOTHING YOU'VE BROKEN THAT GOD CAN'T FIX.

I HEAR THIS KIND OF THING EVERY DAY.

YES, FROM *ME*--

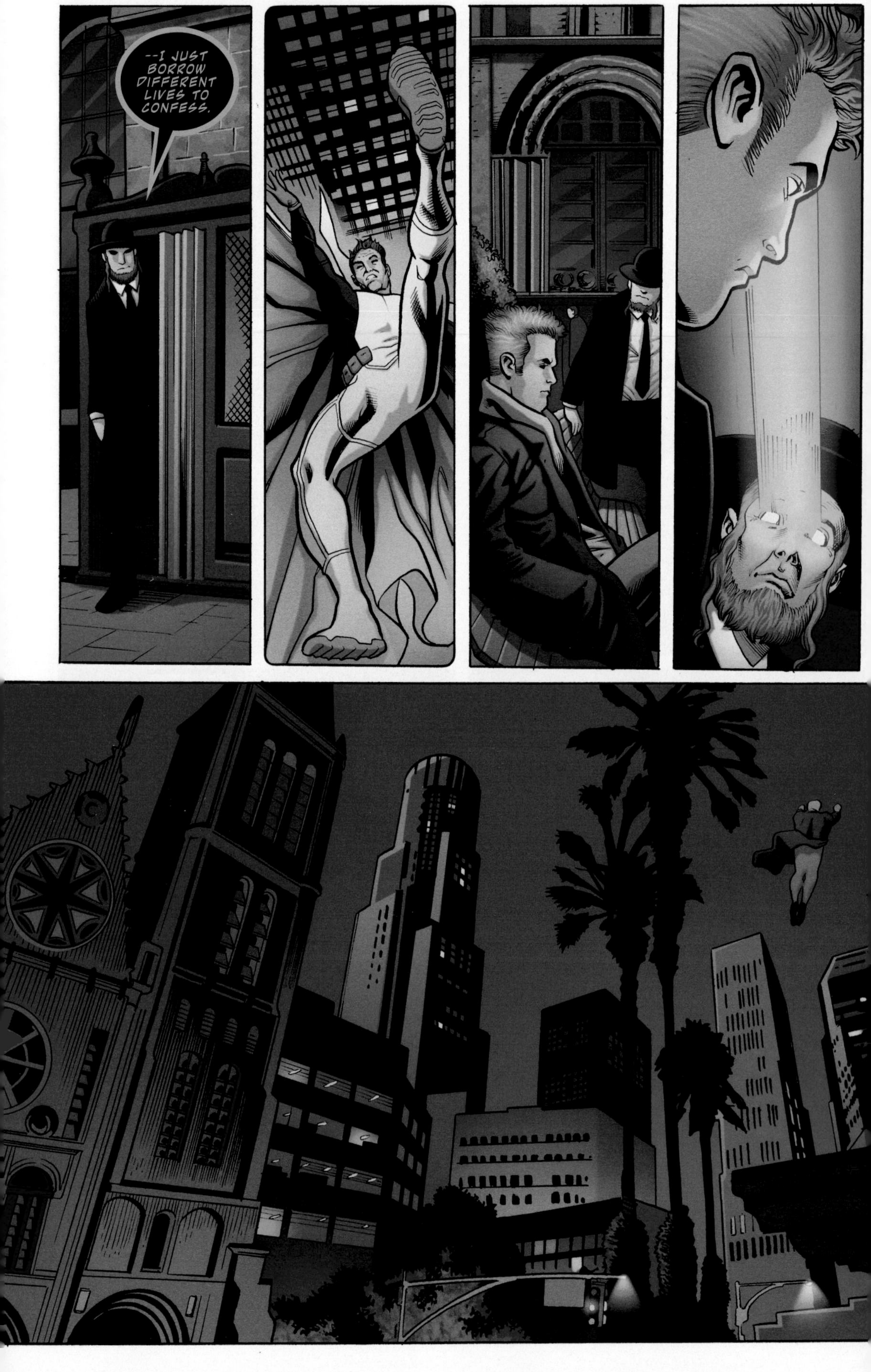
--I JUST BORROW DIFFERENT LIVES TO CONFESS.

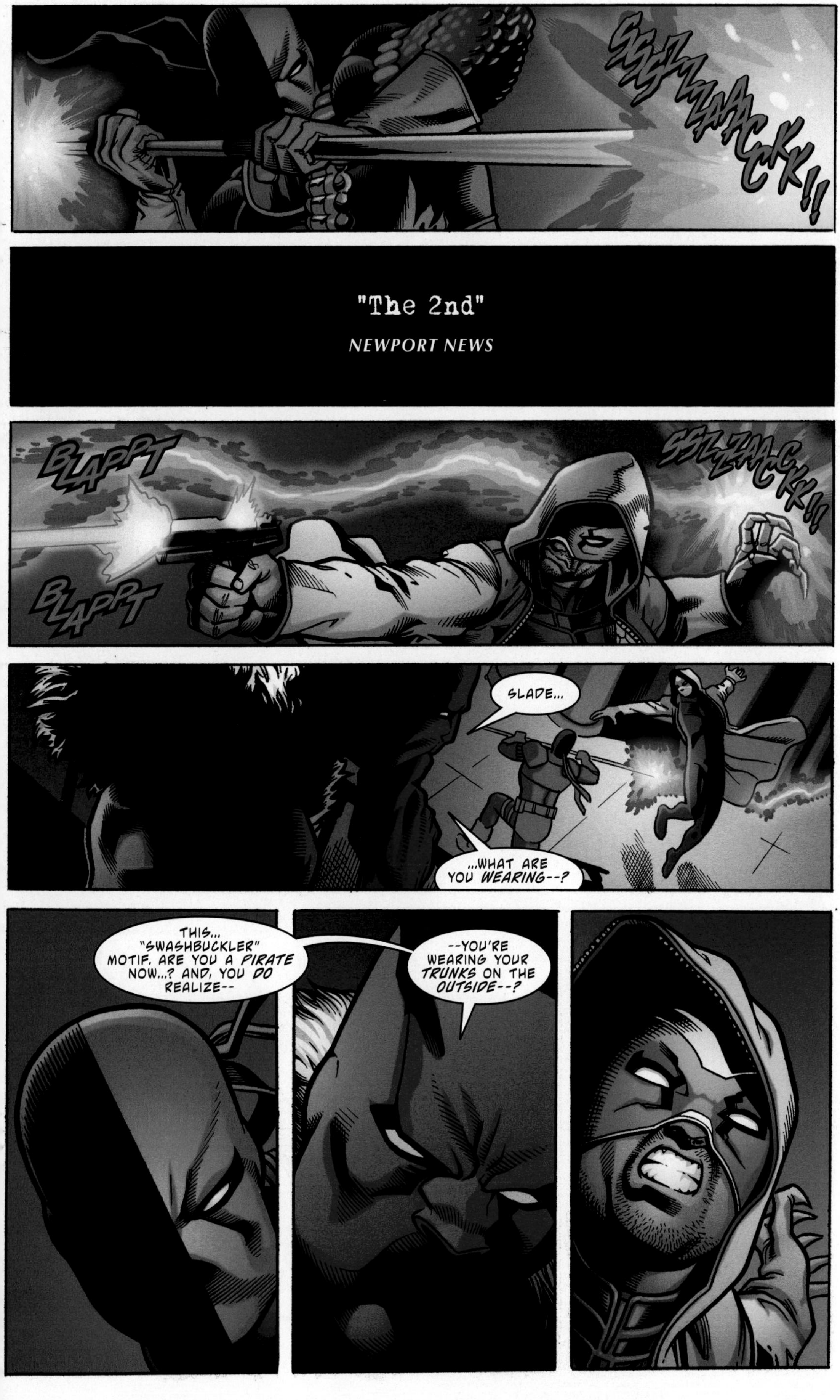

"The 2nd"
NEWPORT NEWS
BLAPPT
BLAPPT
SSZZZAACKK!!
SLADE...
...WHAT ARE YOU *WEARING*--?
THIS... "SWASHBUCKLER" MOTIF. ARE YOU A *PIRATE* NOW...? AND, YOU *DO* REALIZE--
--YOU'RE WEARING YOUR *TRUNKS* ON THE *OUTSIDE*--?

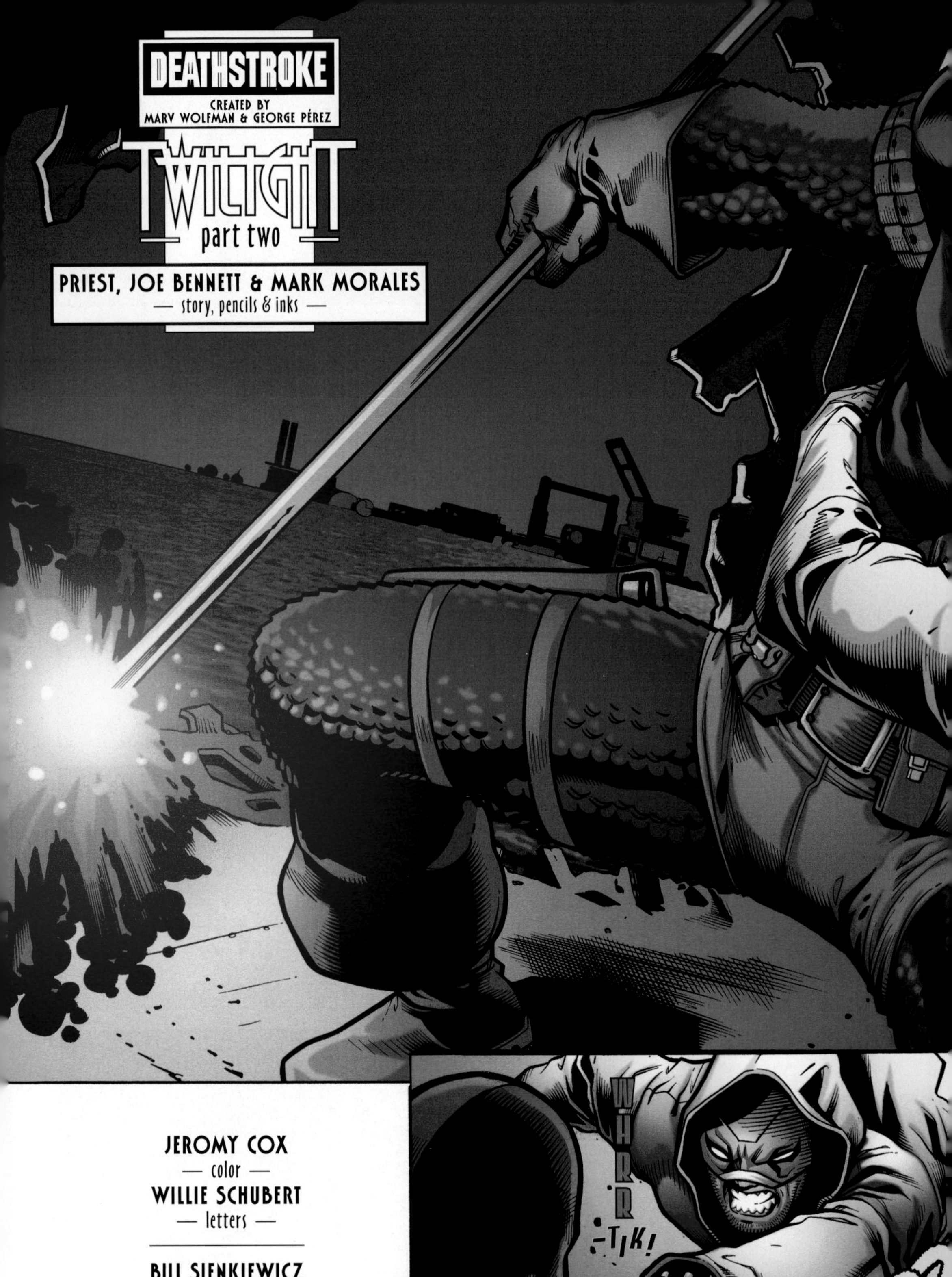
DEATHSTROKE
CREATED BY
MARV WOLFMAN & GEORGE PÉREZ
TWILIGHT
part two
PRIEST, JOE BENNETT & MARK MORALES
— story, pencils & inks —

JEROMY COX
— color —
WILLIE SCHUBERT
— letters —

BILL SIENKIEWICZ
— cover —

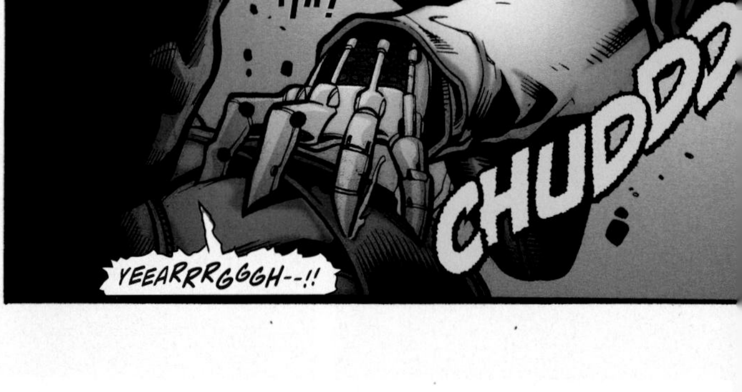
WHARR
-TIK!
CHUDDD
YEEARRRGGGH--!!

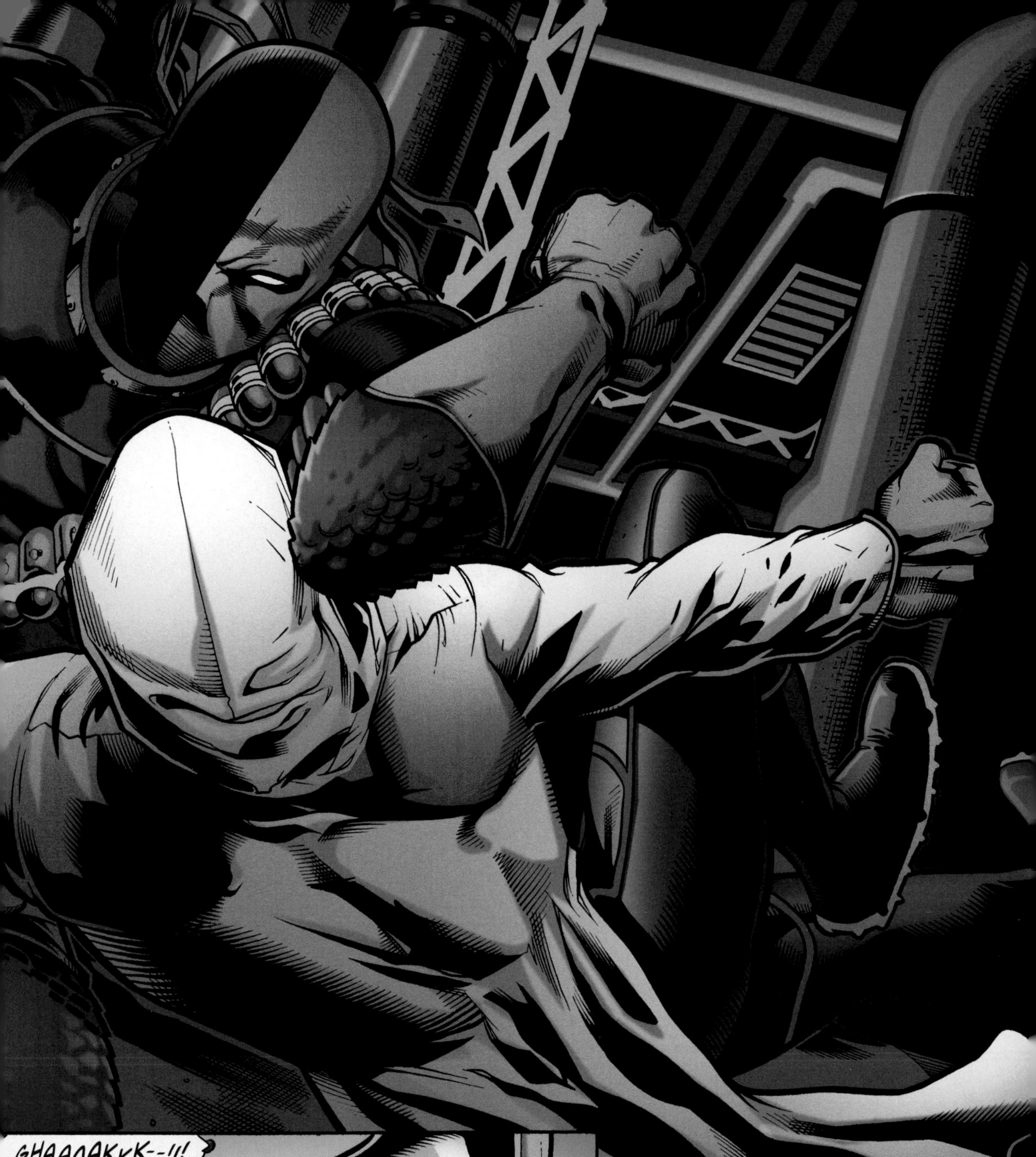

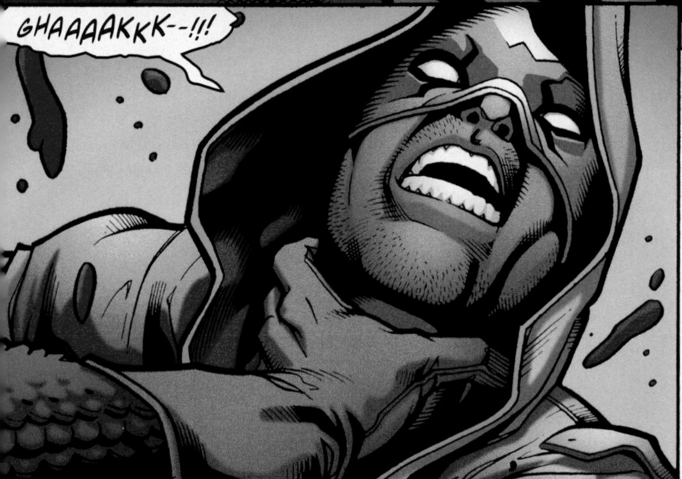
GHAAAAKKK--!!!

**BRITTANY HOLZHERR**
— assistant editor —
**ALEX ANTONE**
— editor —
**MARIE JAVINS**
— group editor —

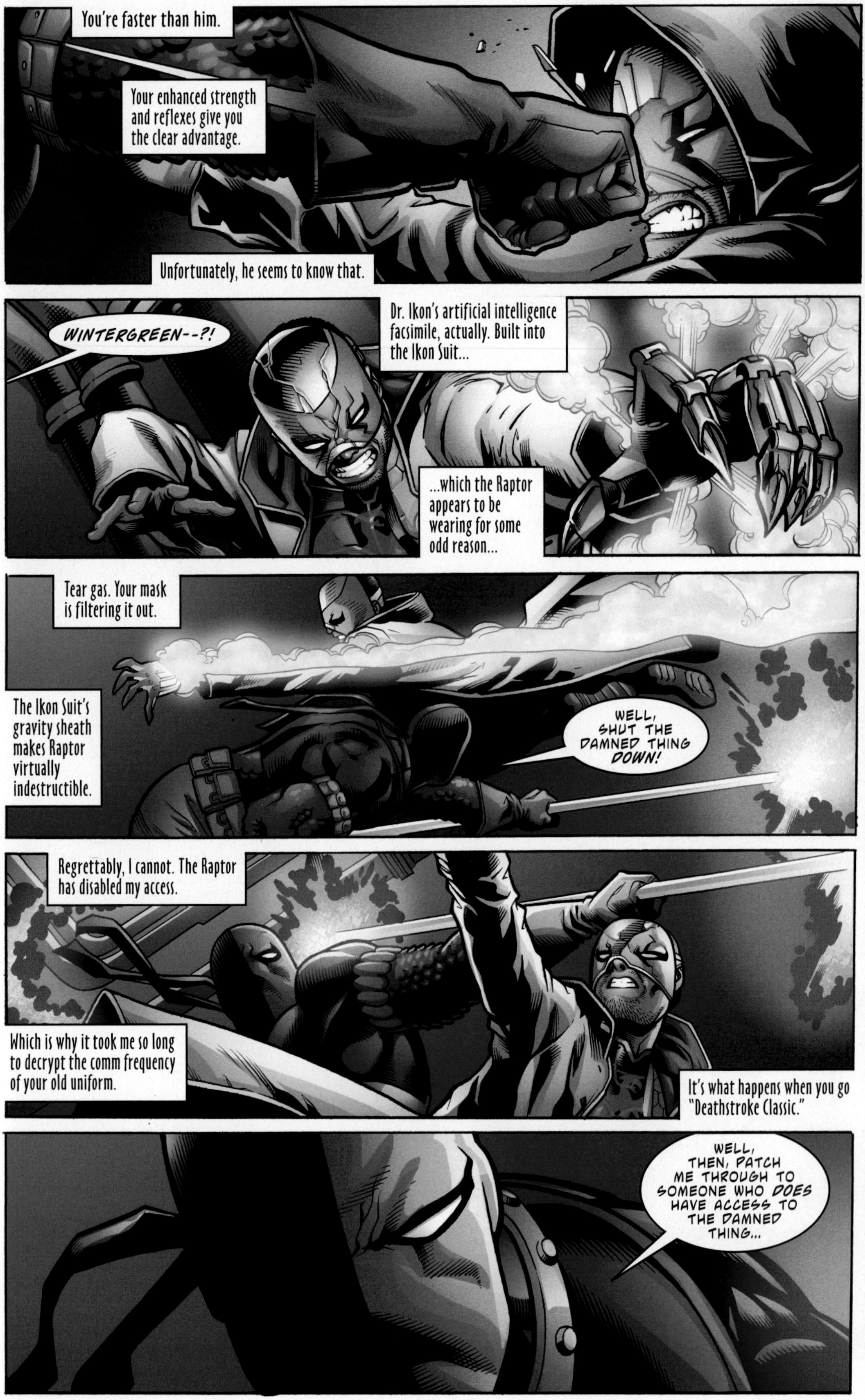
You're faster than him.
Your enhanced strength and reflexes give you the clear advantage.
Unfortunately, he seems to know that.
WINTERGREEN--?!
Dr. Ikon's artificial intelligence facsimile, actually. Built into the Ikon Suit...
...which the Raptor appears to be wearing for some odd reason...
Tear gas. Your mask is filtering it out.
The Ikon Suit's gravity sheath makes Raptor virtually indestructible.
WELL, SHUT THE DAMNED THING DOWN!
Regrettably, I cannot. The Raptor has disabled my access.
Which is why it took me so long to decrypt the comm frequency of your old uniform.
It's what happens when you go "Deathstroke Classic."
WELL, THEN, PATCH ME THROUGH TO SOMEONE WHO DOES HAVE ACCESS TO THE DAMNED THING...

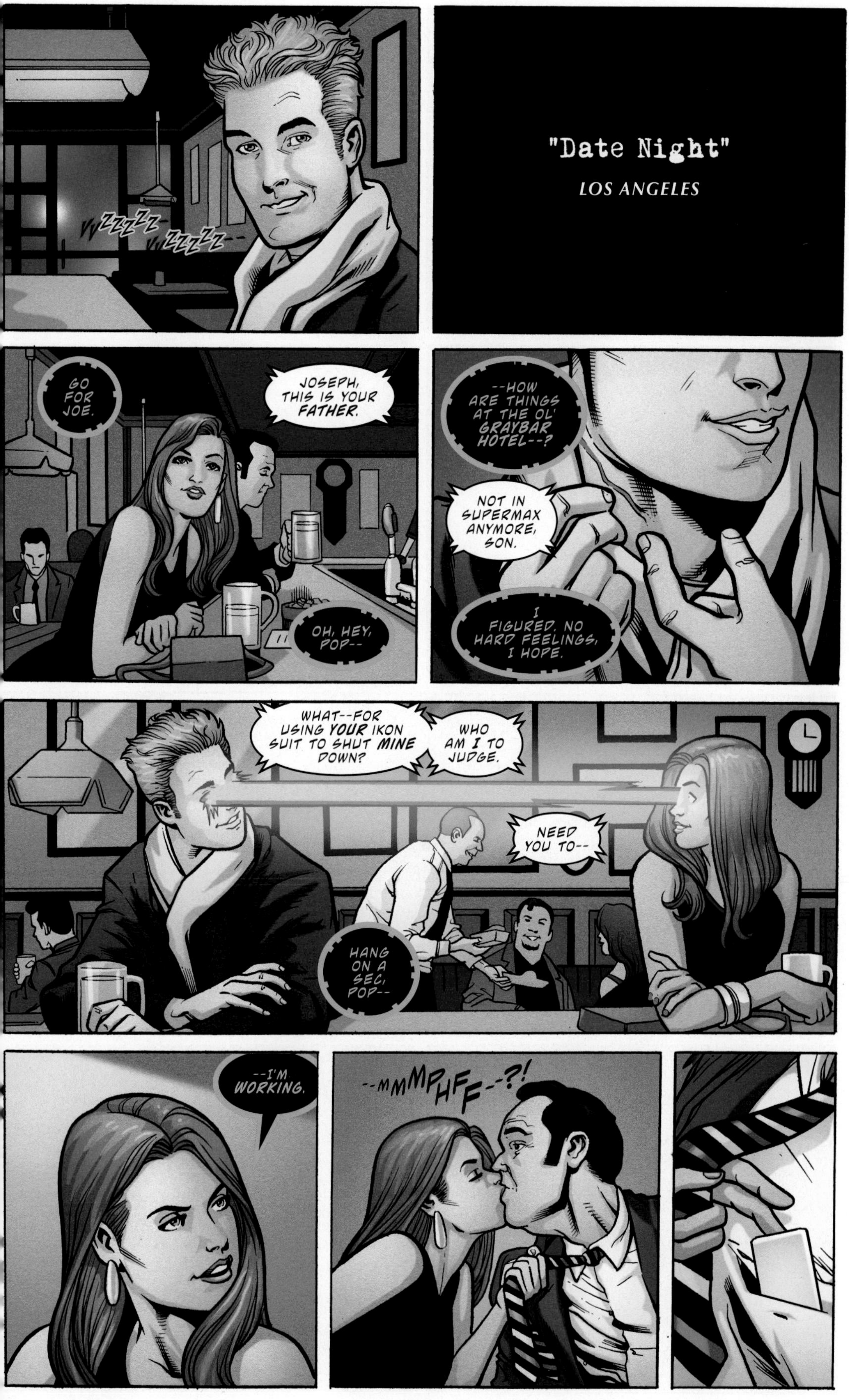
ZZZZZ ZZZZZ
"Date Night"
LOS ANGELES
GO FOR JOE.
JOSEPH, THIS IS YOUR FATHER.
OH, HEY, POP--
--HOW ARE THINGS AT THE OL' GRAYBAR HOTEL--?
NOT IN SUPERMAX ANYMORE, SON.
I FIGURED. NO HARD FEELINGS, I HOPE.
WHAT--FOR USING YOUR IKON SUIT TO SHUT MINE DOWN?
WHO AM I TO JUDGE.
NEED YOU TO--
HANG ON A SEC, POP--
--I'M WORKING.
--MMMPHFF--?!

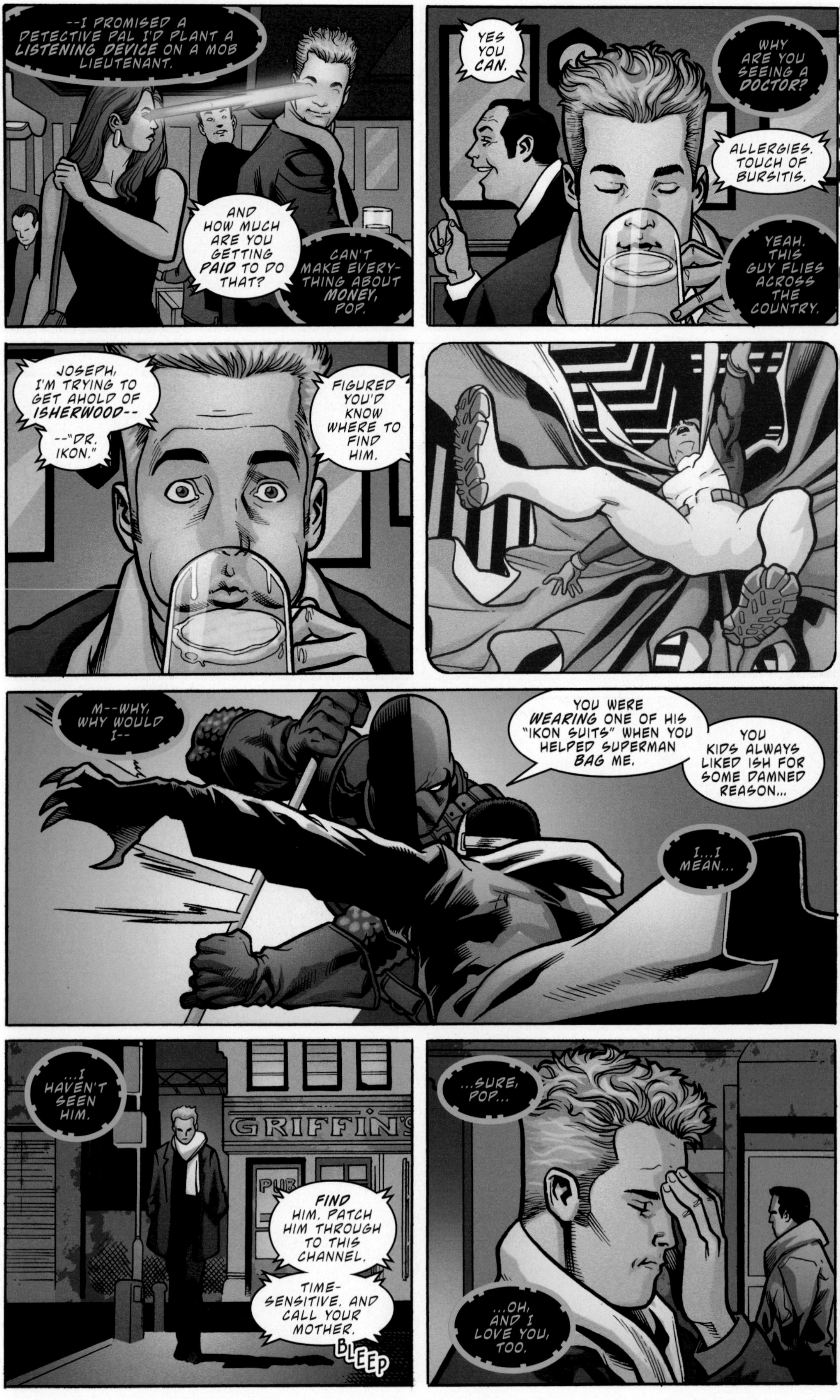
--I PROMISED A DETECTIVE PAL I'D PLANT A LISTENING DEVICE ON A MOB LIEUTENANT.
AND HOW MUCH ARE YOU GETTING PAID TO DO THAT?
CAN'T MAKE EVERYTHING ABOUT MONEY, POP.
YES YOU CAN.
WHY ARE YOU SEEING A DOCTOR?
ALLERGIES. TOUCH OF BURSITIS.
YEAH. THIS GUY FLIES ACROSS THE COUNTRY.
JOSEPH, I'M TRYING TO GET AHOLD OF ISHERWOOD--
--"DR. IKON."
FIGURED YOU'D KNOW WHERE TO FIND HIM.
M--WHY, WHY WOULD I--
YOU WERE WEARING ONE OF HIS "IKON SUITS" WHEN YOU HELPED SUPERMAN BAG ME.
YOU KIDS ALWAYS LIKED ISH FOR SOME DAMNED REASON...
I...I MEAN...
...I HAVEN'T SEEN HIM.
GRIFFIN'S
PUB
FIND HIM. PATCH HIM THROUGH TO THIS CHANNEL.
TIME-SENSITIVE. AND CALL YOUR MOTHER.
BLEEP
...SURE, POP...
...OH, AND I LOVE YOU, TOO.

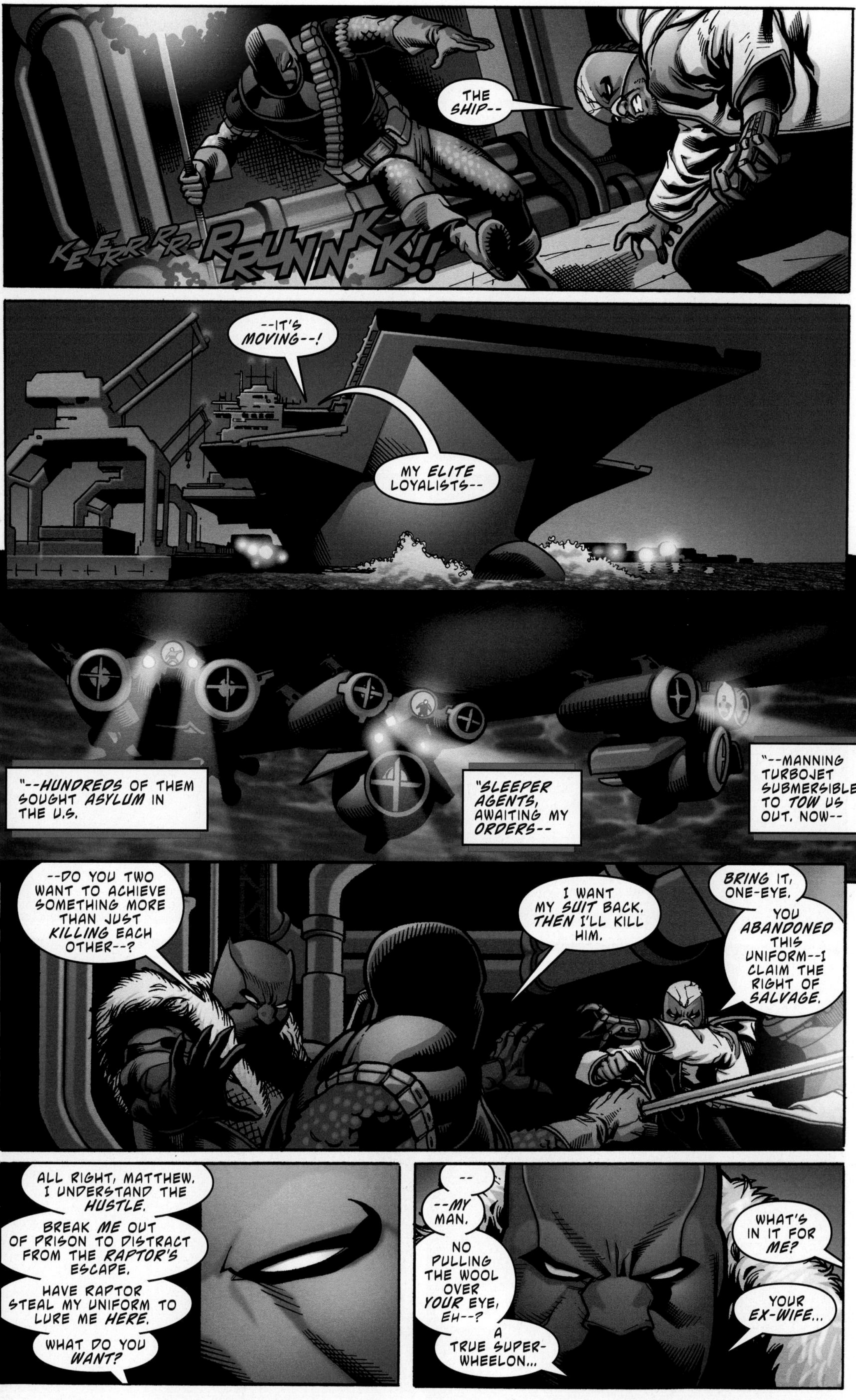

THE SHIP--
KEERRRRR-RRUNNKK!!
--IT'S MOVING--!
MY ELITE LOYALISTS--
"--HUNDREDS OF THEM SOUGHT ASYLUM IN THE U.S.
"SLEEPER AGENTS, AWAITING MY ORDERS--
"--MANNING TURBOJET SUBMERSIBLES TO TOW US OUT. NOW--
--DO YOU TWO WANT TO ACHIEVE SOMETHING MORE THAN JUST KILLING EACH OTHER--?
I WANT MY SUIT BACK. THEN I'LL KILL HIM.
BRING IT, ONE-EYE.
YOU ABANDONED THIS UNIFORM--I CLAIM THE RIGHT OF SALVAGE.
ALL RIGHT, MATTHEW. I UNDERSTAND THE HUSTLE.
BREAK ME OUT OF PRISON TO DISTRACT FROM THE RAPTOR'S ESCAPE.
HAVE RAPTOR STEAL MY UNIFORM TO LURE ME HERE.
WHAT DO YOU WANT?
--
--MY MAN.
NO PULLING THE WOOL OVER YOUR EYE, EH--?
A TRUE SUPER-WHEELON...
WHAT'S IN IT FOR ME?
YOUR EX-WIFE...

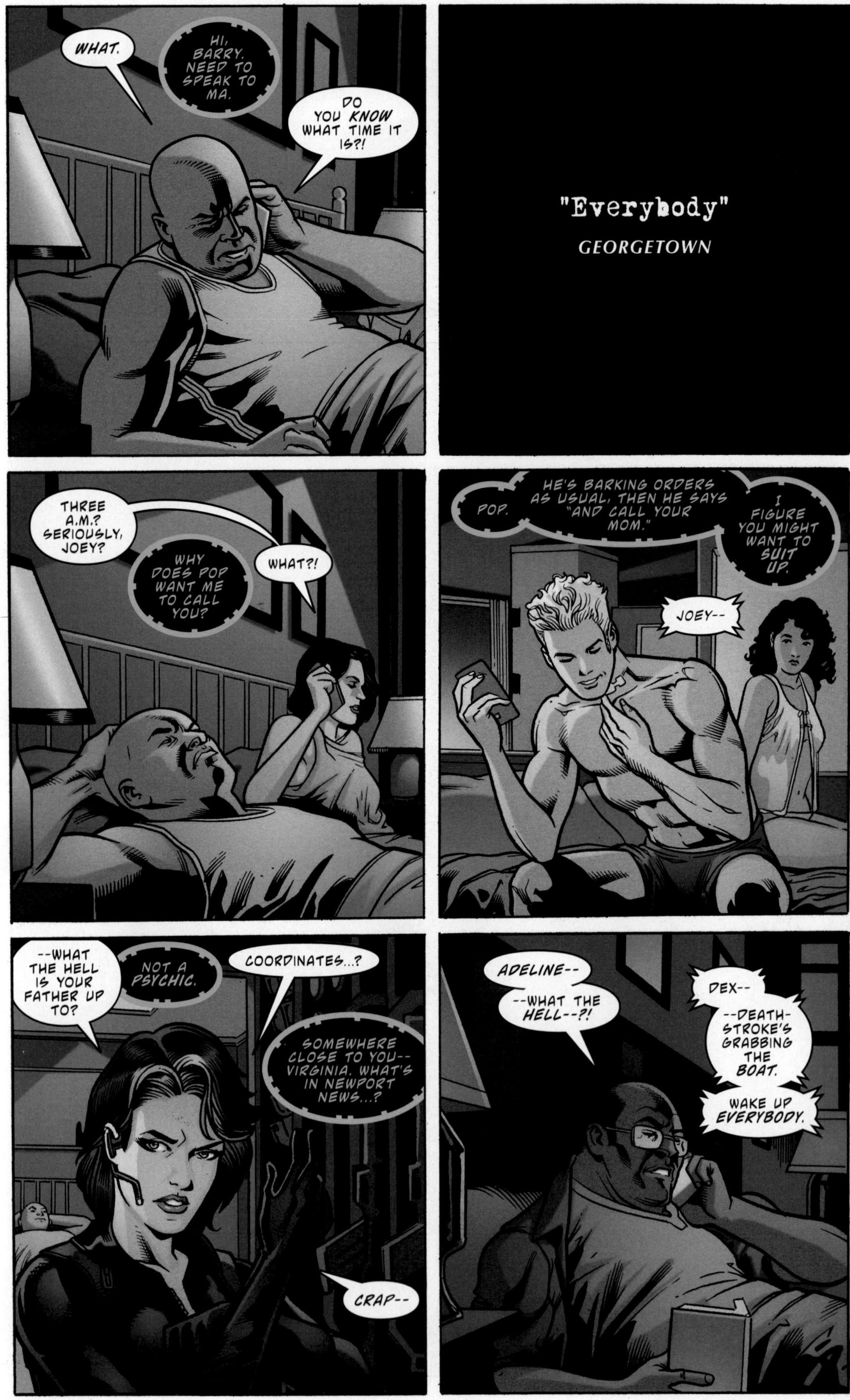
WHAT.
HI, BARRY. NEED TO SPEAK TO MA.
DO YOU KNOW WHAT TIME IT IS?!
"Everybody"
GEORGETOWN
THREE A.M.? SERIOUSLY, JOEY?
WHY DOES POP WANT ME TO CALL YOU?
WHAT?!
POP.
HE'S BARKING ORDERS AS USUAL, THEN HE SAYS "AND CALL YOUR MOM."
I FIGURE YOU MIGHT WANT TO SUIT UP.
JOEY--
--WHAT THE HELL IS YOUR FATHER UP TO?
NOT A PSYCHIC.
COORDINATES...?
SOMEWHERE CLOSE TO YOU-- VIRGINIA. WHAT'S IN NEWPORT NEWS...?
CRAP--
ADELINE--
--WHAT THE HELL--?!
DEX--
--DEATHSTROKE'S GRABBING THE BOAT.
WAKE UP EVERYBODY.

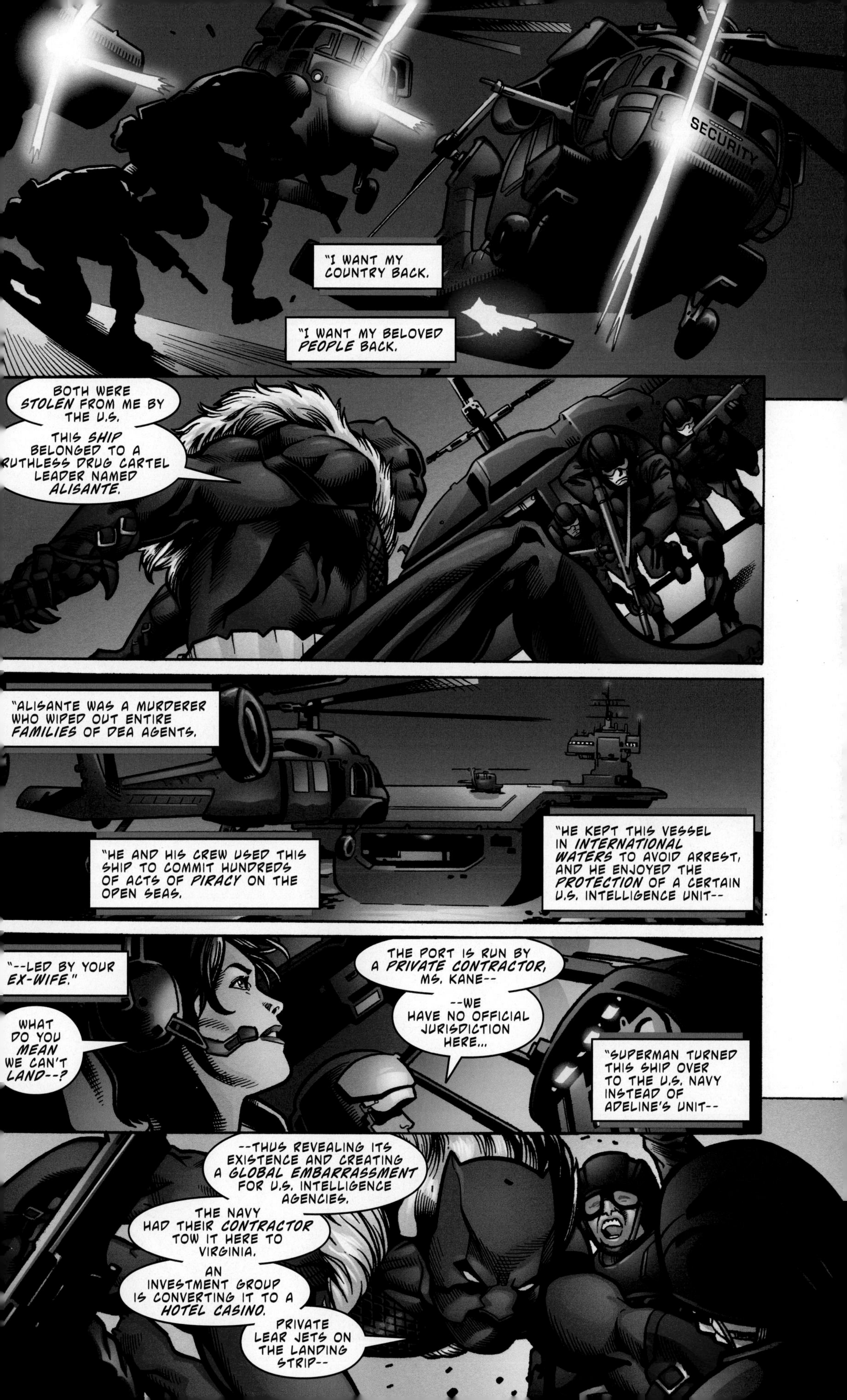

"I WANT MY COUNTRY BACK.
"I WANT MY BELOVED PEOPLE BACK.
BOTH WERE STOLEN FROM ME BY THE U.S.
THIS SHIP BELONGED TO A RUTHLESS DRUG CARTEL LEADER NAMED ALISANTE.
"ALISANTE WAS A MURDERER WHO WIPED OUT ENTIRE FAMILIES OF DEA AGENTS.
"HE AND HIS CREW USED THIS SHIP TO COMMIT HUNDREDS OF ACTS OF PIRACY ON THE OPEN SEAS.
"HE KEPT THIS VESSEL IN INTERNATIONAL WATERS TO AVOID ARREST, AND HE ENJOYED THE PROTECTION OF A CERTAIN U.S. INTELLIGENCE UNIT--
"--LED BY YOUR EX-WIFE."
WHAT DO YOU MEAN WE CAN'T LAND--?
THE PORT IS RUN BY A PRIVATE CONTRACTOR, MS. KANE--
--WE HAVE NO OFFICIAL JURISDICTION HERE...
"SUPERMAN TURNED THIS SHIP OVER TO THE U.S. NAVY INSTEAD OF ADELINE'S UNIT--
--THUS REVEALING ITS EXISTENCE AND CREATING A GLOBAL EMBARRASSMENT FOR U.S. INTELLIGENCE AGENCIES.
THE NAVY HAD THEIR CONTRACTOR TOW IT HERE TO VIRGINIA.
AN INVESTMENT GROUP IS CONVERTING IT TO A HOTEL CASINO.
PRIVATE LEAR JETS ON THE LANDING STRIP--

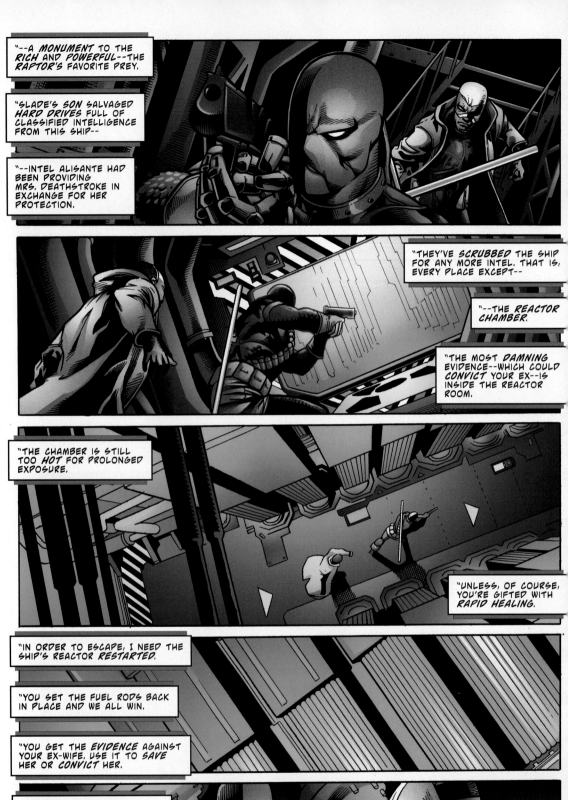

"--A *MONUMENT* TO THE *RICH* AND *POWERFUL*--THE *RAPTOR'S* FAVORITE PREY.

"*SLADE'S SON* SALVAGED *HARD DRIVES* FULL OF CLASSIFIED INTELLIGENCE FROM THIS SHIP--

"--INTEL ALISANTE HAD BEEN PROVIDING MRS. DEATHSTROKE IN EXCHANGE FOR HER PROTECTION.

"THEY'VE *SCRUBBED* THE SHIP FOR ANY MORE INTEL. THAT IS, EVERY PLACE EXCEPT--

"--THE *REACTOR CHAMBER.*

"THE MOST *DAMNING* EVIDENCE--WHICH COULD *CONVICT* YOUR EX--IS INSIDE THE REACTOR ROOM.

"THE CHAMBER IS STILL TOO *HOT* FOR PROLONGED EXPOSURE.

"UNLESS, OF COURSE, YOU'RE GIFTED WITH *RAPID HEALING.*

"IN ORDER TO ESCAPE, I NEED THE SHIP'S REACTOR *RESTARTED.*

"YOU SET THE FUEL RODS BACK IN PLACE AND WE ALL WIN.

"YOU GET THE *EVIDENCE* AGAINST YOUR EX-WIFE. USE IT TO *SAVE* HER OR *CONVICT* HER.

"*RAPTOR* GETS TO *STICK* IT TO THE BILLIONAIRE GROUP WHO *BOUGHT* THIS SHIP.

"I GET MY *COUNTRY BACK.*

"IT'S *WIN-WIN.*"

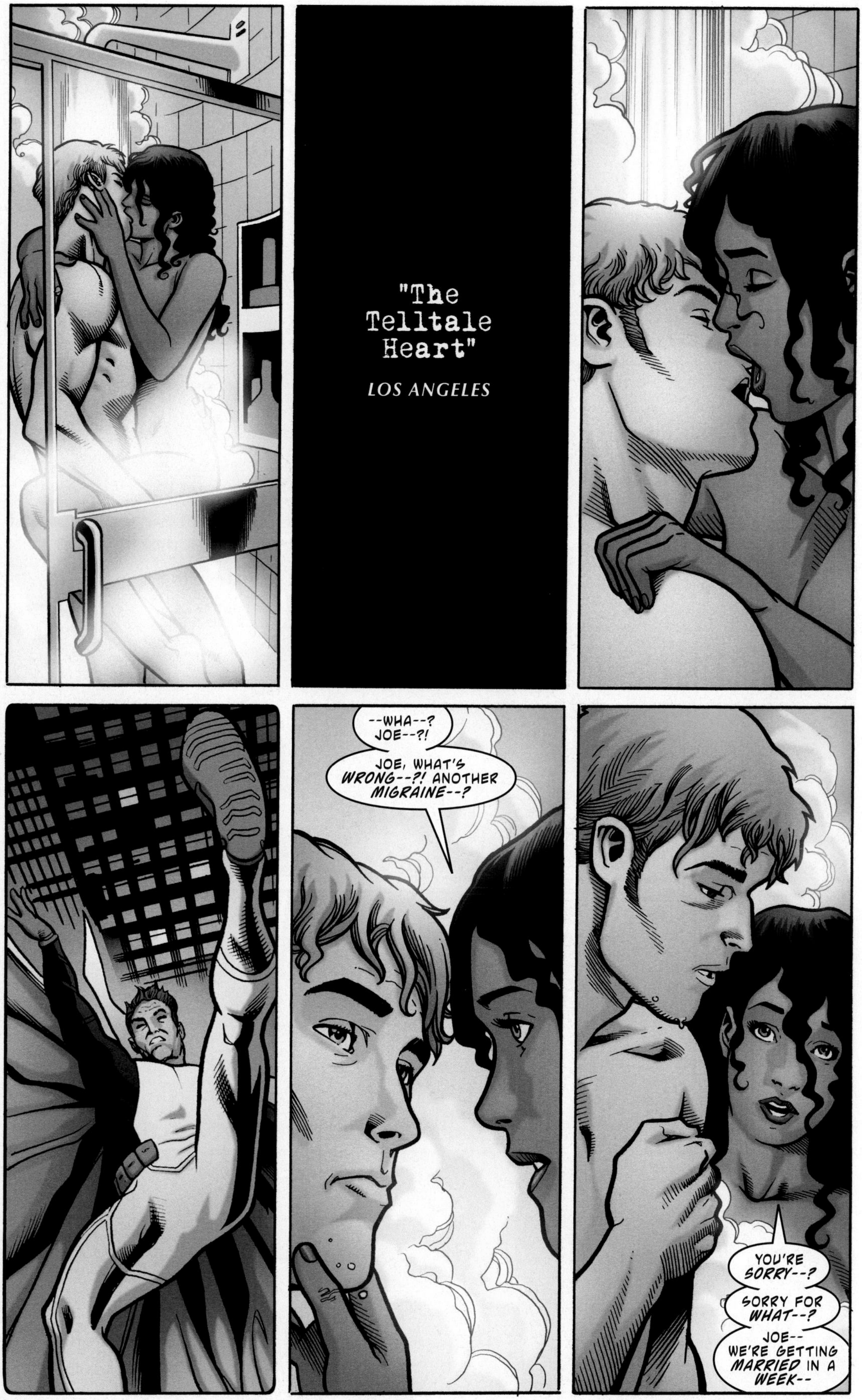
"The Telltale Heart"
LOS ANGELES
--WHA--? JOE--?!
JOE, WHAT'S WRONG--?! ANOTHER MIGRAINE--?
YOU'RE SORRY--?
SORRY FOR WHAT--?
JOE-- WE'RE GETTING MARRIED IN A WEEK--

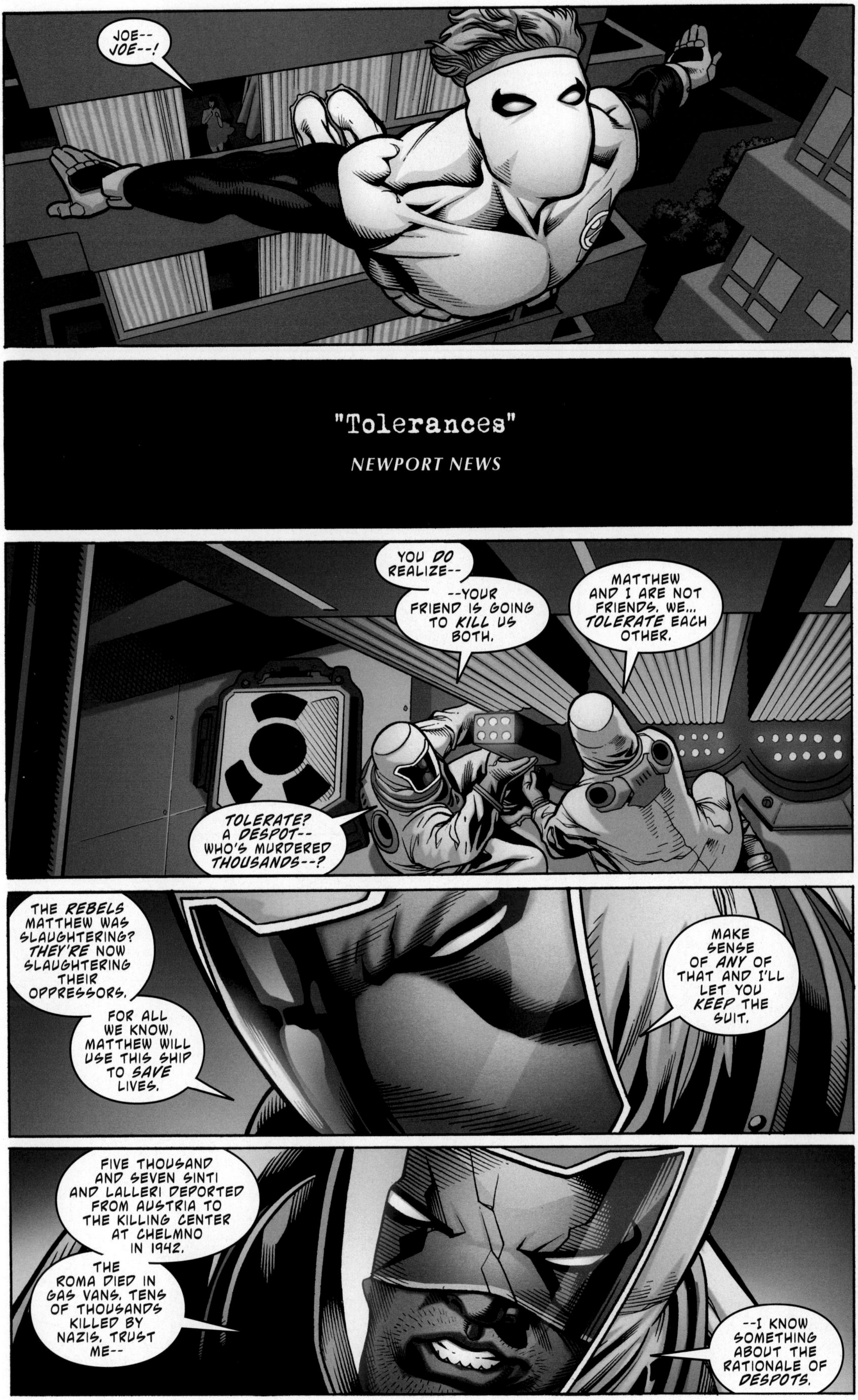
JOE-- JOE--!
"Tolerances"
NEWPORT NEWS
YOU *DO* REALIZE--
--YOUR FRIEND IS GOING TO *KILL* US BOTH.
MATTHEW AND I ARE NOT FRIENDS. WE... *TOLERATE* EACH OTHER.
*TOLERATE?* A *DESPOT*-- WHO'S MURDERED *THOUSANDS*--?
THE *REBELS* MATTHEW WAS SLAUGHTERING? *THEY'RE* NOW SLAUGHTERING THEIR OPPRESSORS.
FOR ALL WE KNOW, MATTHEW WILL USE THIS SHIP TO *SAVE* LIVES.
MAKE SENSE OF *ANY* OF THAT AND I'LL LET YOU *KEEP* THE SUIT.
FIVE THOUSAND AND SEVEN SINTI AND LALLERI DEPORTED FROM AUSTRIA TO THE KILLING CENTER AT CHELMNO IN 1942.
THE ROMA DIED IN GAS VANS, TENS OF THOUSANDS KILLED BY NAZIS. TRUST ME--
--I KNOW SOMETHING ABOUT THE RATIONALE OF *DESPOTS*.

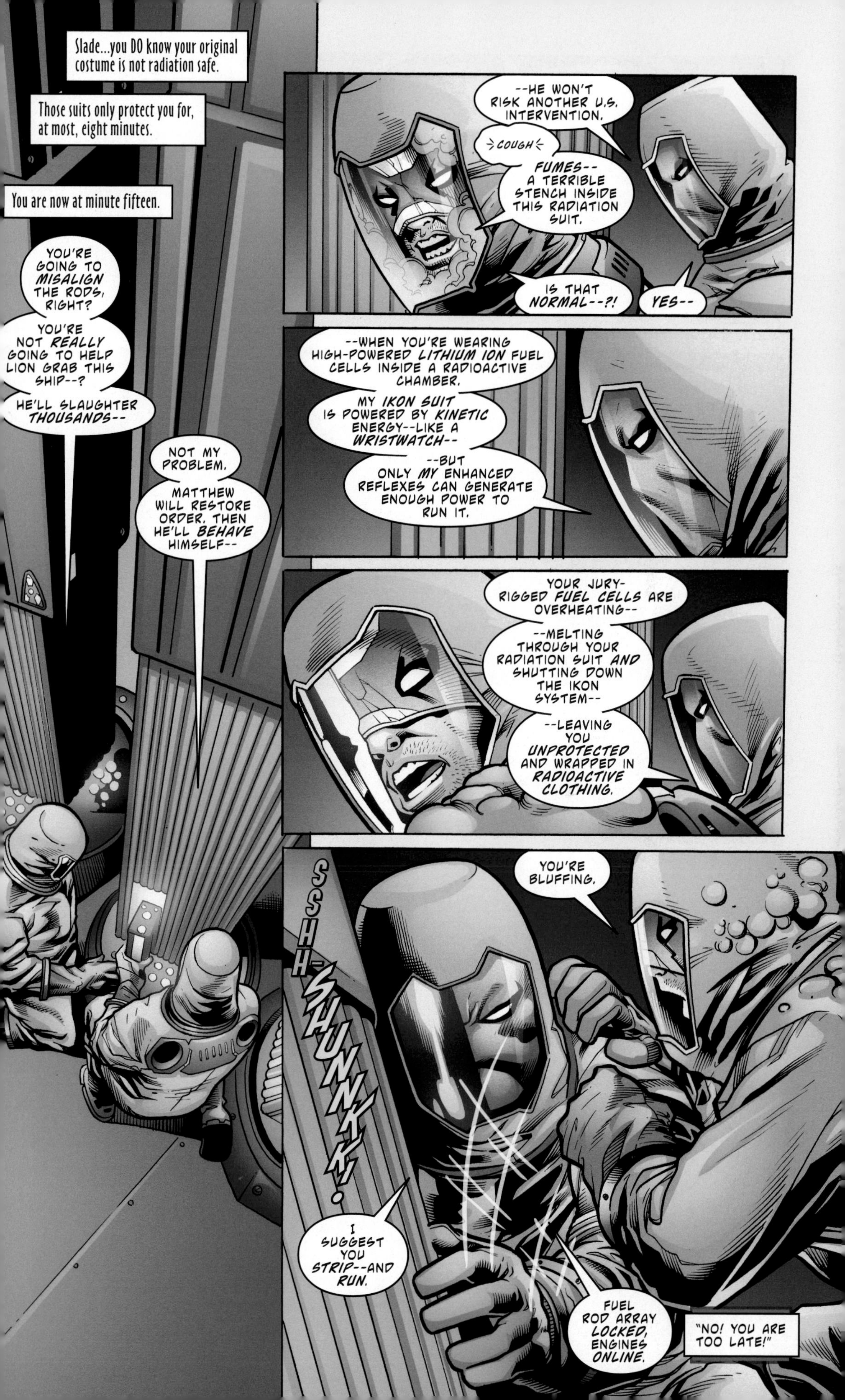
Slade...you DO know your original costume is not radiation safe.
Those suits only protect you for, at most, eight minutes.
You are now at minute fifteen.
YOU'RE GOING TO MISALIGN THE RODS, RIGHT?
YOU'RE NOT REALLY GOING TO HELP LION GRAB THIS SHIP--?
HE'LL SLAUGHTER THOUSANDS--
NOT MY PROBLEM.
MATTHEW WILL RESTORE ORDER. THEN HE'LL BEHAVE HIMSELF--
--HE WON'T RISK ANOTHER U.S. INTERVENTION.
COUGH
FUMES-- A TERRIBLE STENCH INSIDE THIS RADIATION SUIT.
IS THAT NORMAL--?!
YES--
--WHEN YOU'RE WEARING HIGH-POWERED LITHIUM ION FUEL CELLS INSIDE A RADIOACTIVE CHAMBER.
MY IKON SUIT IS POWERED BY KINETIC ENERGY--LIKE A WRISTWATCH--
--BUT ONLY MY ENHANCED REFLEXES CAN GENERATE ENOUGH POWER TO RUN IT.
YOUR JURY-RIGGED FUEL CELLS ARE OVERHEATING--
--MELTING THROUGH YOUR RADIATION SUIT AND SHUTTING DOWN THE IKON SYSTEM--
--LEAVING YOU UNPROTECTED AND WRAPPED IN RADIOACTIVE CLOTHING.
YOU'RE BLUFFING.
SSHH-SHUNNK!
I SUGGEST YOU STRIP--AND RUN.
FUEL ROD ARRAY LOCKED, ENGINES ONLINE.
"NO! YOU ARE TOO LATE!"

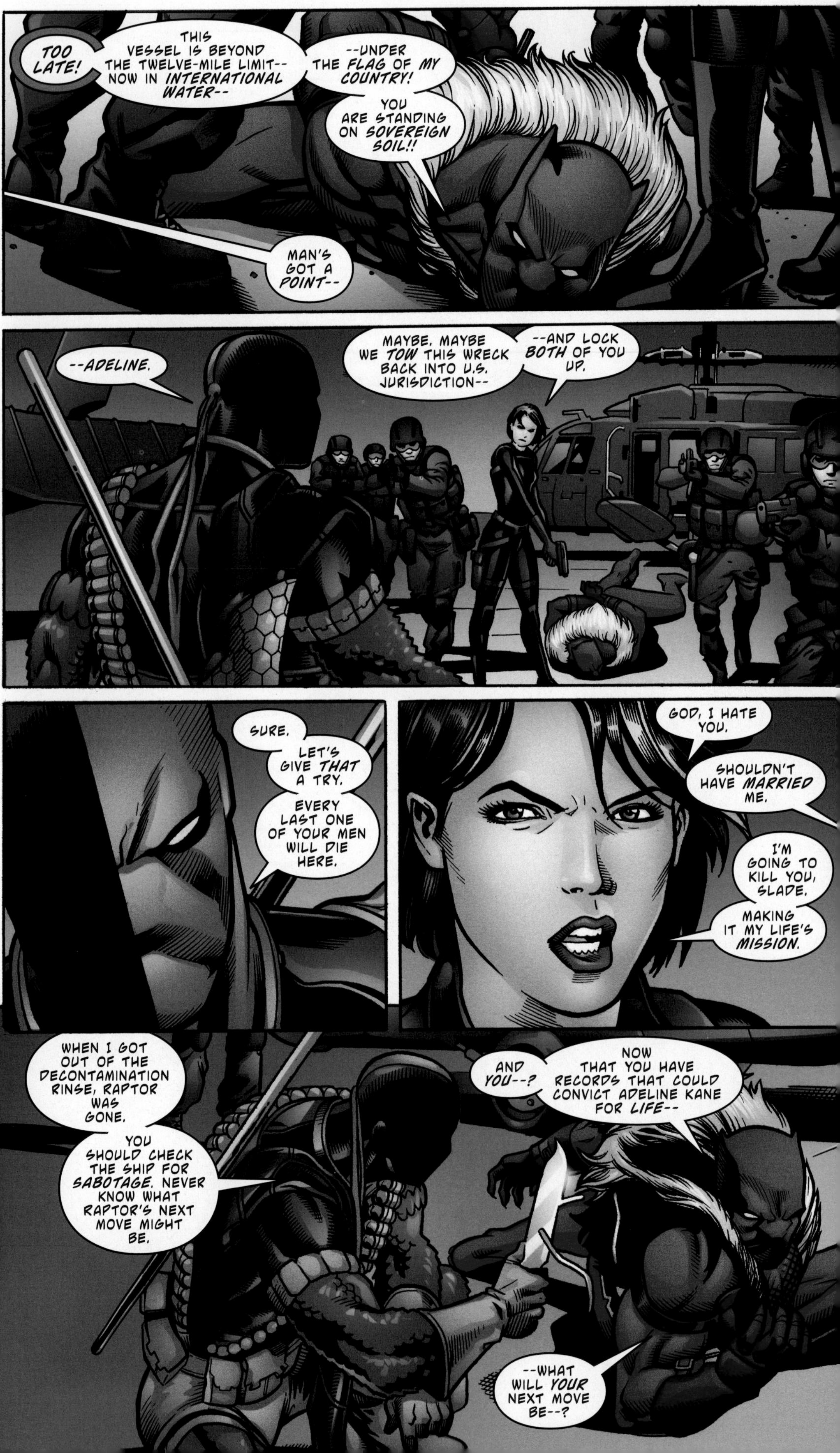

TOO LATE!
THIS VESSEL IS BEYOND THE TWELVE-MILE LIMIT-- NOW IN INTERNATIONAL WATER--
--UNDER THE FLAG OF MY COUNTRY!
YOU ARE STANDING ON SOVEREIGN SOIL!!
MAN'S GOT A POINT--
--ADELINE.
MAYBE. MAYBE WE TOW THIS WRECK BACK INTO U.S. JURISDICTION--
--AND LOCK BOTH OF YOU UP.
SURE.
LET'S GIVE THAT A TRY.
EVERY LAST ONE OF YOUR MEN WILL DIE HERE.
GOD, I HATE YOU.
SHOULDN'T HAVE MARRIED ME.
I'M GOING TO KILL YOU, SLADE.
MAKING IT MY LIFE'S MISSION.
WHEN I GOT OUT OF THE DECONTAMINATION RINSE, RAPTOR WAS GONE.
YOU SHOULD CHECK THE SHIP FOR SABOTAGE. NEVER KNOW WHAT RAPTOR'S NEXT MOVE MIGHT BE.
AND YOU--?
NOW THAT YOU HAVE RECORDS THAT COULD CONVICT ADELINE KANE FOR LIFE--
--WHAT WILL YOUR NEXT MOVE BE--?

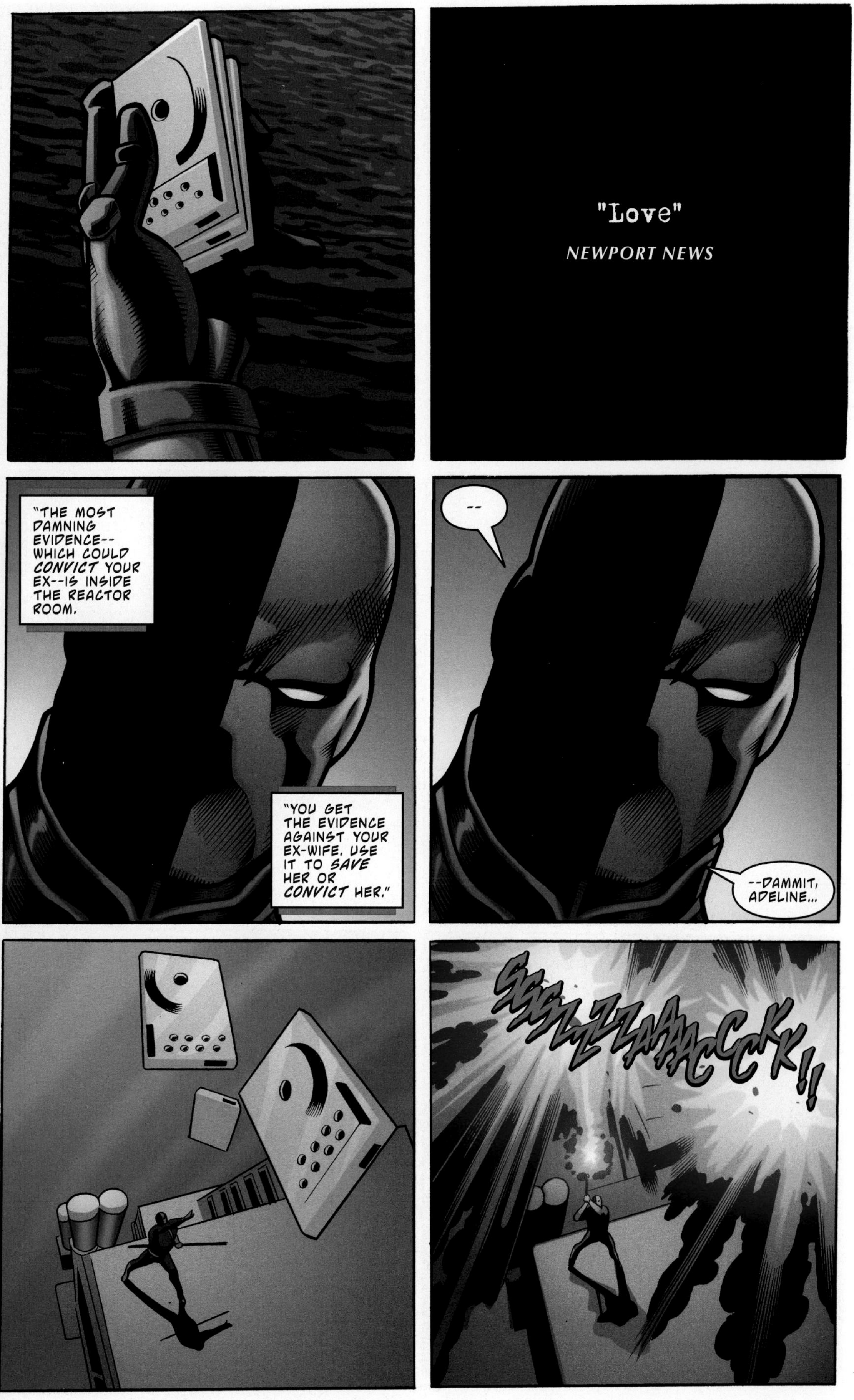
"Love"
NEWPORT NEWS
"THE MOST DAMNING EVIDENCE--WHICH COULD CONVICT YOUR EX--IS INSIDE THE REACTOR ROOM.
"YOU GET THE EVIDENCE AGAINST YOUR EX-WIFE. USE IT TO SAVE HER OR CONVICT HER."
--
--DAMMIT, ADELINE...
GSSZZZAAACCCKK!!

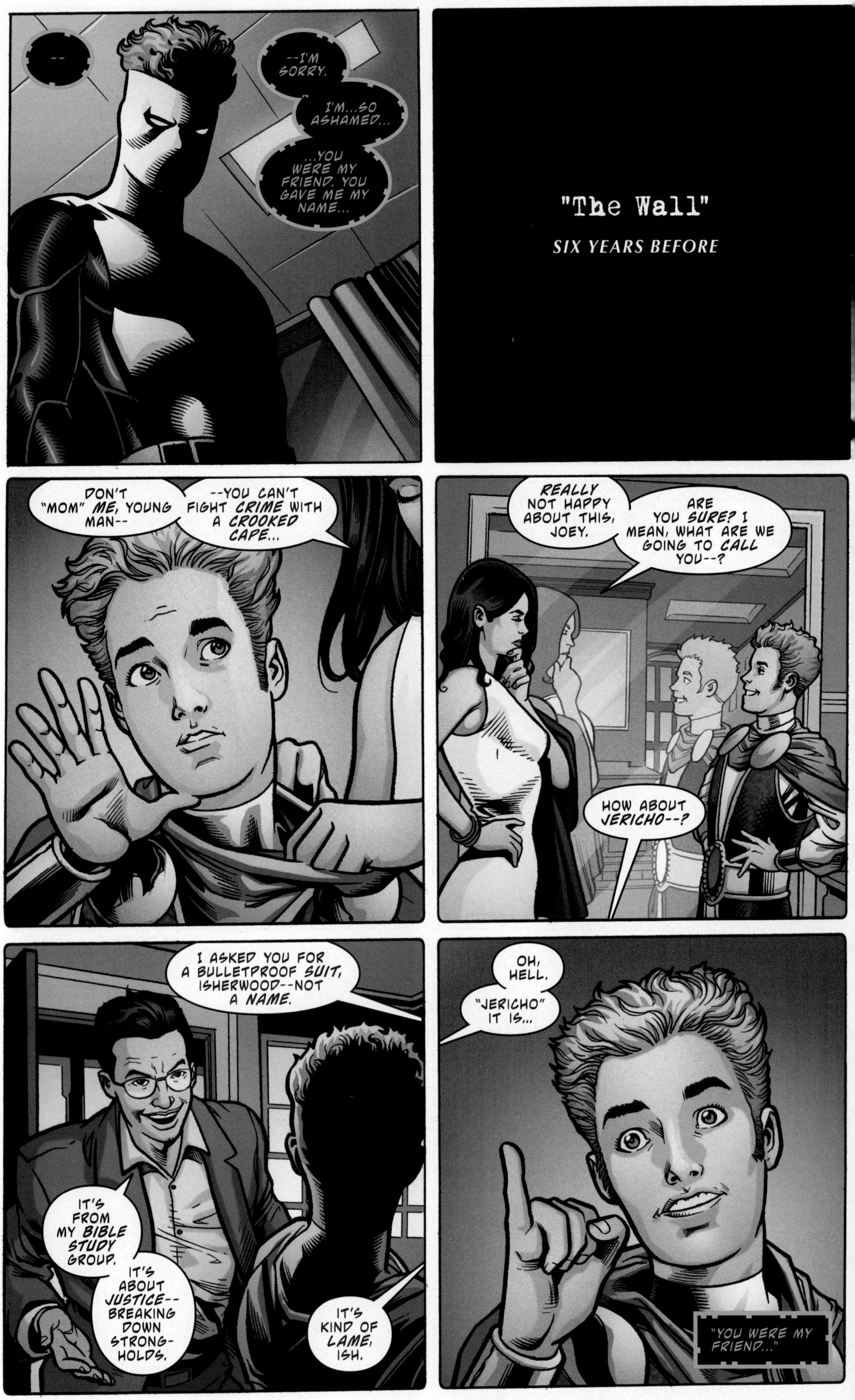
--
--I'M SORRY.
I'M...SO ASHAMED...
...YOU WERE MY FRIEND. YOU GAVE ME MY NAME...
"The Wall"
SIX YEARS BEFORE
DON'T "MOM" ME, YOUNG MAN--
--YOU CAN'T FIGHT CRIME WITH A CROOKED CAPE...
REALLY NOT HAPPY ABOUT THIS, JOEY.
ARE YOU SURE? I MEAN, WHAT ARE WE GOING TO CALL YOU--?
HOW ABOUT JERICHO--?
I ASKED YOU FOR A BULLETPROOF SUIT, ISHERWOOD--NOT A NAME.
IT'S FROM MY BIBLE STUDY GROUP.
IT'S ABOUT JUSTICE--BREAKING DOWN STRONG-HOLDS.
IT'S KIND OF LAME, ISH.
OH, HELL.
"JERICHO" IT IS...
"YOU WERE MY FRIEND..."

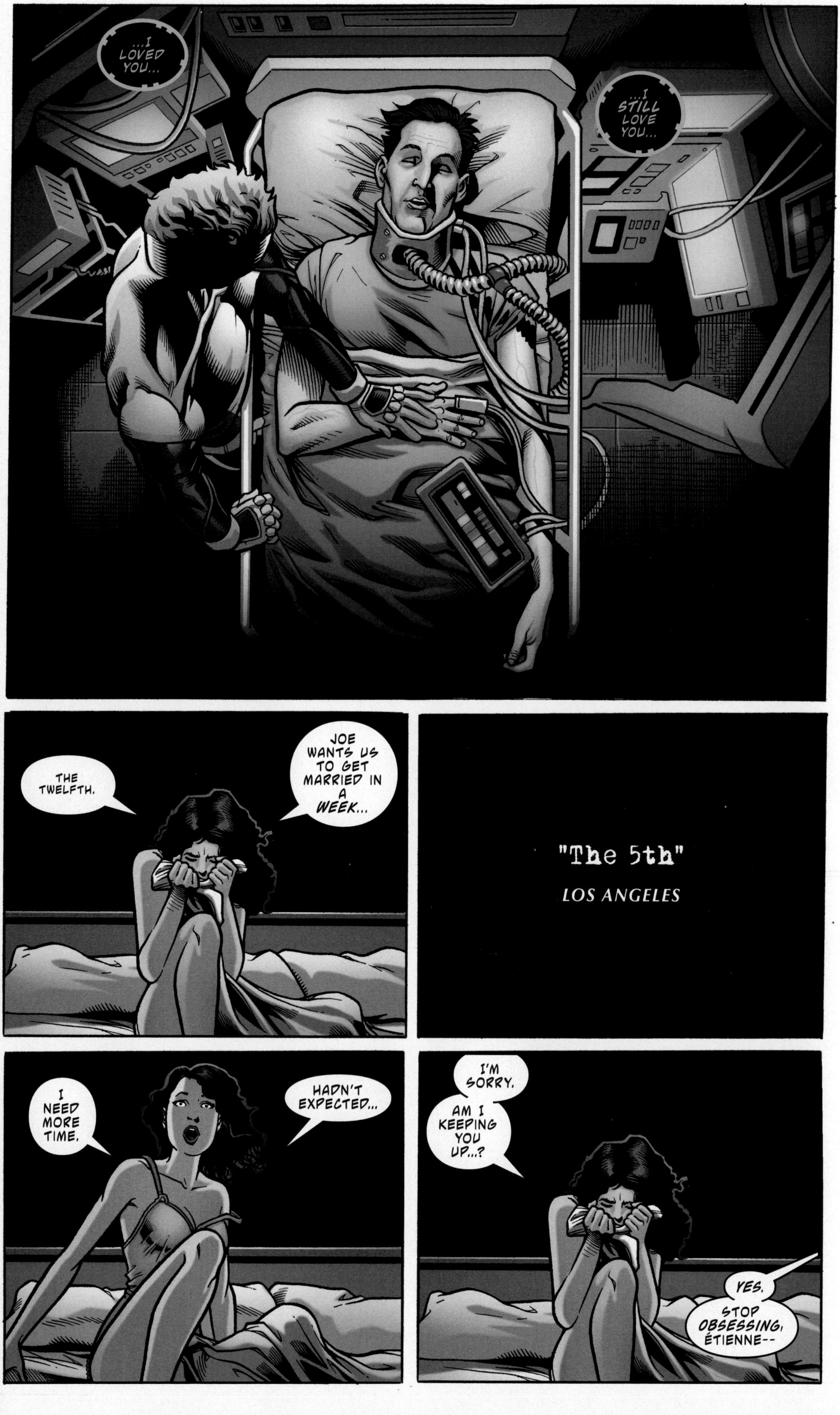
...I LOVED YOU...
...I STILL LOVE YOU...
THE TWELFTH.
JOE WANTS US TO GET MARRIED IN A WEEK...
"The 5th"
LOS ANGELES
I NEED MORE TIME.
HADN'T EXPECTED...
I'M SORRY.
AM I KEEPING YOU UP...?
YES.
STOP OBSESSING, ÉTIENNE--

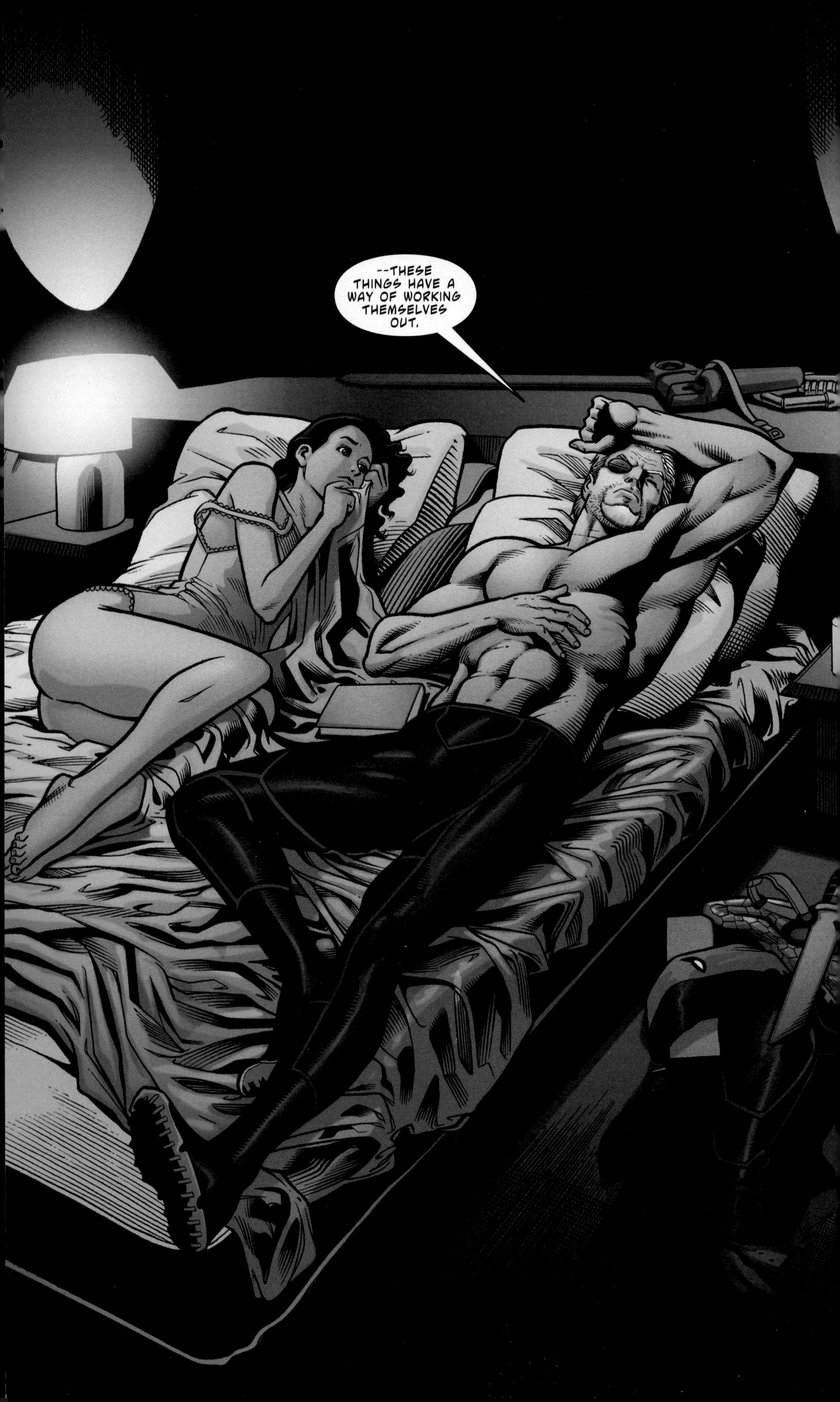
--THESE THINGS HAVE A WAY OF WORKING THEMSELVES OUT.

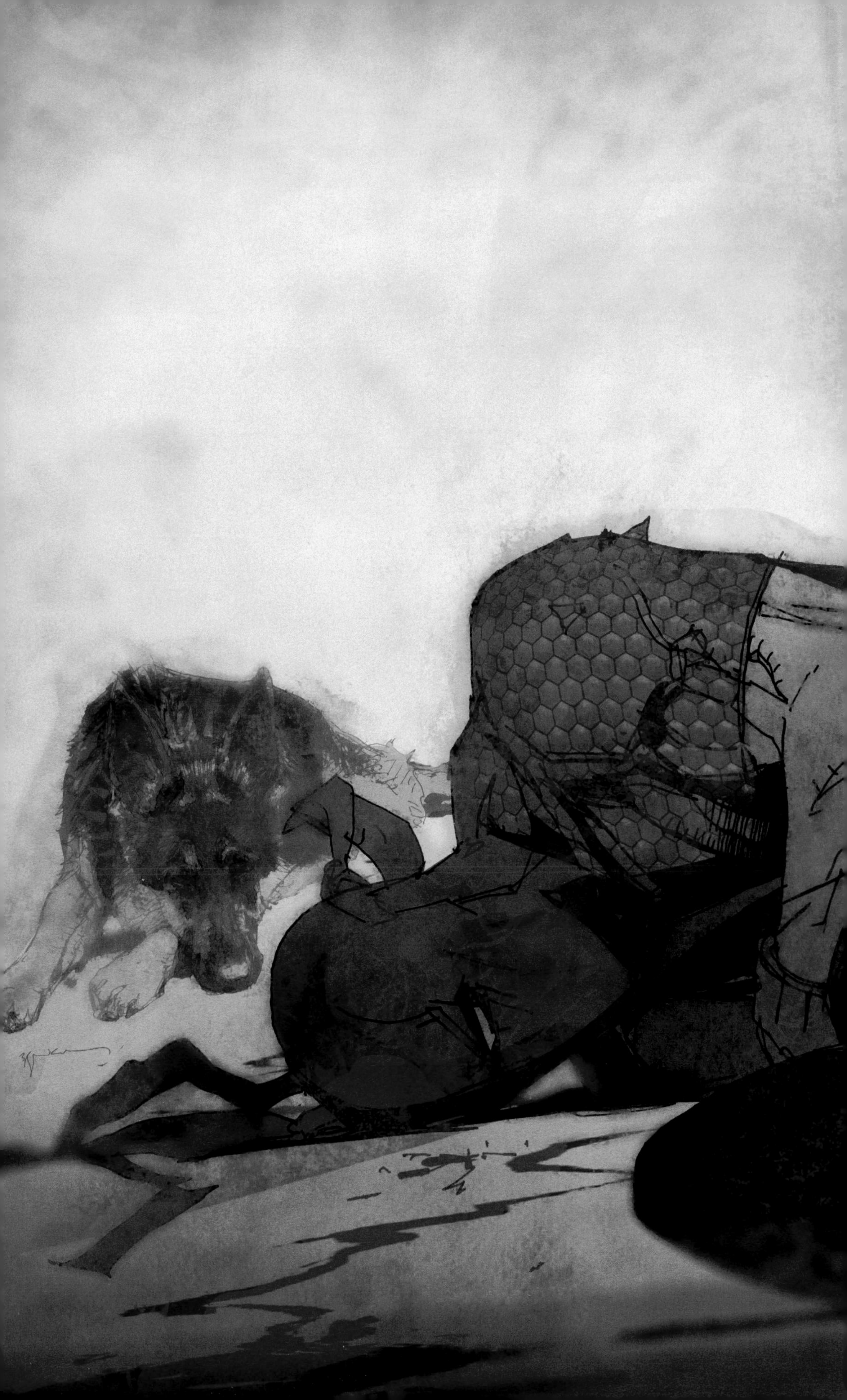

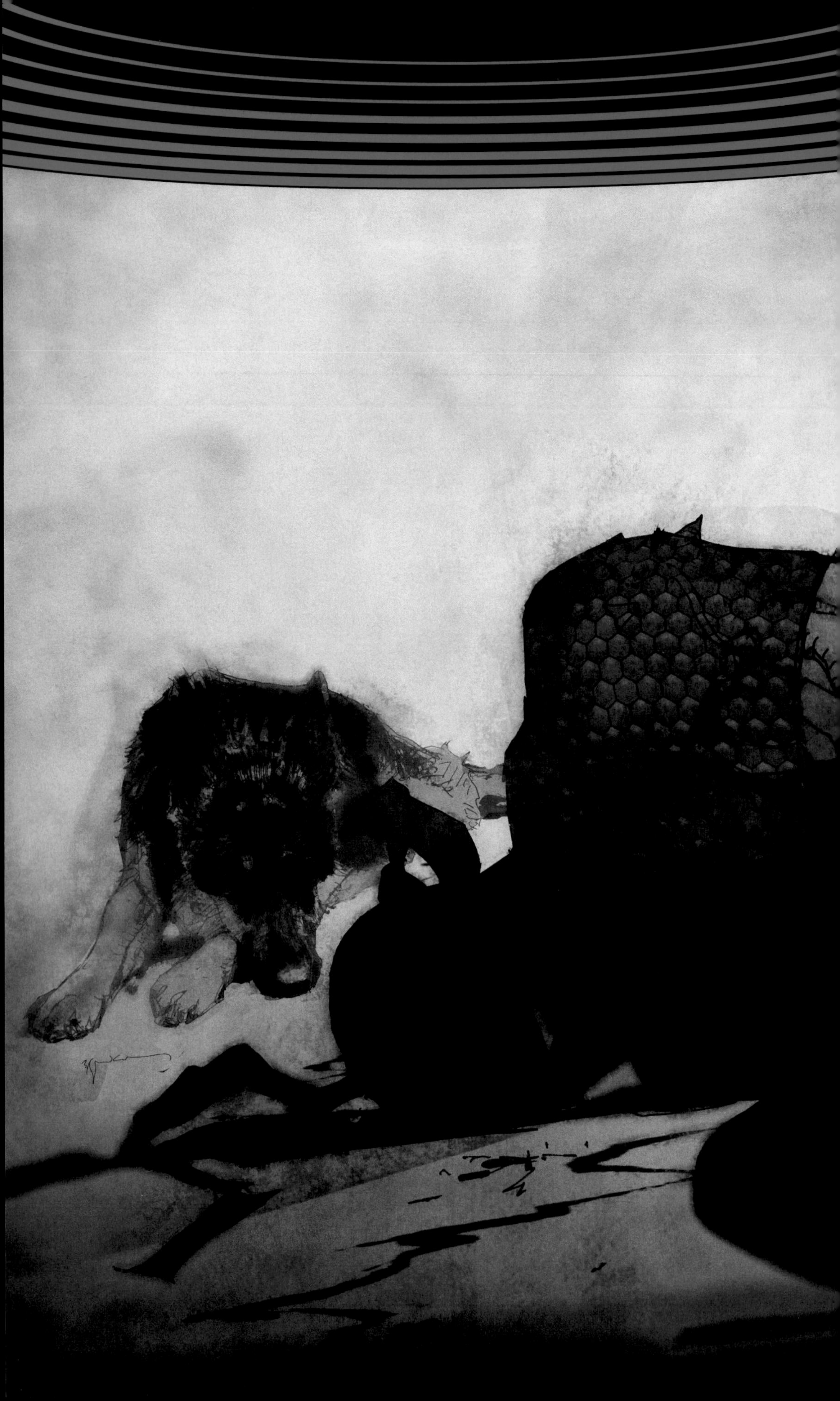

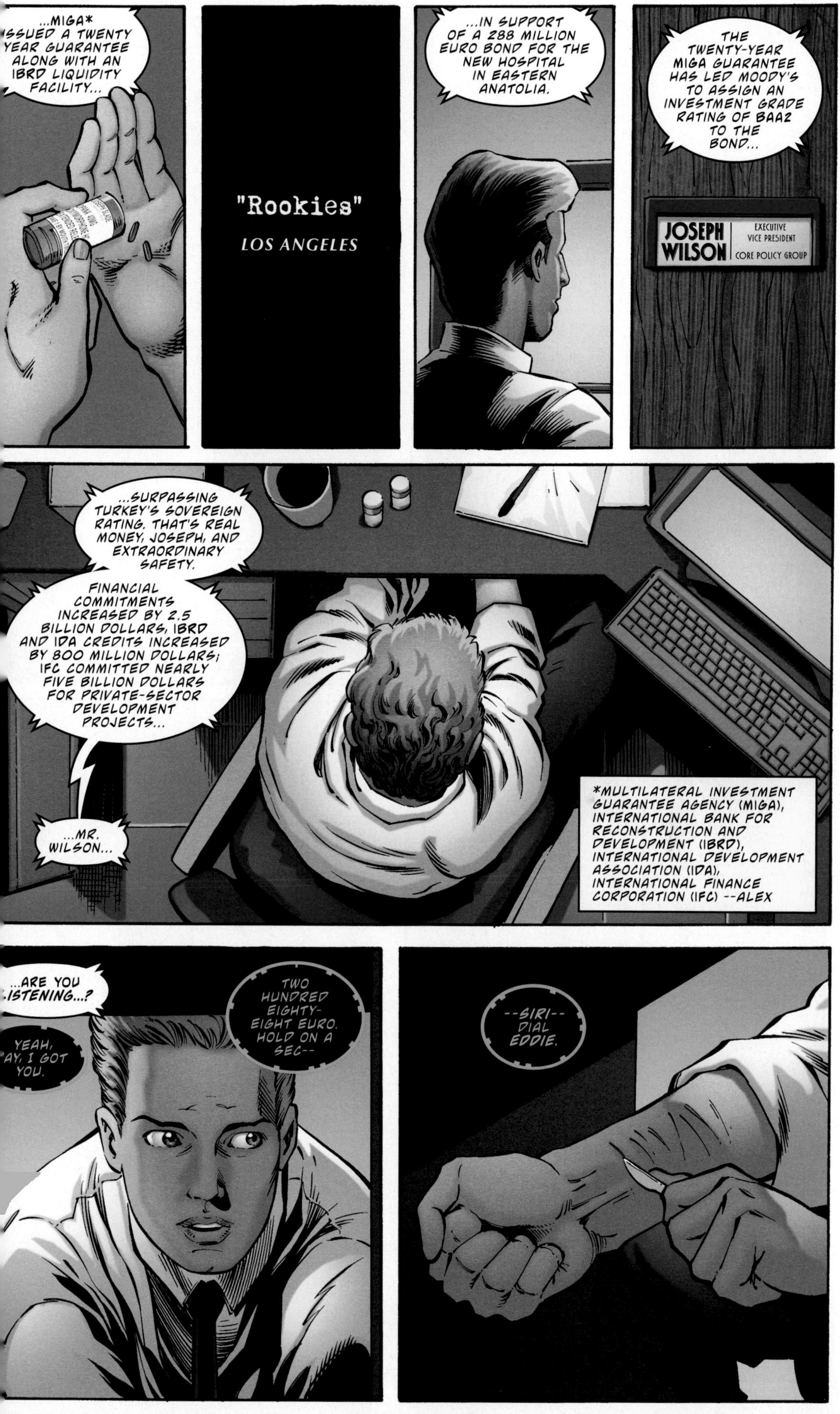
...MIGA*
ISSUED A TWENTY YEAR GUARANTEE ALONG WITH AN IBRD LIQUIDITY FACILITY...
"Rookies"
LOS ANGELES
...IN SUPPORT OF A 288 MILLION EURO BOND FOR THE NEW HOSPITAL IN EASTERN ANATOLIA.
THE TWENTY-YEAR MIGA GUARANTEE HAS LED MOODY'S TO ASSIGN AN INVESTMENT GRADE RATING OF BAA2 TO THE BOND...
JOSEPH WILSON
EXECUTIVE VICE PRESIDENT
CORE POLICY GROUP
...SURPASSING TURKEY'S SOVEREIGN RATING. THAT'S REAL MONEY, JOSEPH, AND EXTRAORDINARY SAFETY.
FINANCIAL COMMITMENTS INCREASED BY 2.5 BILLION DOLLARS, IBRD AND IDA CREDITS INCREASED BY 800 MILLION DOLLARS; IFC COMMITTED NEARLY FIVE BILLION DOLLARS FOR PRIVATE-SECTOR DEVELOPMENT PROJECTS...
...MR. WILSON...
*MULTILATERAL INVESTMENT GUARANTEE AGENCY (MIGA), INTERNATIONAL BANK FOR RECONSTRUCTION AND DEVELOPMENT (IBRD), INTERNATIONAL DEVELOPMENT ASSOCIATION (IDA), INTERNATIONAL FINANCE CORPORATION (IFC) --ALEX
...ARE YOU LISTENING...?
YEAH, YEAH, I GOT YOU.
TWO HUNDRED EIGHTY-EIGHT EURO. HOLD ON A SEC--
--SIRI-- DIAL EDDIE.

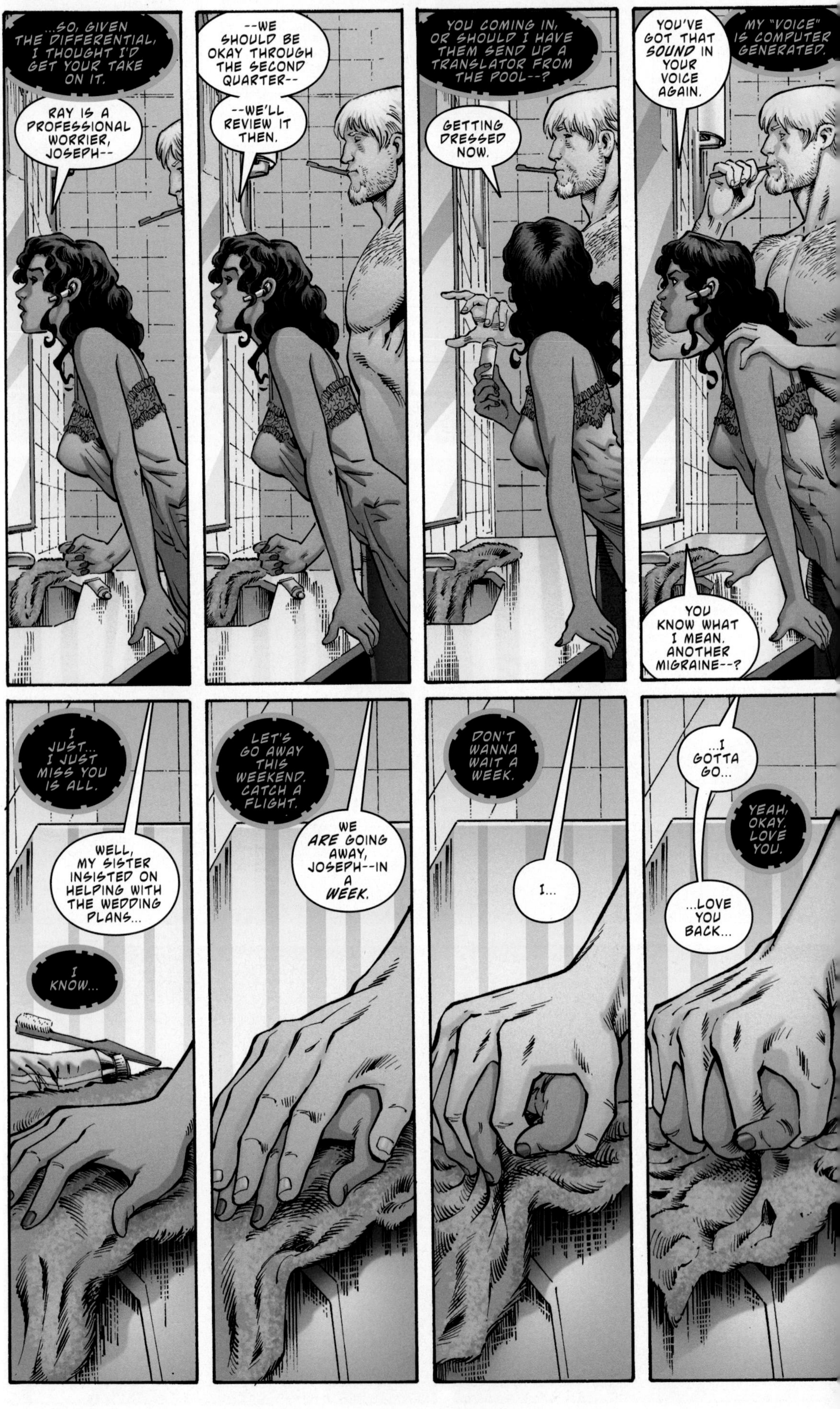
...SO, GIVEN THE DIFFERENTIAL, I THOUGHT I'D GET YOUR TAKE ON IT.
RAY IS A PROFESSIONAL WORRIER, JOSEPH--
--WE SHOULD BE OKAY THROUGH THE SECOND QUARTER--
--WE'LL REVIEW IT THEN.
YOU COMING IN, OR SHOULD I HAVE THEM SEND UP A TRANSLATOR FROM THE POOL--?
GETTING DRESSED NOW.
YOU'VE GOT THAT SOUND IN YOUR VOICE AGAIN.
MY "VOICE" IS COMPUTER GENERATED.
YOU KNOW WHAT I MEAN. ANOTHER MIGRAINE--?
I JUST... I JUST MISS YOU IS ALL.
WELL, MY SISTER INSISTED ON HELPING WITH THE WEDDING PLANS...
I KNOW...
LET'S GO AWAY THIS WEEKEND. CATCH A FLIGHT.
WE ARE GOING AWAY, JOSEPH--IN A WEEK.
DON'T WANNA WAIT A WEEK.
I...
...I GOTTA GO...
YEAH, OKAY. LOVE YOU.
...LOVE YOU BACK...

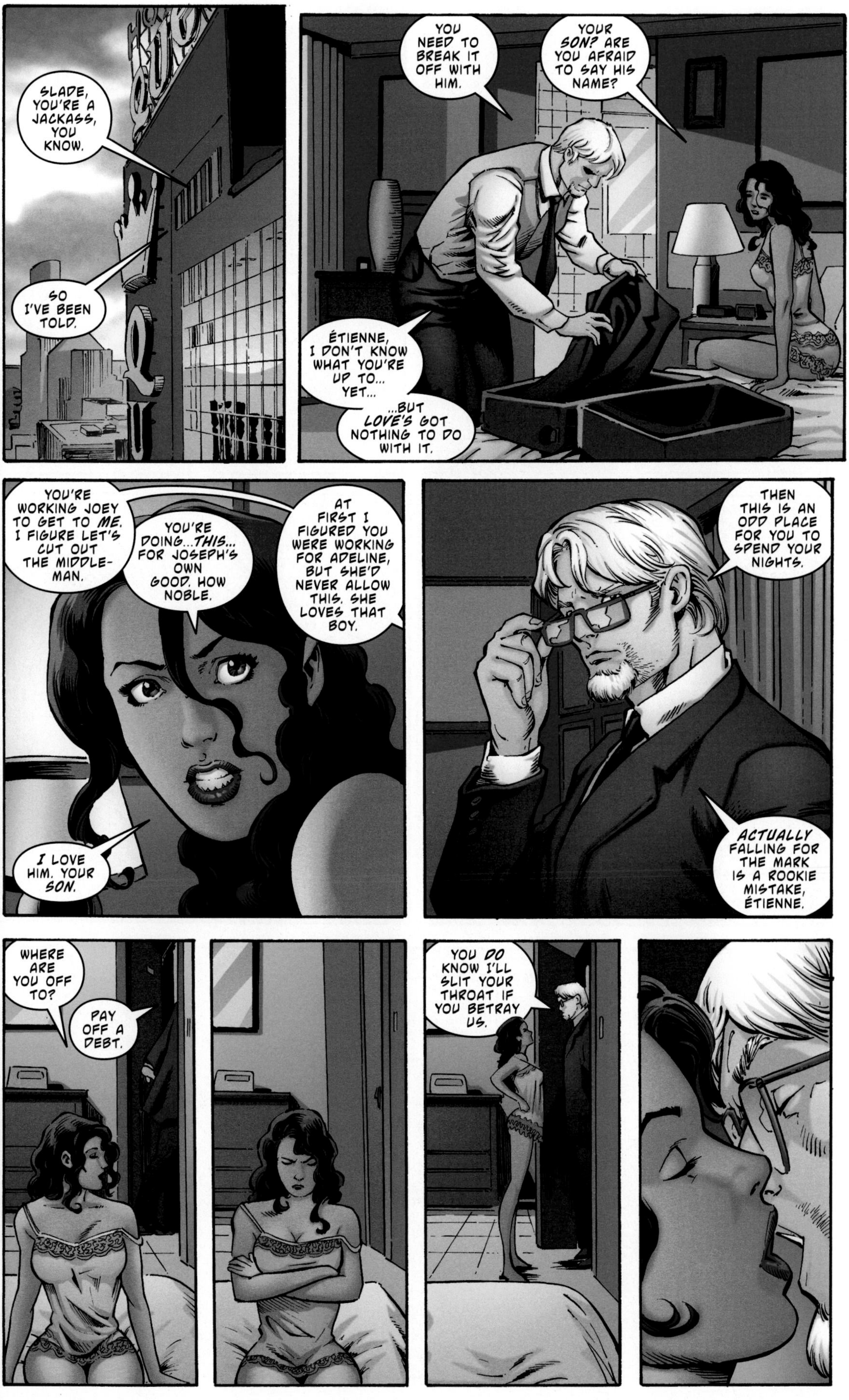
SLADE, YOU'RE A JACKASS, YOU KNOW.
SO I'VE BEEN TOLD.
YOU NEED TO BREAK IT OFF WITH HIM.
YOUR SON? ARE YOU AFRAID TO SAY HIS NAME?
ÉTIENNE, I DON'T KNOW WHAT YOU'RE UP TO... YET...
...BUT LOVE'S GOT NOTHING TO DO WITH IT.
YOU'RE WORKING JOEY TO GET TO ME. I FIGURE LET'S CUT OUT THE MIDDLE-MAN.
YOU'RE DOING...THIS... FOR JOSEPH'S OWN GOOD. HOW NOBLE.
AT FIRST I FIGURED YOU WERE WORKING FOR ADELINE, BUT SHE'D NEVER ALLOW THIS. SHE LOVES THAT BOY.
I LOVE HIM. YOUR SON.
THEN THIS IS AN ODD PLACE FOR YOU TO SPEND YOUR NIGHTS.
ACTUALLY FALLING FOR THE MARK IS A ROOKIE MISTAKE, ÉTIENNE.
WHERE ARE YOU OFF TO?
PAY OFF A DEBT.
YOU DO KNOW I'LL SLIT YOUR THROAT IF YOU BETRAY US.

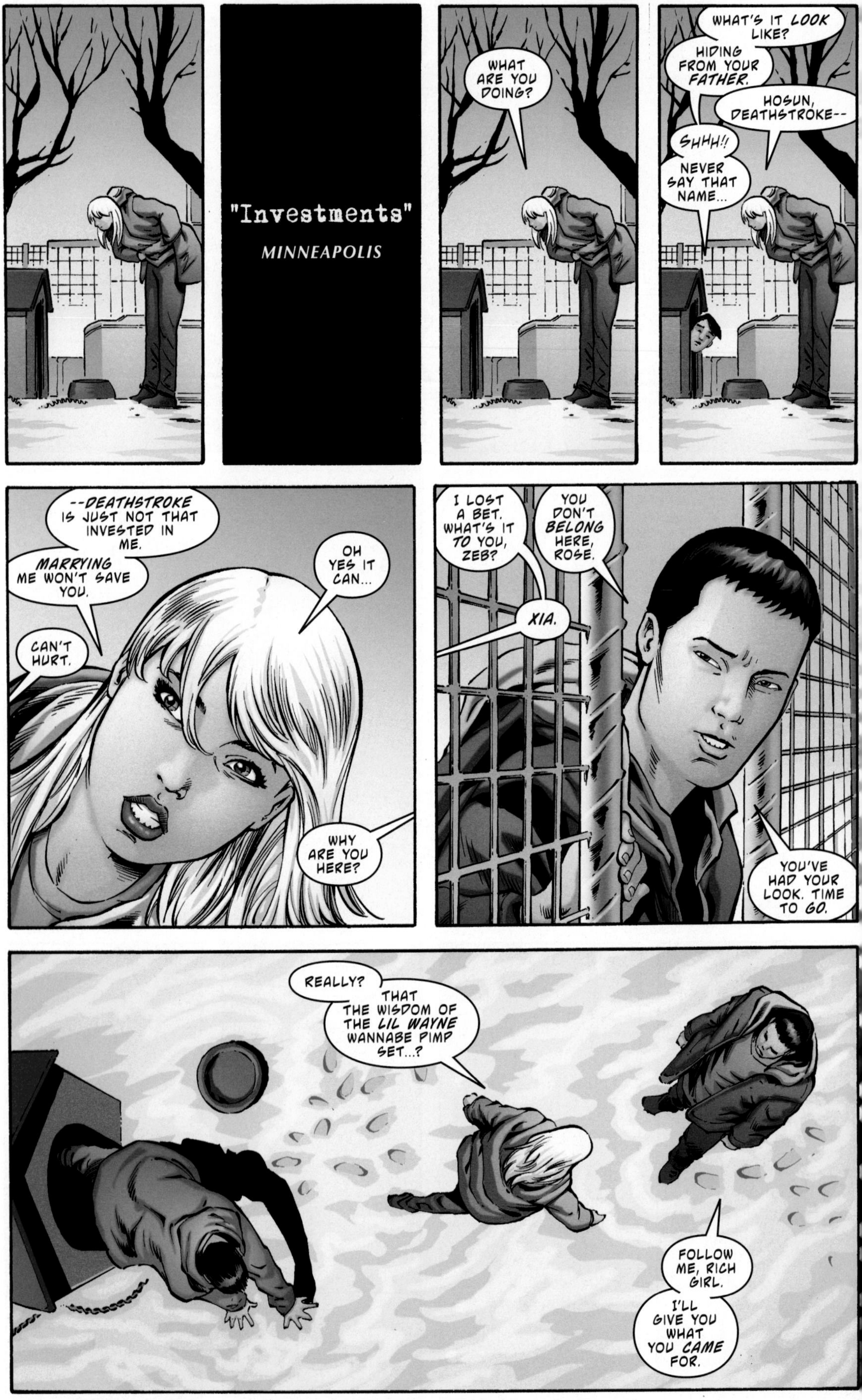
"Investments"
MINNEAPOLIS
WHAT ARE YOU DOING?
WHAT'S IT LOOK LIKE?
HIDING FROM YOUR FATHER.
HOSUN, DEATHSTROKE--
SHHH!!
NEVER SAY THAT NAME...
--DEATHSTROKE IS JUST NOT THAT INVESTED IN ME.
MARRYING ME WON'T SAVE YOU.
CAN'T HURT.
OH YES IT CAN...
WHY ARE YOU HERE?
I LOST A BET. WHAT'S IT TO YOU, ZEB?
XIA.
YOU DON'T BELONG HERE, ROSE.
YOU'VE HAD YOUR LOOK. TIME TO GO.
REALLY?
THAT THE WISDOM OF THE LIL WAYNE WANNABE PIMP SET...?
FOLLOW ME, RICH GIRL.
I'LL GIVE YOU WHAT YOU CAME FOR.

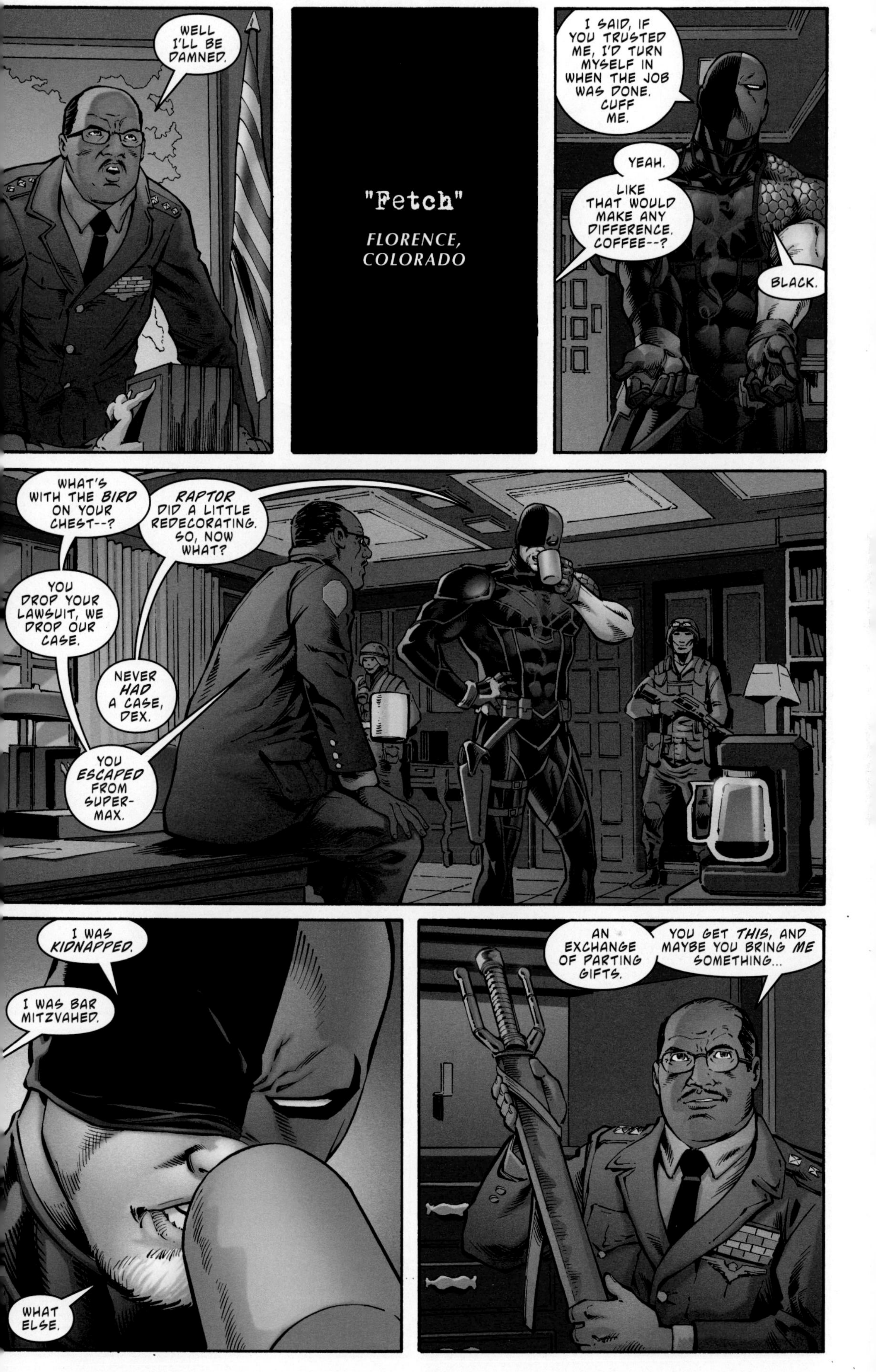
WELL I'LL BE DAMNED.
"Fetch"
FLORENCE, COLORADO
I SAID, IF YOU TRUSTED ME, I'D TURN MYSELF IN WHEN THE JOB WAS DONE. CUFF ME.
YEAH.
LIKE THAT WOULD MAKE ANY DIFFERENCE. COFFEE--?
BLACK.
WHAT'S WITH THE BIRD ON YOUR CHEST--?
RAPTOR DID A LITTLE REDECORATING. SO, NOW WHAT?
YOU DROP YOUR LAWSUIT, WE DROP OUR CASE.
NEVER HAD A CASE, DEX.
YOU ESCAPED FROM SUPER-MAX.
I WAS KIDNAPPED.
I WAS BAR MITZVAHED.
WHAT ELSE.
AN EXCHANGE OF PARTING GIFTS.
YOU GET THIS, AND MAYBE YOU BRING ME SOMETHING...

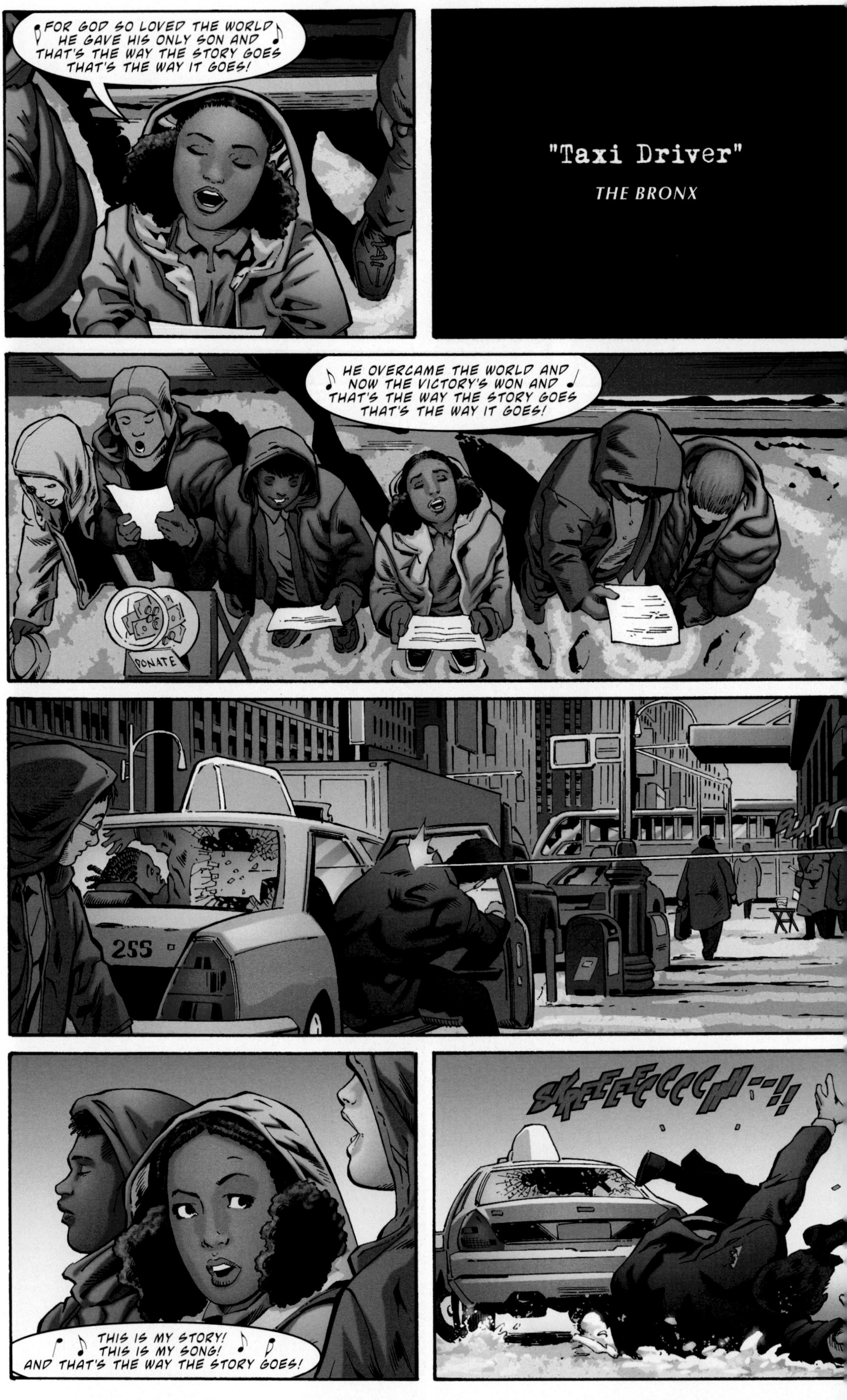
FOR GOD SO LOVED THE WORLD HE GAVE HIS ONLY SON AND THAT'S THE WAY THE STORY GOES THAT'S THE WAY IT GOES!
"Taxi Driver"
THE BRONX
HE OVERCAME THE WORLD AND NOW THE VICTORY'S WON AND THAT'S THE WAY THE STORY GOES THAT'S THE WAY IT GOES!
DONATE
255
THIS IS MY STORY! THIS IS MY SONG! AND THAT'S THE WAY THE STORY GOES!
SKREEECCCCH--!!

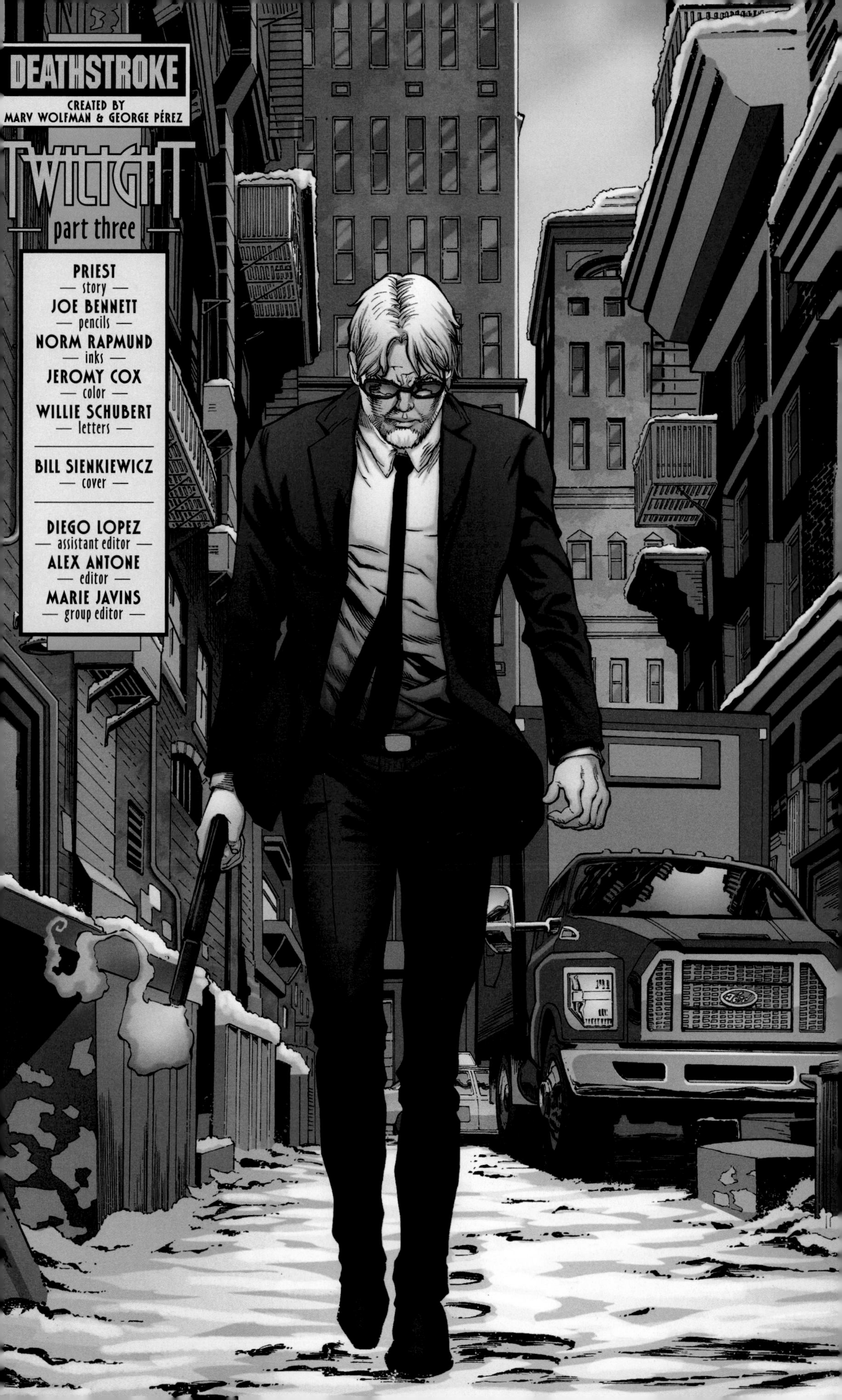

DEATHSTROKE
CREATED BY
MARV WOLFMAN & GEORGE PÉREZ
TWILIGHT
part three
PRIEST
— story —
JOE BENNETT
— pencils —
NORM RAPMUND
— inks —
JEROMY COX
— color —
WILLIE SCHUBERT
— letters —
BILL SIENKIEWICZ
— cover —
DIEGO LOPEZ
— assistant editor —
ALEX ANTONE
— editor —
MARIE JAVINS
— group editor —

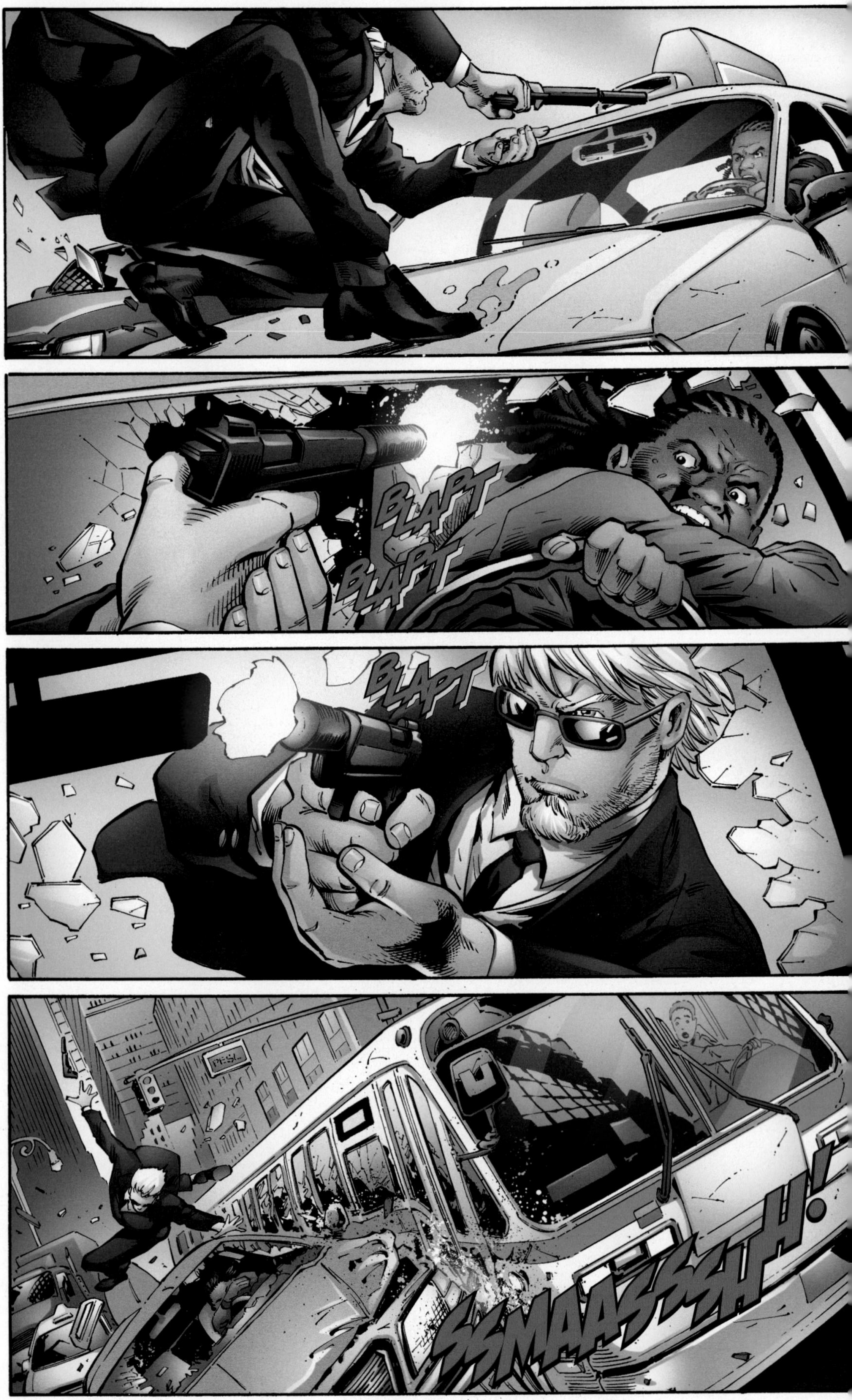
BLAPT
BLAPT
BLAPT
PESL
SSMAASSSH!

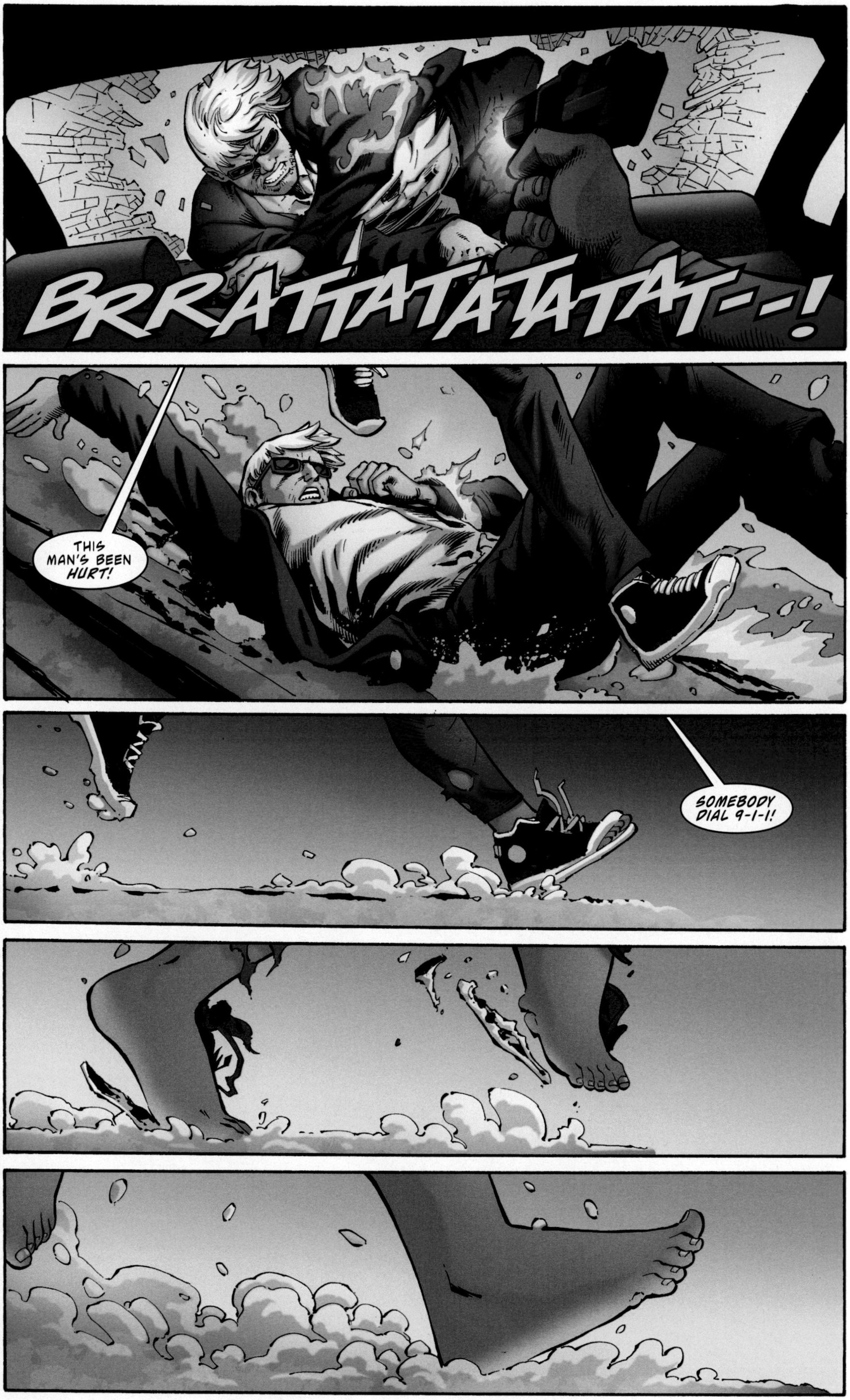
BRRATTATATATAT--!
THIS MAN'S BEEN HURT!
SOMEBODY DIAL 9-1-1!

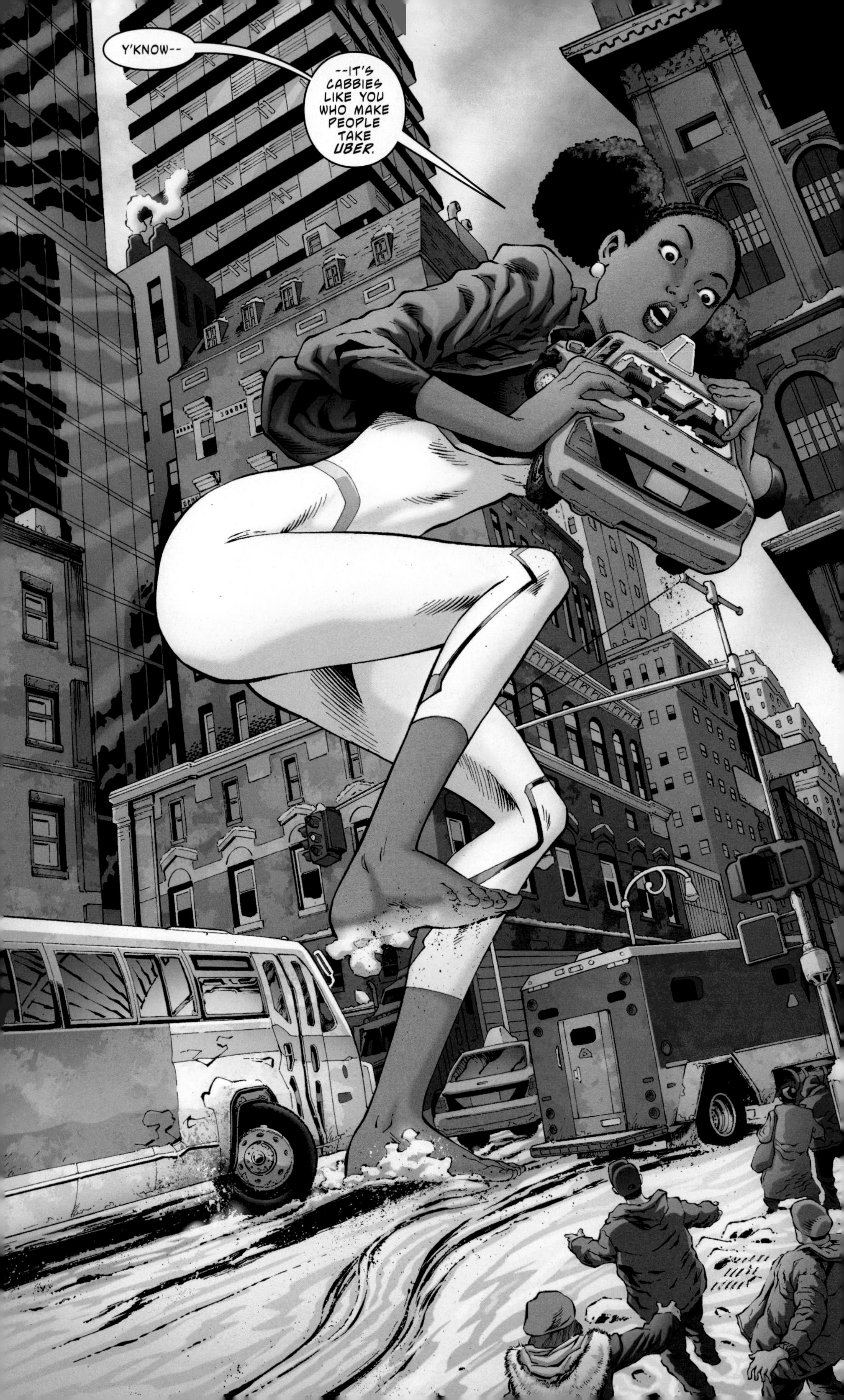
Y'KNOW--
--IT'S CABBIES LIKE YOU WHO MAKE PEOPLE TAKE UBER.

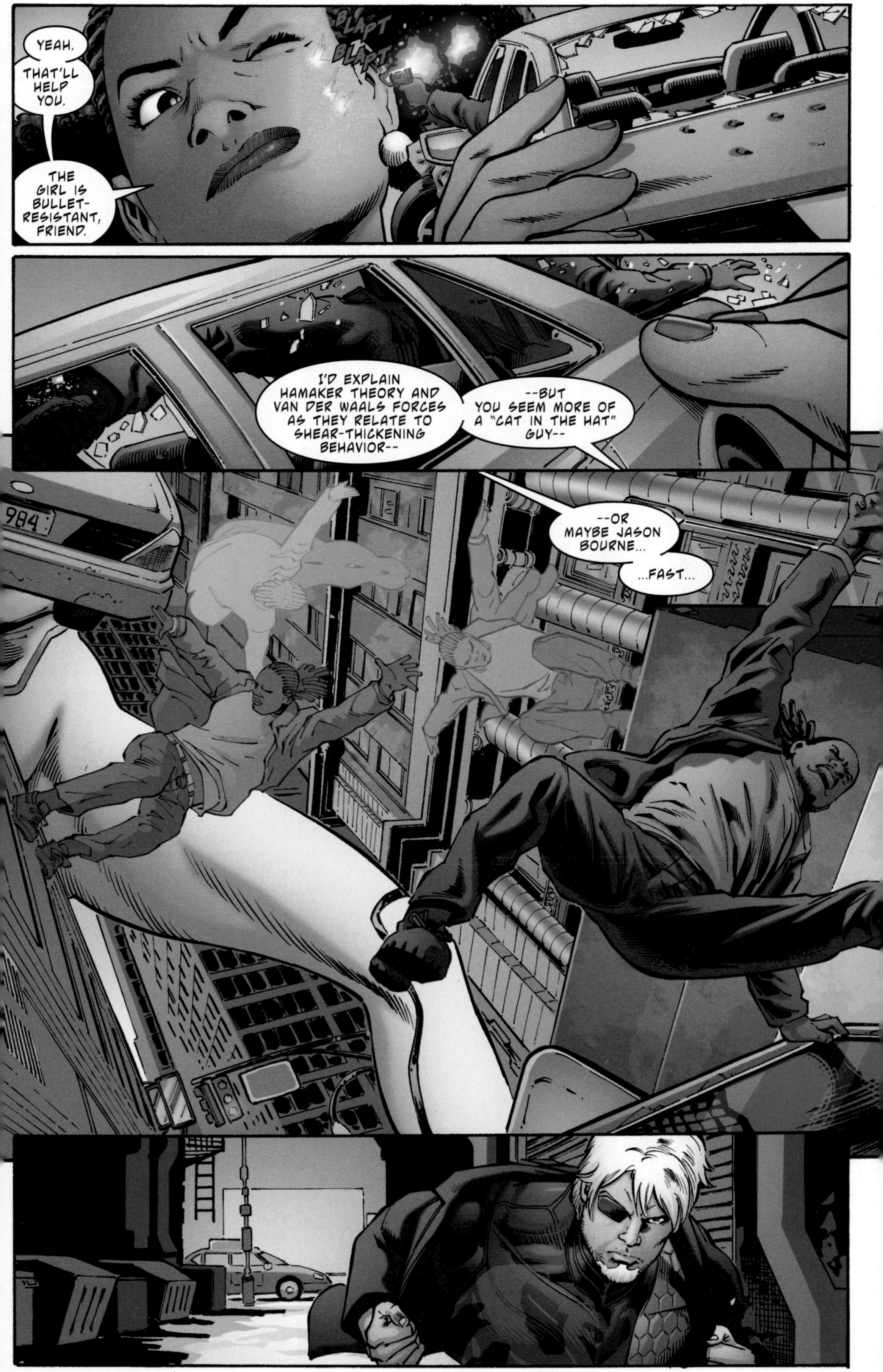
YEAH.
THAT'LL HELP YOU.
THE GIRL IS BULLET-RESISTANT, FRIEND.
BLAPT
BLAPT
I'D EXPLAIN HAMAKER THEORY AND VAN DER WAALS FORCES AS THEY RELATE TO SHEAR-THICKENING BEHAVIOR--
--BUT YOU SEEM MORE OF A "CAT IN THE HAT" GUY--
--OR MAYBE JASON BOURNE...
...FAST...

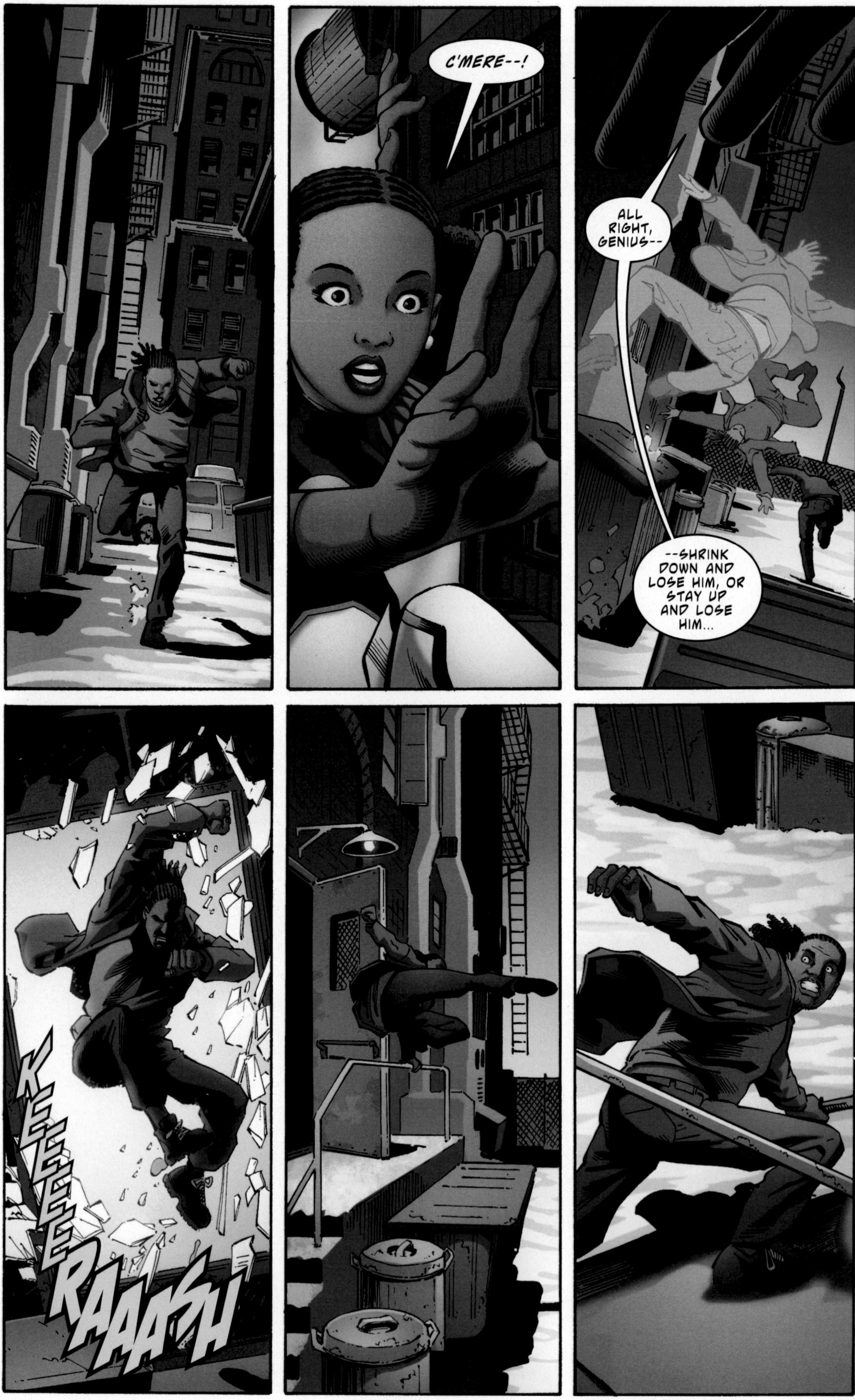
C'MERE--!
ALL RIGHT, GENIUS--
--SHRINK DOWN AND LOSE HIM, OR STAY UP AND LOSE HIM...
KEEEERAAASH

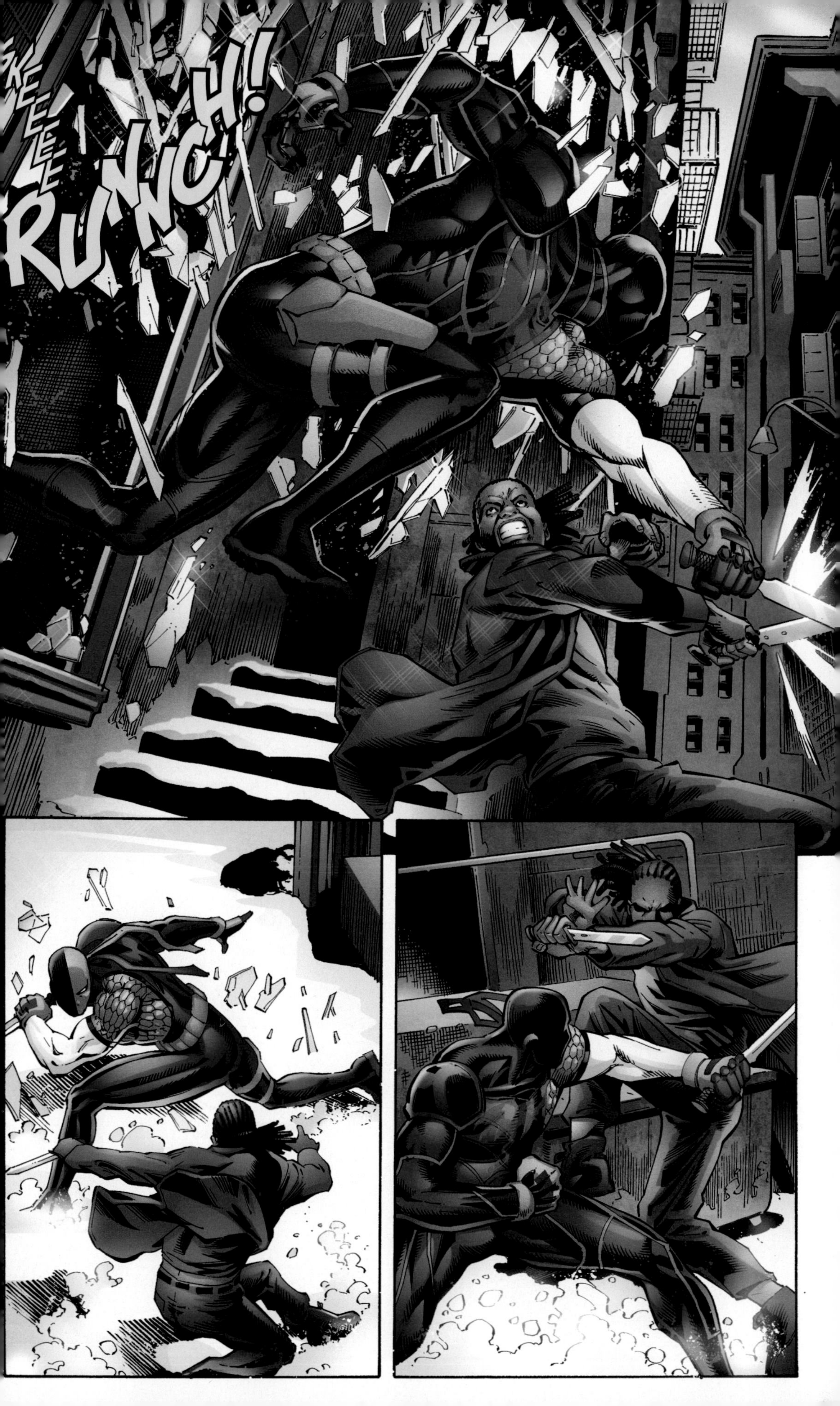
KREEEE
RUNCH!

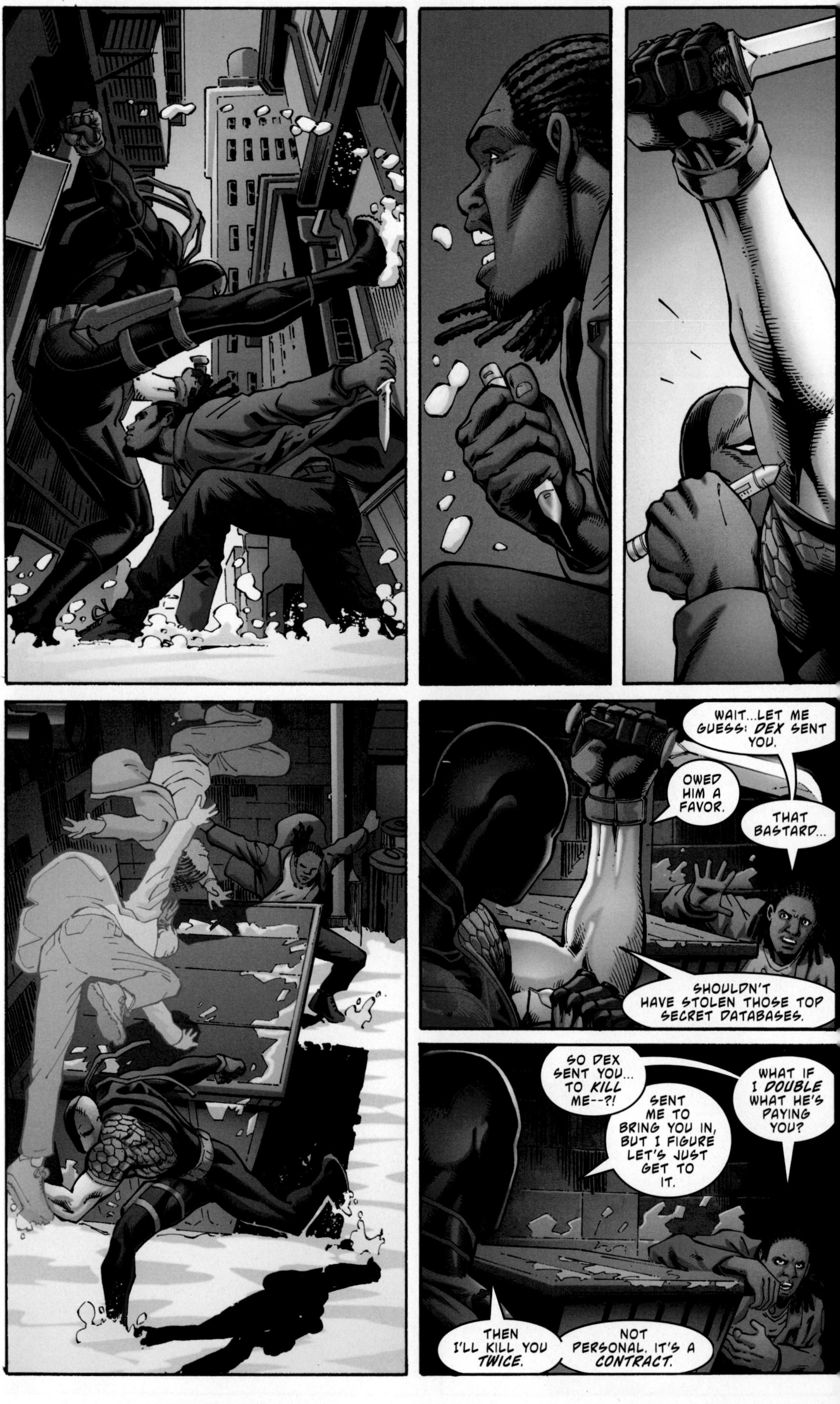

WAIT...LET ME GUESS: DEX SENT YOU.
OWED HIM A FAVOR.
THAT BASTARD...
SHOULDN'T HAVE STOLEN THOSE TOP SECRET DATABASES.
SO DEX SENT YOU... TO KILL ME--?!
SENT ME TO BRING YOU IN, BUT I FIGURE LET'S JUST GET TO IT.
WHAT IF I DOUBLE WHAT HE'S PAYING YOU?
NOT PERSONAL. IT'S A CONTRACT.
THEN I'LL KILL YOU TWICE.

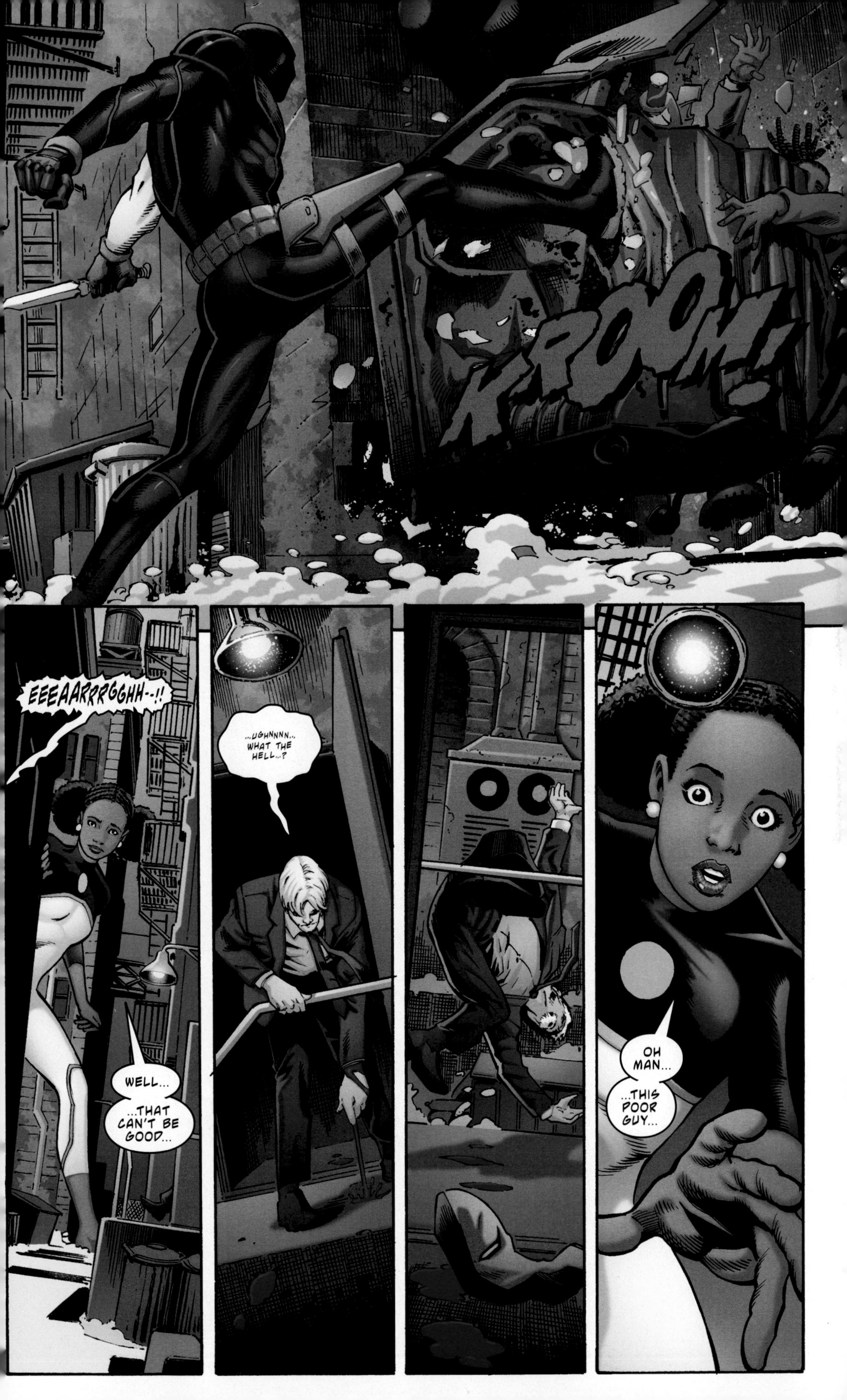
K-POOM!!
EEEAARRRGGHH--!!
WELL... ...THAT CAN'T BE GOOD...
...UGHNNNN... WHAT THE HELL...?
OH MAN... ...THIS POOR GUY...

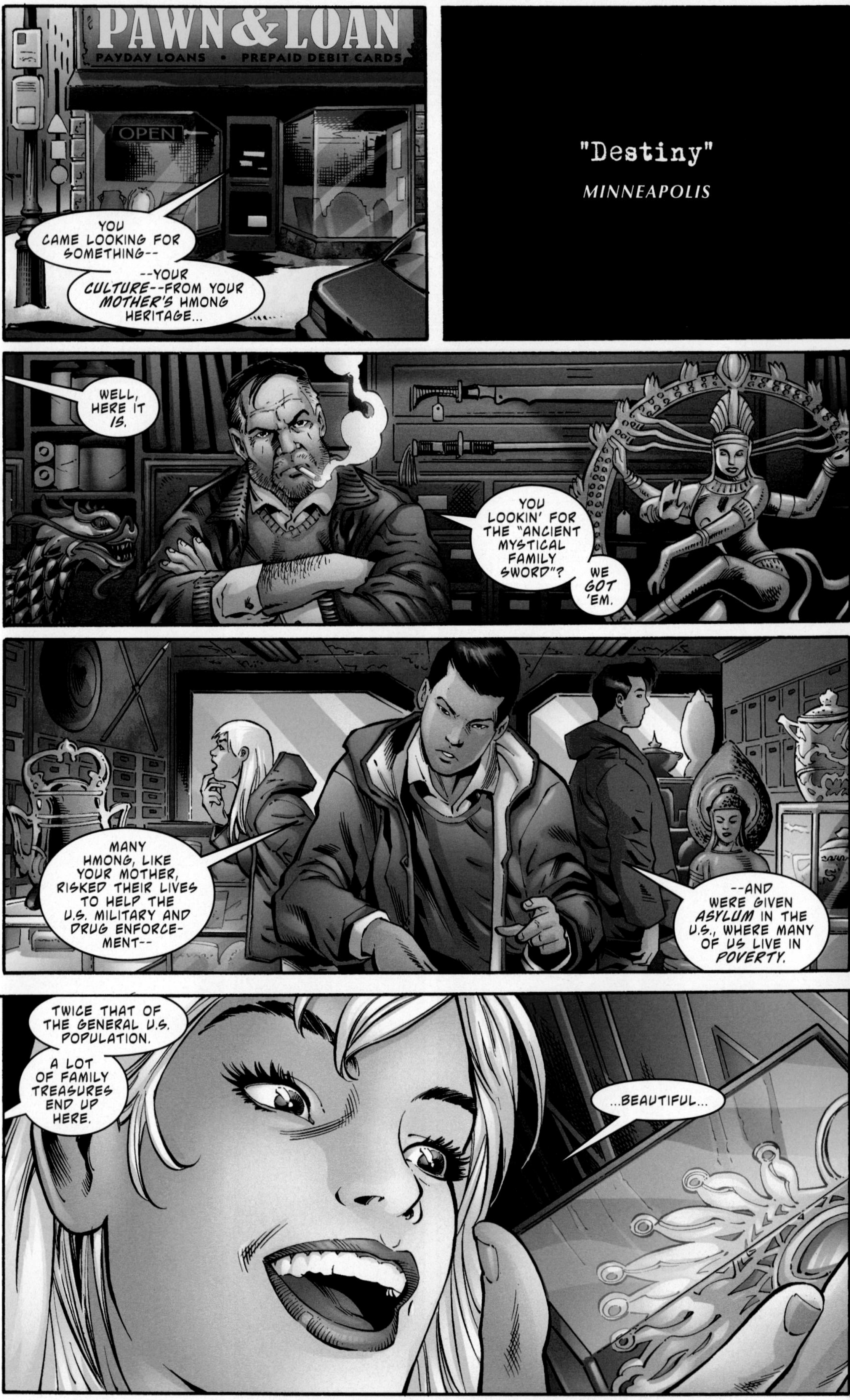
PAWN&LOAN
PAYDAY LOANS • PREPAID DEBIT CARDS
OPEN
YOU CAME LOOKING FOR SOMETHING--
--YOUR *CULTURE*--FROM YOUR *MOTHER'S* HMONG HERITAGE...
"Destiny"
MINNEAPOLIS
WELL, HERE IT *IS*.
YOU LOOKIN' FOR THE "ANCIENT MYSTICAL FAMILY SWORD"?
WE *GOT* 'EM.
MANY HMONG, LIKE YOUR MOTHER, RISKED THEIR LIVES TO HELP THE U.S. MILITARY AND DRUG ENFORCEMENT--
--AND WERE GIVEN *ASYLUM* IN THE U.S., WHERE MANY OF US LIVE IN *POVERTY*.
TWICE THAT OF THE GENERAL U.S. POPULATION.
A LOT OF FAMILY TREASURES END UP HERE.
...BEAUTIFUL...

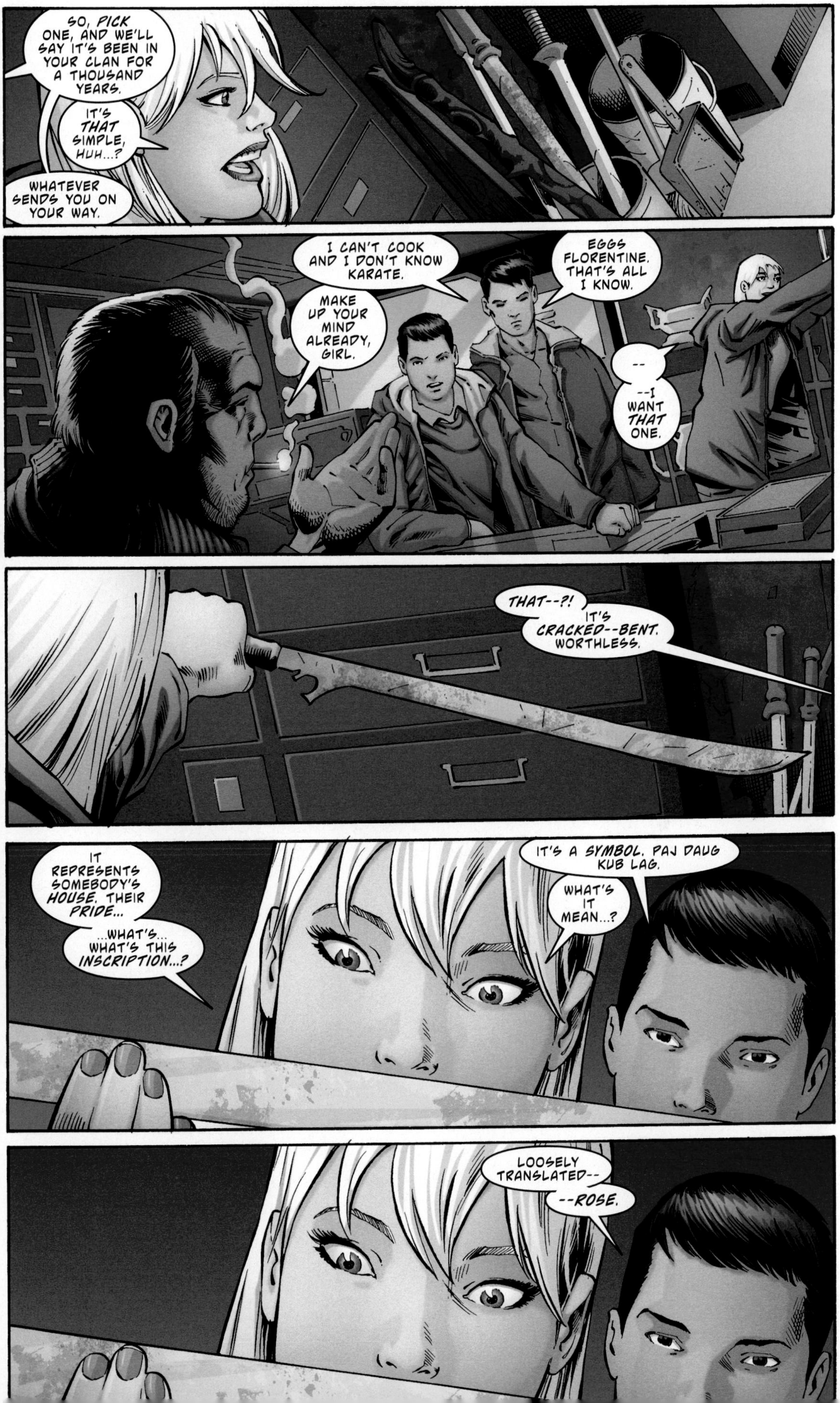
SO, PICK ONE, AND WE'LL SAY IT'S BEEN IN YOUR CLAN FOR A THOUSAND YEARS.
IT'S THAT SIMPLE, HUH...?
WHATEVER SENDS YOU ON YOUR WAY.
I CAN'T COOK AND I DON'T KNOW KARATE.
EGGS FLORENTINE. THAT'S ALL I KNOW.
MAKE UP YOUR MIND ALREADY, GIRL.
--
--I WANT THAT ONE.
THAT--?! IT'S CRACKED--BENT. WORTHLESS.
IT REPRESENTS SOMEBODY'S HOUSE. THEIR PRIDE...
...WHAT'S... WHAT'S THIS INSCRIPTION...?
IT'S A SYMBOL. PAJ DAUG KUB LAG.
WHAT'S IT MEAN...?
LOOSELY TRANSLATED--
--ROSE.

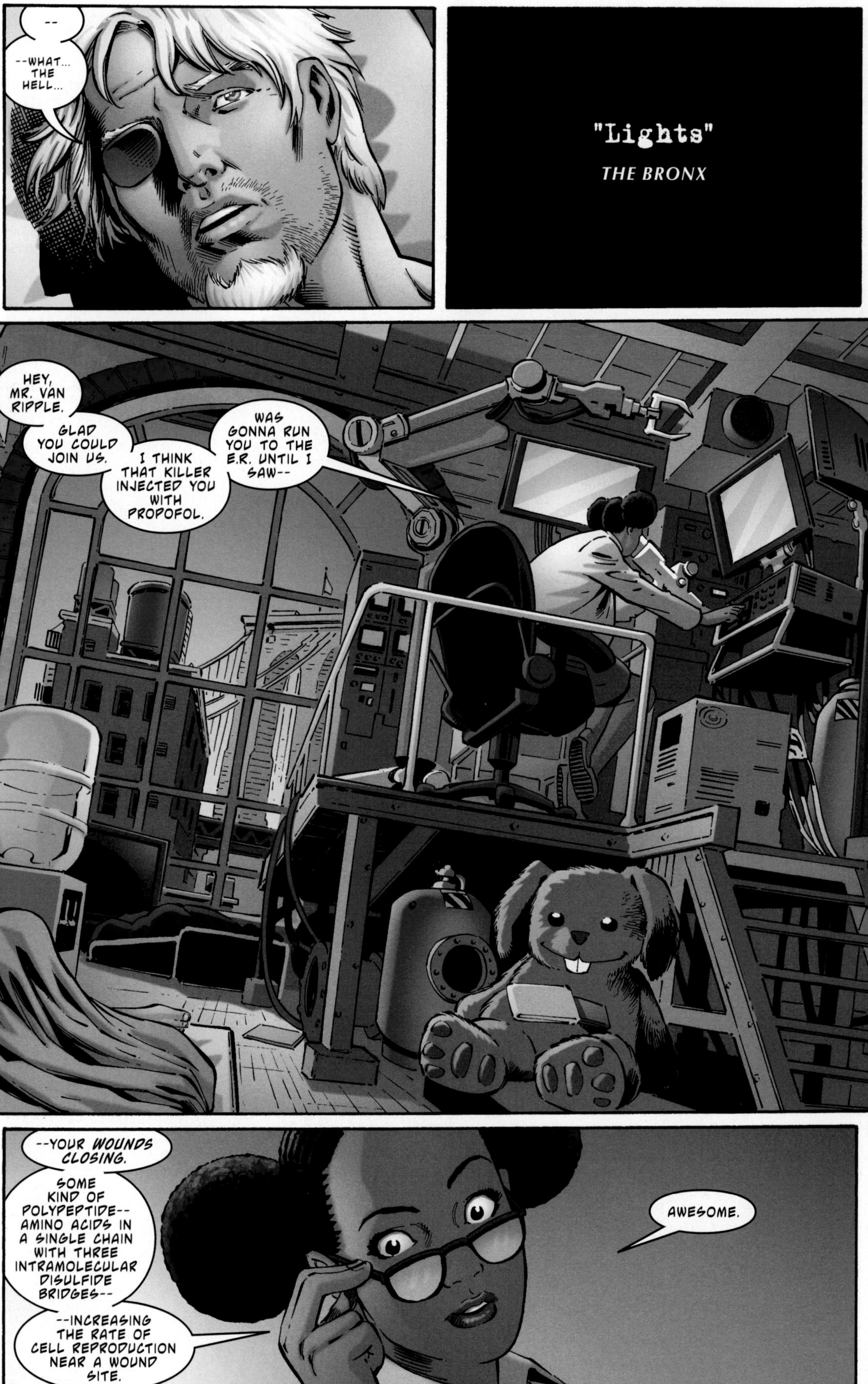
--
--WHAT... THE HELL...
"Lights"
THE BRONX
HEY, MR. VAN RIPPLE.
GLAD YOU COULD JOIN US.
I THINK THAT KILLER INJECTED YOU WITH PROPOFOL.
WAS GONNA RUN YOU TO THE E.R. UNTIL I SAW--
--YOUR WOUNDS CLOSING.
SOME KIND OF POLYPEPTIDE--AMINO ACIDS IN A SINGLE CHAIN WITH THREE INTRAMOLECULAR DISULFIDE BRIDGES--
--INCREASING THE RATE OF CELL REPRODUCTION NEAR A WOUND SITE.
AWESOME.

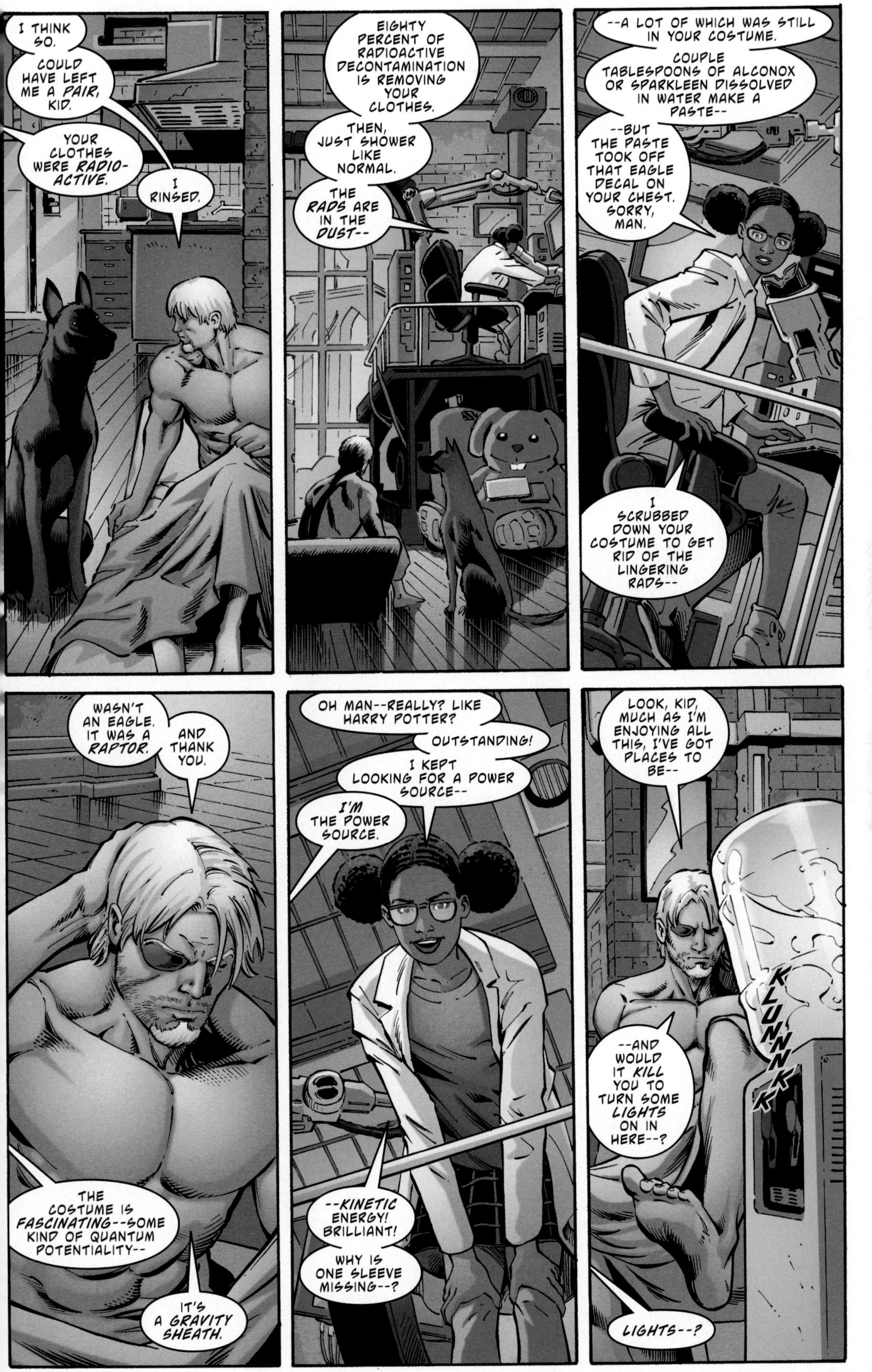
I THINK SO.
COULD HAVE LEFT ME A *PAIR*, KID.
YOUR CLOTHES WERE *RADIO-ACTIVE*.
I RINSED.
EIGHTY PERCENT OF RADIOACTIVE DECONTAMINATION IS REMOVING YOUR CLOTHES.
THEN, JUST SHOWER LIKE NORMAL.
THE *RADS* ARE IN THE *DUST*--
--A LOT OF WHICH WAS STILL IN YOUR COSTUME.
COUPLE TABLESPOONS OF ALCONOX OR SPARKLEEN DISSOLVED IN WATER MAKE A PASTE--
--BUT THE PASTE TOOK OFF THAT EAGLE DECAL ON YOUR CHEST. SORRY, MAN.
I SCRUBBED DOWN YOUR COSTUME TO GET RID OF THE LINGERING RADS--
WASN'T AN EAGLE. IT WAS A *RAPTOR*.
AND THANK YOU.
THE COSTUME IS *FASCINATING*--SOME KIND OF QUANTUM POTENTIALITY--
IT'S A *GRAVITY SHEATH*.
OH MAN--REALLY? LIKE HARRY POTTER?
OUTSTANDING!
I KEPT LOOKING FOR A POWER SOURCE--
*I'M* THE POWER SOURCE.
--*KINETIC* ENERGY! BRILLIANT!
WHY IS ONE SLEEVE MISSING--?
LOOK, KID, MUCH AS I'M ENJOYING ALL THIS, I'VE GOT PLACES TO BE--
--AND WOULD IT *KILL* YOU TO TURN SOME *LIGHTS* ON IN HERE--?
KLUNNKK
*LIGHTS*--?

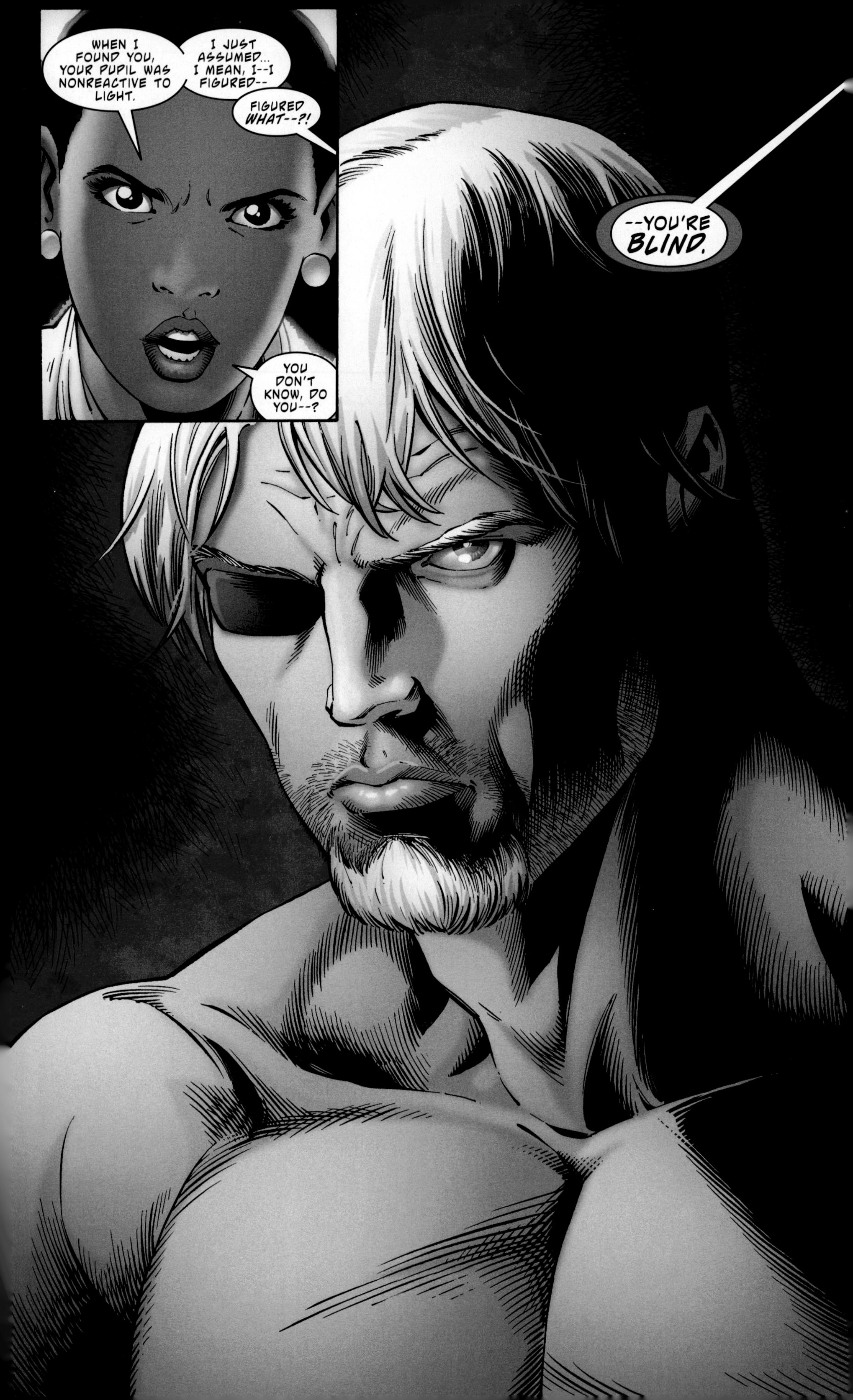
WHEN I FOUND YOU, YOUR PUPIL WAS NONREACTIVE TO LIGHT.
I JUST ASSUMED... I MEAN, I--I FIGURED--
FIGURED WHAT--?!
YOU DON'T KNOW, DO YOU--?
--YOU'RE BLIND.

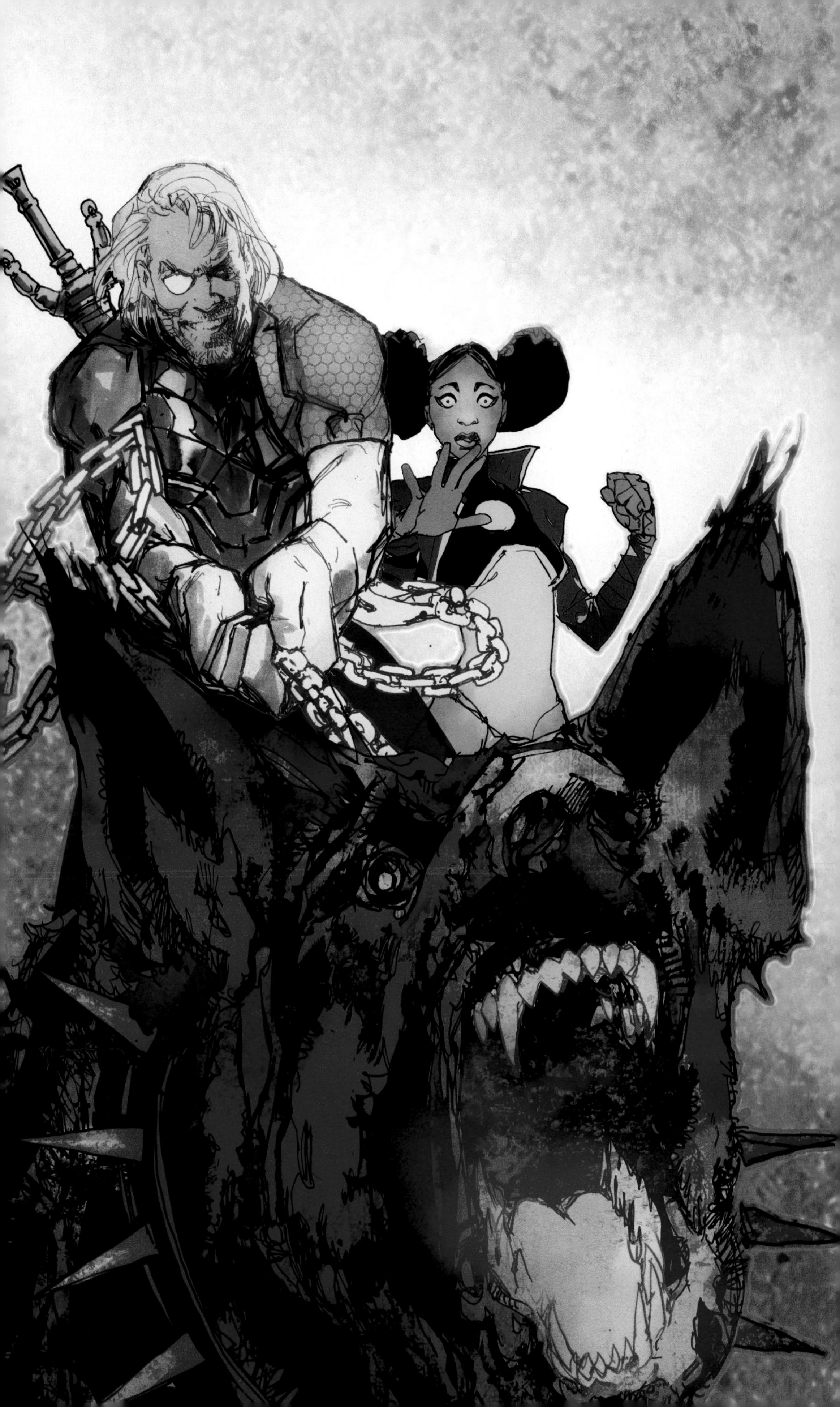

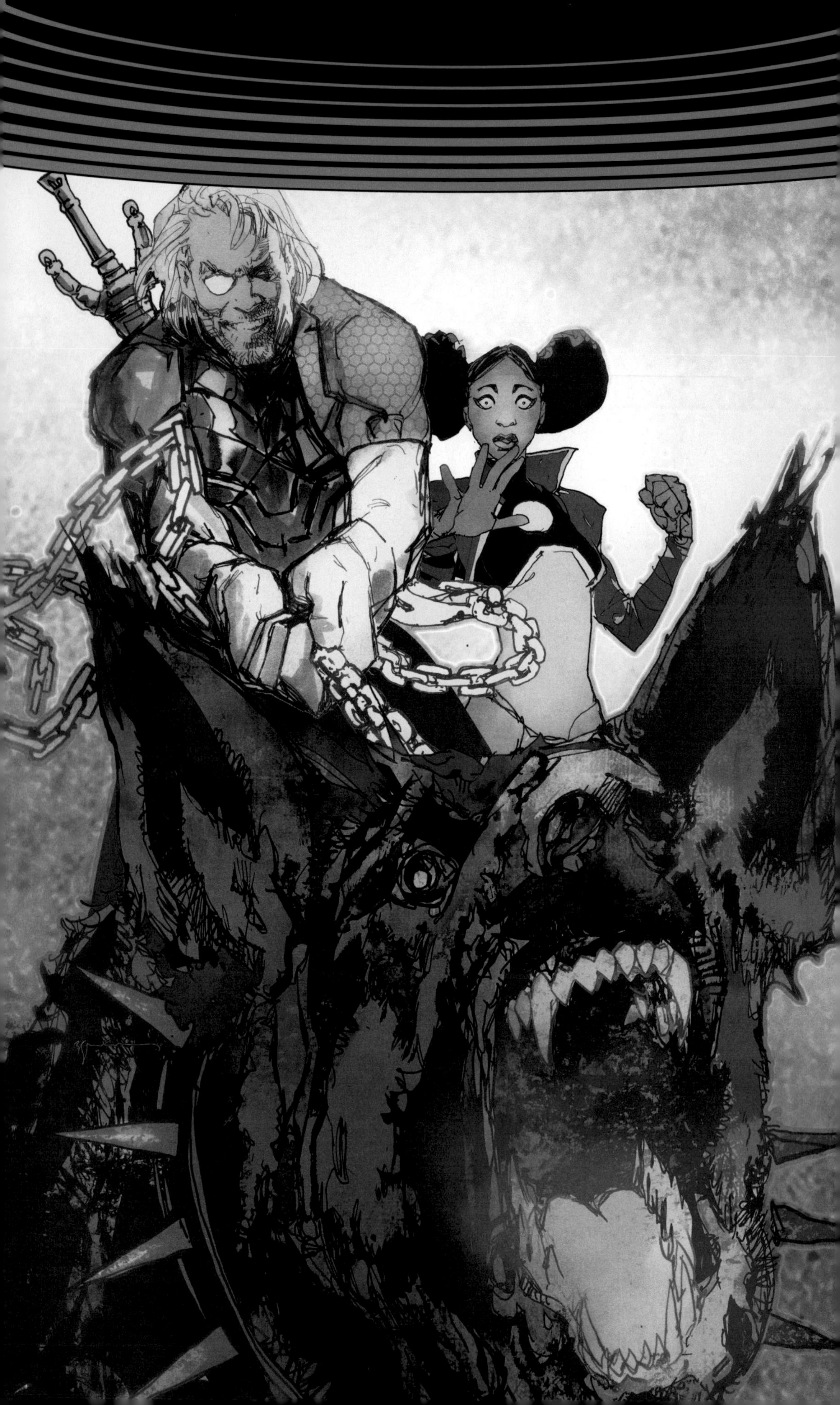

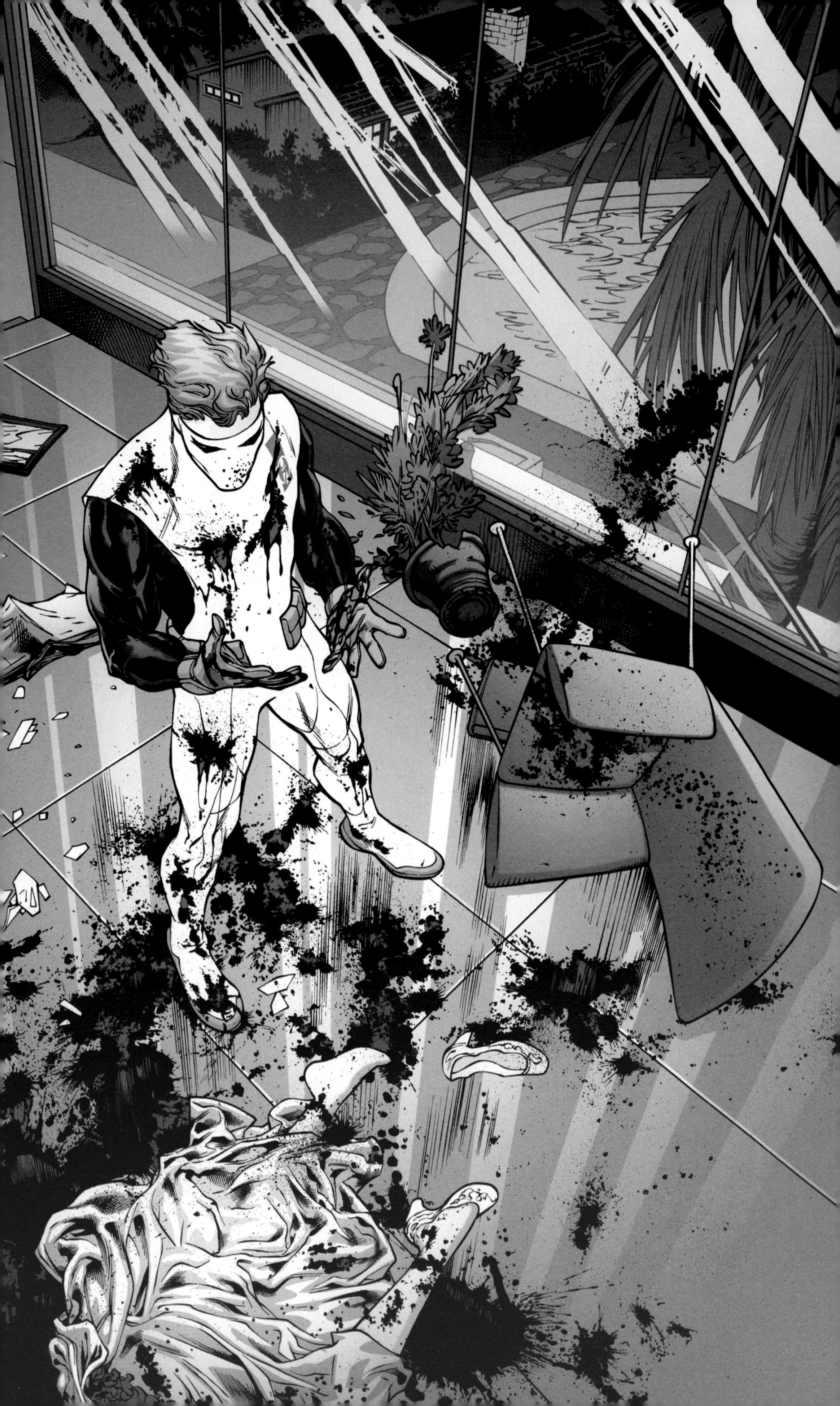

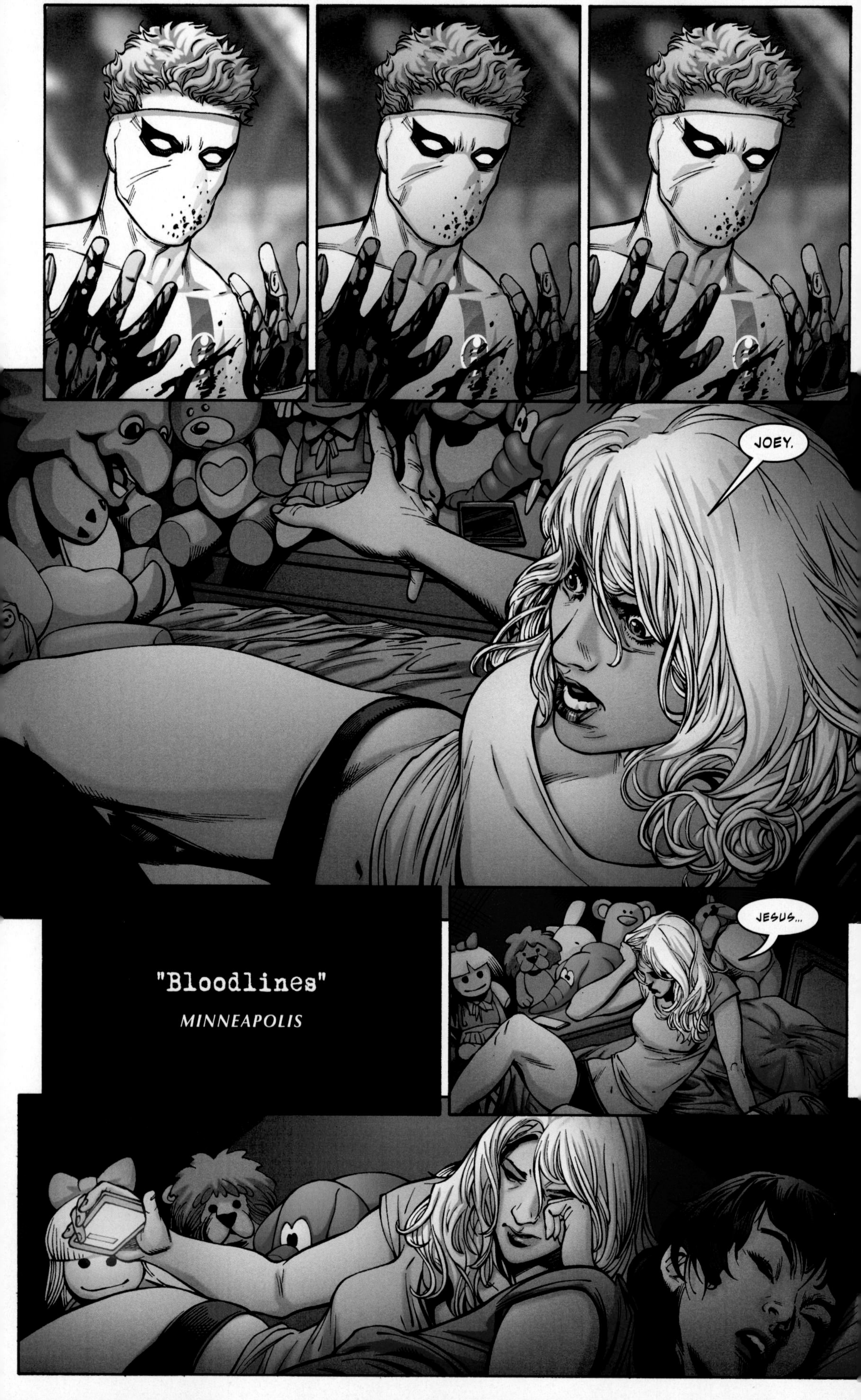
JOEY.
"Bloodlines"
MINNEAPOLIS
JESUS...

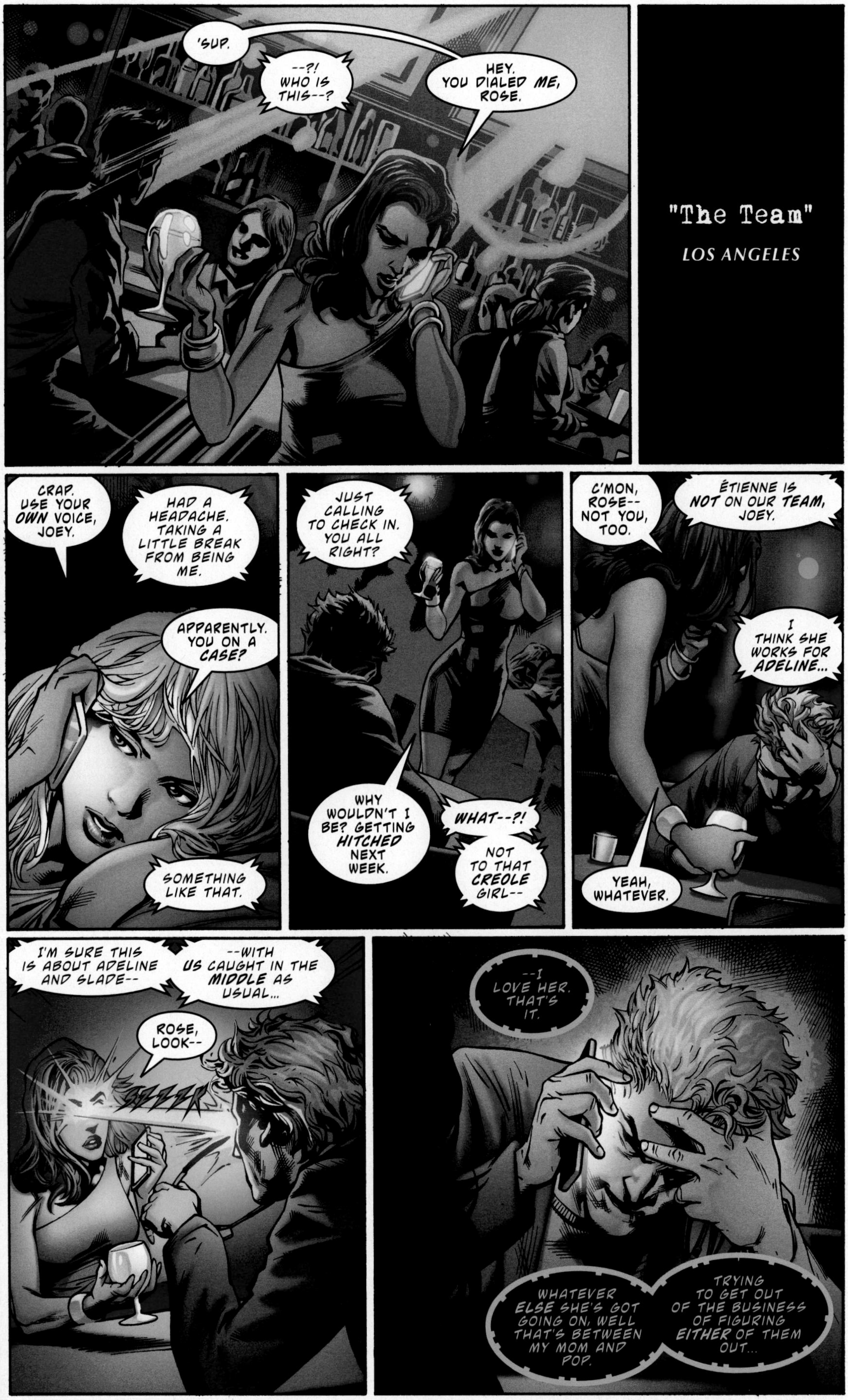
"The Team"
LOS ANGELES
'SUP.
--?! WHO IS THIS--?
HEY. YOU DIALED ME, ROSE.
CRAP. USE YOUR OWN VOICE, JOEY.
HAD A HEADACHE. TAKING A LITTLE BREAK FROM BEING ME.
APPARENTLY. YOU ON A CASE?
SOMETHING LIKE THAT.
JUST CALLING TO CHECK IN. YOU ALL RIGHT?
WHY WOULDN'T I BE? GETTING HITCHED NEXT WEEK.
WHAT--?!
NOT TO THAT CREOLE GIRL--
C'MON, ROSE-- NOT YOU, TOO.
ÉTIENNE IS NOT ON OUR TEAM, JOEY.
I THINK SHE WORKS FOR ADELINE...
YEAH, WHATEVER.
I'M SURE THIS IS ABOUT ADELINE AND SLADE--
--WITH US CAUGHT IN THE MIDDLE AS USUAL...
ROSE, LOOK--
--I LOVE HER. THAT'S IT.
WHATEVER ELSE SHE'S GOT GOING ON, WELL THAT'S BETWEEN MY MOM AND POP.
TRYING TO GET OUT OF THE BUSINESS OF FIGURING EITHER OF THEM OUT...

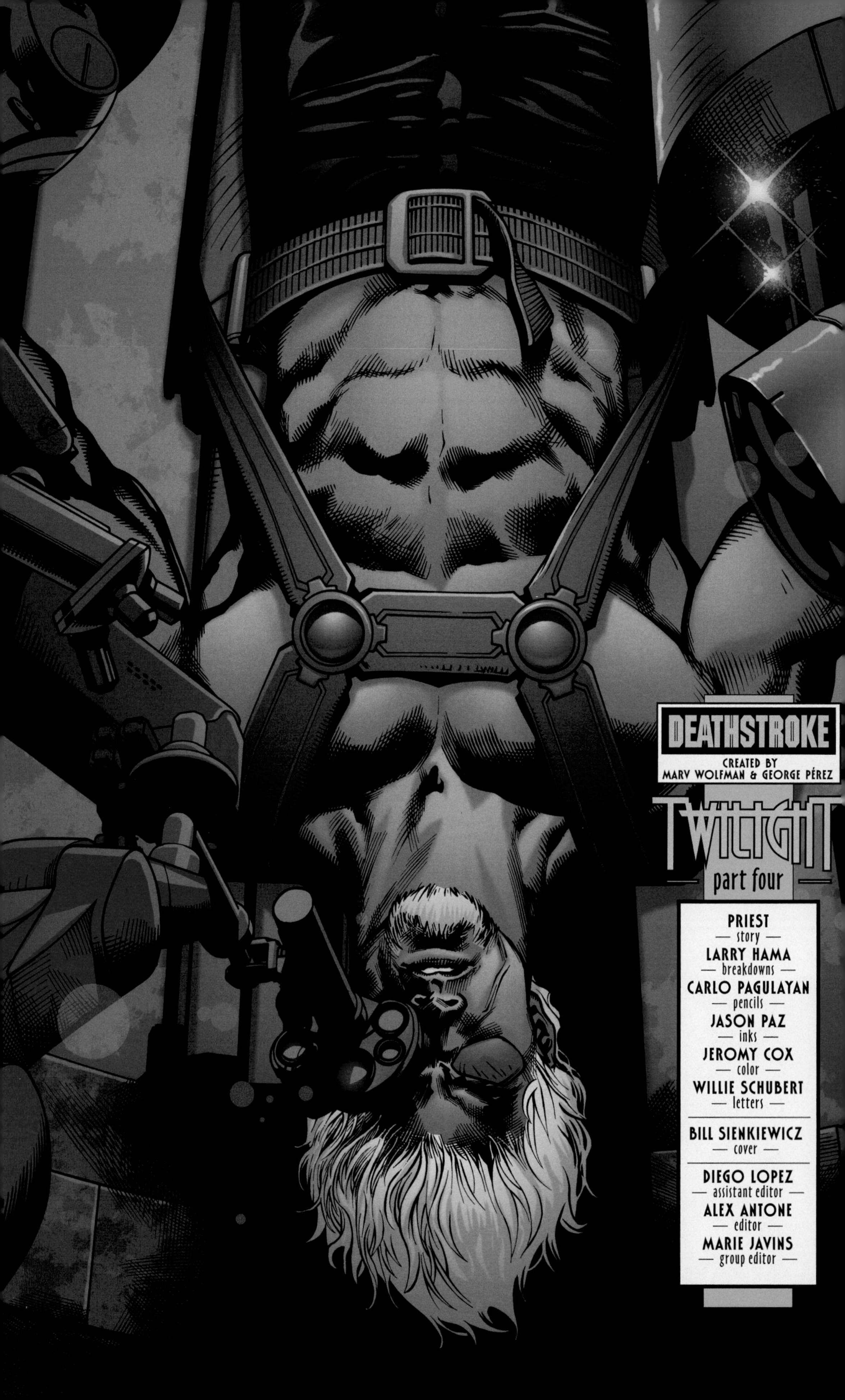

DEATHSTROKE
CREATED BY
MARV WOLFMAN & GEORGE PÉREZ
TWILIGHT
part four
PRIEST
— story —
LARRY HAMA
— breakdowns —
CARLO PAGULAYAN
— pencils —
JASON PAZ
— inks —
JEROMY COX
— color —
WILLIE SCHUBERT
— letters —
BILL SIENKIEWICZ
— cover —
DIEGO LOPEZ
— assistant editor —
ALEX ANTONE
— editor —
MARIE JAVINS
— group editor —

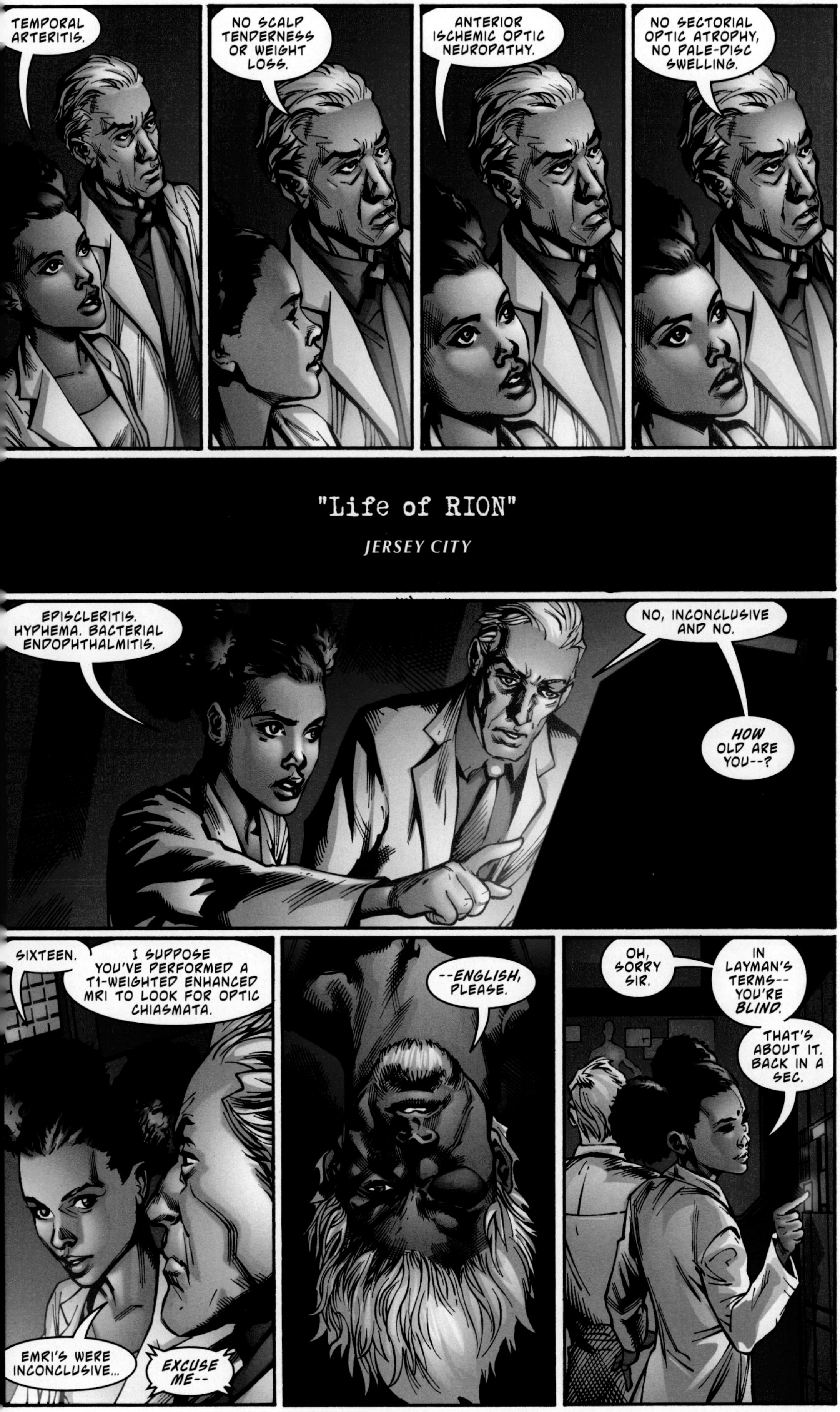
TEMPORAL ARTERITIS.
NO SCALP TENDERNESS OR WEIGHT LOSS.
ANTERIOR ISCHEMIC OPTIC NEUROPATHY.
NO SECTORIAL OPTIC ATROPHY, NO PALE-DISC SWELLING.
"Life of RION"
JERSEY CITY
EPISCLERITIS. HYPHEMA. BACTERIAL ENDOPHTHALMITIS.
NO, INCONCLUSIVE AND NO.
HOW OLD ARE YOU--?
SIXTEEN.
I SUPPOSE YOU'VE PERFORMED A T1-WEIGHTED ENHANCED MRI TO LOOK FOR OPTIC CHIASMATA.
EMRI'S WERE INCONCLUSIVE...
EXCUSE ME--
--ENGLISH, PLEASE.
OH, SORRY SIR.
IN LAYMAN'S TERMS-- YOU'RE BLIND.
THAT'S ABOUT IT. BACK IN A SEC.

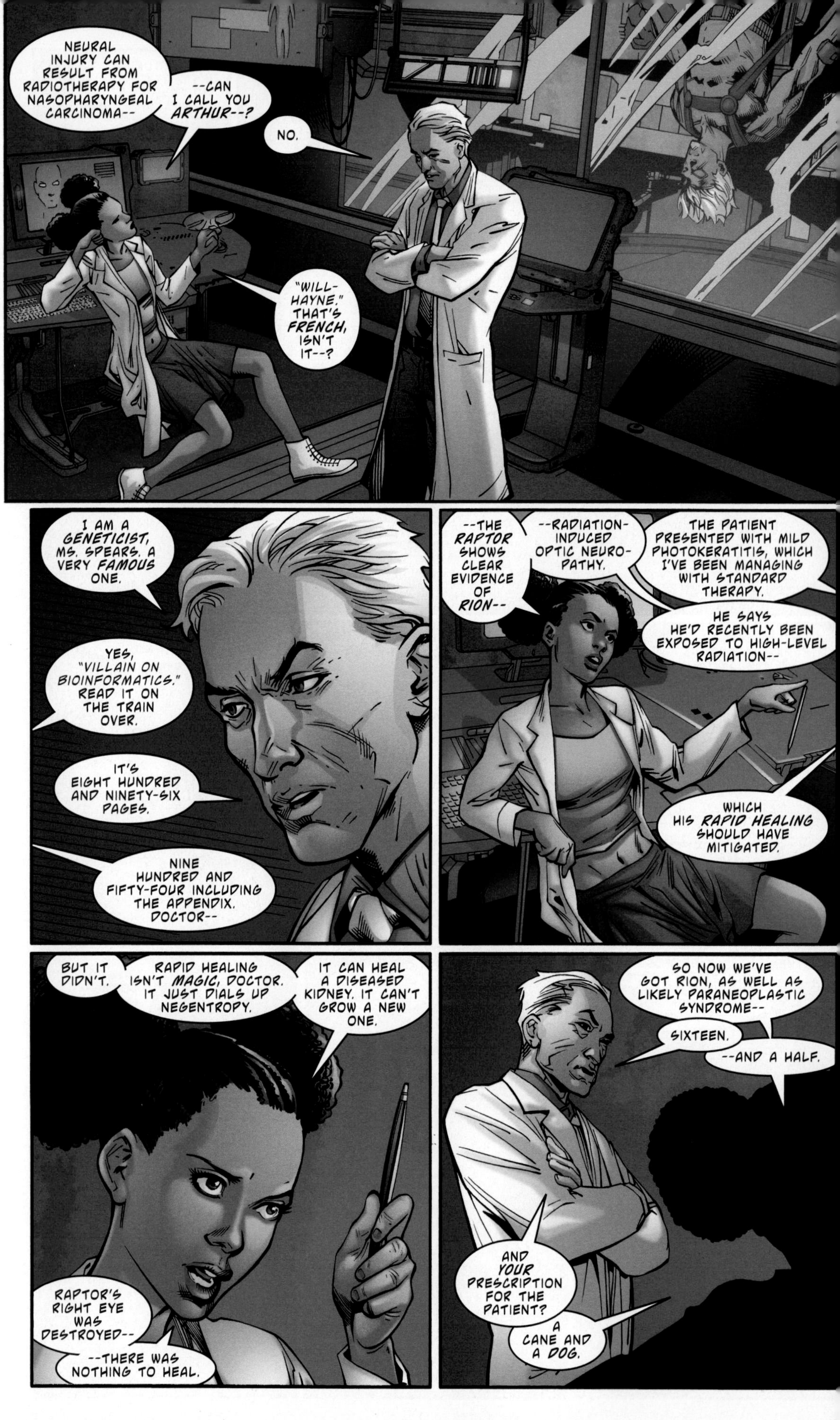
NEURAL INJURY CAN RESULT FROM RADIOTHERAPY FOR NASOPHARYNGEAL CARCINOMA--
--CAN I CALL YOU ARTHUR--?
NO.
"WILL-HAYNE." THAT'S FRENCH, ISN'T IT--?
I AM A GENETICIST, MS. SPEARS. A VERY FAMOUS ONE.
YES, "VILLAIN ON BIOINFORMATICS." READ IT ON THE TRAIN OVER.
IT'S EIGHT HUNDRED AND NINETY-SIX PAGES.
NINE HUNDRED AND FIFTY-FOUR INCLUDING THE APPENDIX. DOCTOR--
THE PATIENT PRESENTED WITH MILD PHOTOKERATITIS, WHICH I'VE BEEN MANAGING WITH STANDARD THERAPY.
HE SAYS HE'D RECENTLY BEEN EXPOSED TO HIGH-LEVEL RADIATION--
--RADIATION-INDUCED OPTIC NEURO-PATHY.
--THE RAPTOR SHOWS CLEAR EVIDENCE OF RION--
WHICH HIS RAPID HEALING SHOULD HAVE MITIGATED.
BUT IT DIDN'T.
RAPID HEALING ISN'T MAGIC, DOCTOR. IT JUST DIALS UP NEGENTROPY.
IT CAN HEAL A DISEASED KIDNEY. IT CAN'T GROW A NEW ONE.
RAPTOR'S RIGHT EYE WAS DESTROYED--
--THERE WAS NOTHING TO HEAL.
SO NOW WE'VE GOT RION, AS WELL AS LIKELY PARANEOPLASTIC SYNDROME--
SIXTEEN.
--AND A HALF.
AND YOUR PRESCRIPTION FOR THE PATIENT?
A CANE AND A DOG.

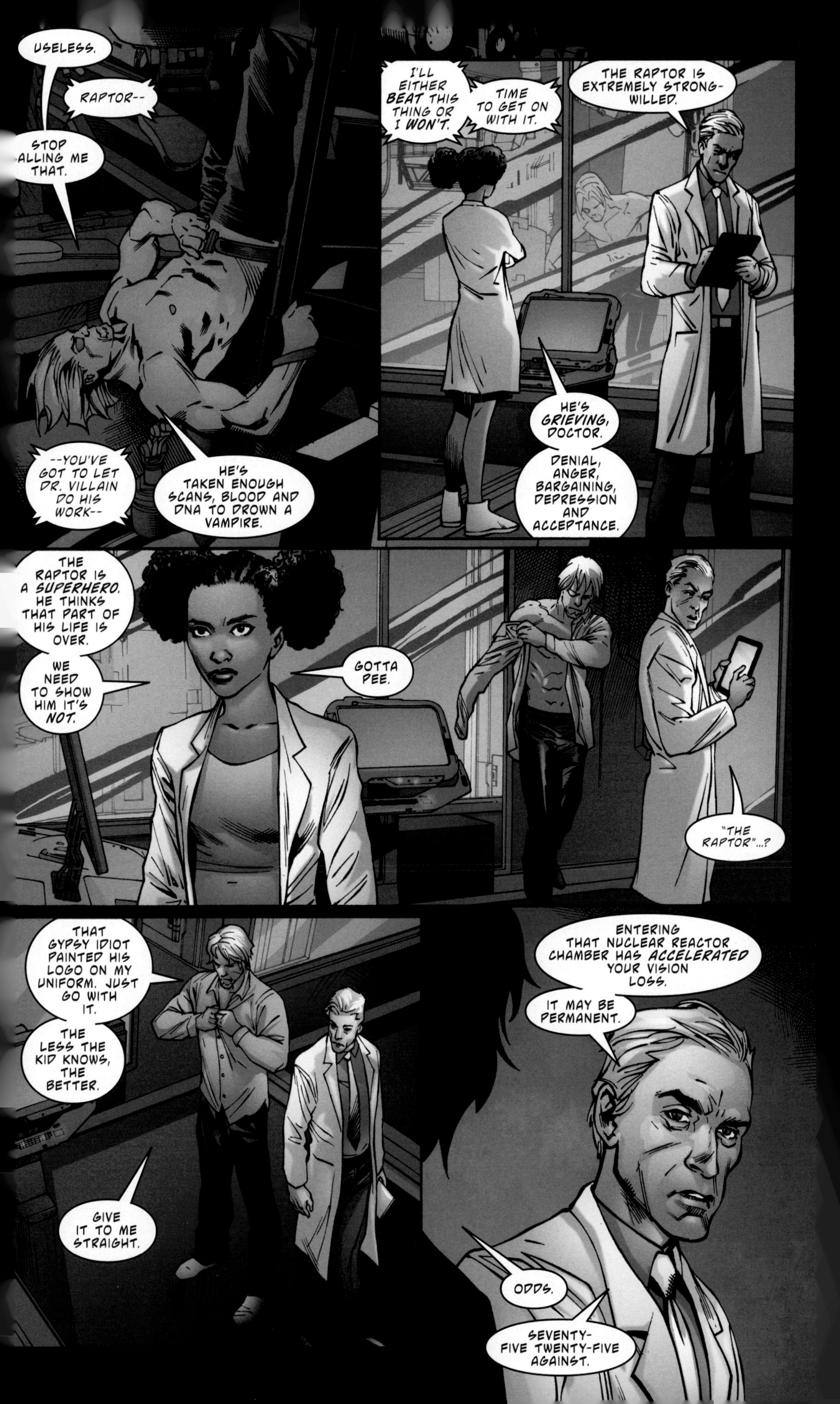
USELESS.
RAPTOR--
STOP CALLING ME THAT.
--YOU'VE GOT TO LET DR. VILLAIN DO HIS WORK--
HE'S TAKEN ENOUGH SCANS, BLOOD AND DNA TO DROWN A VAMPIRE.
I'LL EITHER BEAT THIS THING OR I WON'T.
TIME TO GET ON WITH IT.
THE RAPTOR IS EXTREMELY STRONG-WILLED.
HE'S GRIEVING, DOCTOR.
DENIAL, ANGER, BARGAINING, DEPRESSION AND ACCEPTANCE.
THE RAPTOR IS A SUPERHERO. HE THINKS THAT PART OF HIS LIFE IS OVER.
WE NEED TO SHOW HIM IT'S NOT.
GOTTA PEE.
"THE RAPTOR"...?
THAT GYPSY IDIOT PAINTED HIS LOGO ON MY UNIFORM. JUST GO WITH IT.
THE LESS THE KID KNOWS, THE BETTER.
GIVE IT TO ME STRAIGHT.
ENTERING THAT NUCLEAR REACTOR CHAMBER HAS ACCELERATED YOUR VISION LOSS.
IT MAY BE PERMANENT.
ODDS.
SEVENTY-FIVE TWENTY-FIVE AGAINST.

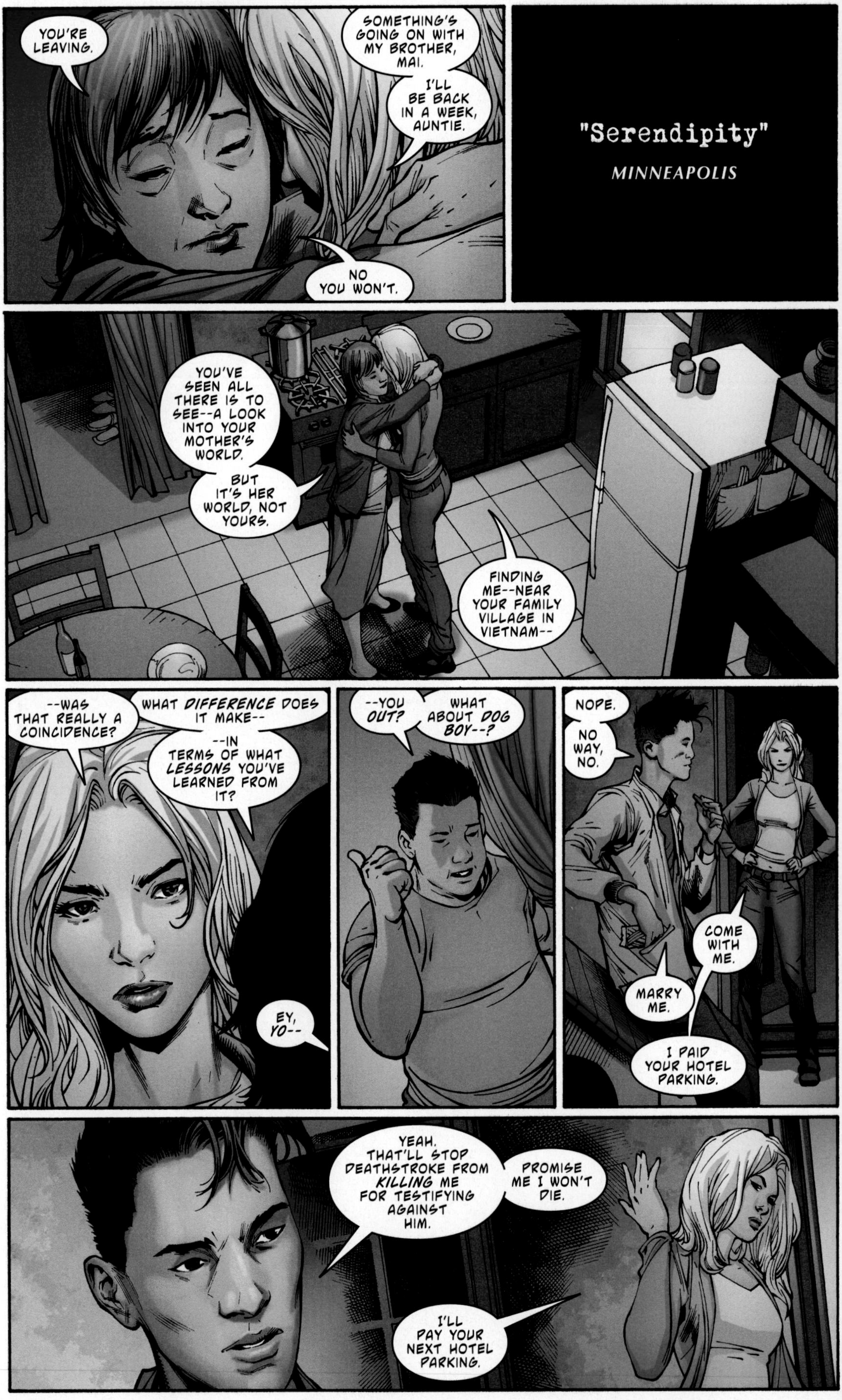

YOU'RE LEAVING.
SOMETHING'S GOING ON WITH MY BROTHER, MAI.
I'LL BE BACK IN A WEEK, AUNTIE.
NO YOU WON'T.
"Serendipity"
MINNEAPOLIS
YOU'VE SEEN ALL THERE IS TO SEE--A LOOK INTO YOUR MOTHER'S WORLD.
BUT IT'S HER WORLD, NOT YOURS.
FINDING ME--NEAR YOUR FAMILY VILLAGE IN VIETNAM--
--WAS THAT REALLY A COINCIDENCE?
WHAT DIFFERENCE DOES IT MAKE--
--IN TERMS OF WHAT LESSONS YOU'VE LEARNED FROM IT?
EY, YO--
--YOU OUT?
WHAT ABOUT DOG BOY--?
NOPE.
NO WAY, NO.
COME WITH ME.
MARRY ME.
I PAID YOUR HOTEL PARKING.
YEAH. THAT'LL STOP DEATHSTROKE FROM KILLING ME FOR TESTIFYING AGAINST HIM.
PROMISE ME I WON'T DIE.
I'LL PAY YOUR NEXT HOTEL PARKING.

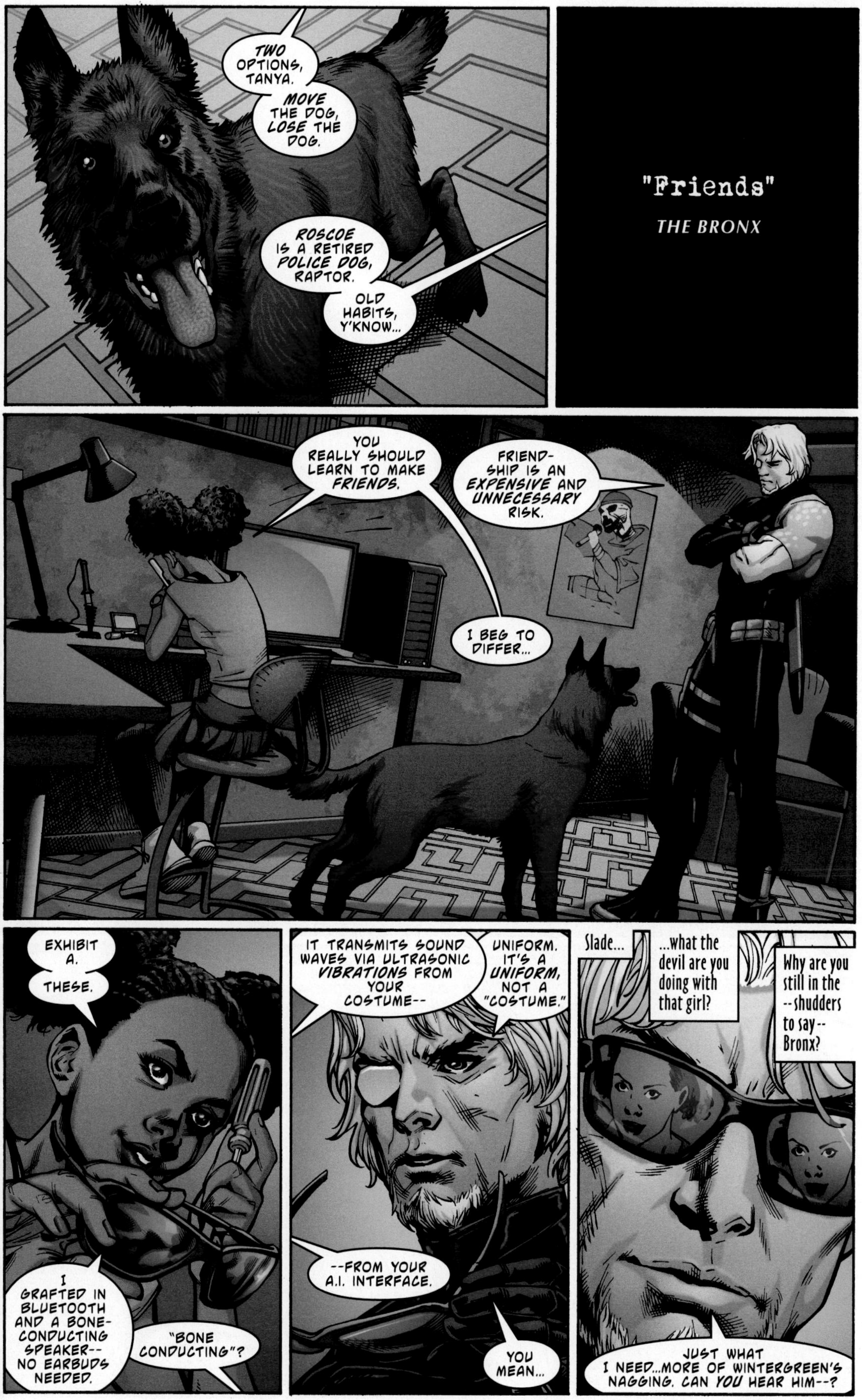
TWO OPTIONS, TANYA.
MOVE THE DOG, LOSE THE DOG.
ROSCOE IS A RETIRED POLICE DOG, RAPTOR.
OLD HABITS, Y'KNOW...
"Friends"
THE BRONX
YOU REALLY SHOULD LEARN TO MAKE FRIENDS.
FRIEND-SHIP IS AN EXPENSIVE AND UNNECESSARY RISK.
I BEG TO DIFFER...
EXHIBIT A.
THESE.
I GRAFTED IN BLUETOOTH AND A BONE-CONDUCTING SPEAKER--NO EARBUDS NEEDED.
"BONE CONDUCTING"?
IT TRANSMITS SOUND WAVES VIA ULTRASONIC VIBRATIONS FROM YOUR COSTUME--
UNIFORM. IT'S A UNIFORM, NOT A "COSTUME."
--FROM YOUR A.I. INTERFACE.
YOU MEAN...
Slade...
...what the devil are you doing with that girl?
Why are you still in the --shudders to say--Bronx?
JUST WHAT I NEED...MORE OF WINTERGREEN'S NAGGING. CAN YOU HEAR HIM--?

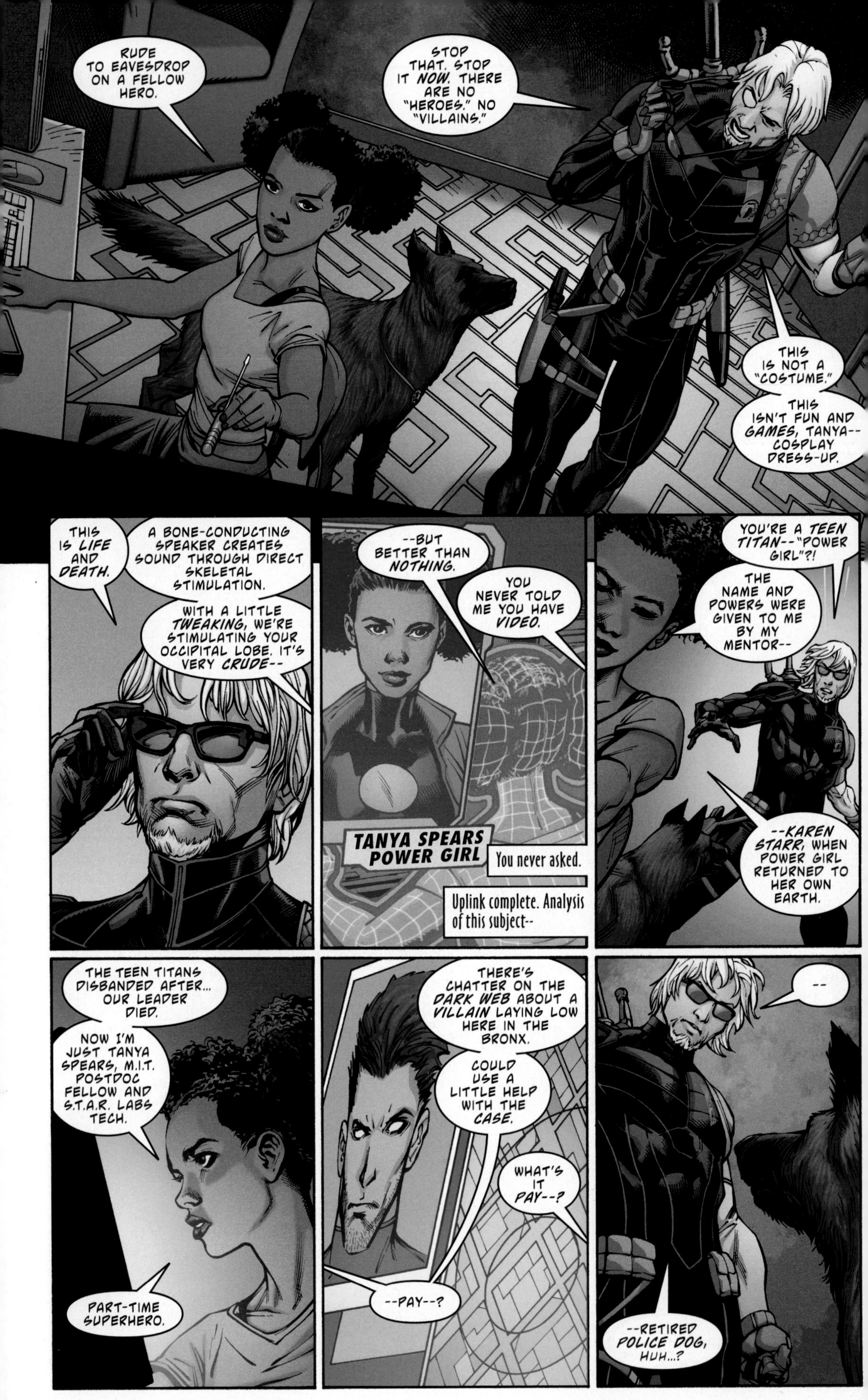
RUDE TO EAVESDROP ON A FELLOW HERO.
STOP THAT. STOP IT NOW. THERE ARE NO "HEROES." NO "VILLAINS."
THIS IS NOT A "COSTUME."
THIS ISN'T FUN AND GAMES, TANYA--COSPLAY DRESS-UP.
THIS IS LIFE AND DEATH.
A BONE-CONDUCTING SPEAKER CREATES SOUND THROUGH DIRECT SKELETAL STIMULATION.
WITH A LITTLE TWEAKING, WE'RE STIMULATING YOUR OCCIPITAL LOBE. IT'S VERY CRUDE--
--BUT BETTER THAN NOTHING.
YOU NEVER TOLD ME YOU HAVE VIDEO.
TANYA SPEARS
POWER GIRL
You never asked.
Uplink complete. Analysis of this subject--
YOU'RE A TEEN TITAN--"POWER GIRL"?!
THE NAME AND POWERS WERE GIVEN TO ME BY MY MENTOR--
--KAREN STARR, WHEN POWER GIRL RETURNED TO HER OWN EARTH.
THE TEEN TITANS DISBANDED AFTER... OUR LEADER DIED.
NOW I'M JUST TANYA SPEARS, M.I.T. POSTDOC FELLOW AND S.T.A.R. LABS TECH.
PART-TIME SUPERHERO.
THERE'S CHATTER ON THE DARK WEB ABOUT A VILLAIN LAYING LOW HERE IN THE BRONX.
COULD USE A LITTLE HELP WITH THE CASE.
WHAT'S IT PAY--?
--PAY--?
--
--RETIRED POLICE DOG, HUH...?

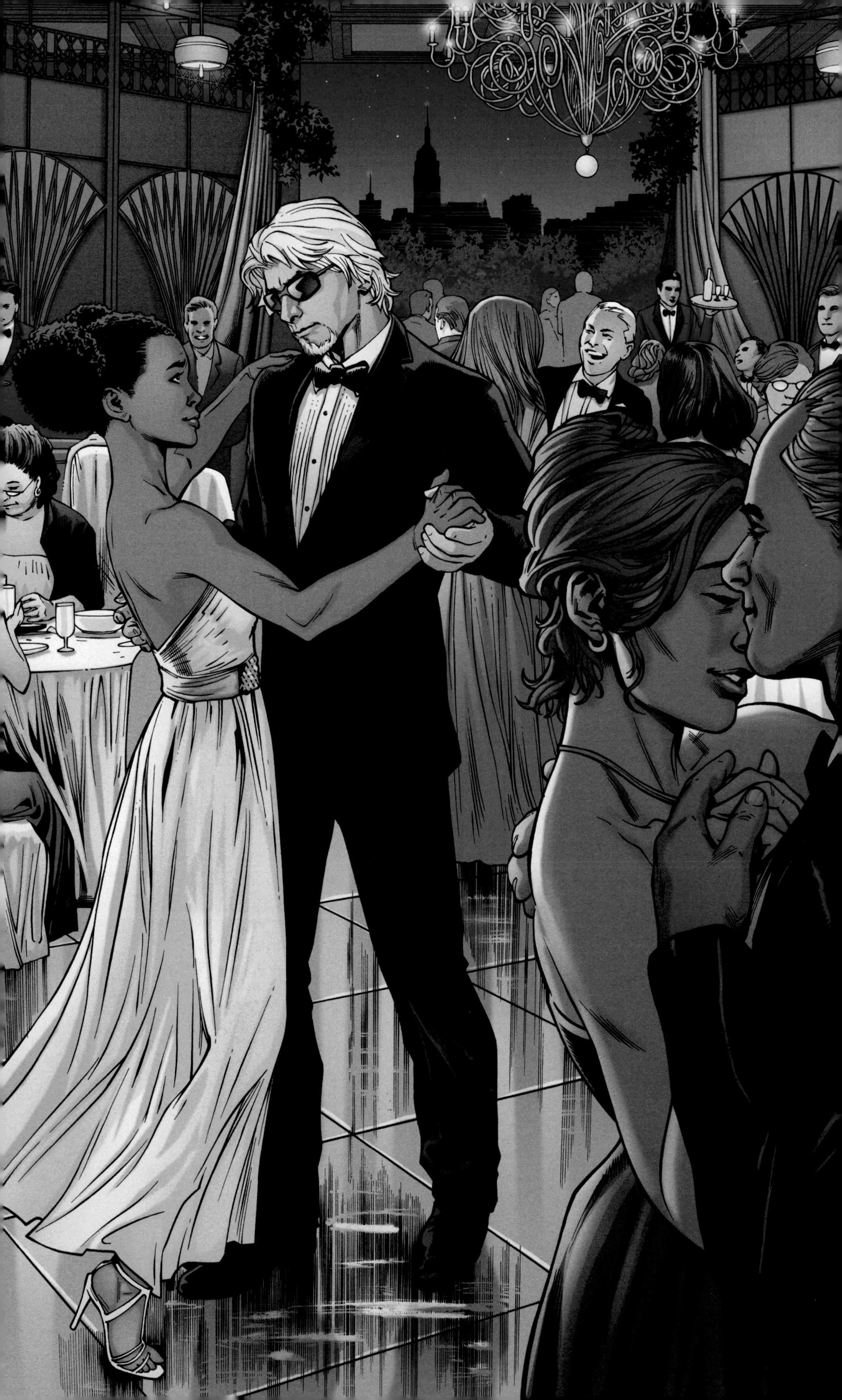

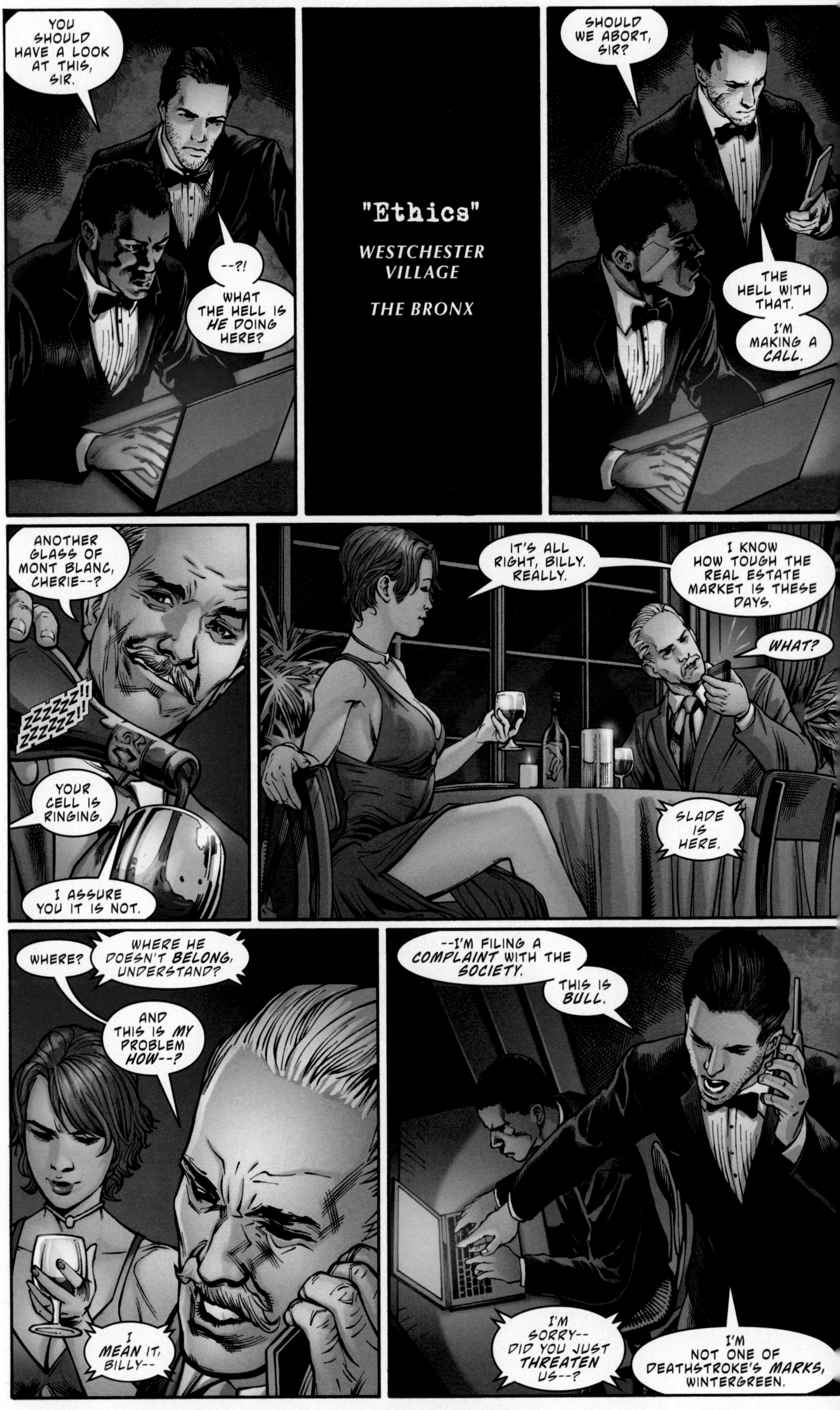
YOU SHOULD HAVE A LOOK AT THIS, SIR.
--?! WHAT THE HELL IS HE DOING HERE?
"Ethics"
WESTCHESTER VILLAGE
THE BRONX
SHOULD WE ABORT, SIR?
THE HELL WITH THAT.
I'M MAKING A CALL.
ANOTHER GLASS OF MONT BLANC, CHERIE--?
ZZZZZZ!! ZZZZZZ!!
YOUR CELL IS RINGING.
I ASSURE YOU IT IS NOT.
IT'S ALL RIGHT, BILLY. REALLY.
I KNOW HOW TOUGH THE REAL ESTATE MARKET IS THESE DAYS.
WHAT?
SLADE IS HERE.
WHERE?
WHERE HE DOESN'T BELONG, UNDERSTAND?
AND THIS IS MY PROBLEM HOW--?
I MEAN IT, BILLY--
--I'M FILING A COMPLAINT WITH THE SOCIETY.
THIS IS BULL.
I'M SORRY-- DID YOU JUST THREATEN US--?
I'M NOT ONE OF DEATHSTROKE'S MARKS, WINTERGREEN.

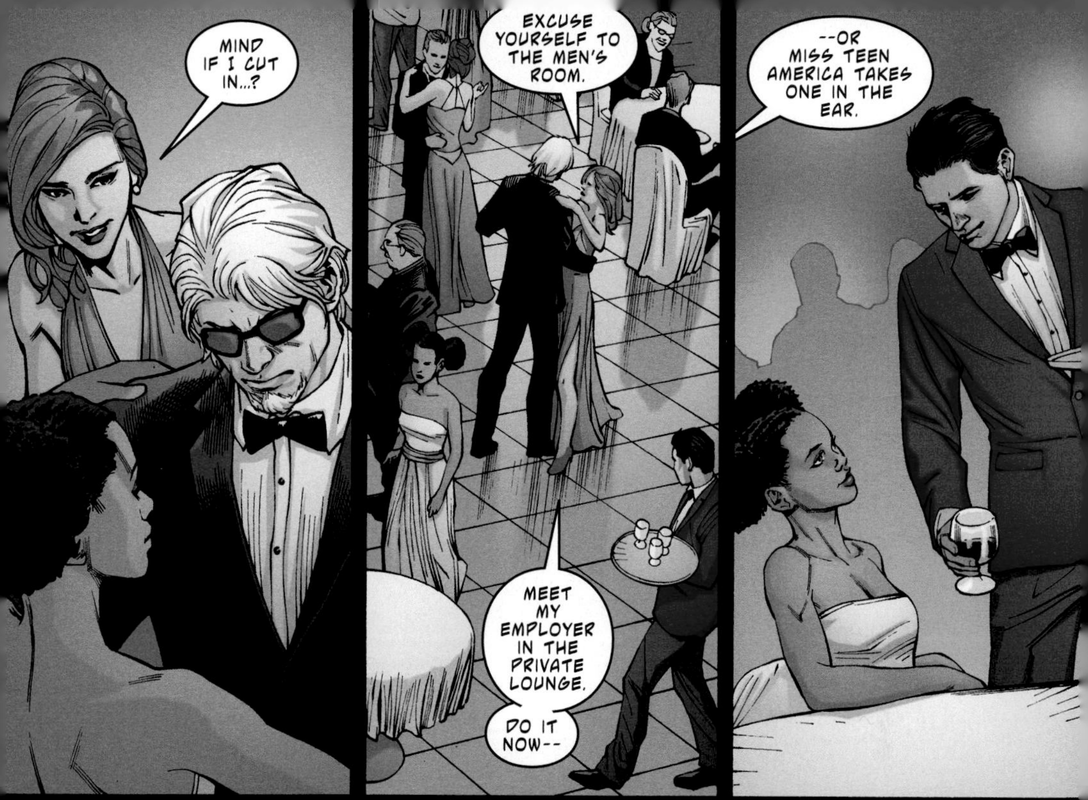

MIND IF I CUT IN...?
EXCUSE YOURSELF TO THE MEN'S ROOM.
MEET MY EMPLOYER IN THE PRIVATE LOUNGE.
DO IT NOW--
--OR MISS TEEN AMERICA TAKES ONE IN THE EAR.


"Redline"

*LOS ANGELES*

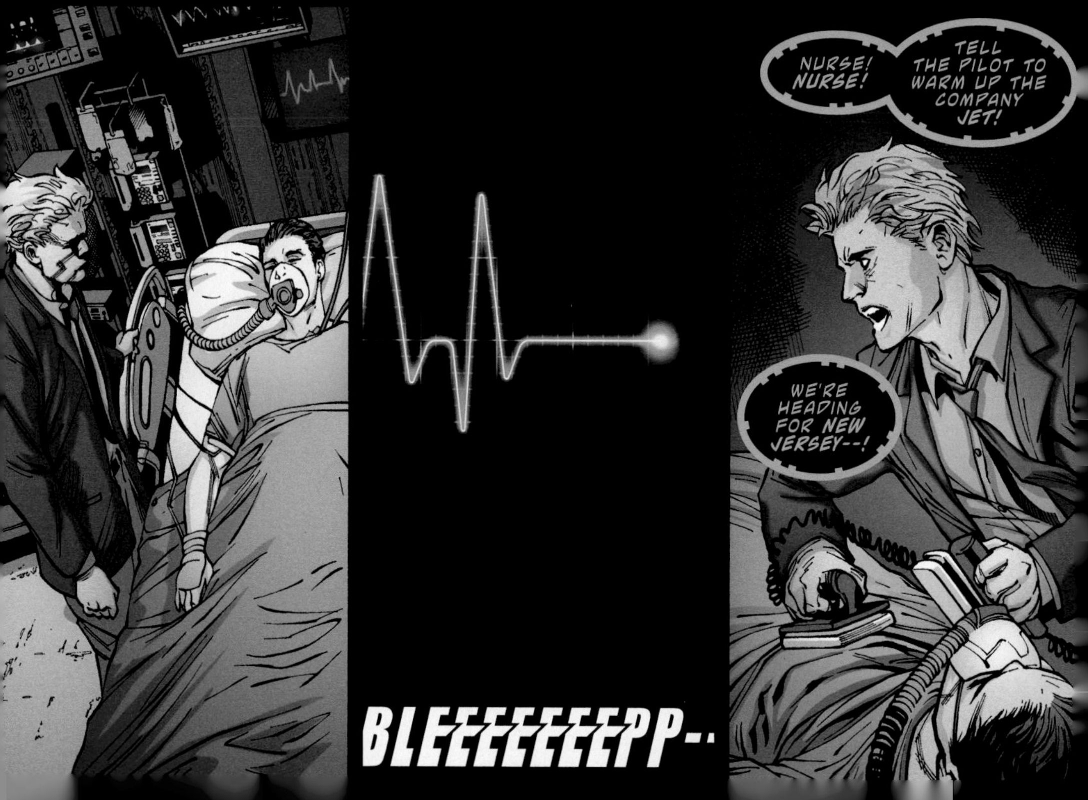

BLEEEEEEEPP--.
NURSE! NURSE!
TELL THE PILOT TO WARM UP THE COMPANY JET!
WE'RE HEADING FOR NEW JERSEY--!

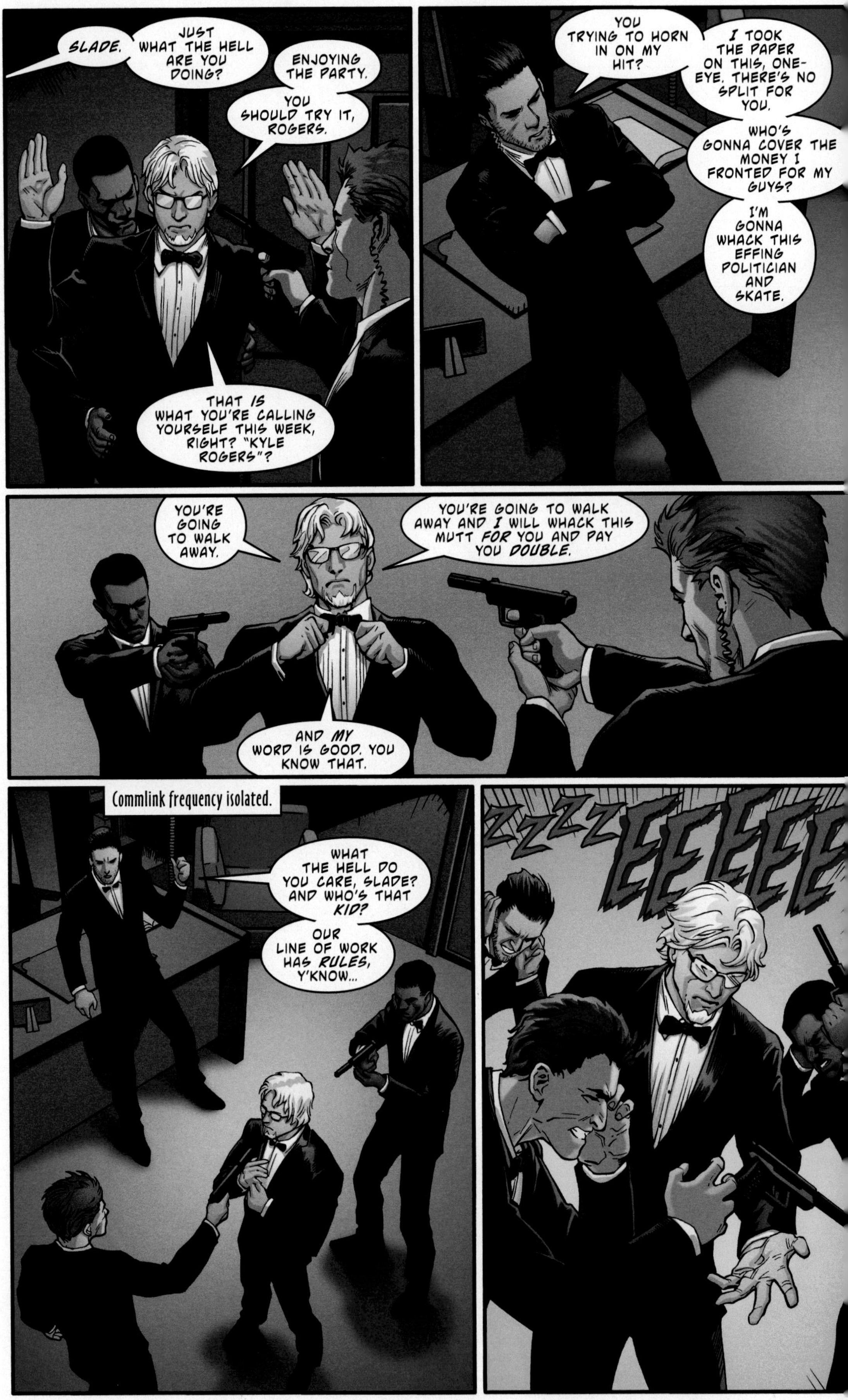
SLADE.
JUST WHAT THE HELL ARE YOU DOING?
ENJOYING THE PARTY.
YOU SHOULD TRY IT, ROGERS.
THAT IS WHAT YOU'RE CALLING YOURSELF THIS WEEK, RIGHT? "KYLE ROGERS"?
YOU TRYING TO HORN IN ON MY HIT?
I TOOK THE PAPER ON THIS, ONE-EYE. THERE'S NO SPLIT FOR YOU.
WHO'S GONNA COVER THE MONEY I FRONTED FOR MY GUYS?
I'M GONNA WHACK THIS EFFING POLITICIAN AND SKATE.
YOU'RE GOING TO WALK AWAY.
YOU'RE GOING TO WALK AWAY AND I WILL WHACK THIS MUTT FOR YOU AND PAY YOU DOUBLE.
AND MY WORD IS GOOD. YOU KNOW THAT.
Commlink frequency isolated.
WHAT THE HELL DO YOU CARE, SLADE? AND WHO'S THAT KID?
OUR LINE OF WORK HAS RULES, Y'KNOW...
ZZZZZEEEEEE

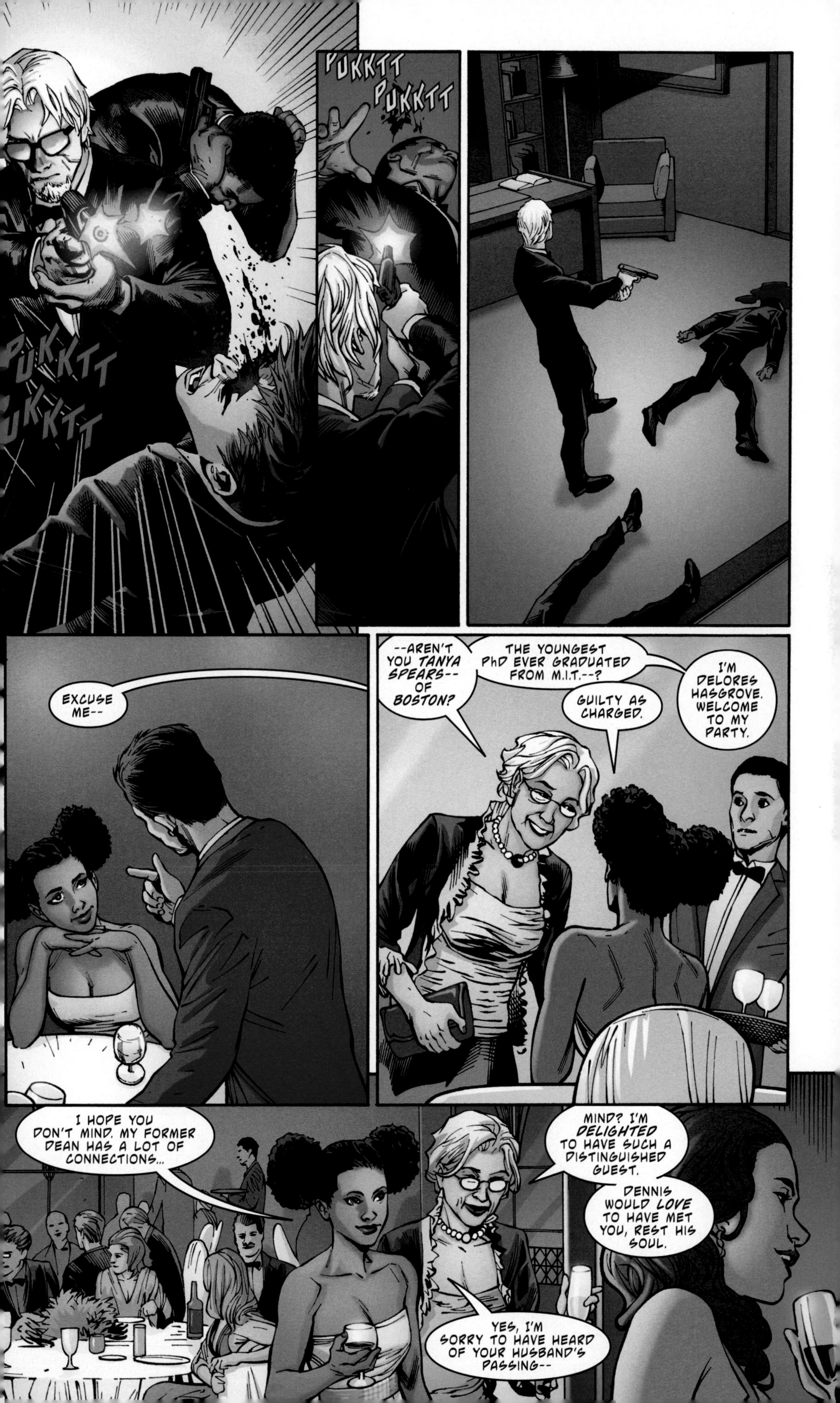
PUKKTT
PUKKTT
PUKKTT
PUKKTT
EXCUSE ME--
--AREN'T YOU TANYA SPEARS-- OF BOSTON?
THE YOUNGEST PhD EVER GRADUATED FROM M.I.T.--?
GUILTY AS CHARGED.
I'M DELORES HASGROVE. WELCOME TO MY PARTY.
I HOPE YOU DON'T MIND. MY FORMER DEAN HAS A LOT OF CONNECTIONS...
MIND? I'M DELIGHTED TO HAVE SUCH A DISTINGUISHED GUEST.
DENNIS WOULD LOVE TO HAVE MET YOU, REST HIS SOUL.
YES, I'M SORRY TO HAVE HEARD OF YOUR HUSBAND'S PASSING--

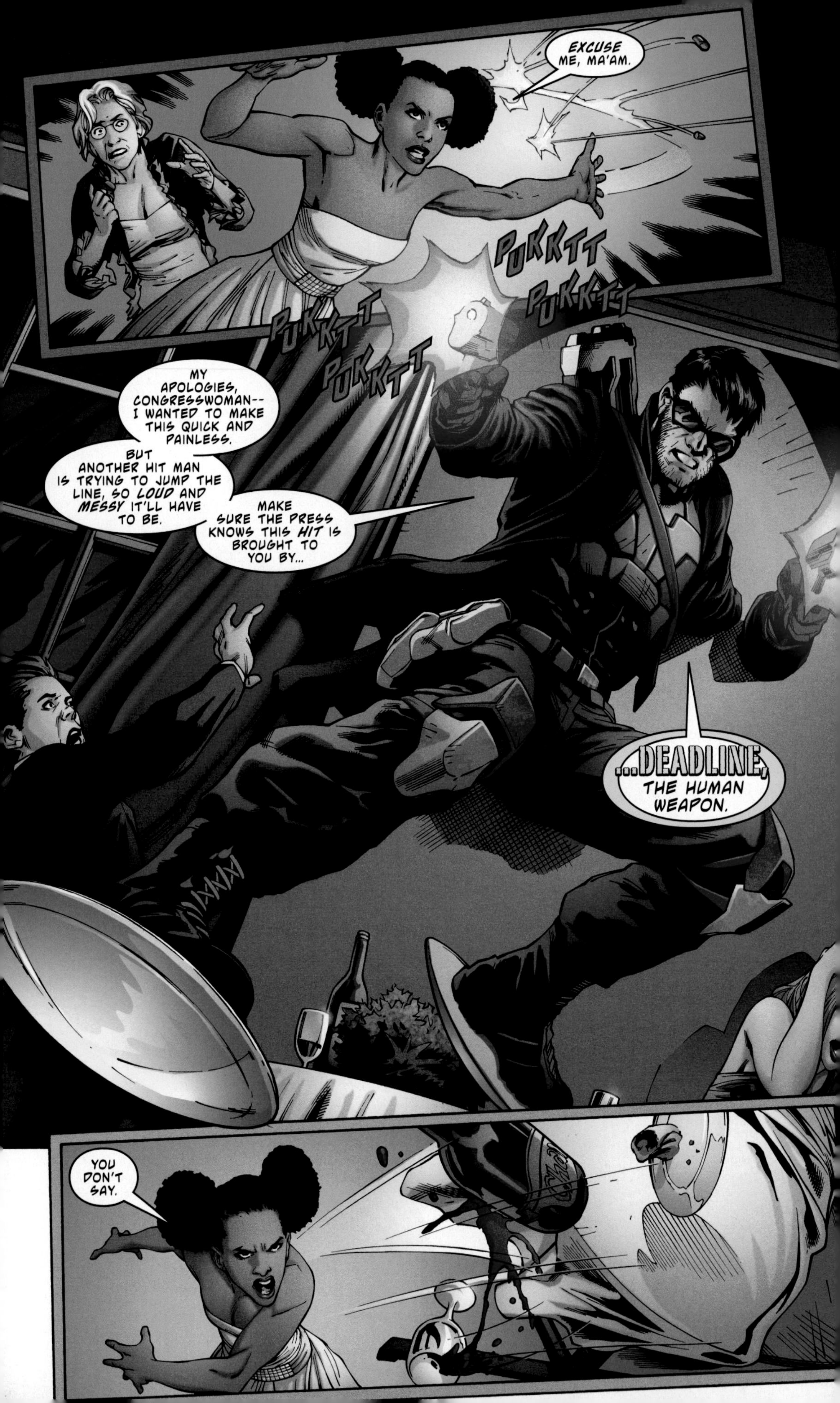
EXCUSE ME, MA'AM.
PUKKTT
PUKKTT
PUKKTT
PUKKTT
MY APOLOGIES, CONGRESSWOMAN-- I WANTED TO MAKE THIS QUICK AND PAINLESS.
BUT ANOTHER HIT MAN IS TRYING TO JUMP THE LINE, SO LOUD AND MESSY IT'LL HAVE TO BE.
MAKE SURE THE PRESS KNOWS THIS HIT IS BROUGHT TO YOU BY...
...DEADLINE, THE HUMAN WEAPON.
YOU DON'T SAY.

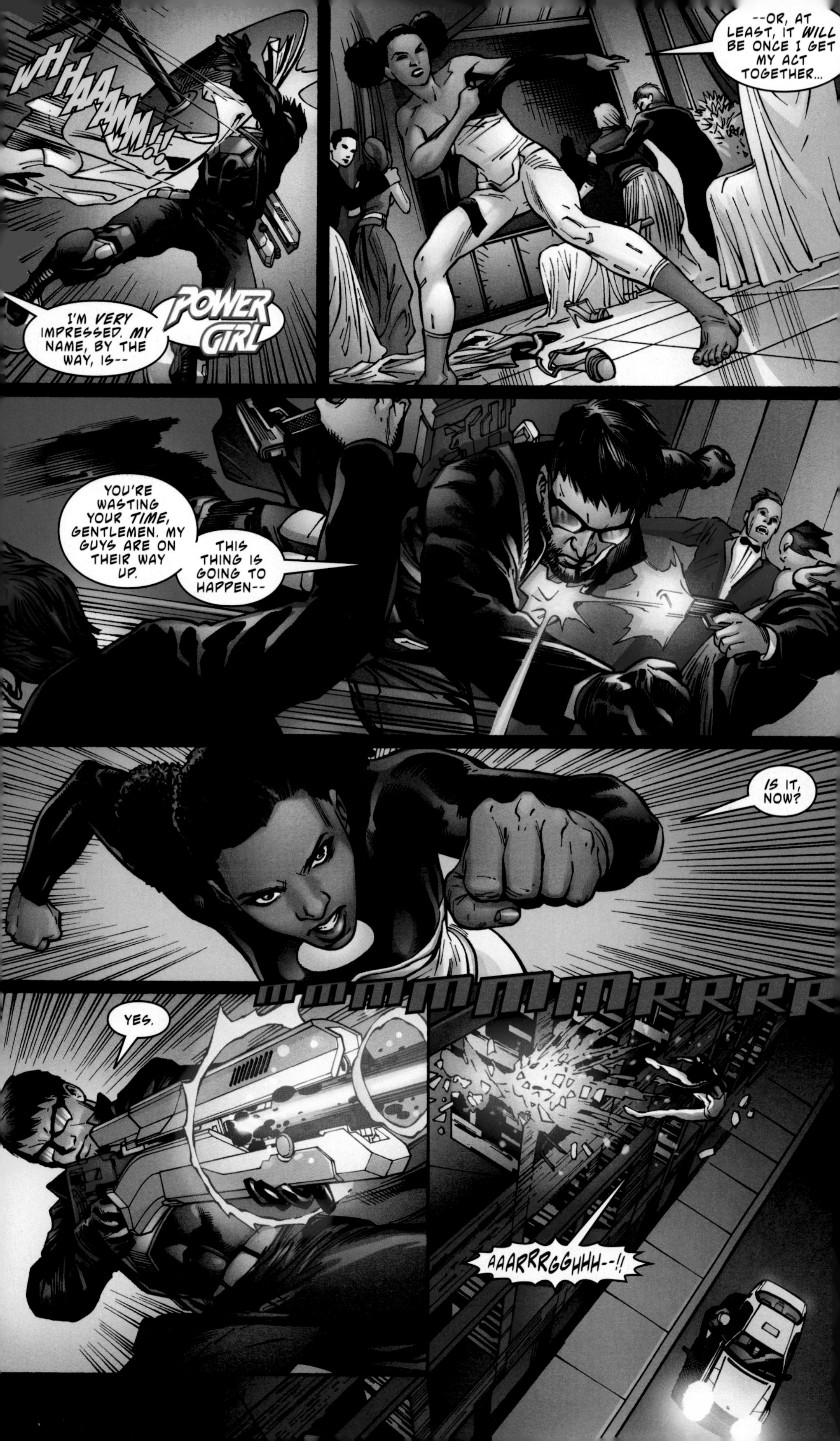
WHHAAAMM!!!
I'M VERY IMPRESSED. MY NAME, BY THE WAY, IS--
POWER GIRL
--OR, AT LEAST, IT WILL BE ONCE I GET MY ACT TOGETHER...
YOU'RE WASTING YOUR TIME, GENTLEMEN. MY GUYS ARE ON THEIR WAY UP.
THIS THING IS GOING TO HAPPEN--
IS IT, NOW?
MMMMMMMRRRRR
YES.
AAARRRGGHHH--!!

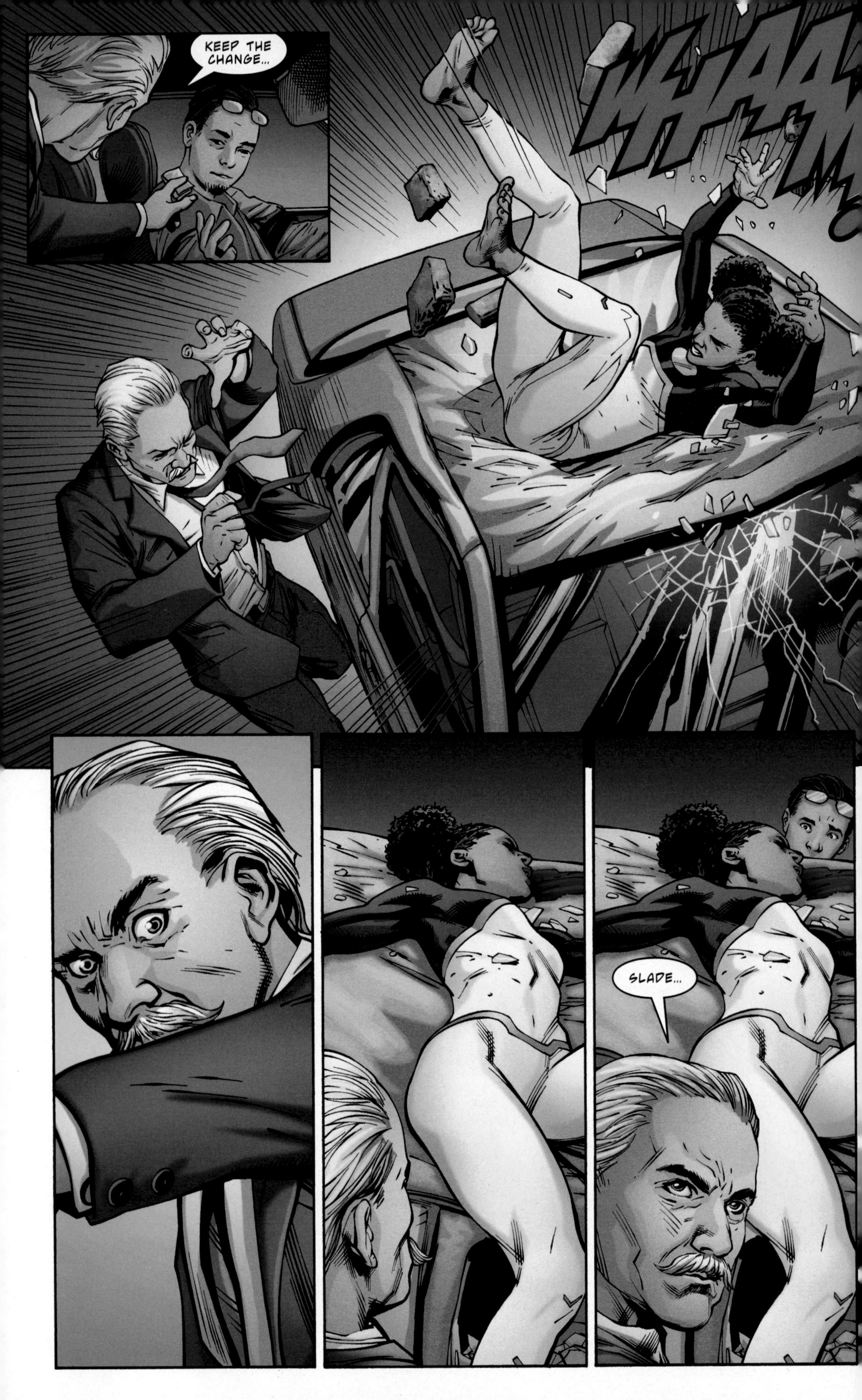
KEEP THE CHANGE...
SLADE...

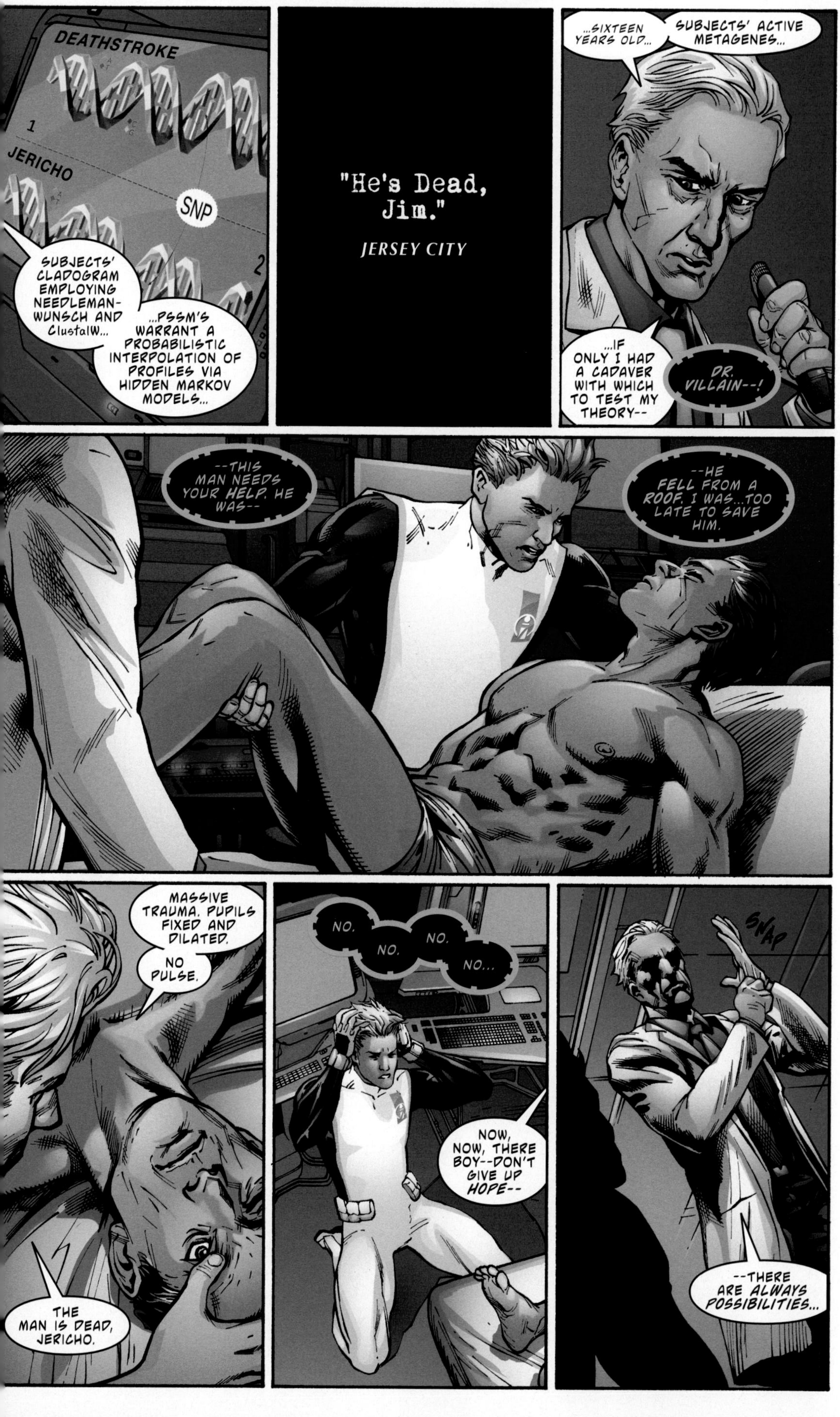
DEATHSTROKE
1
JERICHO
SNP
2
SUBJECTS' CLADOGRAM EMPLOYING NEEDLEMAN-WUNSCH AND ClustalW...
...PSSM'S WARRANT A PROBABILISTIC INTERPOLATION OF PROFILES VIA HIDDEN MARKOV MODELS...
"He's Dead, Jim."
JERSEY CITY
...SIXTEEN YEARS OLD...
SUBJECTS' ACTIVE METAGENES...
...IF ONLY I HAD A CADAVER WITH WHICH TO TEST MY THEORY--
DR. VILLAIN--!
--THIS MAN NEEDS YOUR HELP. HE WAS--
--HE FELL FROM A ROOF. I WAS...TOO LATE TO SAVE HIM.
MASSIVE TRAUMA. PUPILS FIXED AND DILATED.
NO PULSE.
THE MAN IS DEAD, JERICHO.
NO.
NO.
NO.
NO...
NOW, NOW, THERE BOY--DON'T GIVE UP HOPE--
SNAP
--THERE ARE ALWAYS POSSIBILITIES...

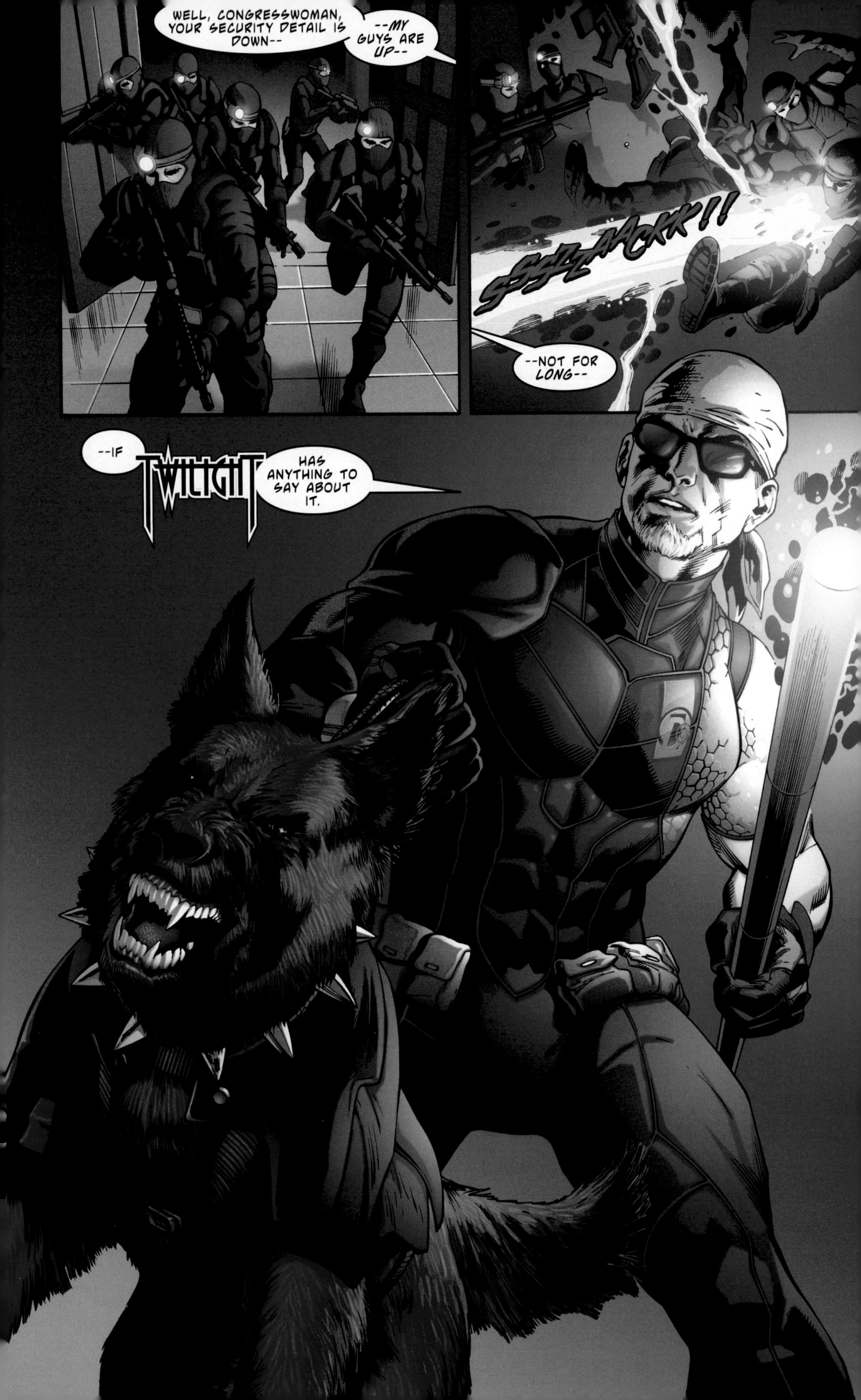
WELL, CONGRESSWOMAN, YOUR SECURITY DETAIL IS DOWN--
--MY GUYS ARE UP--
SSSZZAACKK!!
--NOT FOR LONG--
--IF
TWILIGHT
HAS ANYTHING TO SAY ABOUT IT.

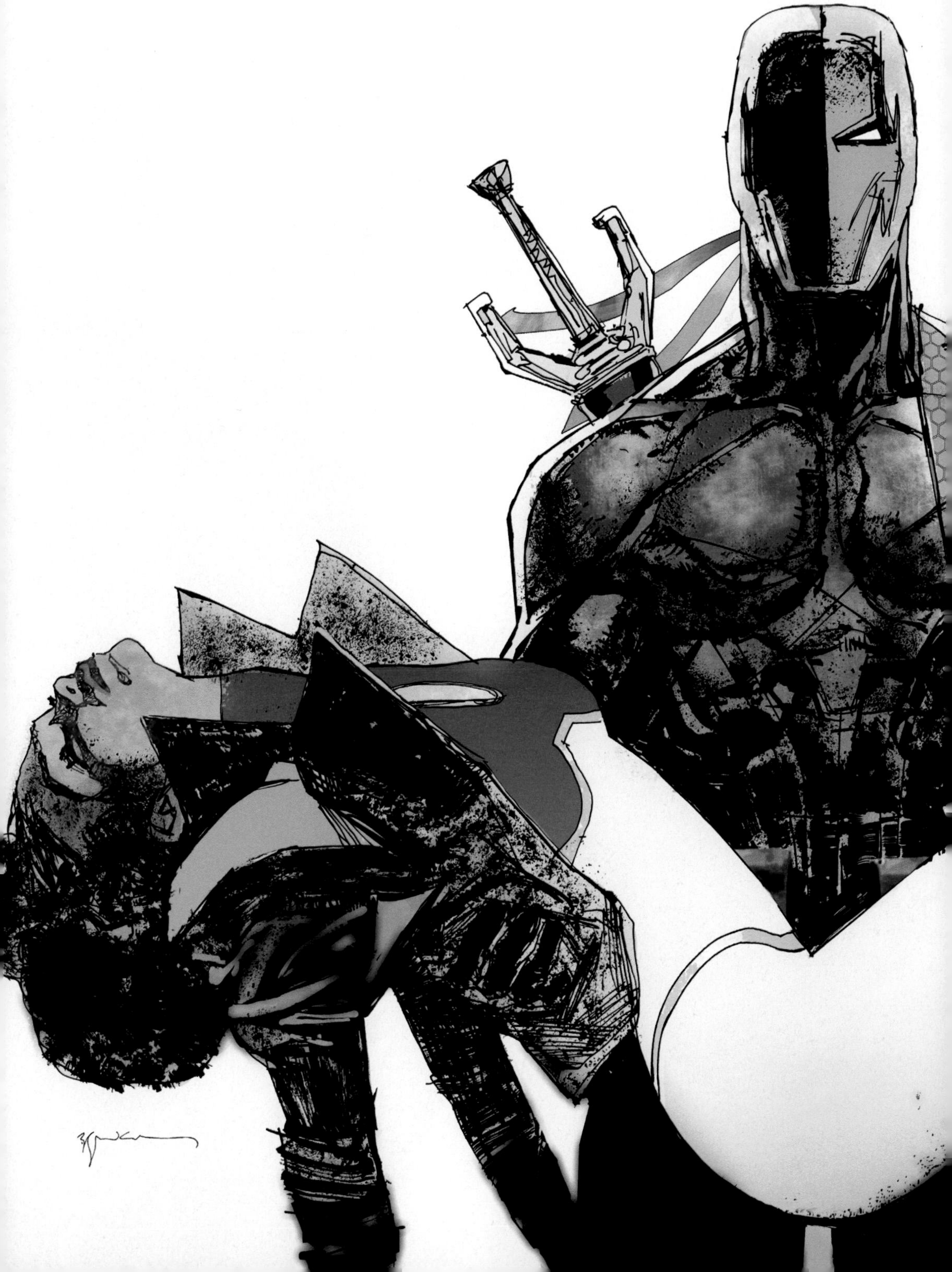

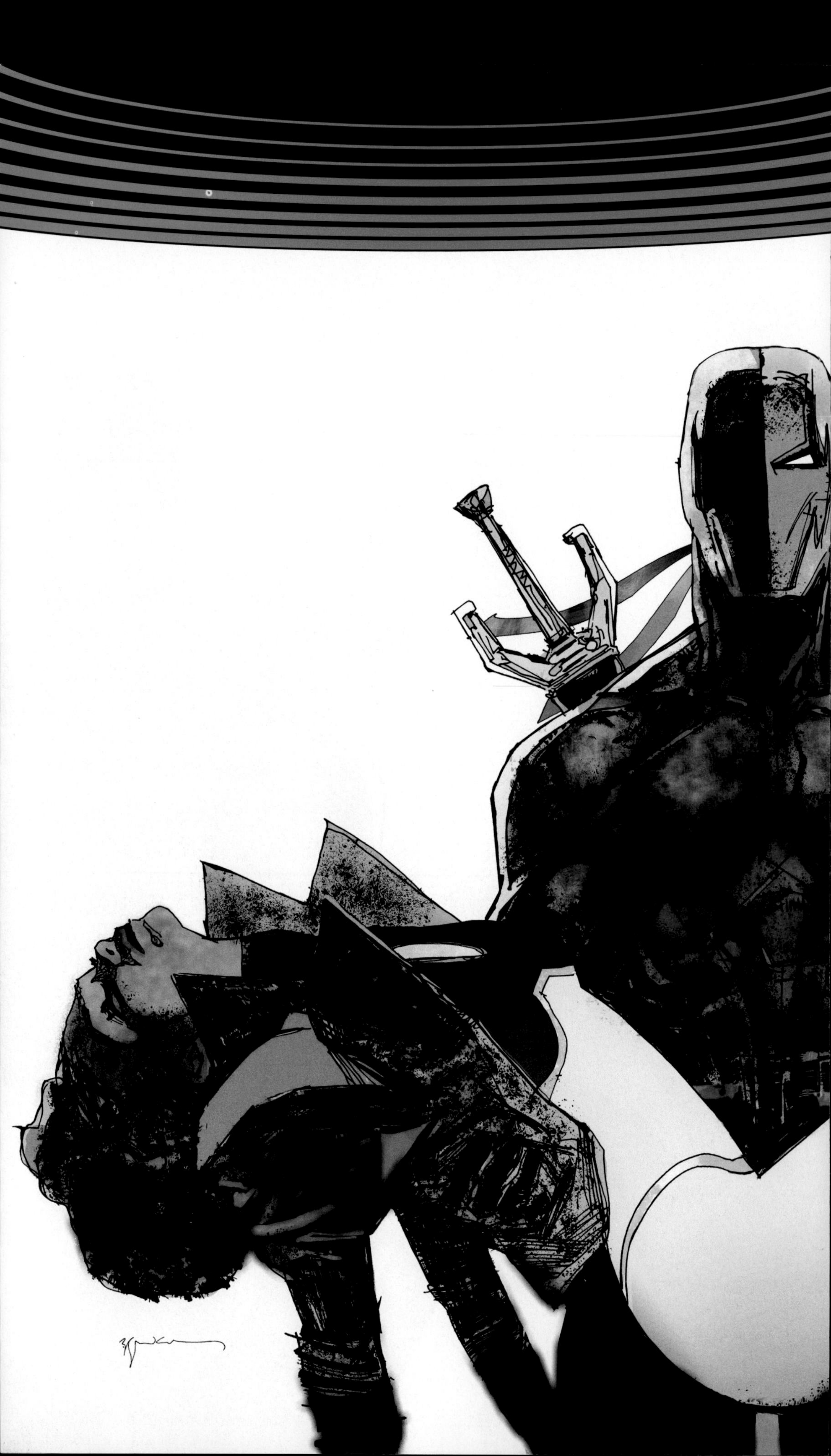

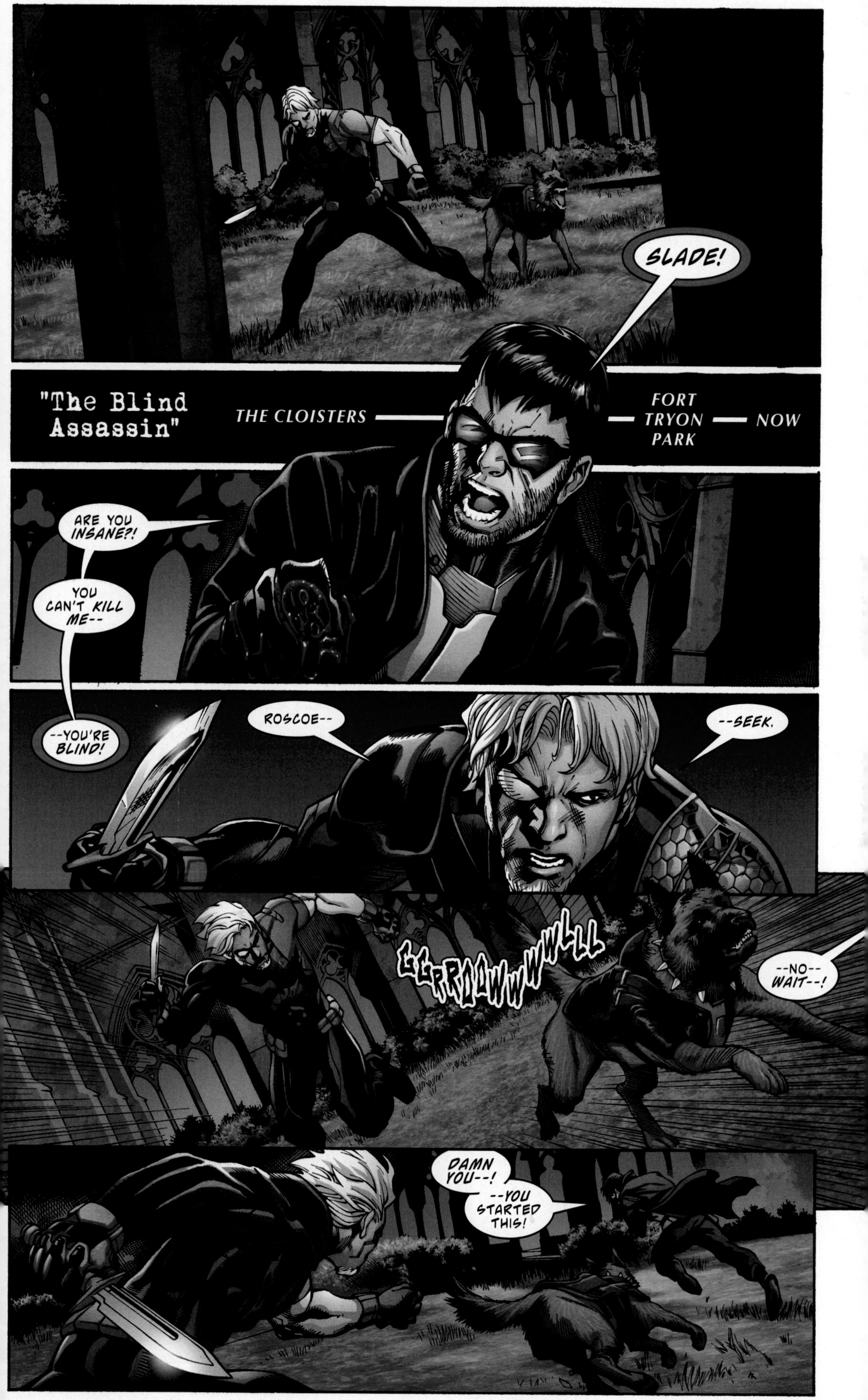
SLADE!
"The Blind Assassin"
THE CLOISTERS — FORT TRYON PARK — NOW
ARE YOU INSANE?!
YOU CAN'T KILL ME--
--YOU'RE BLIND!
ROSCOE--
--SEEK.
GGRRROOWWWWLLL
--NO-- WAIT--!
DAMN YOU--!
--YOU STARTED THIS!

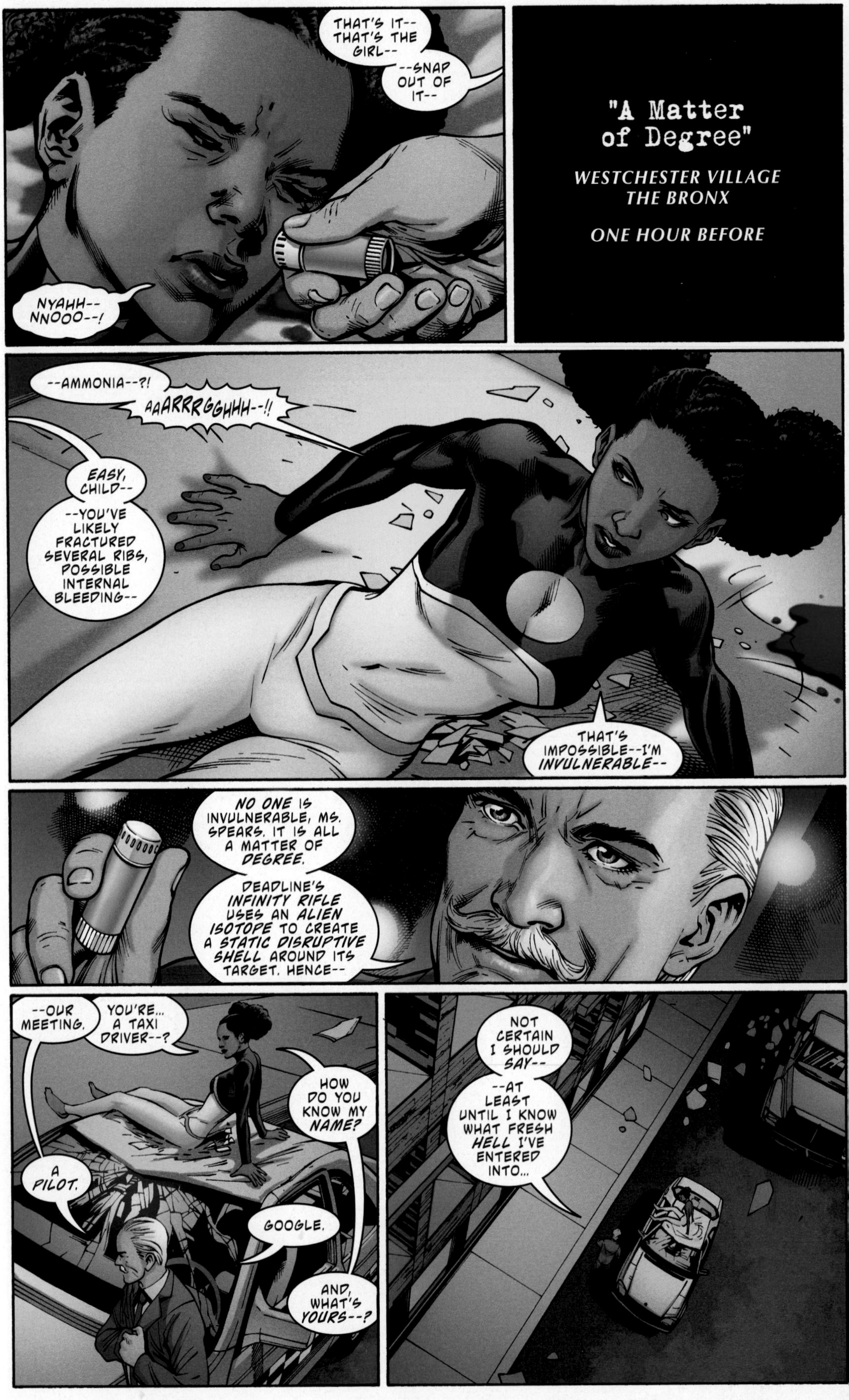
THAT'S IT-- THAT'S THE GIRL--
--SNAP OUT OF IT--
NYAHH-- NNOOO--!
"A Matter of Degree"
WESTCHESTER VILLAGE THE BRONX
ONE HOUR BEFORE
--AMMONIA--?!
AAARRRGGHHH--!!
EASY, CHILD--
--YOU'VE LIKELY FRACTURED SEVERAL RIBS, POSSIBLE INTERNAL BLEEDING--
THAT'S IMPOSSIBLE--I'M INVULNERABLE--
NO ONE IS INVULNERABLE, MS. SPEARS. IT IS ALL A MATTER OF DEGREE.
DEADLINE'S INFINITY RIFLE USES AN ALIEN ISOTOPE TO CREATE A STATIC DISRUPTIVE SHELL AROUND ITS TARGET. HENCE--
--OUR MEETING.
YOU'RE... A TAXI DRIVER--?
A PILOT.
HOW DO YOU KNOW MY NAME?
GOOGLE.
AND, WHAT'S YOURS--?
NOT CERTAIN I SHOULD SAY--
--AT LEAST UNTIL I KNOW WHAT FRESH HELL I'VE ENTERED INTO...

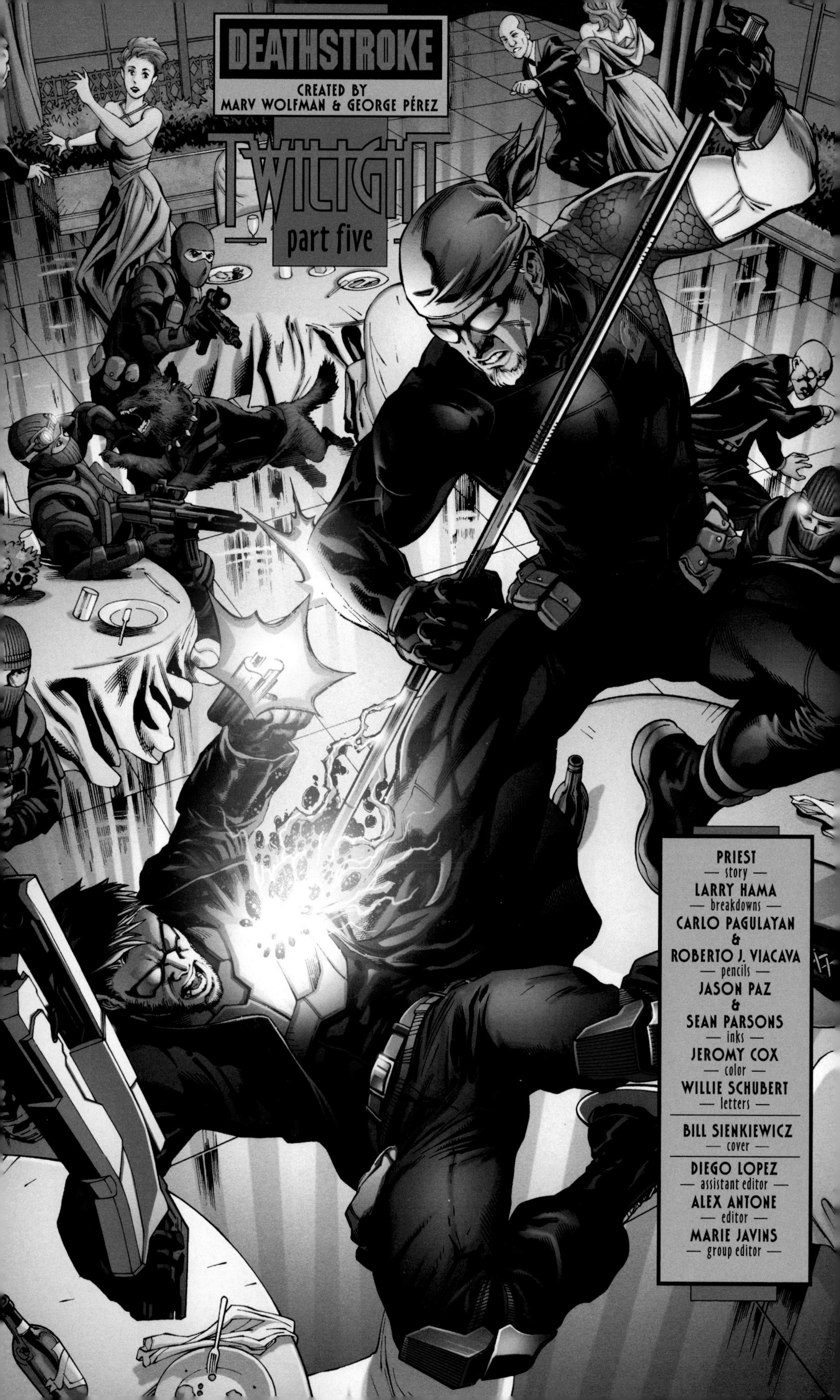
DEATHSTROKE
CREATED BY
MARV WOLFMAN & GEORGE PÉREZ
TWILIGHT
part five
PRIEST
— story —
LARRY HAMA
— breakdowns —
CARLO PAGULAYAN
&
ROBERTO J. VIACAVA
— pencils —
JASON PAZ
&
SEAN PARSONS
— inks —
JEROMY COX
— color —
WILLIE SCHUBERT
— letters —
BILL SIENKIEWICZ
— cover —
DIEGO LOPEZ
— assistant editor —
ALEX ANTONE
— editor —
MARIE JAVINS
— group editor —

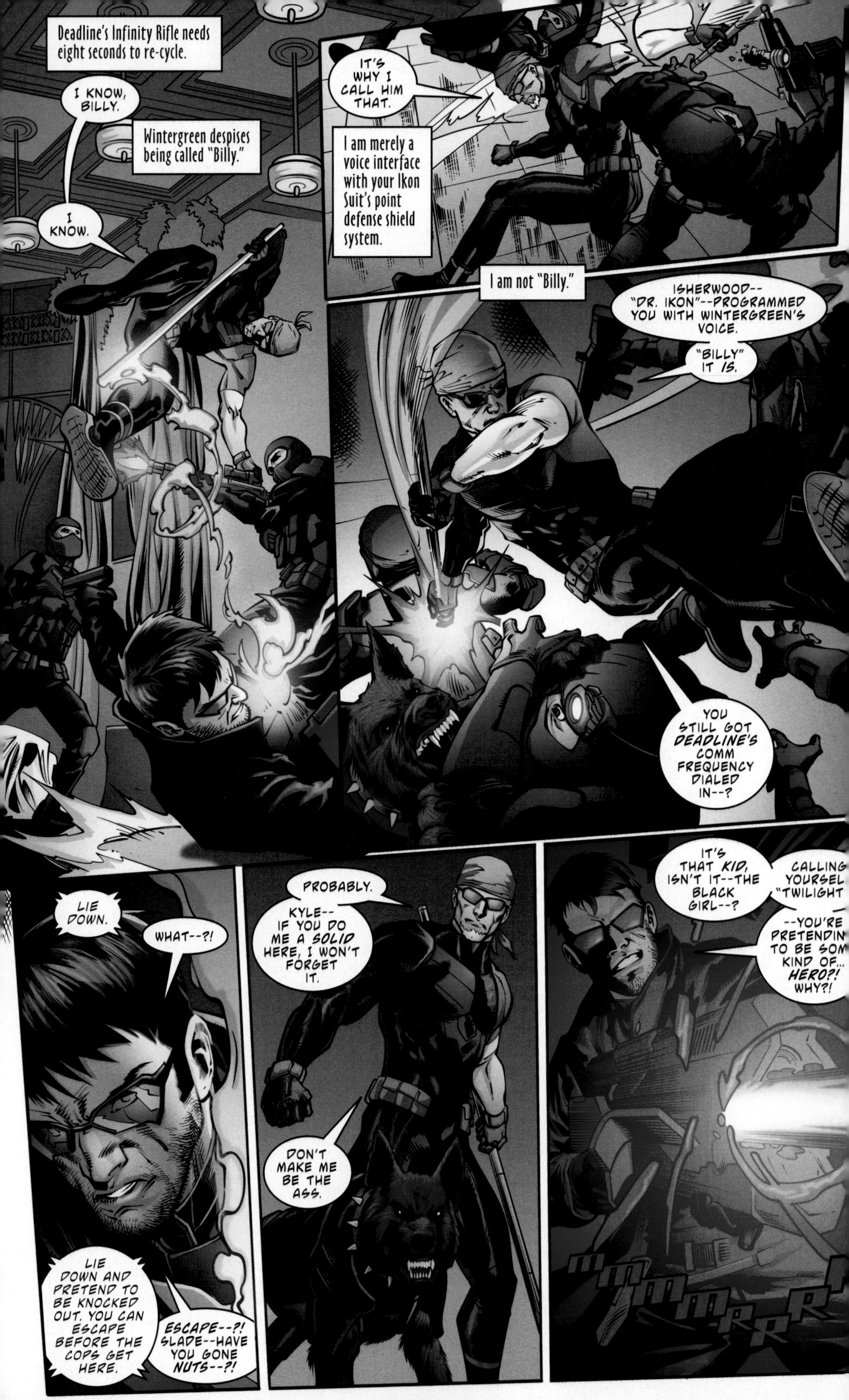
Deadline's Infinity Rifle needs eight seconds to re-cycle.
I KNOW, BILLY.
Wintergreen despises being called "Billy."
I KNOW.
IT'S WHY I CALL HIM THAT.
I am merely a voice interface with your Ikon Suit's point defense shield system.
I am not "Billy."
ISHERWOOD-- "DR. IKON"--PROGRAMMED YOU WITH WINTERGREEN'S VOICE.
"BILLY" IT *IS*.
YOU STILL GOT *DEADLINE'S* COMM FREQUENCY DIALED IN--?
LIE DOWN.
WHAT--?!
LIE DOWN AND PRETEND TO BE KNOCKED OUT. YOU CAN ESCAPE BEFORE THE COPS GET HERE.
*ESCAPE--?!* SLADE--HAVE YOU GONE *NUTS--?!*
PROBABLY.
KYLE-- IF YOU DO ME A *SOLID* HERE, I WON'T FORGET IT.
DON'T MAKE ME BE THE ASS.
IT'S THAT *KID*, ISN'T IT--THE BLACK GIRL--?
CALLING YOURSEL "TWILIGHT
--YOU'RE PRETENDIN TO BE SOM KIND OF... *HERO?!* WHY?!
MMMMRRR

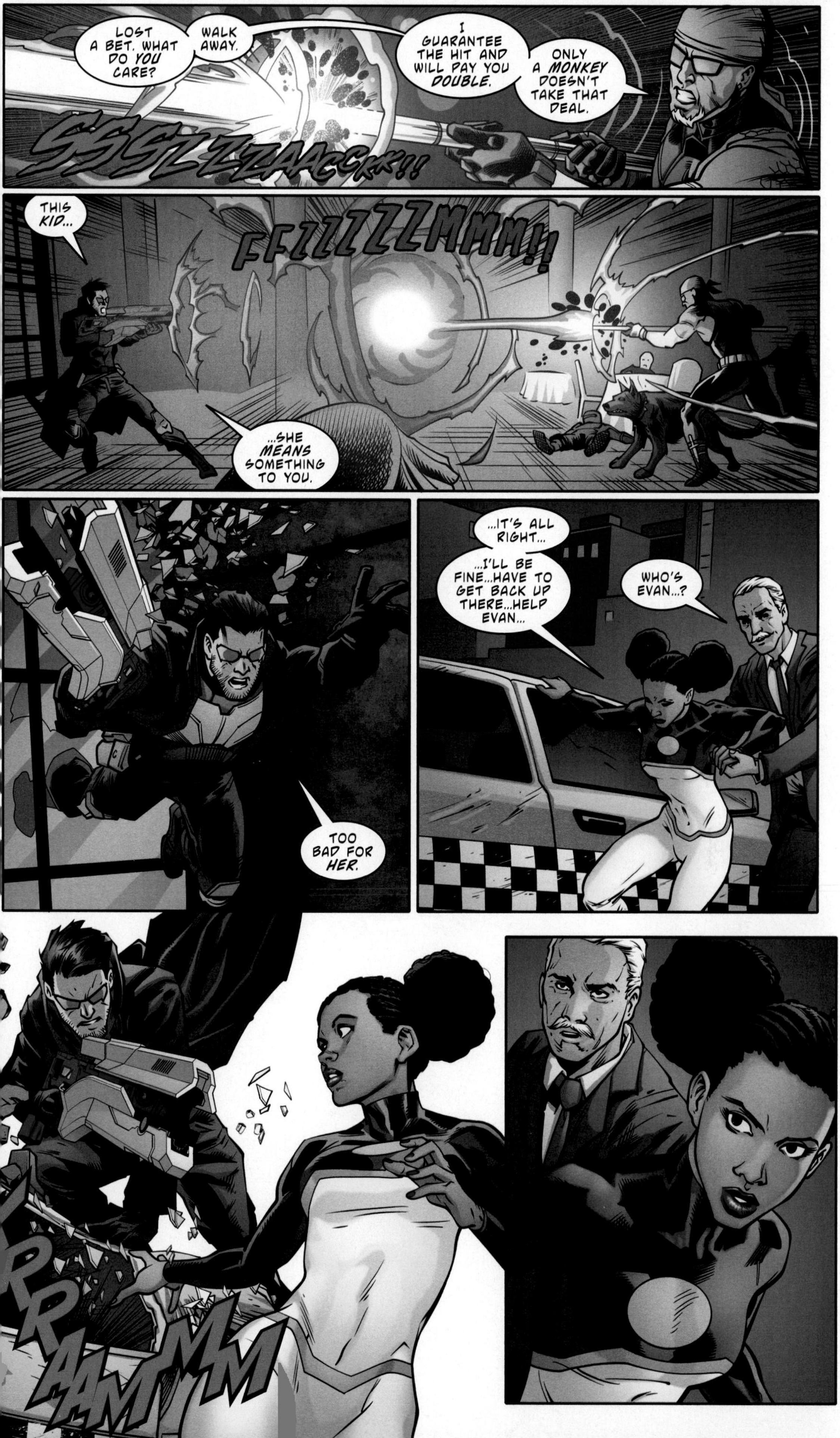
LOST A BET. WHAT DO YOU CARE?
WALK AWAY.
I GUARANTEE THE HIT AND WILL PAY YOU DOUBLE.
ONLY A MONKEY DOESN'T TAKE THAT DEAL.
SSSZZZZAACCKK!!
THIS KID...
FFZZZZZMMMM!!
...SHE MEANS SOMETHING TO YOU.
TOO BAD FOR HER.
...IT'S ALL RIGHT...
...I'LL BE FINE...HAVE TO GET BACK UP THERE...HELP EVAN...
WHO'S EVAN...?
RRAAMMM

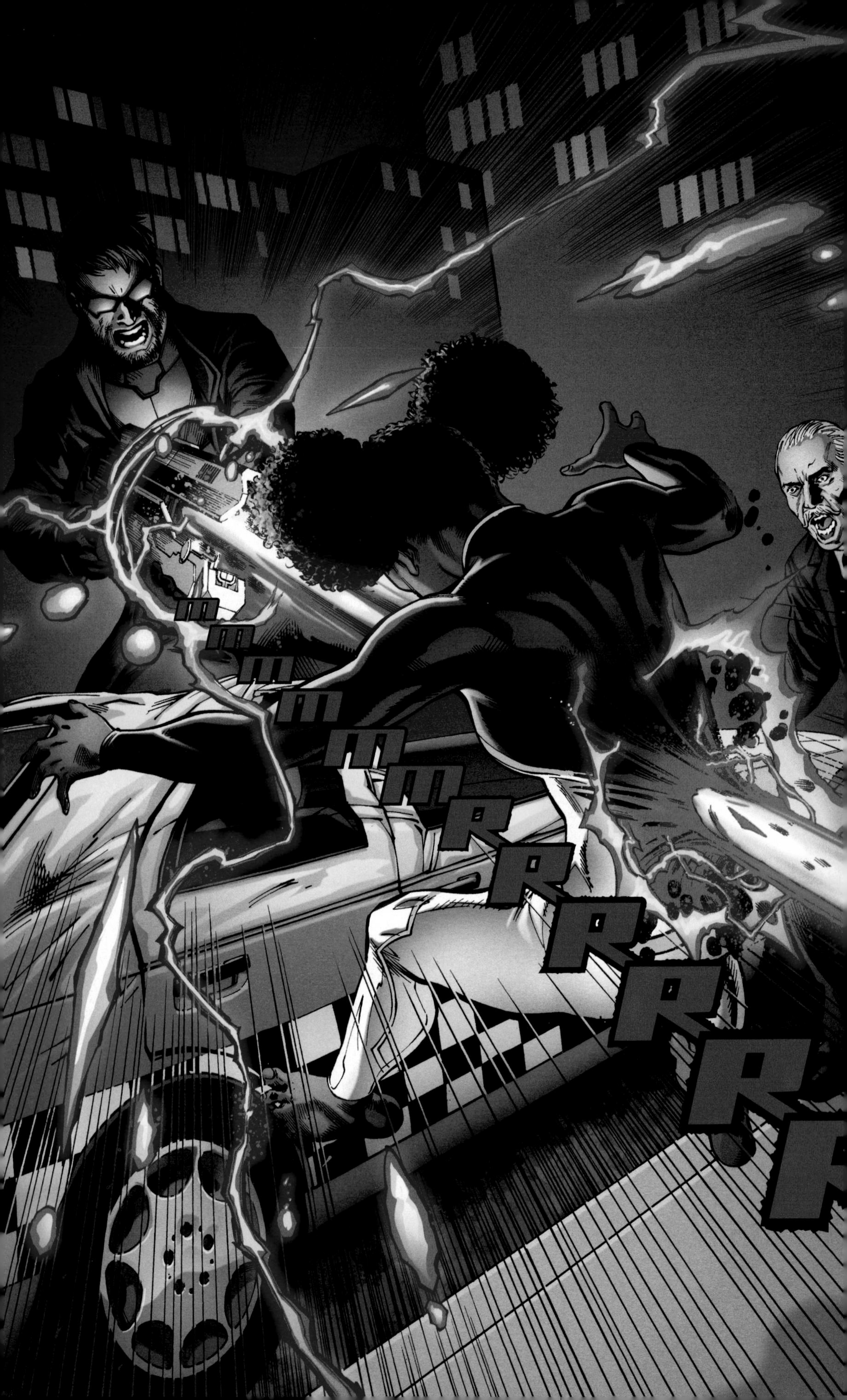
MMMMMMRRRRRR

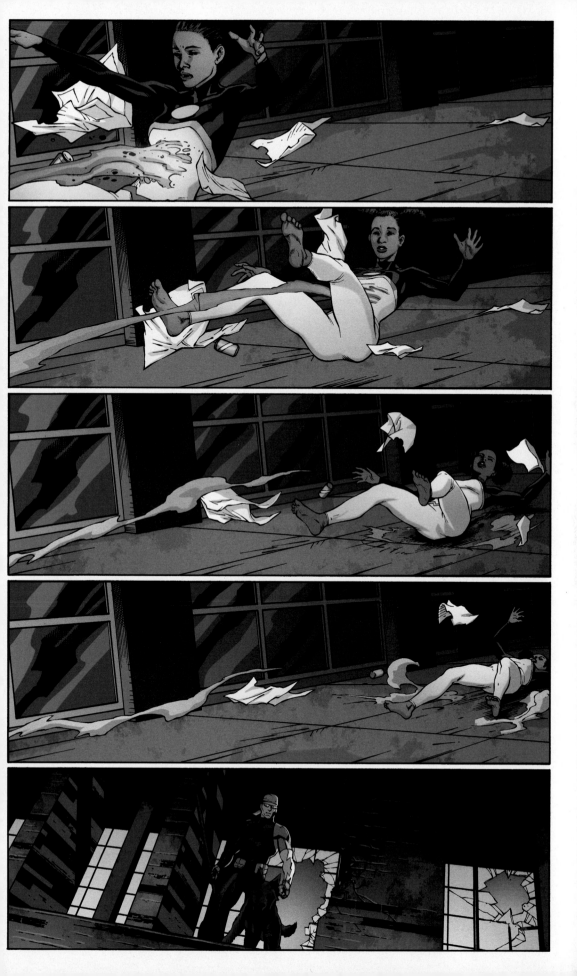

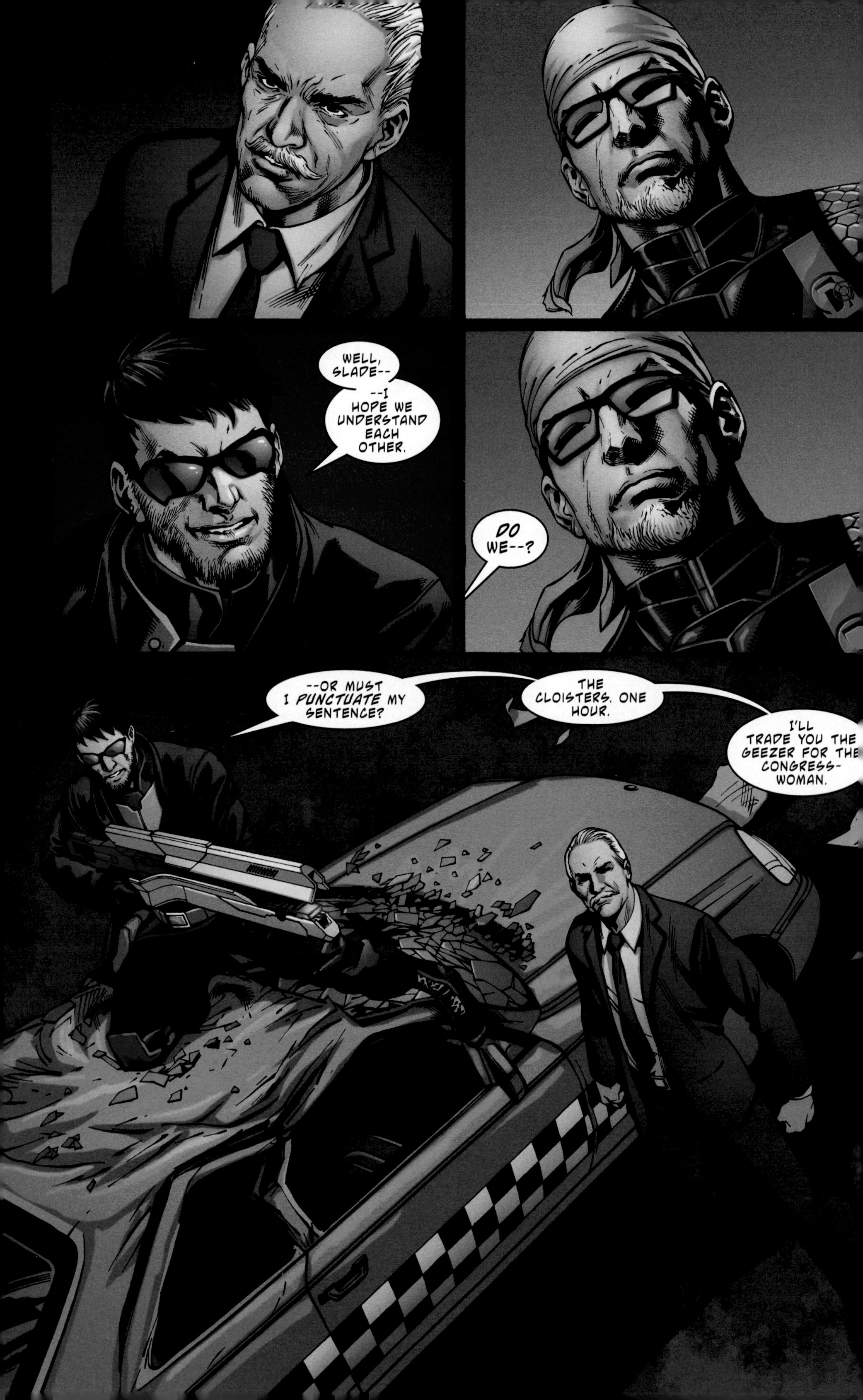
WELL, SLADE--
--I HOPE WE UNDERSTAND EACH OTHER.
DO WE--?
--OR MUST I PUNCTUATE MY SENTENCE?
THE CLOISTERS. ONE HOUR.
I'LL TRADE YOU THE GEEZER FOR THE CONGRESS-WOMAN.

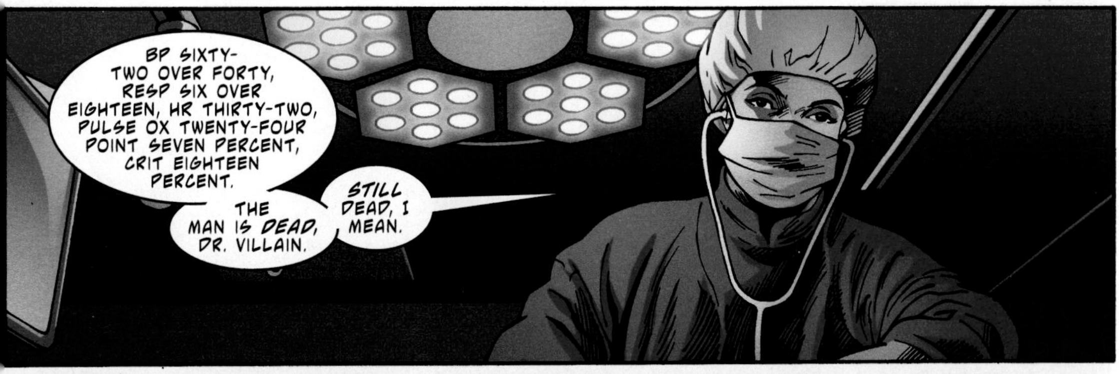
BP SIXTY-TWO OVER FORTY, RESP SIX OVER EIGHTEEN, HR THIRTY-TWO, PULSE OX TWENTY-FOUR POINT SEVEN PERCENT, CRIT EIGHTEEN PERCENT.
THE MAN IS *DEAD,* DR. VILLAIN.
*STILL* DEAD, I MEAN.

## "Res Pulchritudinis"

*JERSEY CITY*

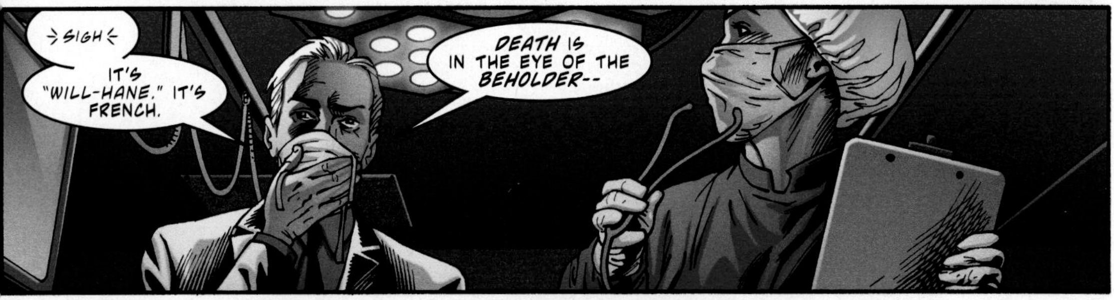
SIGH
IT'S "WILL-HANE." IT'S FRENCH.
*DEATH* IS IN THE EYE OF THE *BEHOLDER--*

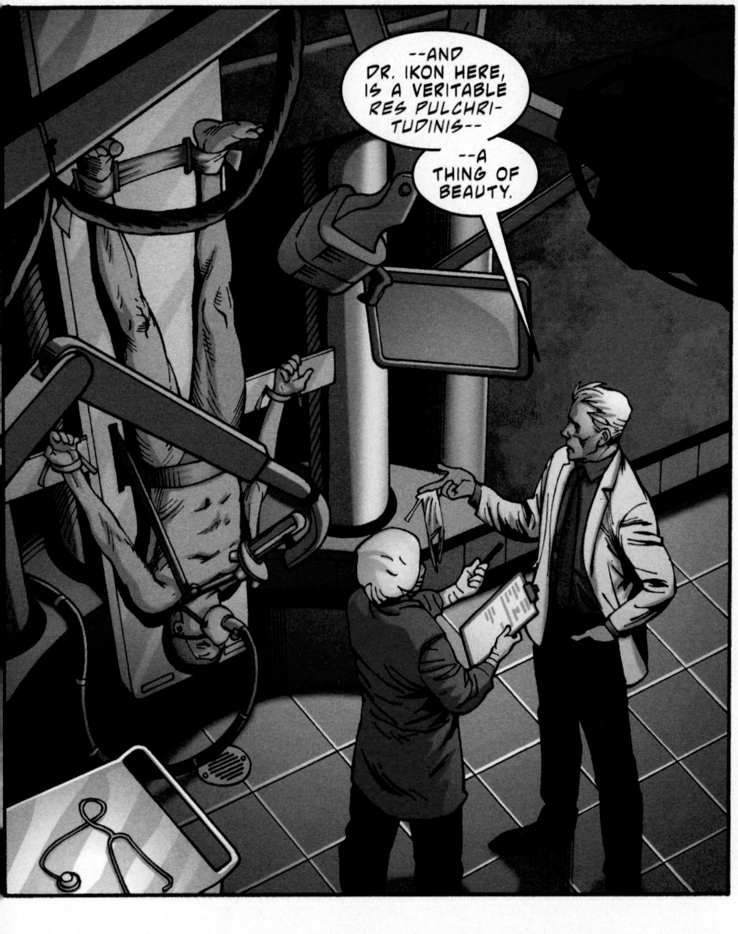
--AND DR. IKON HERE, IS A VERITABLE *RES PULCHRITUDINIS--*
--A THING OF BEAUTY.

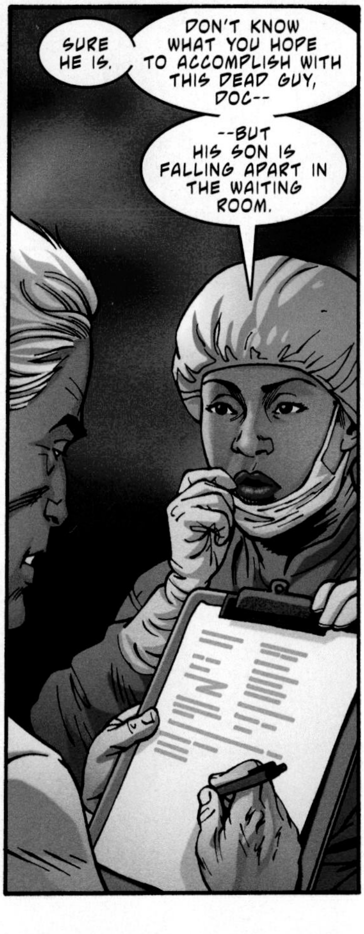
SURE HE IS.
DON'T KNOW WHAT YOU HOPE TO ACCOMPLISH WITH THIS DEAD GUY, DOC--
--BUT HIS SON IS FALLING APART IN THE WAITING ROOM.

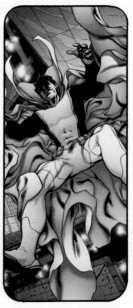

DR. IKON REMAINS...*STABLE,* JERICHO. DON'T GIVE UP HOPE.

YOUR *MIGRAINES* HAVE NO *PHSYIOLOGICAL* CAUSE, THUS, I CANNOT PRESCRIBE ANYTHING FOR YOU.

YOU SHOULD SEE A THERAPIST... THERE MUST BE SOMEONE YOU *TRUST--*

JOSEPH W. WILSON
EXECUTIVE VICE PRESIDENT
CORE POLICY GROUP

THAT'S QUITE A *MESS* YOU'VE MADE, ÉTIENNE.

YOU WERE SUPPOSED TO HELP US KEEP AN EYE ON *SLADE--*

--NOT PLAN A *WEDDING.* WE'RE PULLING YOU OUT.

NO--NOT *YET--*

WHAT TIME WOULD BE *BETTER?* AFTER YOU GIVE SLADE HIS FIRST GRANDKID?

YOU'RE TOO INVESTED, *EDDIE.* BOOK A FLIGHT *TODAY--*

HOLD ON A SEC--

--GETTING A CALL ON JOSEPH'S PHONE...

BEEP

ROSE. HI.

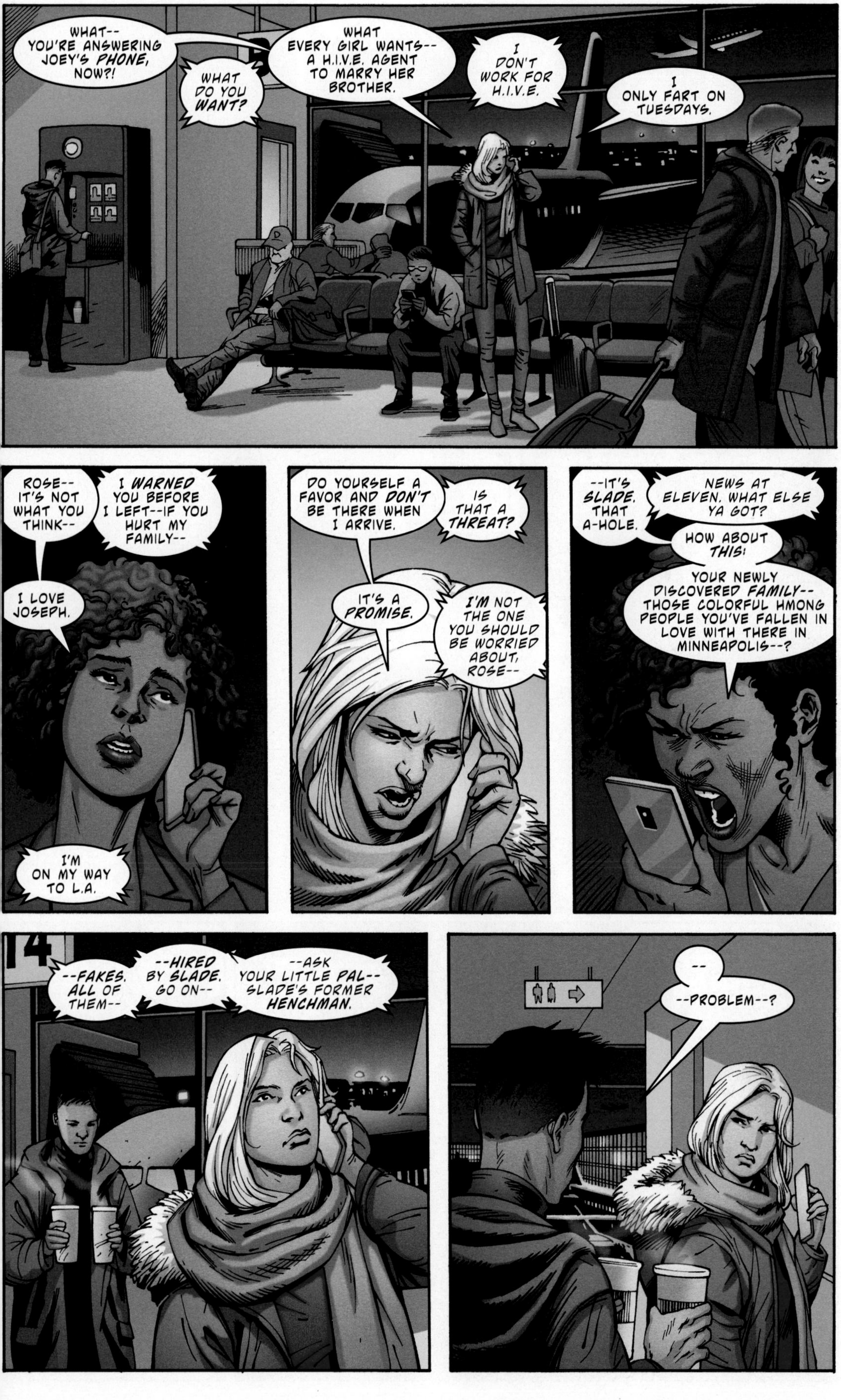

WHAT-- YOU'RE ANSWERING JOEY'S PHONE, NOW?!
WHAT DO YOU WANT?
WHAT EVERY GIRL WANTS-- A H.I.V.E. AGENT TO MARRY HER BROTHER.
I DON'T WORK FOR H.I.V.E.
I ONLY FART ON TUESDAYS.
ROSE-- IT'S NOT WHAT YOU THINK--
I WARNED YOU BEFORE I LEFT--IF YOU HURT MY FAMILY--
I LOVE JOSEPH.
I'M ON MY WAY TO L.A.
DO YOURSELF A FAVOR AND DON'T BE THERE WHEN I ARRIVE.
IS THAT A THREAT?
IT'S A PROMISE.
I'M NOT THE ONE YOU SHOULD BE WORRIED ABOUT, ROSE--
--IT'S SLADE. THAT A-HOLE.
NEWS AT ELEVEN. WHAT ELSE YA GOT?
HOW ABOUT THIS:
YOUR NEWLY DISCOVERED FAMILY-- THOSE COLORFUL HMONG PEOPLE YOU'VE FALLEN IN LOVE WITH THERE IN MINNEAPOLIS--?
14
--FAKES. ALL OF THEM--
--HIRED BY SLADE. GO ON--
--ASK YOUR LITTLE PAL-- SLADE'S FORMER HENCHMAN.
--
--PROBLEM--?

DEATHSTROKE IS LATE...DEFYING MY DEADLINE.

YOU GUARANTEE YOUR WORK.

I DO. IT'S MY HOOK. THE JOB IS DONE BY THE DEADLINE OR IT'S FREE.

SLADE'S COSTING ME A FORTUNE.

## "Ethics"

*THE CLOISTERS FORT TRYON PARK*

*FIVE MINUTES BEFORE*

I NEVER STEP ON ANOTHER MAN'S WORK, WINTERGREEN. SLADE IS WAY OUT OF LINE.

SO...YOU KILLED A CHILD TO EXPRESS...ETHICAL CONCERNS--?

THAT'S ON SLADE'S HEAD.

YES, I WOULD IMAGINE IT IS. WHAT, MIGHT I ASK, IS ON YOURS?

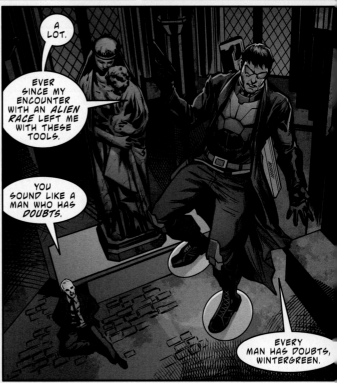

A LOT.

EVER SINCE MY ENCOUNTER WITH AN ALIEN RACE LEFT ME WITH THESE TOOLS.

YOU SOUND LIKE A MAN WHO HAS DOUBTS.

EVERY MAN HAS DOUBTS, WINTERGREEN.

SOME MEN HAVE WIVES...CHILDREN. THIS ISN'T THE LIFE FOR IT.

THERE ARE OTHER JOBS, DEADLINE. I HEAR FEDEX IS HIRING.

THIS IS WHAT I AM, WINTERGREEN-- A KILLER. I'VE LEARNED TO ACCEPT IT.

MAKES ME A TAD SANER THAN YOUR BOSS.

SLADE IS NOT MY BOSS. HE'S MY FRIEND.

GUYS LIKE US-- DEATHSTROKE AND MYSELF-- DON'T HAVE FRIENDS.

WHICH IS WHY HE NEEDS ME.

IMAGINE HOW DANGEROUS HE'D BE WITHOUT FRIENDS.

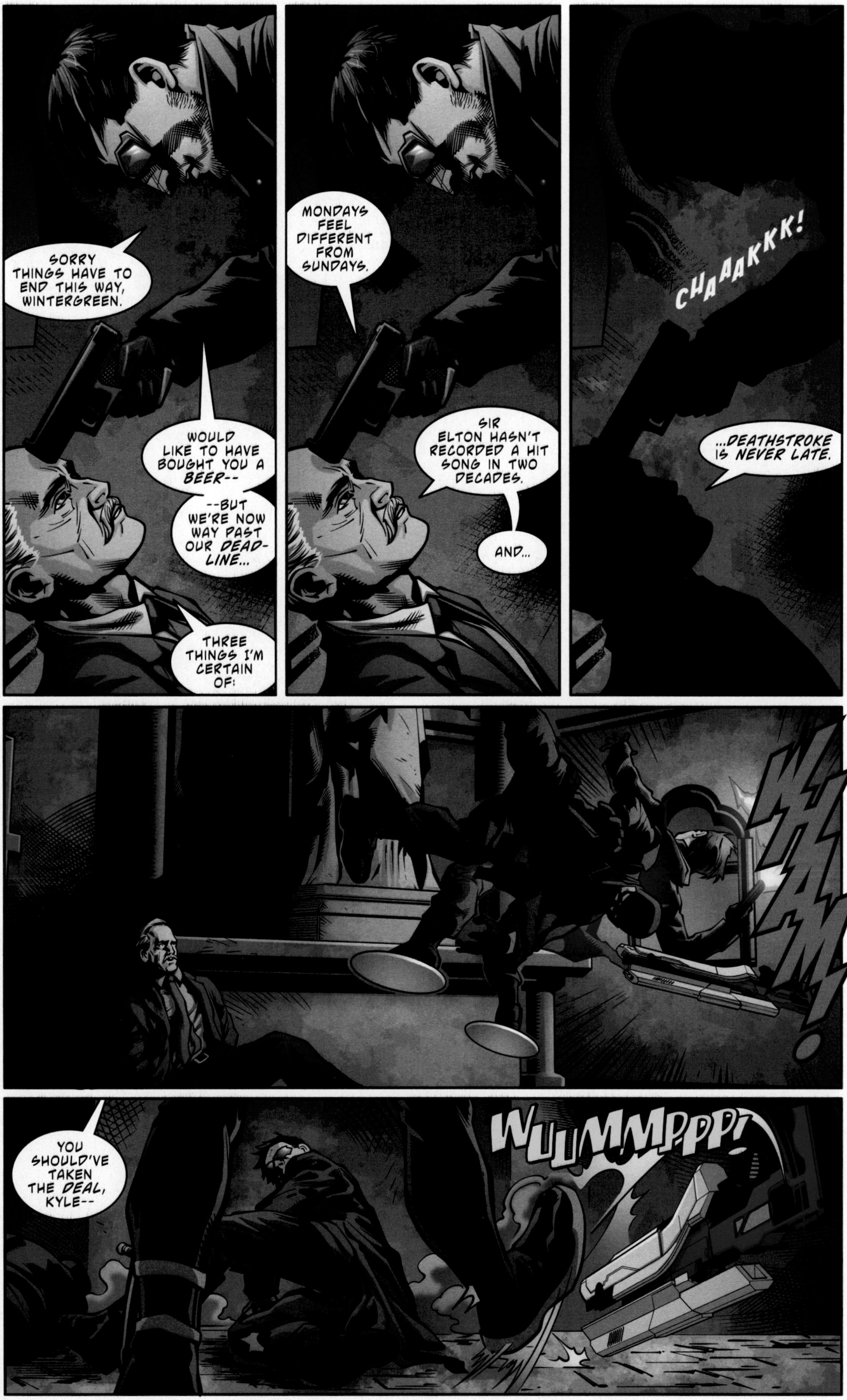

SORRY THINGS HAVE TO END THIS WAY, WINTERGREEN.
WOULD LIKE TO HAVE BOUGHT YOU A BEER--
--BUT WE'RE NOW WAY PAST OUR DEAD-LINE...
THREE THINGS I'M CERTAIN OF:
MONDAYS FEEL DIFFERENT FROM SUNDAYS.
SIR ELTON HASN'T RECORDED A HIT SONG IN TWO DECADES.
AND...
CHAAAKKK!
...DEATHSTROKE IS NEVER LATE.
WHAM!
YOU SHOULD'VE TAKEN THE DEAL, KYLE--
WUUMMPPP!

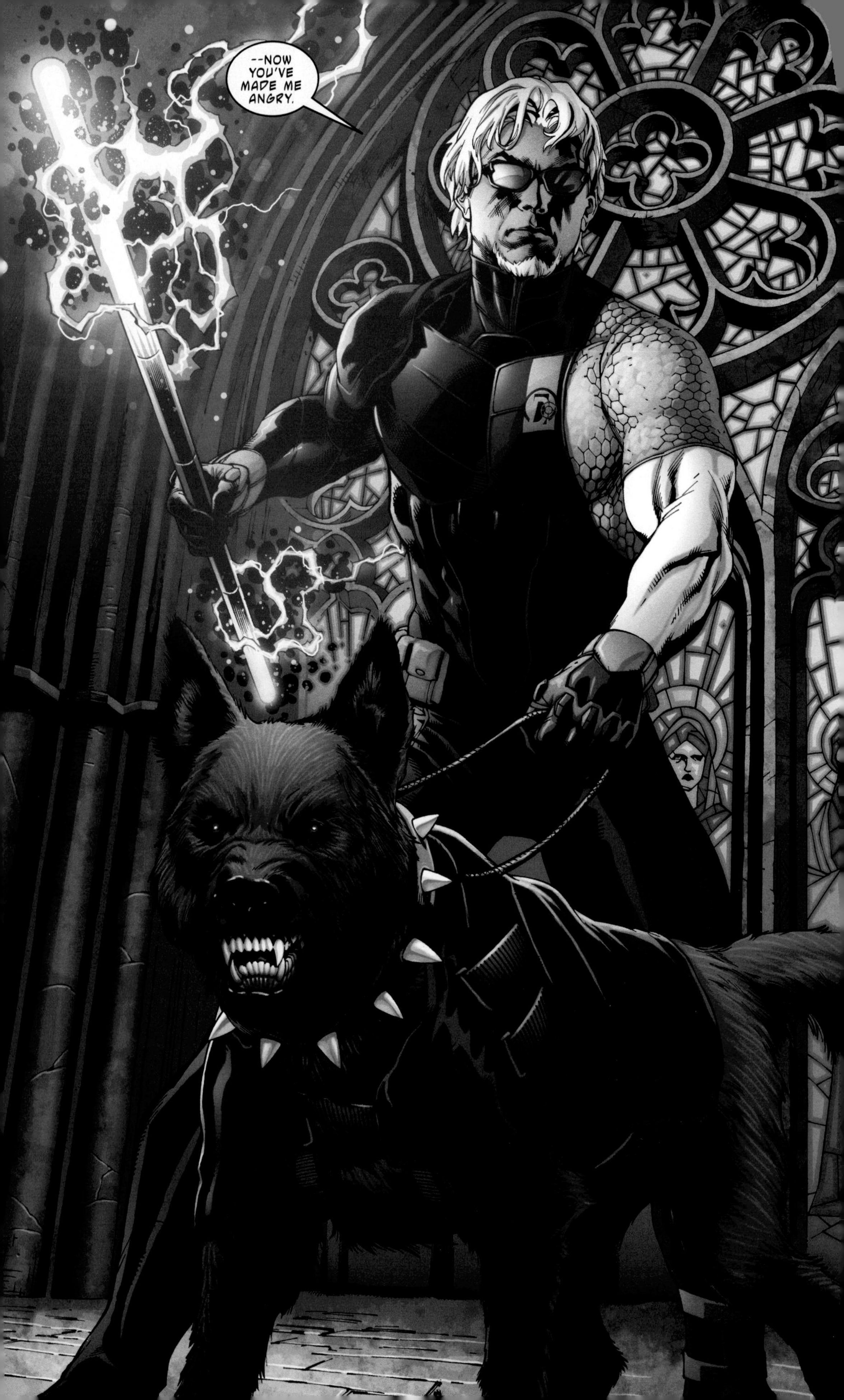
--NOW YOU'VE MADE ME ANGRY.

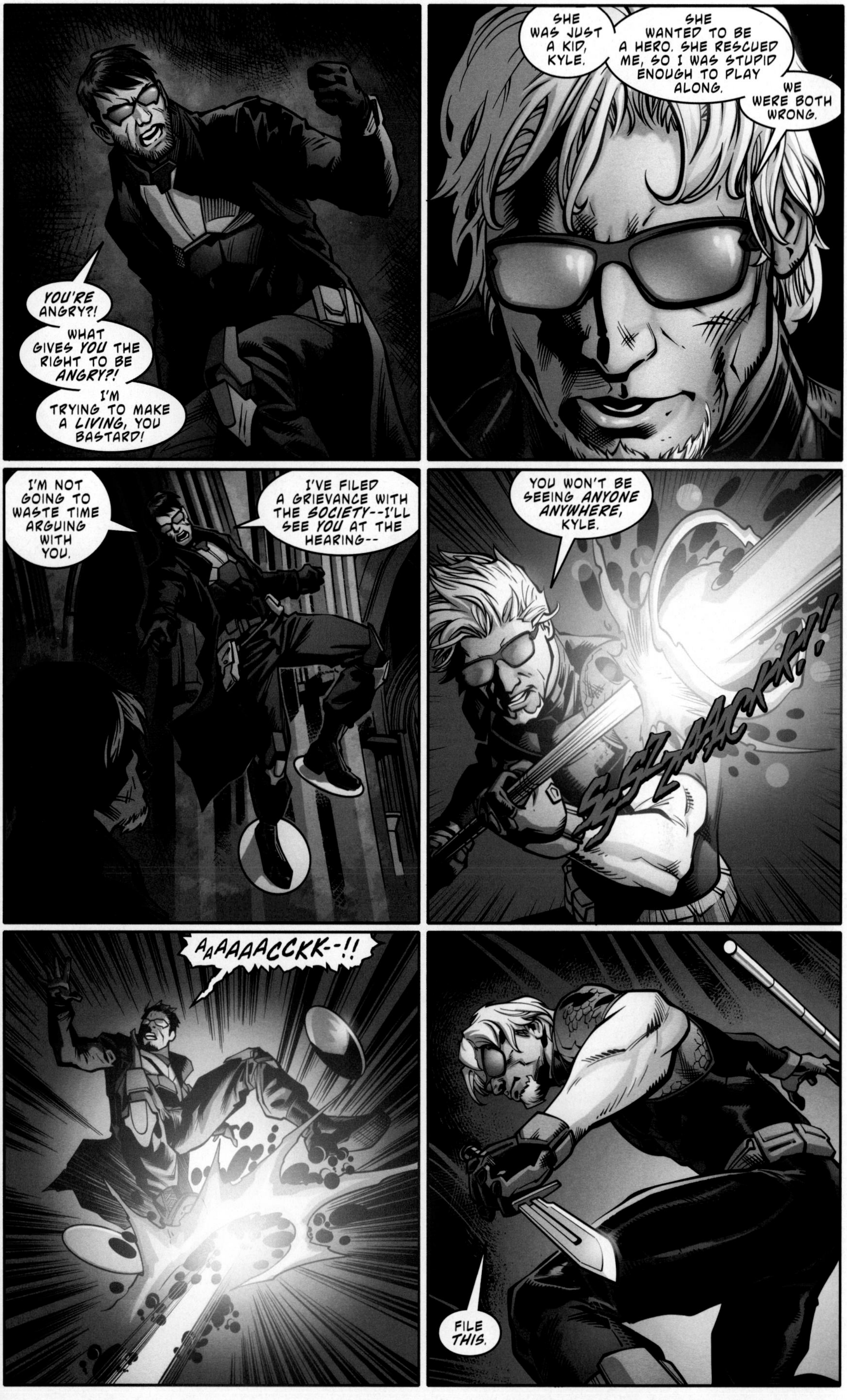
YOU'RE ANGRY?!
WHAT GIVES YOU THE RIGHT TO BE ANGRY?!
I'M TRYING TO MAKE A LIVING, YOU BASTARD!
SHE WAS JUST A KID, KYLE.
SHE WANTED TO BE A HERO. SHE RESCUED ME, SO I WAS STUPID ENOUGH TO PLAY ALONG.
WE WERE BOTH WRONG.
I'M NOT GOING TO WASTE TIME ARGUING WITH YOU.
I'VE FILED A GRIEVANCE WITH THE SOCIETY--I'LL SEE YOU AT THE HEARING--
YOU WON'T BE SEEING ANYONE ANYWHERE, KYLE.
SSSZZAACKK!!
AAAAAACCKK--!!
FILE THIS.

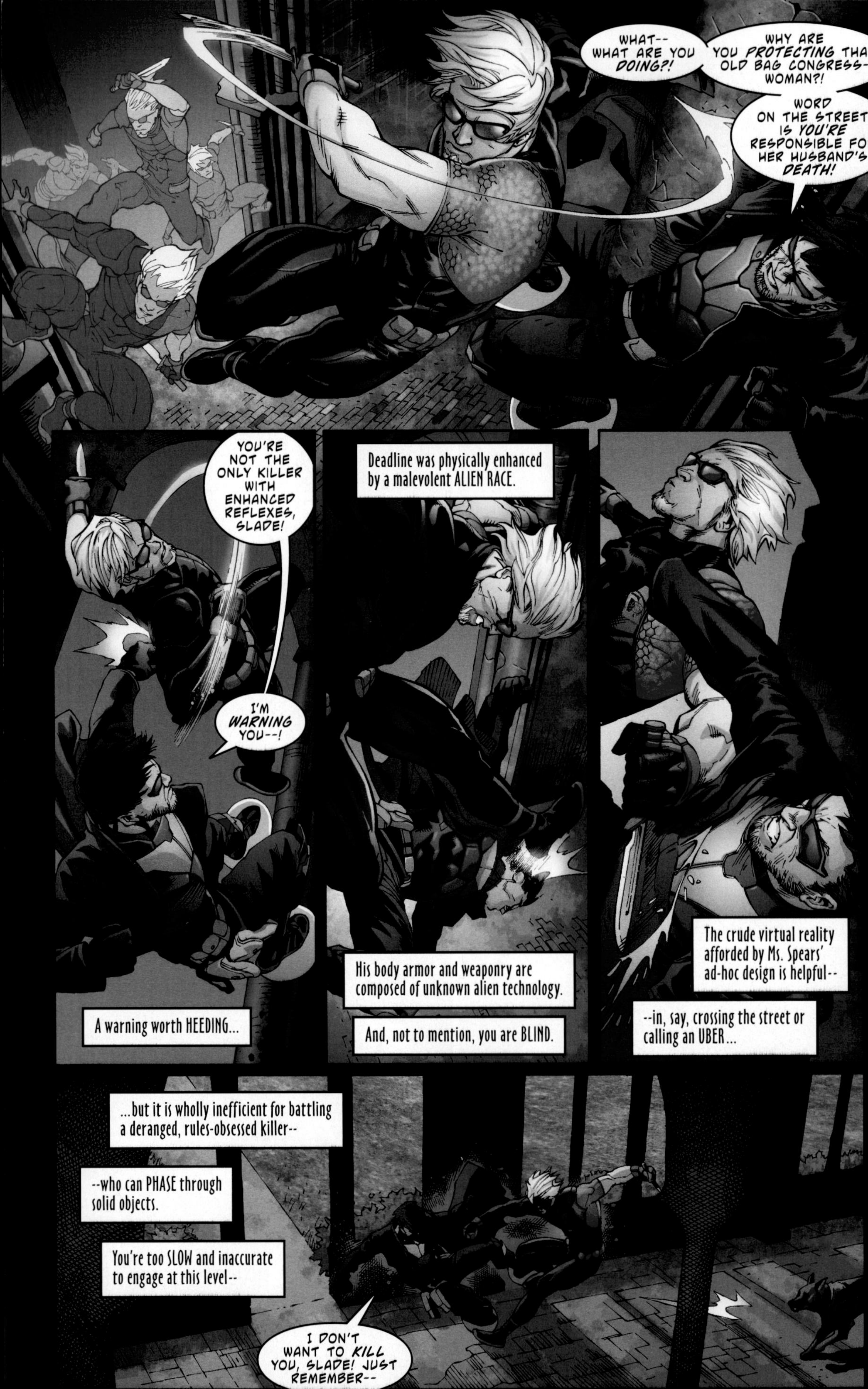

WHAT-- WHAT ARE YOU DOING?!
WHY ARE YOU PROTECTING THA OLD BAG CONGRESS-WOMAN?!
WORD ON THE STREET IS YOU'RE RESPONSIBLE FO HER HUSBAND'S DEATH!
YOU'RE NOT THE ONLY KILLER WITH ENHANCED REFLEXES, SLADE!
I'M WARNING YOU--!
A warning worth HEEDING...
Deadline was physically enhanced by a malevolent ALIEN RACE.
His body armor and weaponry are composed of unknown alien technology.
And, not to mention, you are BLIND.
The crude virtual reality afforded by Ms. Spears' ad-hoc design is helpful--
--in, say, crossing the street or calling an UBER...
...but it is wholly inefficient for battling a deranged, rules-obsessed killer--
--who can PHASE through solid objects.
You're too SLOW and inaccurate to engage at this level--
I DON'T WANT TO KILL YOU, SLADE! JUST REMEMBER--

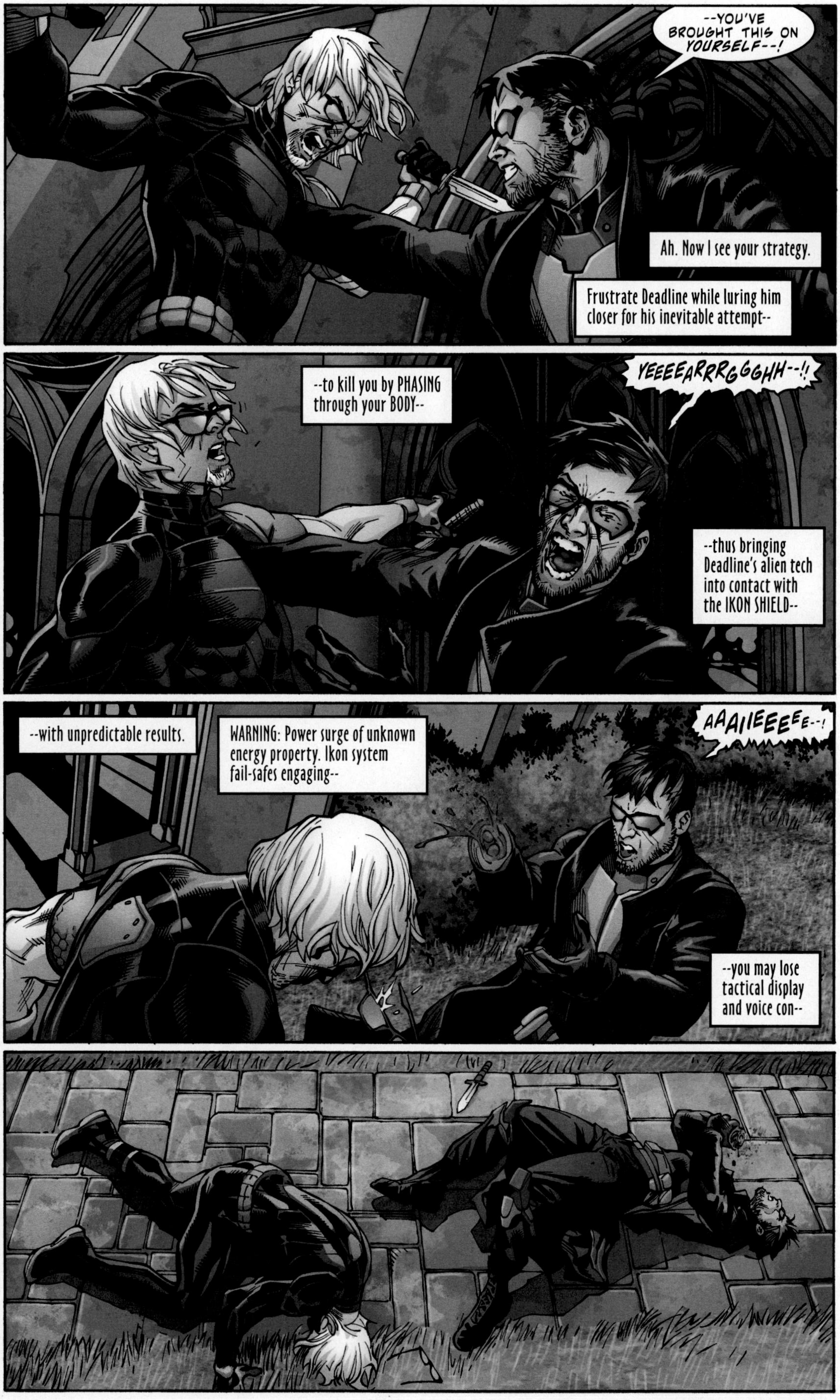
--YOU'VE BROUGHT THIS ON YOURSELF--!
Ah. Now I see your strategy.
Frustrate Deadline while luring him closer for his inevitable attempt--
--to kill you by PHASING through your BODY--
YEEEEARRRGGGHH--!!
--thus bringing Deadline's alien tech into contact with the IKON SHIELD--
--with unpredictable results.
WARNING: Power surge of unknown energy property. Ikon system fail-safes engaging--
AAAIIEEEEE--!
--you may lose tactical display and voice con--

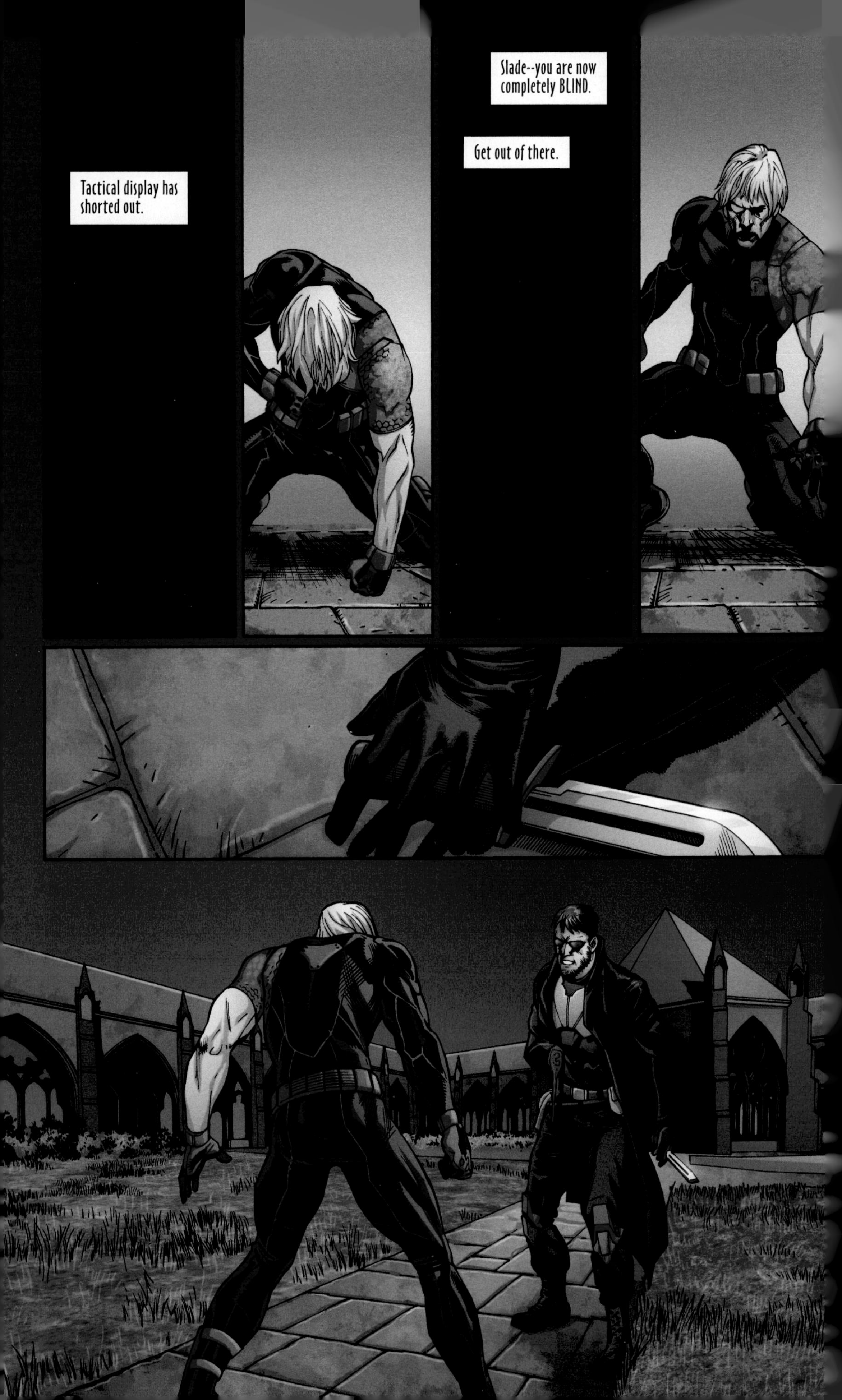

Tactical display has shorted out.
Slade--you are now completely BLIND.
Get out of there.

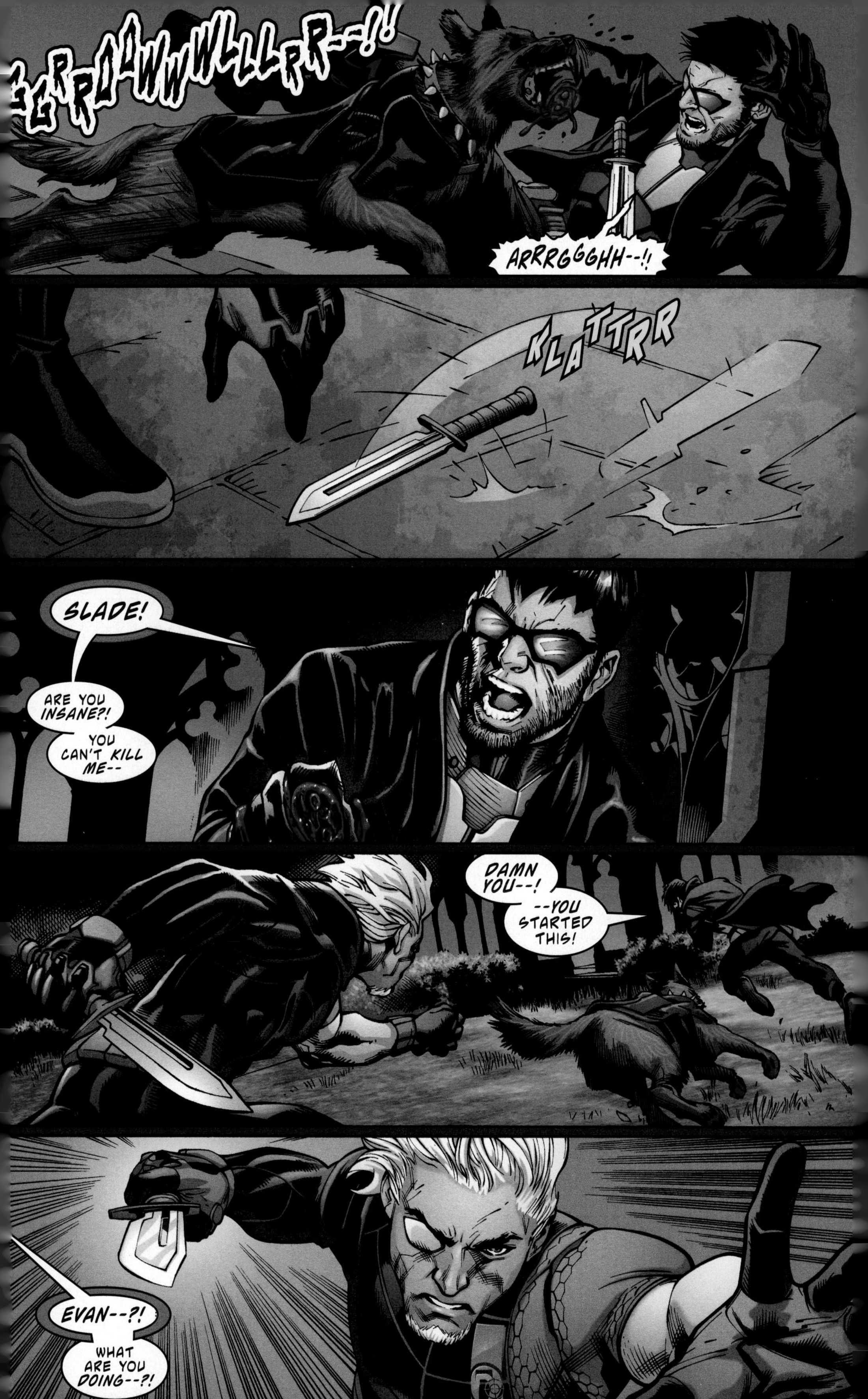
GRROOWWWLLLRR--!!
ARRRGGGHH--!!
KLATTRR
SLADE!
ARE YOU INSANE?!
YOU CAN'T KILL ME--
DAMN YOU--!
--YOU STARTED THIS!
EVAN--?!
WHAT ARE YOU DOING--?!

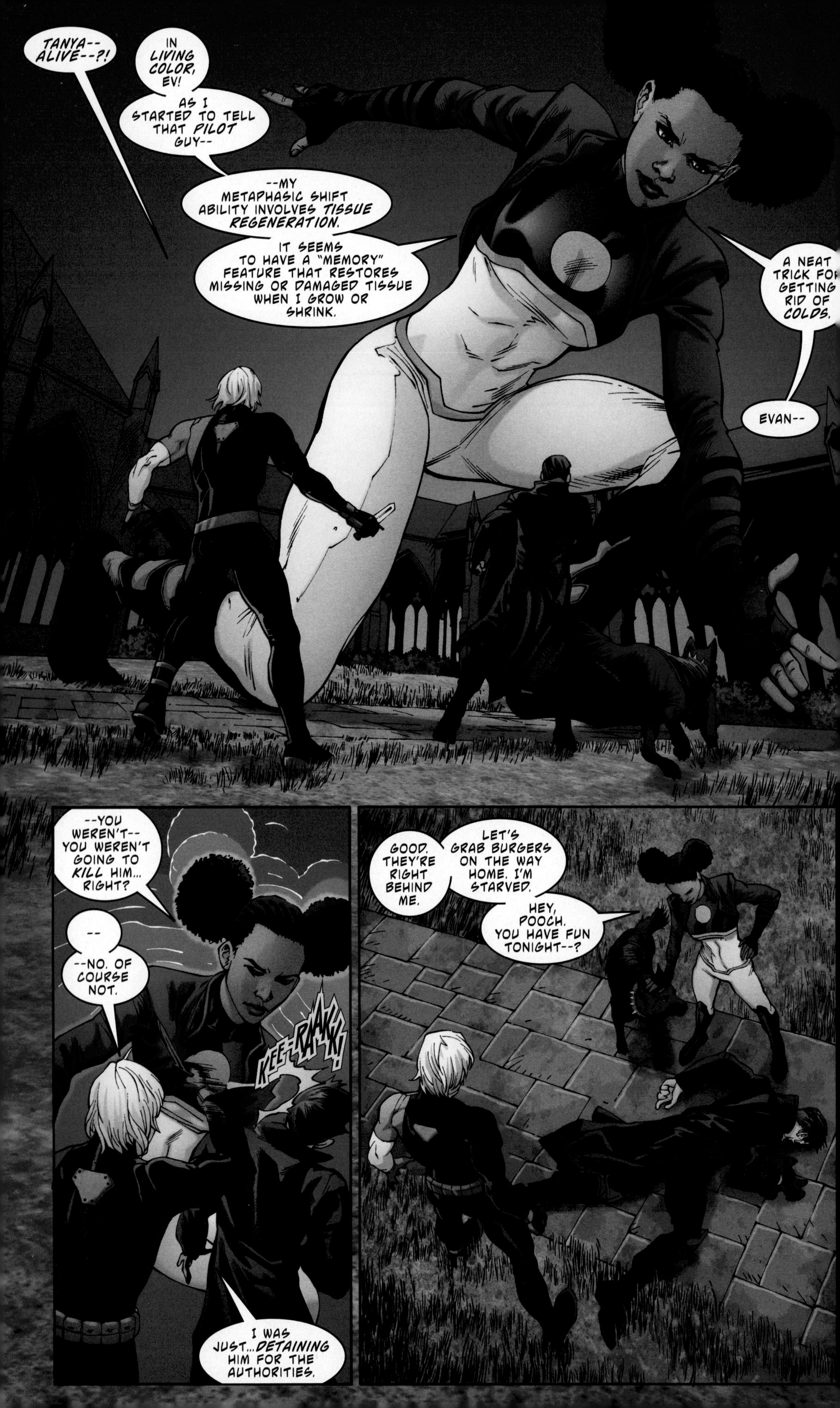

TANYA-- ALIVE--?!
IN LIVING COLOR, EV!
AS I STARTED TO TELL THAT PILOT GUY--
--MY METAPHASIC SHIFT ABILITY INVOLVES TISSUE REGENERATION.
IT SEEMS TO HAVE A "MEMORY" FEATURE THAT RESTORES MISSING OR DAMAGED TISSUE WHEN I GROW OR SHRINK.
A NEAT TRICK FOR GETTING RID OF COLDS.
EVAN--
--YOU WEREN'T-- YOU WEREN'T GOING TO KILL HIM... RIGHT?
--
--NO. OF COURSE NOT.
KEE-RAKK!
I WAS JUST...DETAINING HIM FOR THE AUTHORITIES.
GOOD. THEY'RE RIGHT BEHIND ME.
LET'S GRAB BURGERS ON THE WAY HOME. I'M STARVED.
HEY, POOCH. YOU HAVE FUN TONIGHT--?

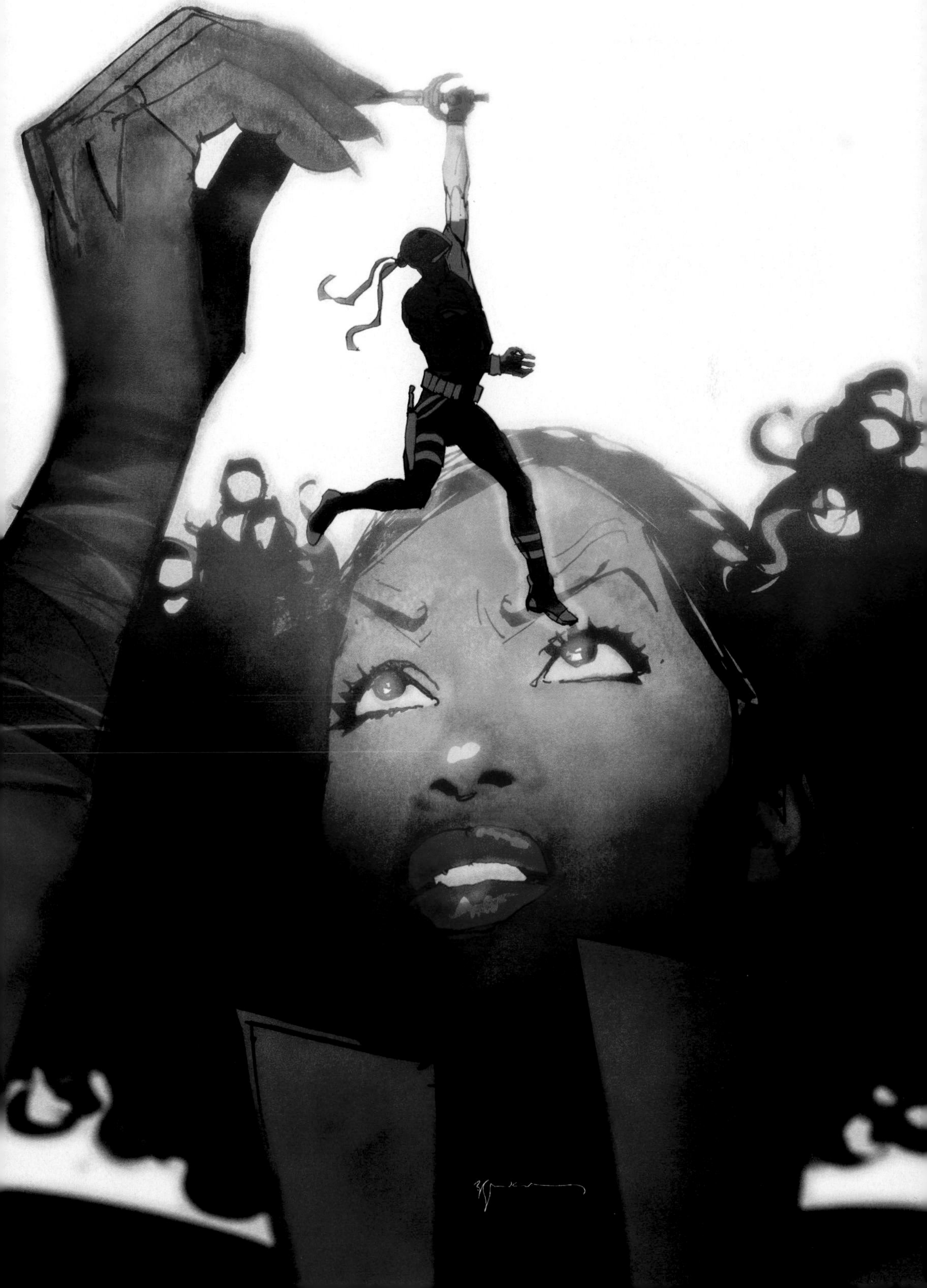

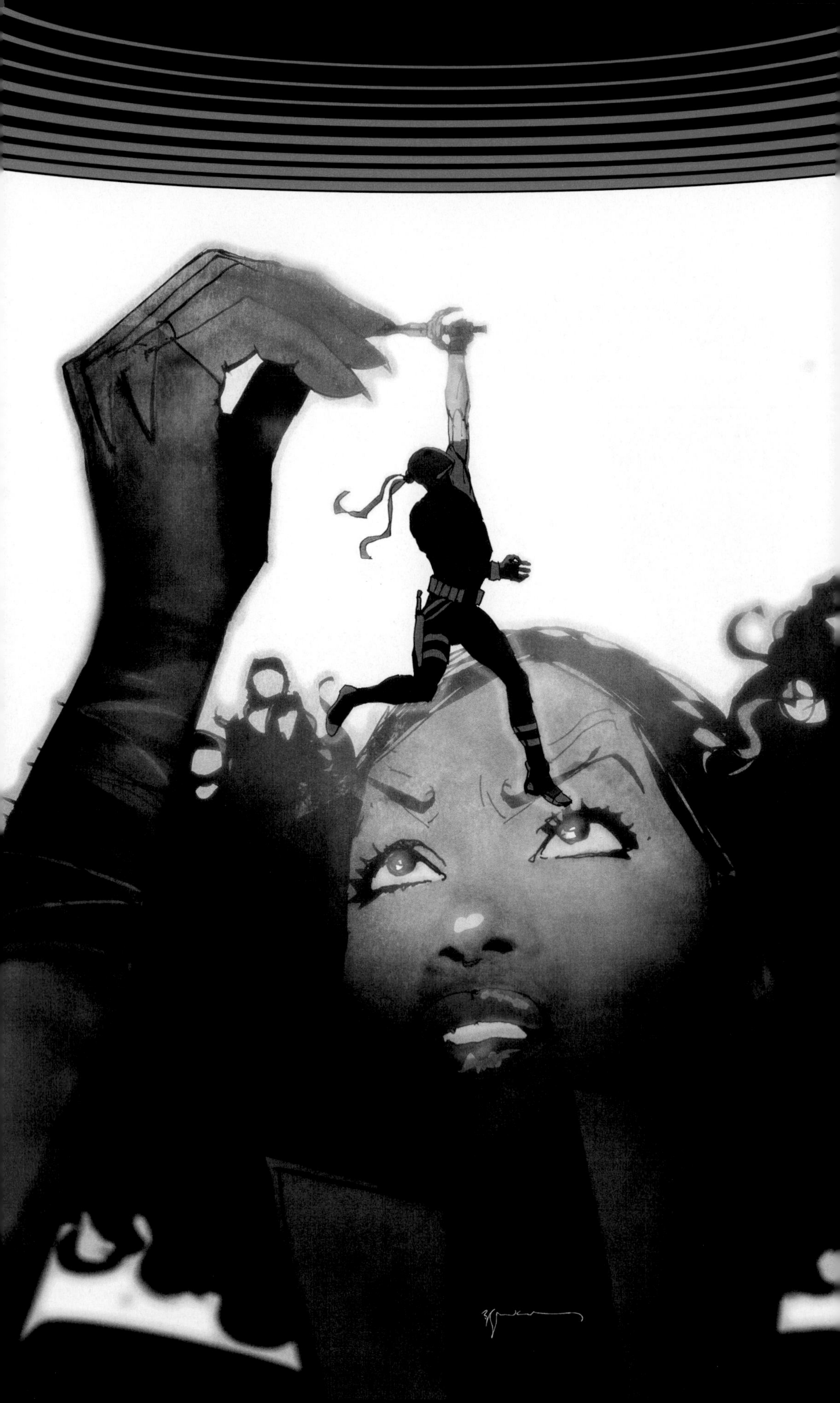

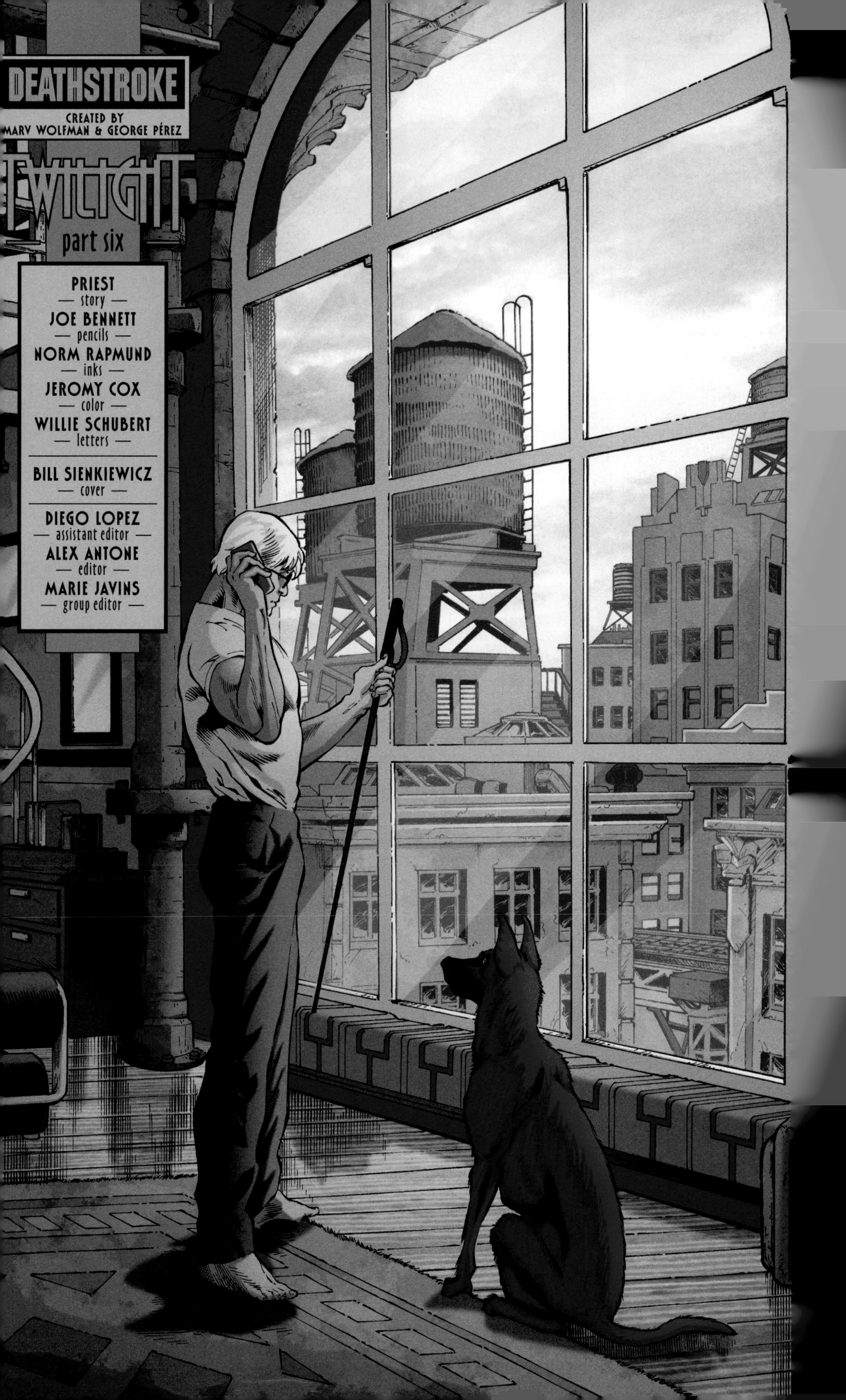
DEATHSTROKE
CREATED BY
MARV WOLFMAN & GEORGE PÉREZ
TWILIGHT
part six
PRIEST
— story —
JOE BENNETT
— pencils —
NORM RAPMUND
— inks —
JEROMY COX
— color —
WILLIE SCHUBERT
— letters —
BILL SIENKIEWICZ
— cover —
DIEGO LOPEZ
— assistant editor —
ALEX ANTONE
— editor —
MARIE JAVINS
— group editor —

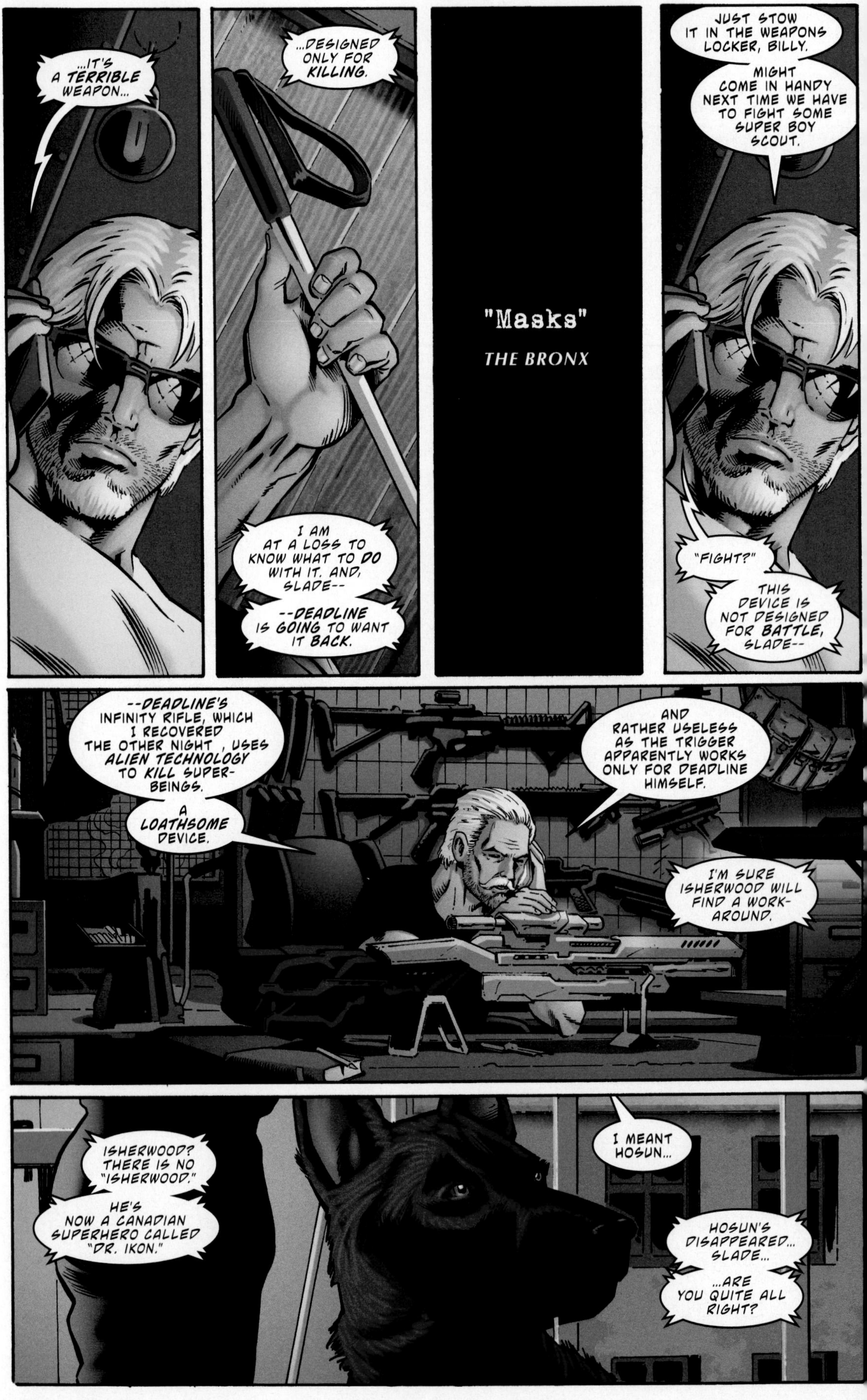
...IT'S A TERRIBLE WEAPON...
...DESIGNED ONLY FOR KILLING.
I AM AT A LOSS TO KNOW WHAT TO DO WITH IT. AND, SLADE--
--DEADLINE IS GOING TO WANT IT BACK.
"Masks"
THE BRONX
JUST STOW IT IN THE WEAPONS LOCKER, BILLY.
MIGHT COME IN HANDY NEXT TIME WE HAVE TO FIGHT SOME SUPER BOY SCOUT.
"FIGHT?"
THIS DEVICE IS NOT DESIGNED FOR BATTLE, SLADE--
--DEADLINE'S INFINITY RIFLE, WHICH I RECOVERED THE OTHER NIGHT , USES ALIEN TECHNOLOGY TO KILL SUPER-BEINGS.
A LOATHSOME DEVICE.
AND RATHER USELESS AS THE TRIGGER APPARENTLY WORKS ONLY FOR DEADLINE HIMSELF.
I'M SURE ISHERWOOD WILL FIND A WORK-AROUND.
ISHERWOOD? THERE IS NO "ISHERWOOD."
HE'S NOW A CANADIAN SUPERHERO CALLED "DR. IKON."
I MEANT HOSUN...
HOSUN'S DISAPPEARED... SLADE...
...ARE YOU QUITE ALL RIGHT?

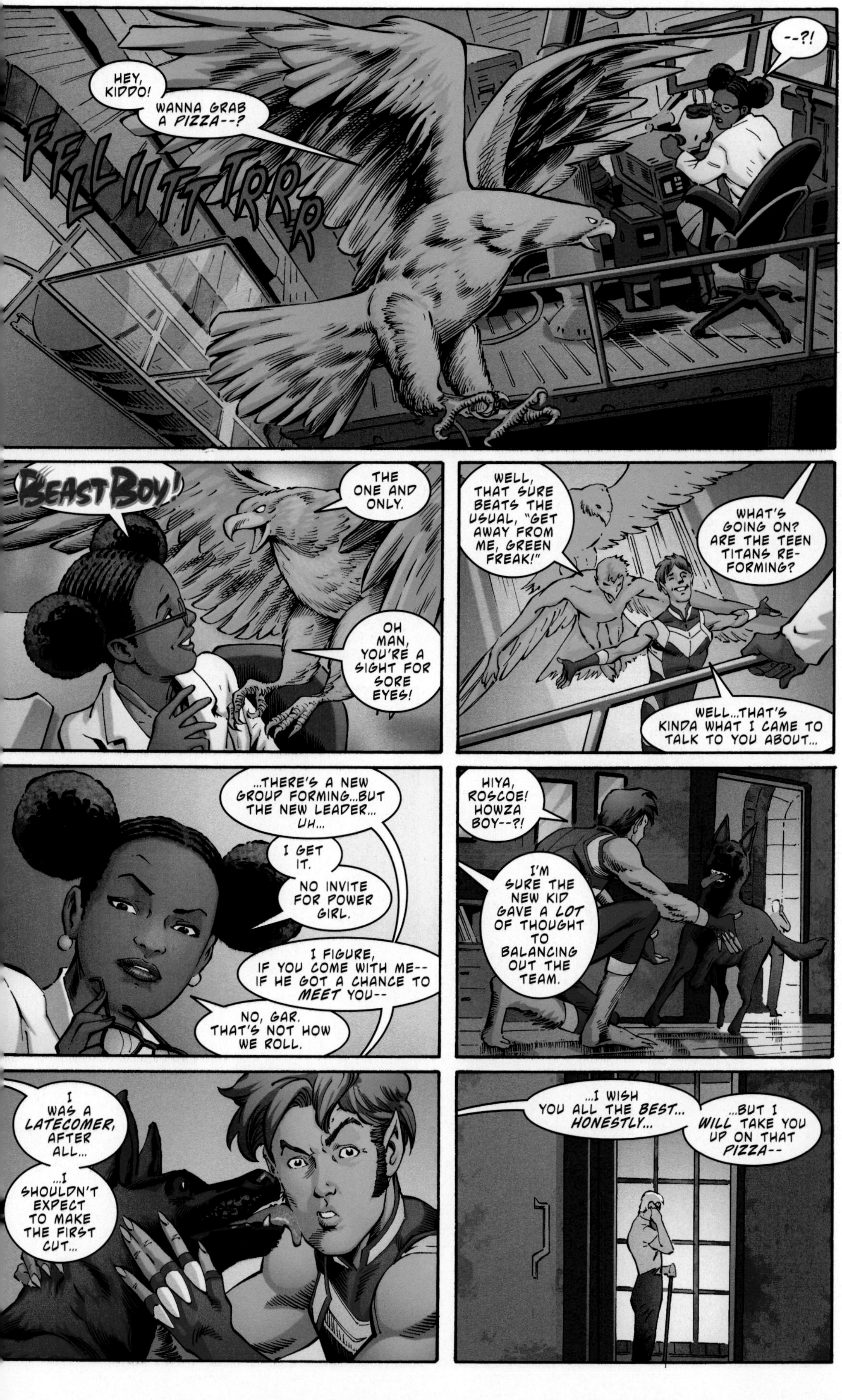
HEY, KIDDO!
WANNA GRAB A PIZZA--?
FFLLIITTRRR
--?!
BEAST BOY!
THE ONE AND ONLY.
OH MAN, YOU'RE A SIGHT FOR SORE EYES!
WELL, THAT SURE BEATS THE USUAL, "GET AWAY FROM ME, GREEN FREAK!"
WHAT'S GOING ON? ARE THE TEEN TITANS RE-FORMING?
WELL...THAT'S KINDA WHAT I CAME TO TALK TO YOU ABOUT...
...THERE'S A NEW GROUP FORMING...BUT THE NEW LEADER... UH...
I GET IT.
NO INVITE FOR POWER GIRL.
I FIGURE, IF YOU COME WITH ME-- IF HE GOT A CHANCE TO MEET YOU--
NO, GAR. THAT'S NOT HOW WE ROLL.
HIYA, ROSCOE! HOWZA BOY--?!
I'M SURE THE NEW KID GAVE A LOT OF THOUGHT TO BALANCING OUT THE TEAM.
I WAS A LATECOMER, AFTER ALL...
...I SHOULDN'T EXPECT TO MAKE THE FIRST CUT...
...I WISH YOU ALL THE BEST... HONESTLY...
...BUT I WILL TAKE YOU UP ON THAT PIZZA--

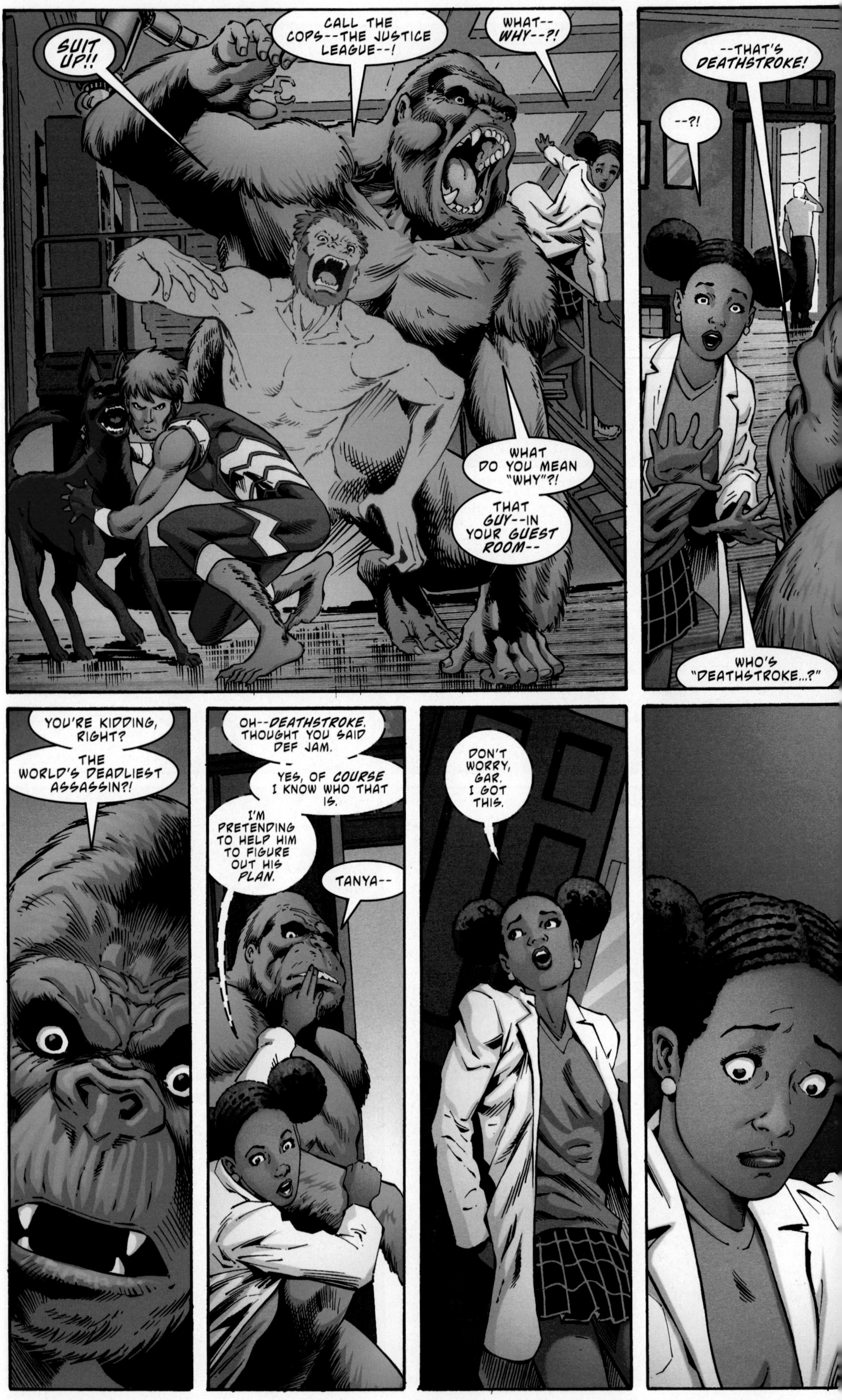
SUIT UP!!
CALL THE COPS--THE JUSTICE LEAGUE--!
WHAT--WHY--?!
WHAT DO YOU MEAN "WHY"?!
THAT GUY--IN YOUR GUEST ROOM--
--THAT'S DEATHSTROKE!
--?!
WHO'S "DEATHSTROKE...?"
YOU'RE KIDDING, RIGHT?
THE WORLD'S DEADLIEST ASSASSIN?!
OH--DEATHSTROKE. THOUGHT YOU SAID DEF JAM.
YES, OF COURSE I KNOW WHO THAT IS.
I'M PRETENDING TO HELP HIM TO FIGURE OUT HIS PLAN.
TANYA--
DON'T WORRY, GAR. I GOT THIS.

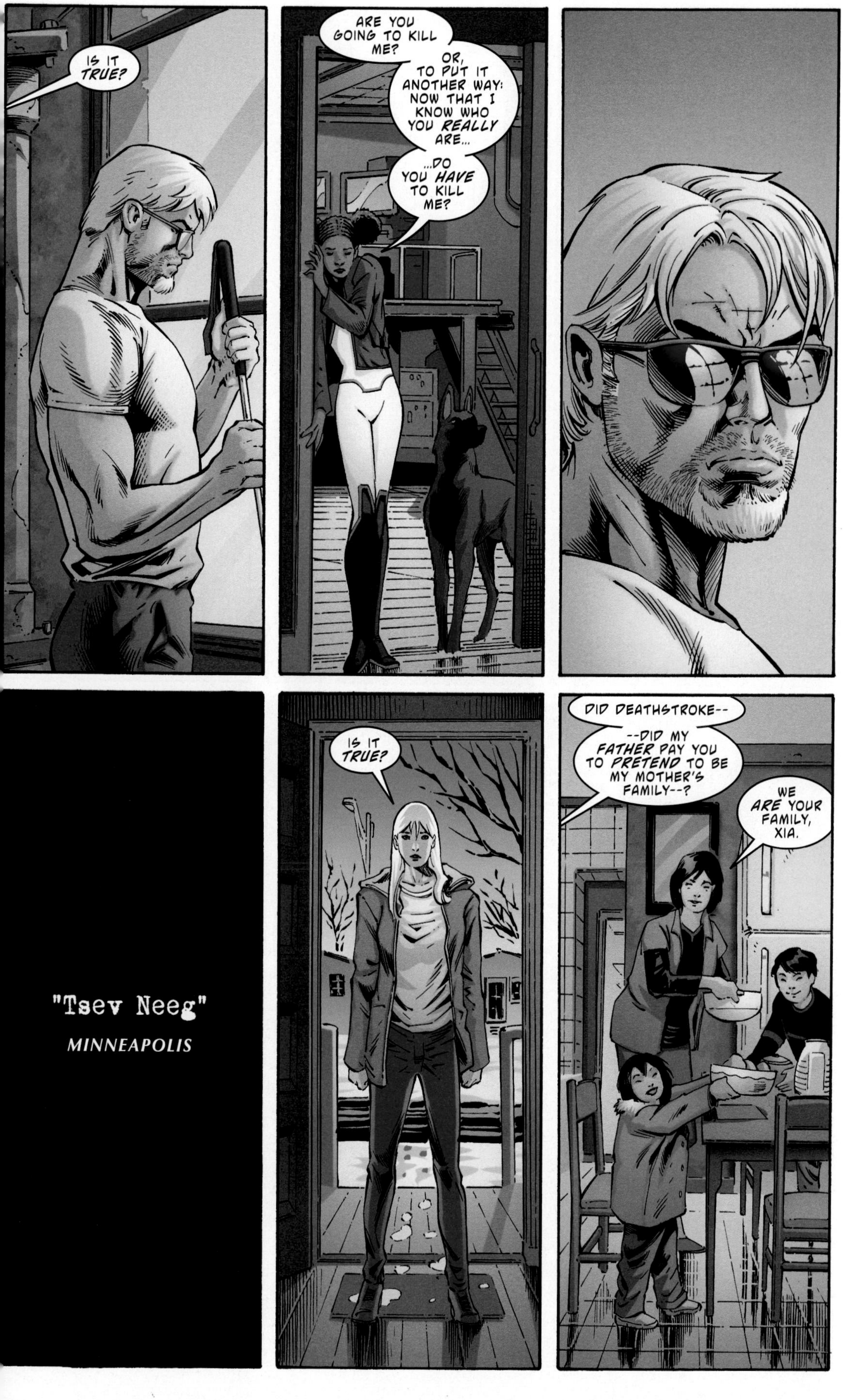
IS IT TRUE?
ARE YOU GOING TO KILL ME?
OR, TO PUT IT ANOTHER WAY: NOW THAT I KNOW WHO YOU REALLY ARE...
...DO YOU HAVE TO KILL ME?
"Tsev Neeg"
MINNEAPOLIS
IS IT TRUE?
DID DEATHSTROKE--
--DID MY FATHER PAY YOU TO PRETEND TO BE MY MOTHER'S FAMILY--?
WE ARE YOUR FAMILY, XIA.

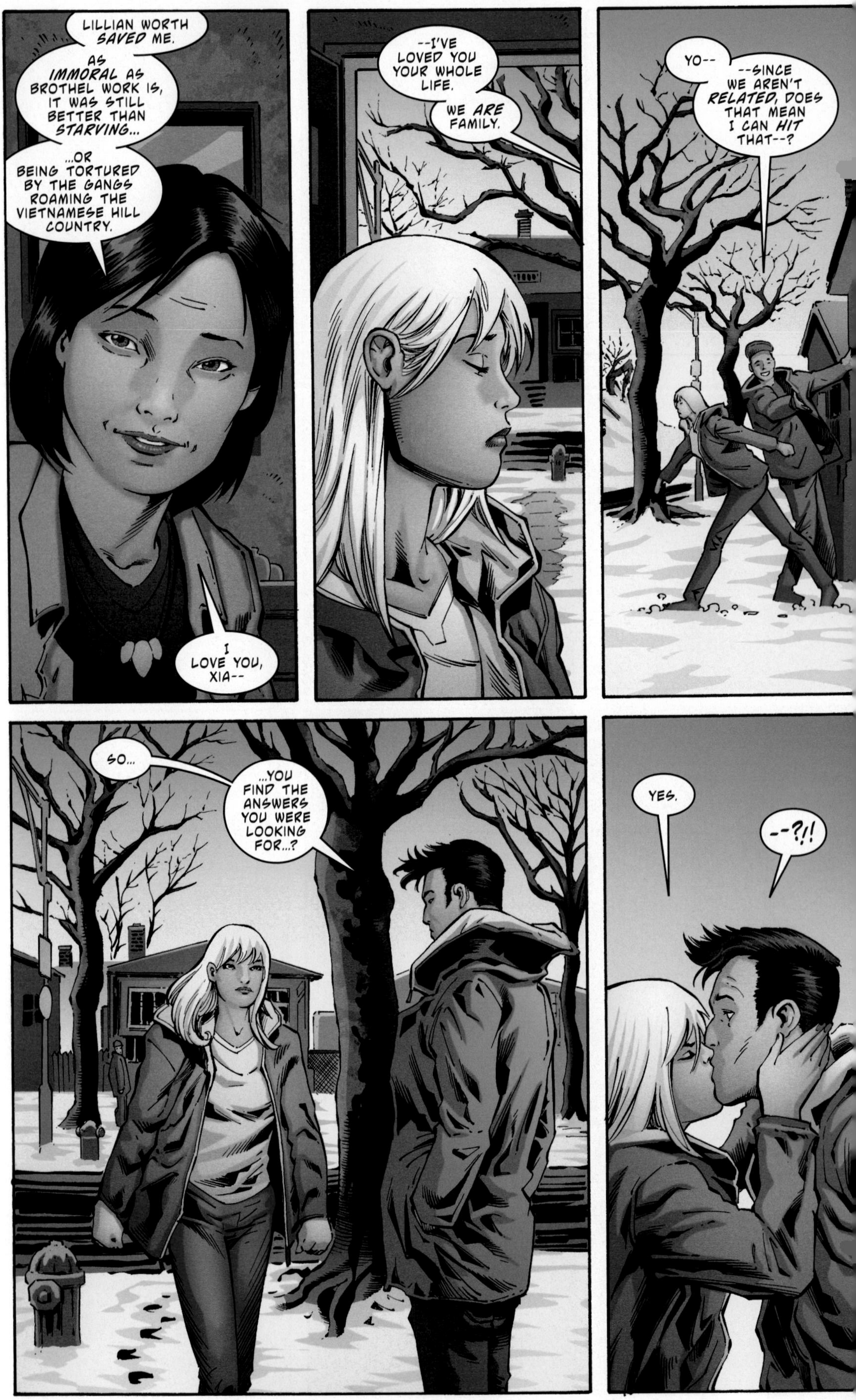
LILLIAN WORTH *SAVED* ME.
AS *IMMORAL* AS BROTHEL WORK IS, IT WAS STILL BETTER THAN *STARVING*...
...OR BEING TORTURED BY THE GANGS ROAMING THE VIETNAMESE HILL COUNTRY.
I LOVE YOU, XIA--
--I'VE LOVED YOU YOUR WHOLE LIFE.
WE *ARE* FAMILY.
YO--
--SINCE WE AREN'T *RELATED*, DOES THAT MEAN I CAN *HIT* THAT--?
SO...
...YOU FIND THE ANSWERS YOU WERE LOOKING FOR...?
YES.
--?!!

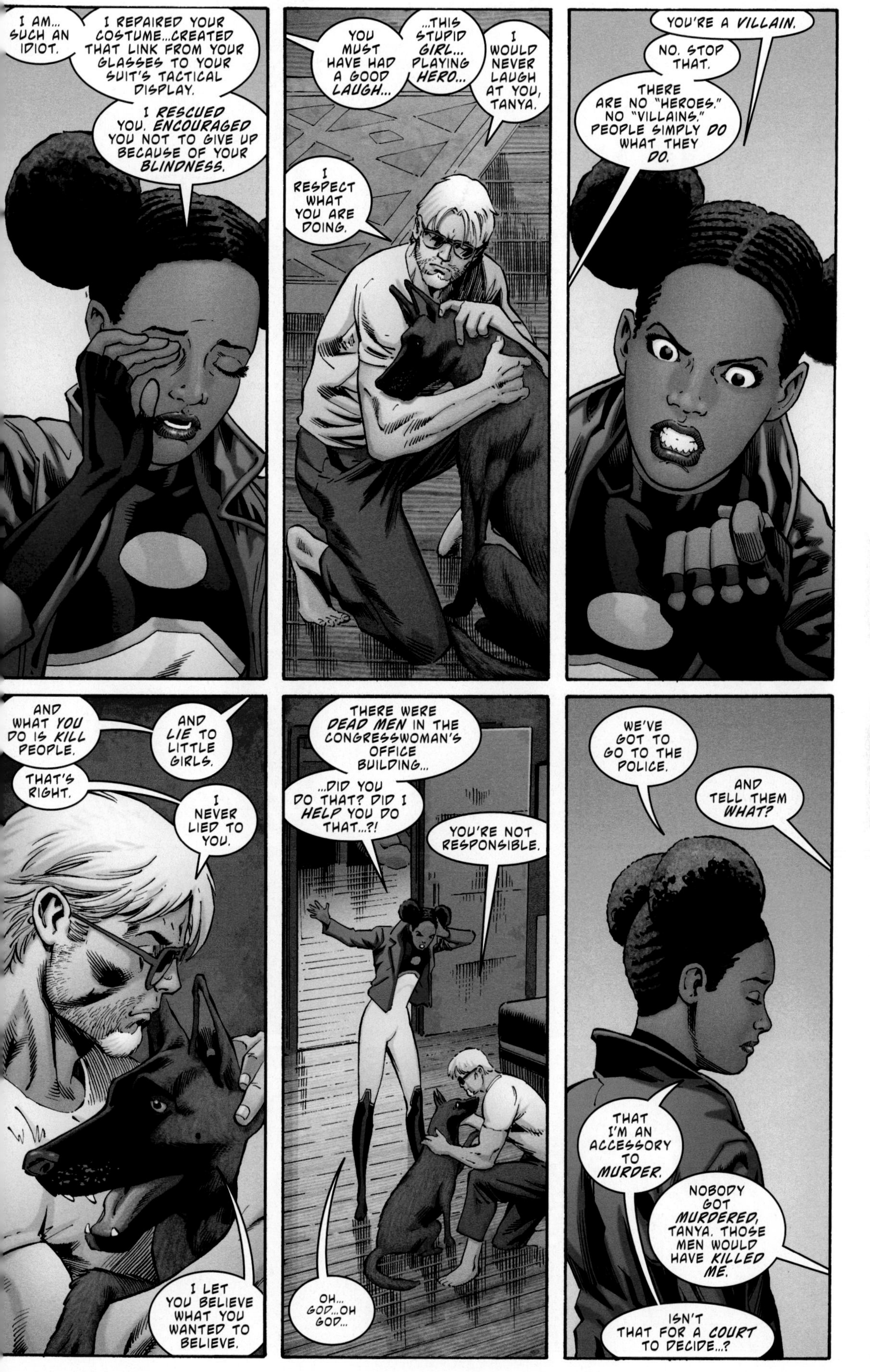
I AM... SUCH AN IDIOT.
I REPAIRED YOUR COSTUME...CREATED THAT LINK FROM YOUR GLASSES TO YOUR SUIT'S TACTICAL DISPLAY.
I RESCUED YOU. ENCOURAGED YOU NOT TO GIVE UP BECAUSE OF YOUR BLINDNESS.
YOU MUST HAVE HAD A GOOD LAUGH...
...THIS STUPID GIRL... PLAYING HERO...
I WOULD NEVER LAUGH AT YOU, TANYA.
I RESPECT WHAT YOU ARE DOING.
YOU'RE A VILLAIN.
NO. STOP THAT.
THERE ARE NO "HEROES." NO "VILLAINS." PEOPLE SIMPLY DO WHAT THEY DO.
AND WHAT YOU DO IS KILL PEOPLE.
AND LIE TO LITTLE GIRLS.
THAT'S RIGHT.
I NEVER LIED TO YOU.
I LET YOU BELIEVE WHAT YOU WANTED TO BELIEVE.
THERE WERE DEAD MEN IN THE CONGRESSWOMAN'S OFFICE BUILDING...
...DID YOU DO THAT? DID I HELP YOU DO THAT...?!
YOU'RE NOT RESPONSIBLE.
OH... GOD...OH GOD...
WE'VE GOT TO GO TO THE POLICE.
AND TELL THEM WHAT?
THAT I'M AN ACCESSORY TO MURDER.
NOBODY GOT MURDERED, TANYA. THOSE MEN WOULD HAVE KILLED ME.
ISN'T THAT FOR A COURT TO DECIDE...?

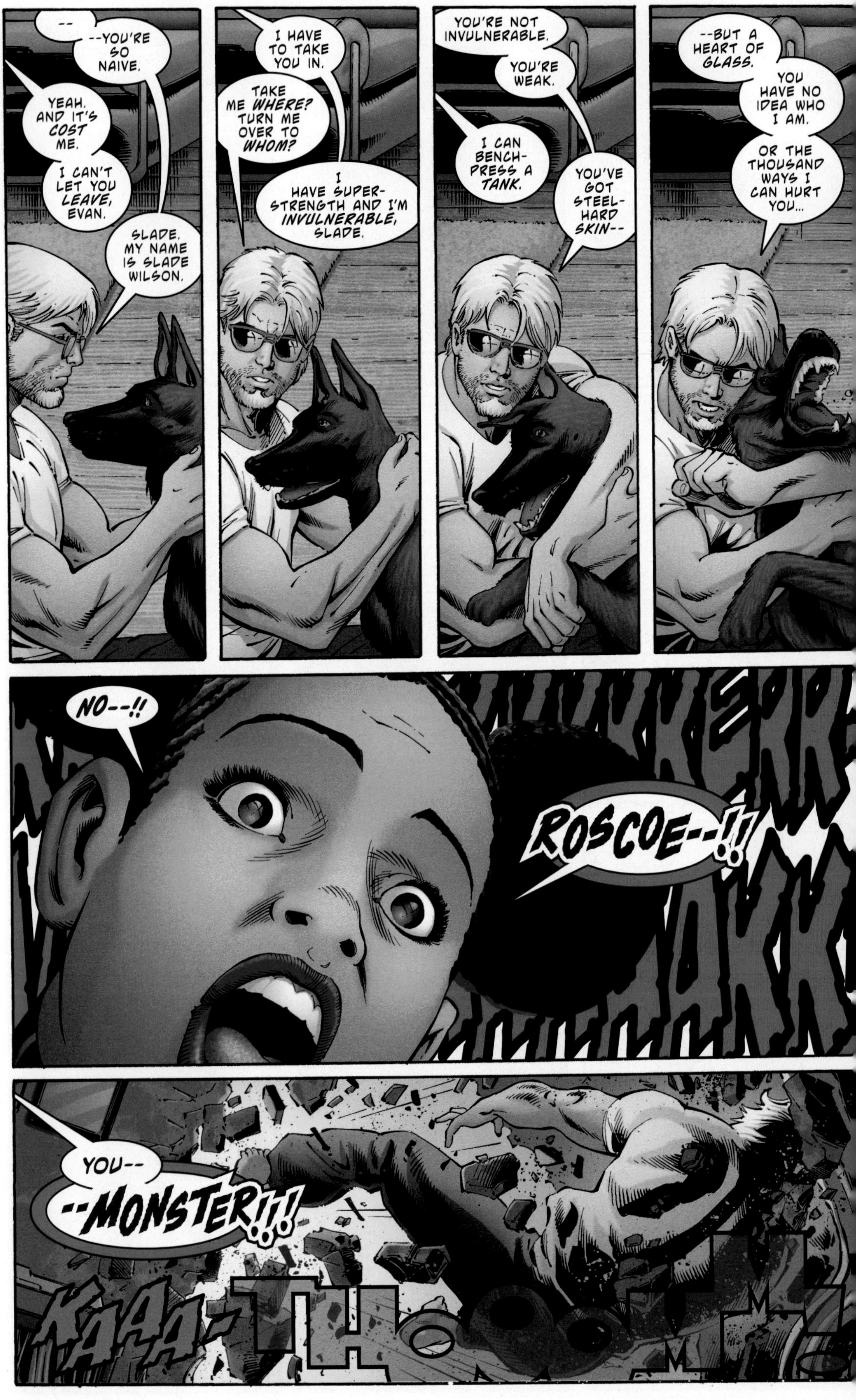
--
--YOU'RE SO NAIVE.
YEAH. AND IT'S COST ME.
I CAN'T LET YOU LEAVE, EVAN.
SLADE. MY NAME IS SLADE WILSON.
I HAVE TO TAKE YOU IN.
TAKE ME WHERE? TURN ME OVER TO WHOM?
I HAVE SUPER-STRENGTH AND I'M INVULNERABLE, SLADE.
YOU'RE NOT INVULNERABLE.
YOU'RE WEAK.
I CAN BENCH-PRESS A TANK.
YOU'VE GOT STEEL-HARD SKIN--
--BUT A HEART OF GLASS.
YOU HAVE NO IDEA WHO I AM.
OR THE THOUSAND WAYS I CAN HURT YOU...
NO--!!
ROSCOE--!!
YOU--
--MONSTER!!!
KAAA-THOOOM

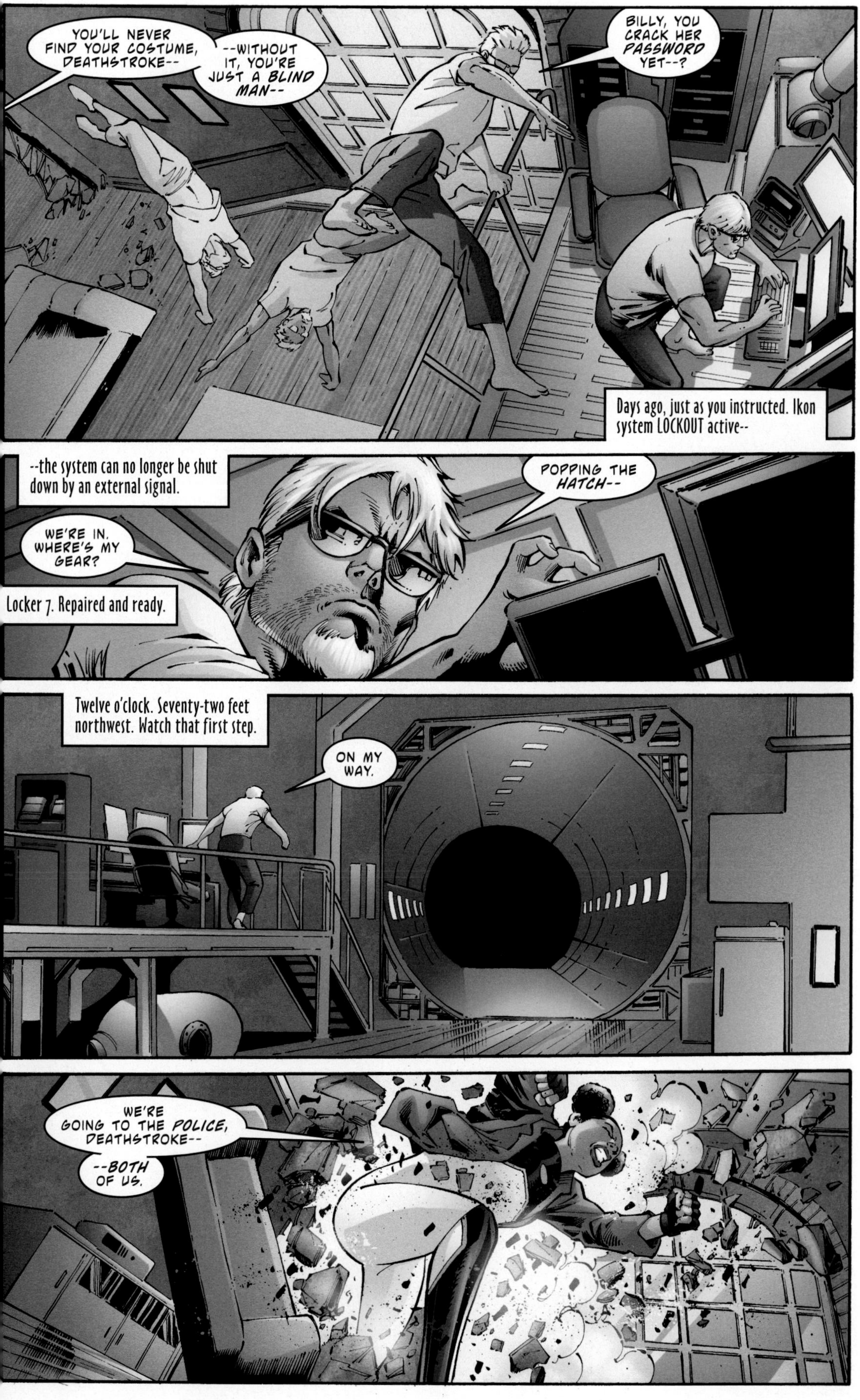

YOU'LL NEVER FIND YOUR COSTUME, DEATHSTROKE--
--WITHOUT IT, YOU'RE JUST A BLIND MAN--
BILLY, YOU CRACK HER PASSWORD YET--?
Days ago, just as you instructed. Ikon system LOCKOUT active--
--the system can no longer be shut down by an external signal.
POPPING THE HATCH--
WE'RE IN. WHERE'S MY GEAR?
Locker 7. Repaired and ready.
Twelve o'clock. Seventy-two feet northwest. Watch that first step.
ON MY WAY.
WE'RE GOING TO THE POLICE, DEATHSTROKE--
--BOTH OF US.

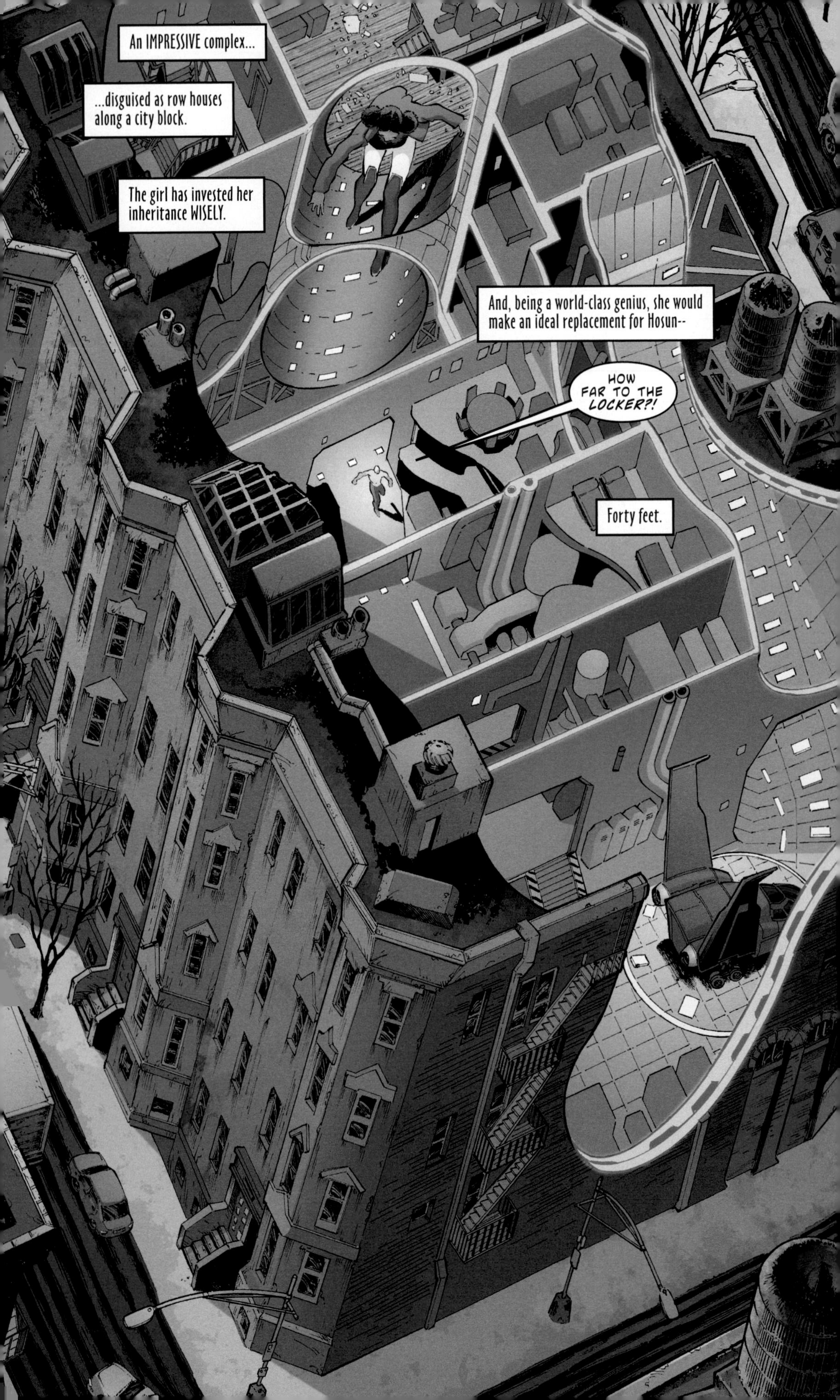
An IMPRESSIVE complex...
...disguised as row houses along a city block.
The girl has invested her inheritance WISELY.
And, being a world-class genius, she would make an ideal replacement for Hosun--
HOW FAR TO THE LOCKER?!
Forty feet.

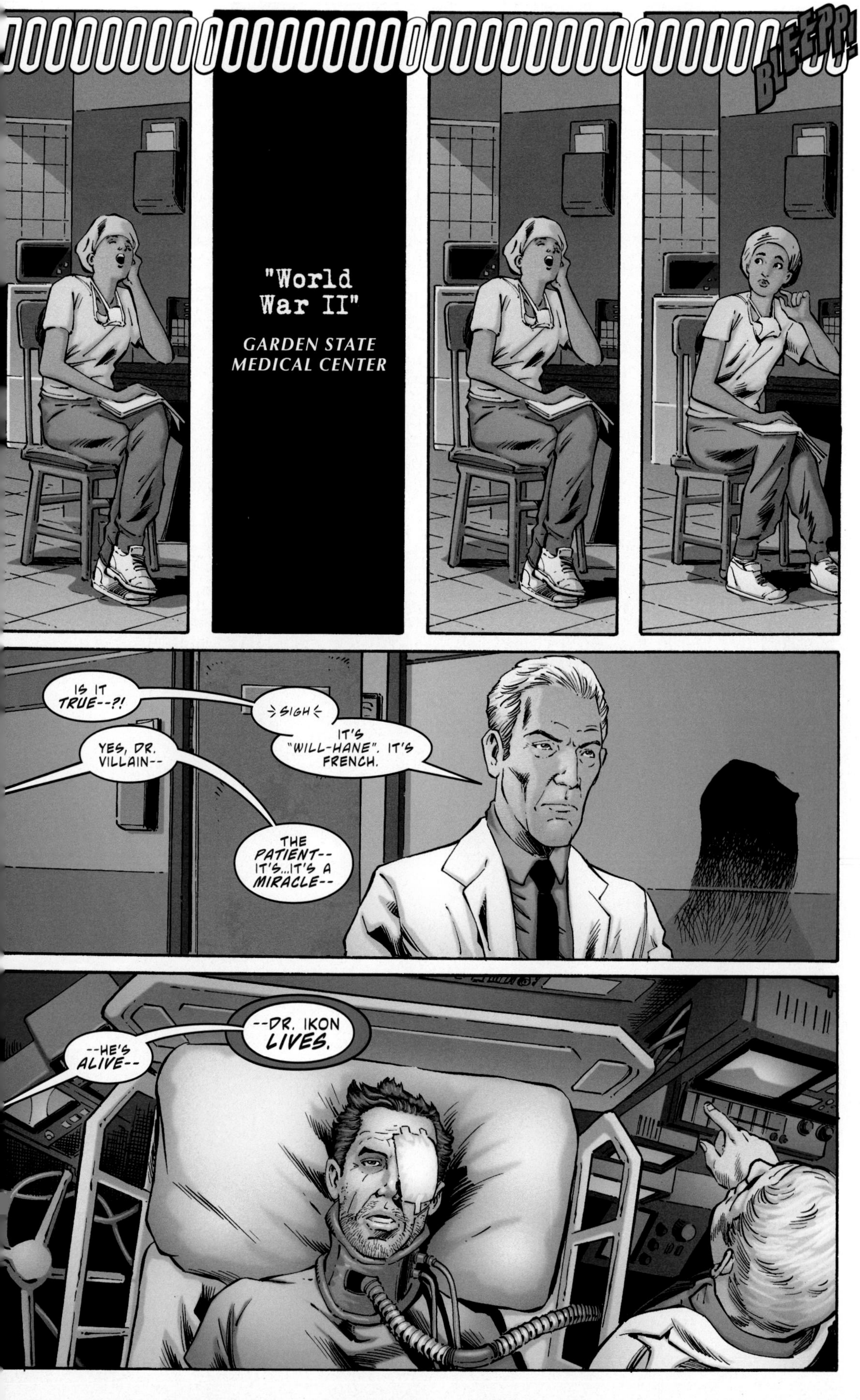

OOOOOOOOOOOOOOOOOOOOOOOOOOOOOOOOOOOOOOOOOOOOOO
BLEEPP!
"World War II"
GARDEN STATE MEDICAL CENTER
IS IT TRUE--?!
SIGH
IT'S "WILL-HANE". IT'S FRENCH.
YES, DR. VILLAIN--
THE PATIENT--IT'S...IT'S A MIRACLE--
--HE'S ALIVE--
--DR. IKON LIVES.

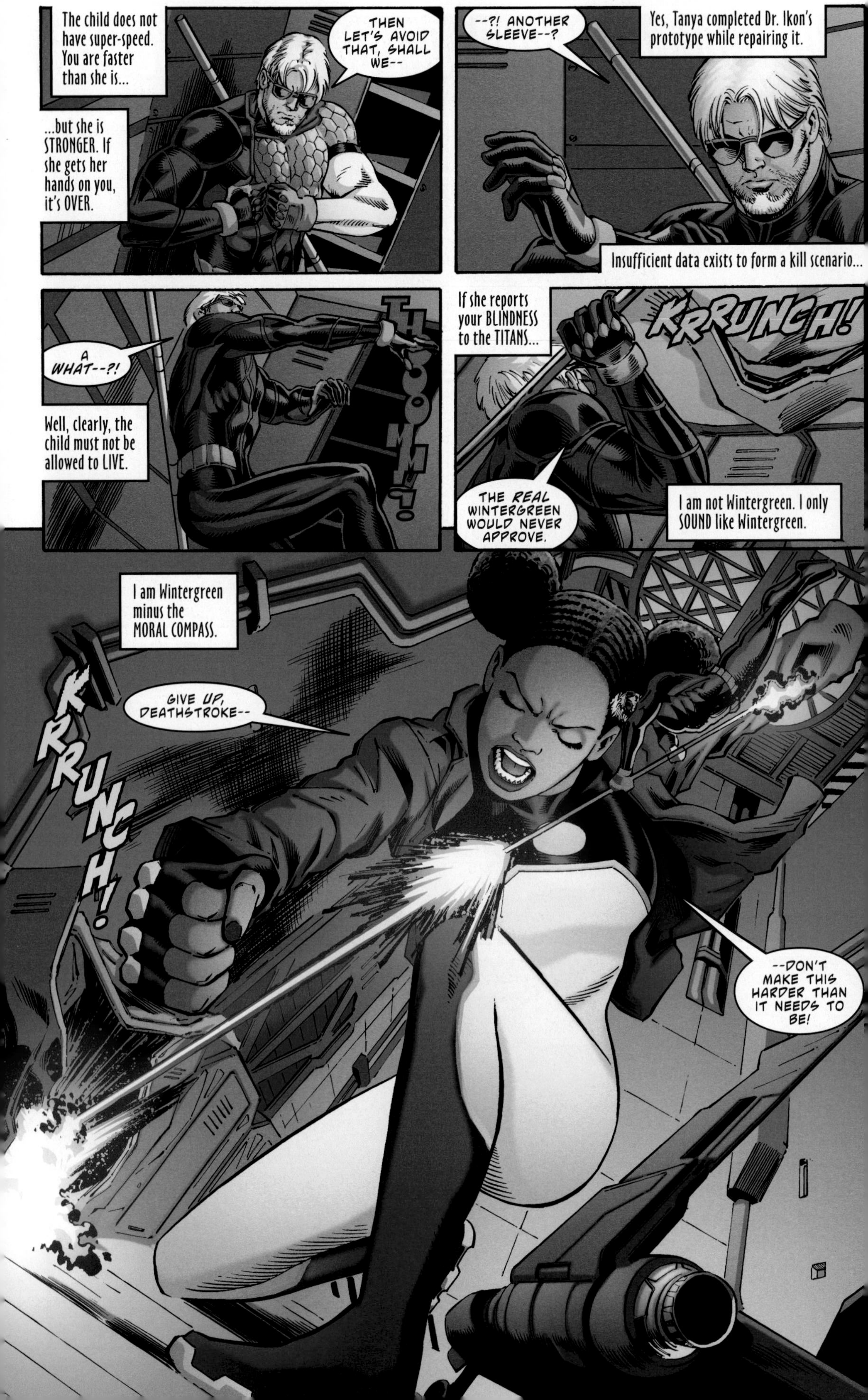

The child does not have super-speed. You are faster than she is...
THEN LET'S AVOID THAT, SHALL WE--
...but she is STRONGER. If she gets her hands on you, it's OVER.
--?! ANOTHER SLEEVE--?
Yes, Tanya completed Dr. Ikon's prototype while repairing it.
Insufficient data exists to form a kill scenario...
A WHAT--?!
THOOOMM!
Well, clearly, the child must not be allowed to LIVE.
If she reports your BLINDNESS to the TITANS...
KRRUNCH!
THE REAL WINTERGREEN WOULD NEVER APPROVE.
I am not Wintergreen. I only SOUND like Wintergreen.
I am Wintergreen minus the MORAL COMPASS.
KRRUNCH!
GIVE UP, DEATHSTROKE--
--DON'T MAKE THIS HARDER THAN IT NEEDS TO BE!

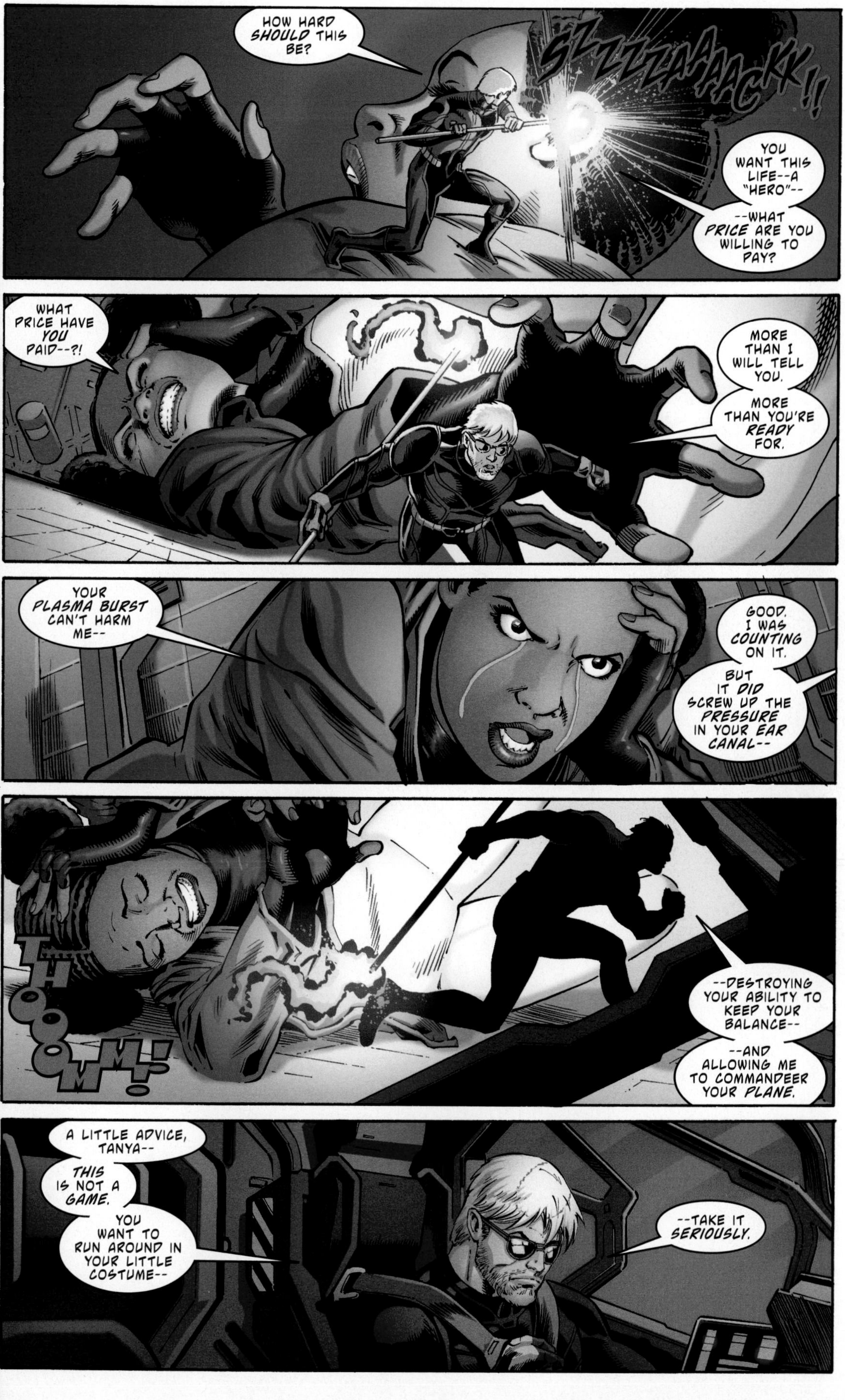

HOW HARD *SHOULD* THIS BE?
SZZZZAAAACKK!!
YOU WANT THIS LIFE--A "HERO"--
--WHAT *PRICE* ARE YOU WILLING TO PAY?
WHAT PRICE HAVE *YOU* PAID--?!
MORE THAN I WILL TELL YOU.
MORE THAN YOU'RE *READY* FOR.
YOUR *PLASMA BURST* CAN'T HARM ME--
GOOD. I WAS *COUNTING* ON IT.
BUT IT *DID* SCREW UP THE *PRESSURE* IN YOUR *EAR CANAL*--
THOOOOM!
--DESTROYING YOUR ABILITY TO KEEP YOUR BALANCE--
--AND ALLOWING ME TO COMMANDEER YOUR *PLANE*.
A LITTLE ADVICE, TANYA--
*THIS* IS NOT A *GAME*.
YOU WANT TO RUN AROUND IN YOUR LITTLE COSTUME--
--TAKE IT *SERIOUSLY*.

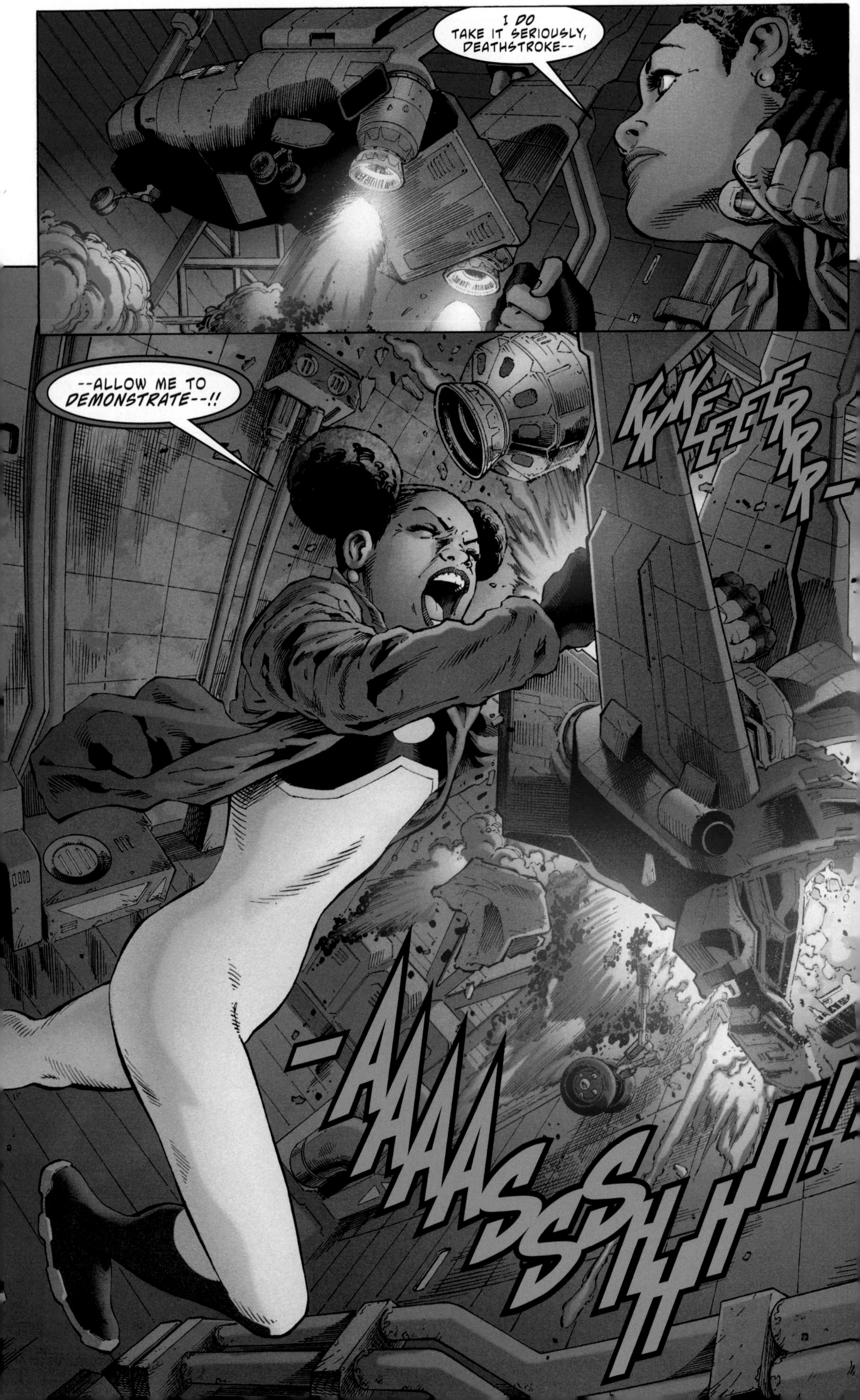

I DO TAKE IT SERIOUSLY, DEATHSTROKE--
--ALLOW ME TO DEMONSTRATE--!!
KKKEEEERRR--
-AAAASSSHHH!!

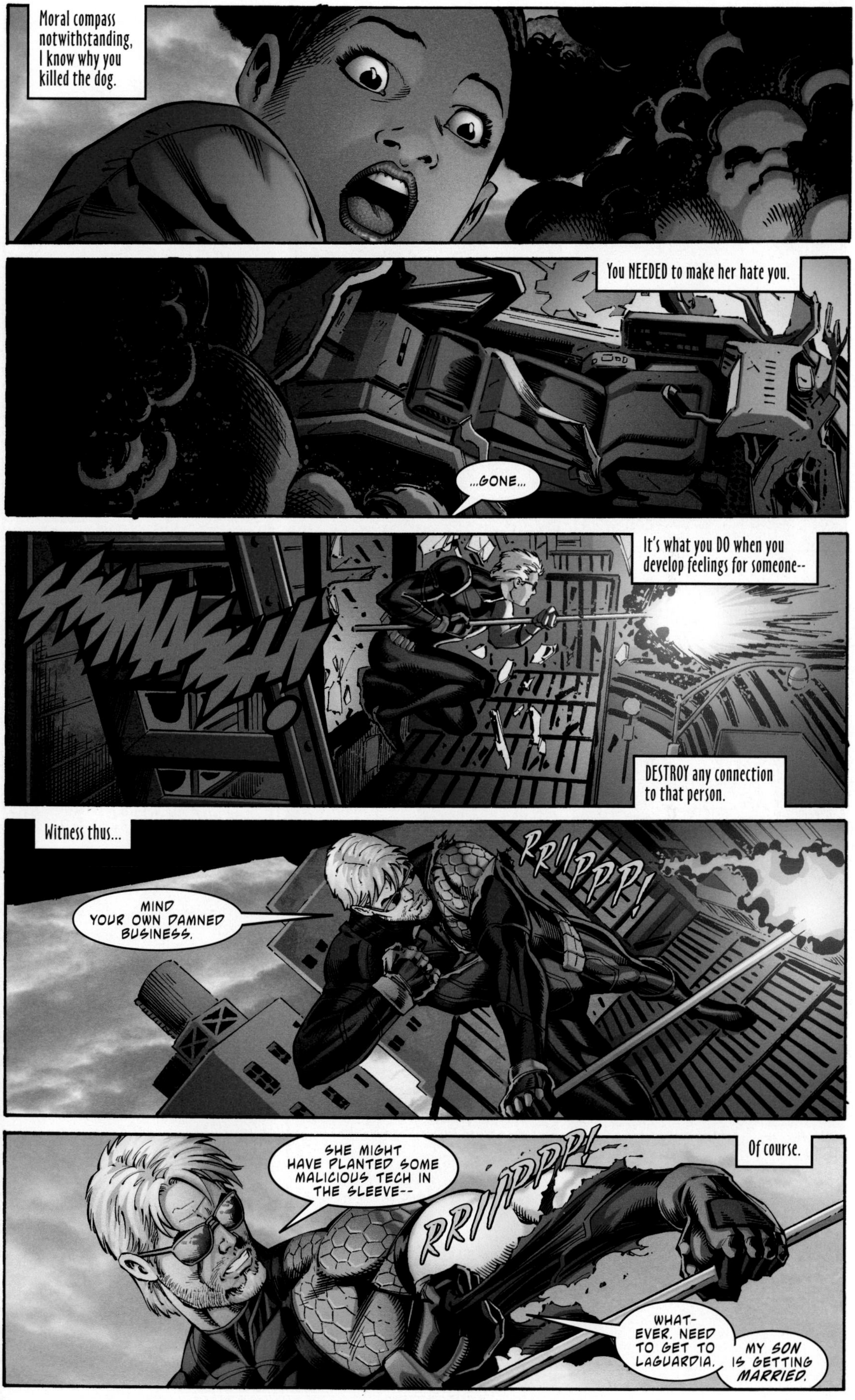
Moral compass notwithstanding, I know why you killed the dog.
You NEEDED to make her hate you.
...GONE...
SMASH!
It's what you DO when you develop feelings for someone--
DESTROY any connection to that person.
Witness thus...
RRIIPPPP!
MIND YOUR OWN DAMNED BUSINESS.
Of course.
SHE MIGHT HAVE PLANTED SOME MALICIOUS TECH IN THE SLEEVE--
RRIIPPPP!
RRIIPPPP!
WHAT-EVER. NEED TO GET TO LAGUARDIA.
MY SON IS GETTING MARRIED.

9 APRIL

Getting harder to police Slade's conscience.

Not certain I even care to try.

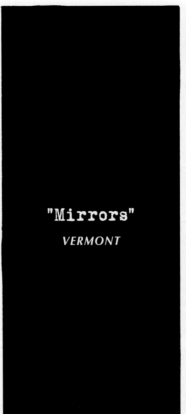

"Mirrors"

*VERMONT*

Playing house with some CHILD...

...intending to use this terrible WEAPON...

...I've grown much too old for this...

BLEE'P

WINTERGREEN.

GOD...OH GOD...HE'S SUCH A MONSTER...

ROSE--?!

WINTERGREEN... MY DAD...HE JUST... HE NEVER STOPS!

MY OWN *FATHER*... TRYING TO *KILL* ME... HIRING *RICHARD* TO PRETEND TO LOVE ME...

...HIRING THIS *HMONG* FAMILY TO *LIE* TO ME--!

ROSE-- ROSE--CALM YOURSELF, CHILD--

--SLADE WAS NEVER *ACTUALLY* TRYING TO KILL YOU.

HE ONLY POSTED THE *HIT* ON YOU SO HE'D HAVE AN EXCUSE TO STAY BY YOUR SIDE...

...HE JUST WANTED TO SPEND TIME WITH HIS *DAUGHTER*.

THAT'S INSANE.

THAT'S SLADE.

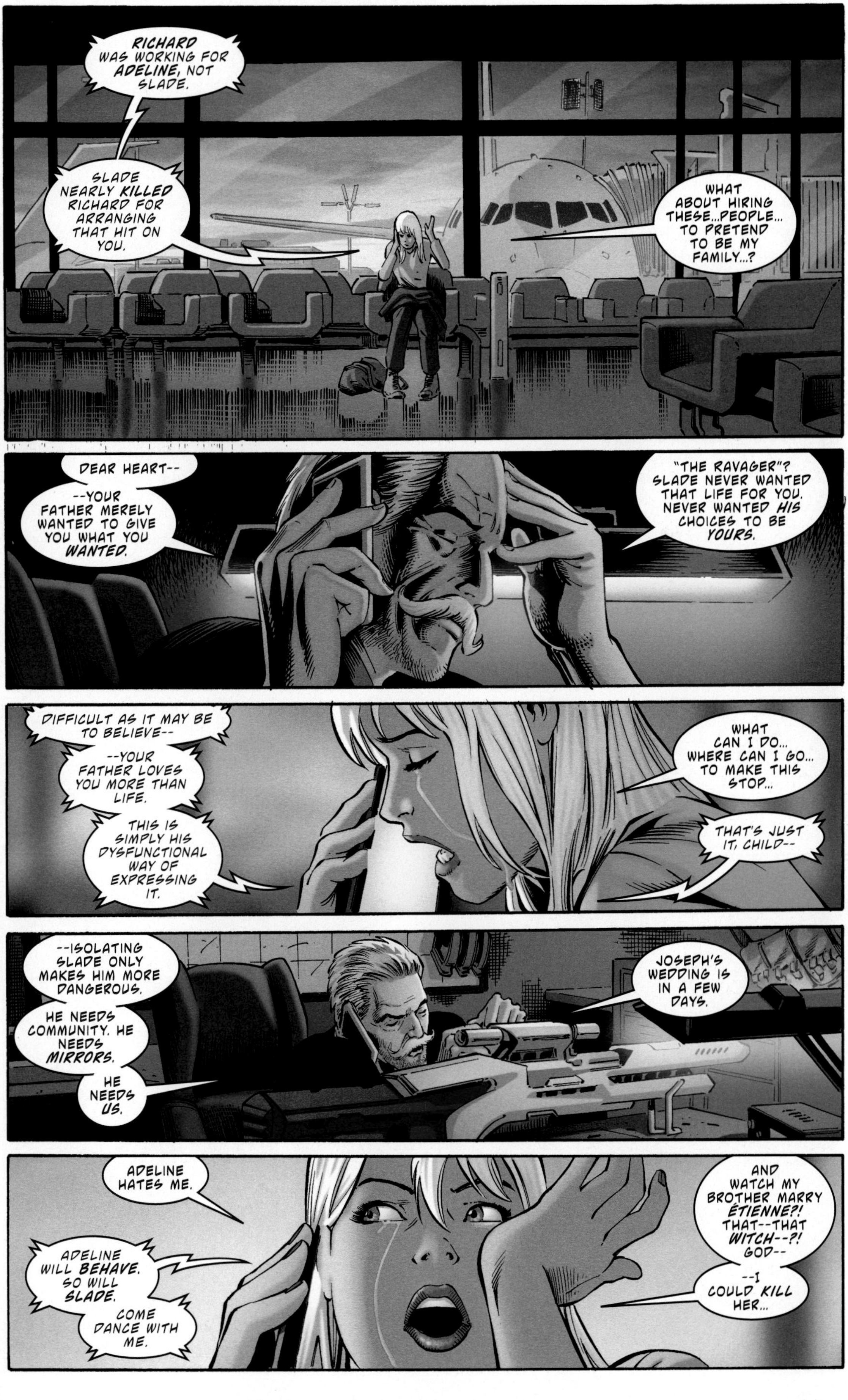

RICHARD WAS WORKING FOR ADELINE, NOT SLADE.
SLADE NEARLY KILLED RICHARD FOR ARRANGING THAT HIT ON YOU.
WHAT ABOUT HIRING THESE...PEOPLE... TO PRETEND TO BE MY FAMILY...?
DEAR HEART--
--YOUR FATHER MERELY WANTED TO GIVE YOU WHAT YOU WANTED.
"THE RAVAGER"? SLADE NEVER WANTED THAT LIFE FOR YOU. NEVER WANTED HIS CHOICES TO BE YOURS.
DIFFICULT AS IT MAY BE TO BELIEVE--
--YOUR FATHER LOVES YOU MORE THAN LIFE.
THIS IS SIMPLY HIS DYSFUNCTIONAL WAY OF EXPRESSING IT.
WHAT CAN I DO... WHERE CAN I GO... TO MAKE THIS STOP...
THAT'S JUST IT, CHILD--
--ISOLATING SLADE ONLY MAKES HIM MORE DANGEROUS.
HE NEEDS COMMUNITY. HE NEEDS MIRRORS.
HE NEEDS US.
JOSEPH'S WEDDING IS IN A FEW DAYS.
ADELINE HATES ME.
ADELINE WILL BEHAVE. SO WILL SLADE.
COME DANCE WITH ME.
AND WATCH MY BROTHER MARRY ÉTIENNE?! THAT--THAT WITCH--?! GOD--
--I COULD KILL HER...

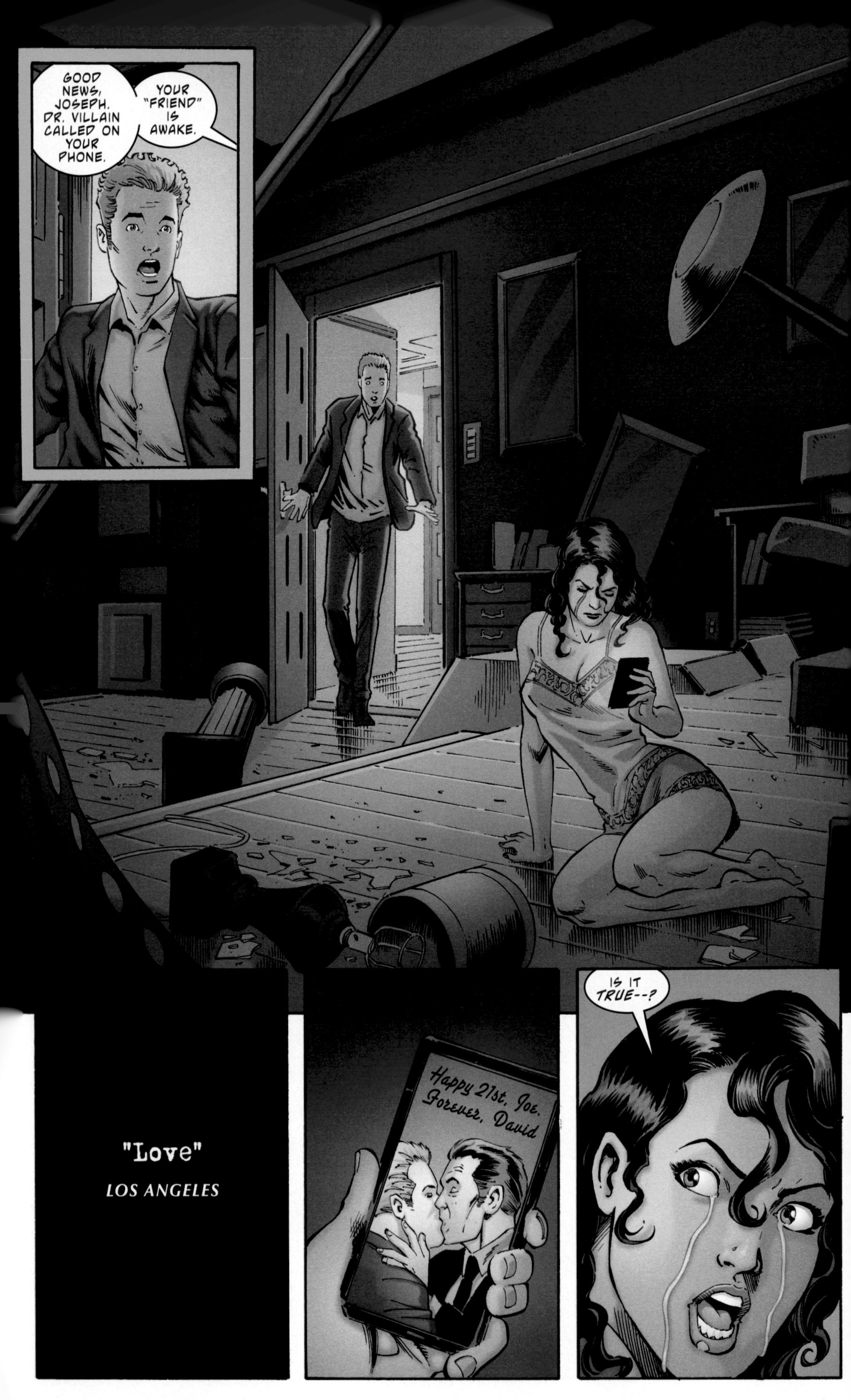

GOOD NEWS, JOSEPH. DR. VILLAIN CALLED ON YOUR PHONE.
YOUR "FRIEND" IS AWAKE.
"Love"
LOS ANGELES
Happy 21st, Joe. Forever, David
IS IT TRUE--?

--?! ÉTIENNE-- WHAT THE HELL HAPPENED--?

LEFT YOUR PHONE AT THE OFFICE, JOSEPH.

YOU AND DAVID ISHERWOOD-- DR. IKON--

--IS IT *TRUE*--?!

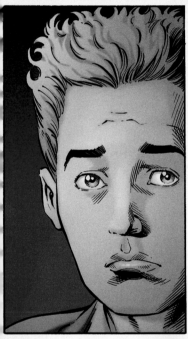

I WANTED TO TELL YOU...

EDDIE-- IT WAS ONLY A FEW MONTHS-- I LOVE YOU--

OKAY, STOP.

I GET IT.

AT LEAST NOW I DON'T FEEL SO BAD ABOUT SCREWING YOUR FATHER BEHIND YOUR BACK.

--

--WHAT--?

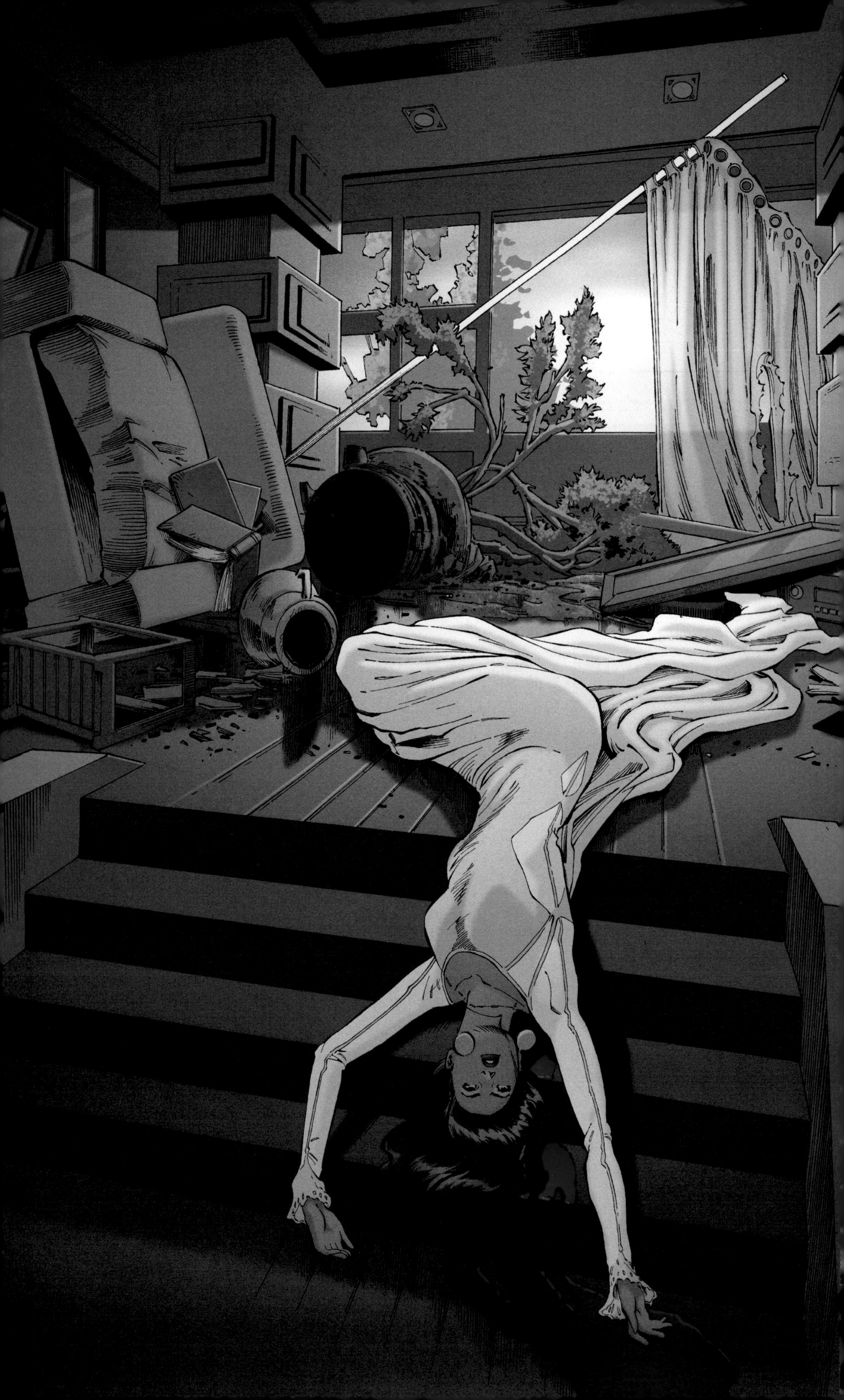

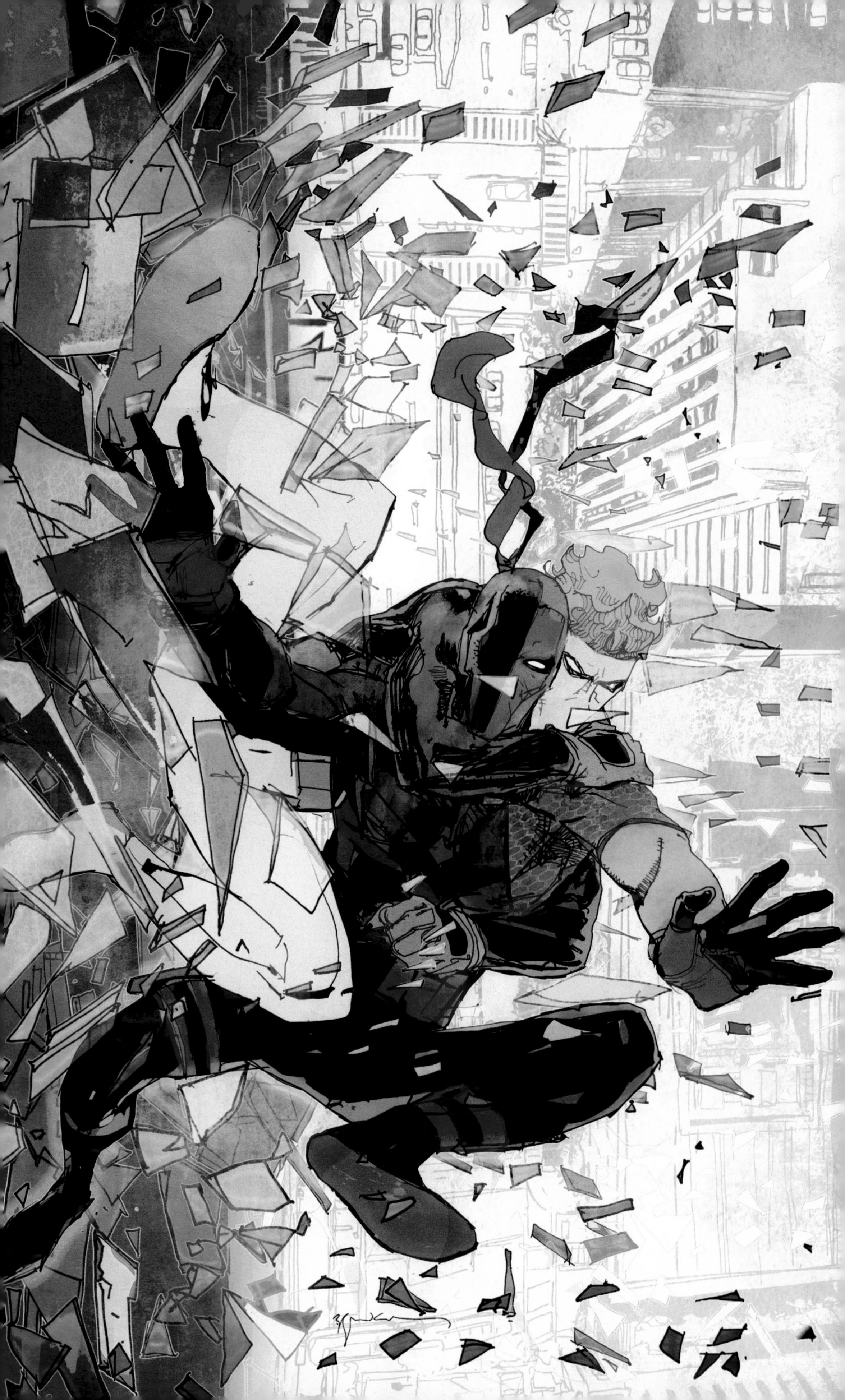

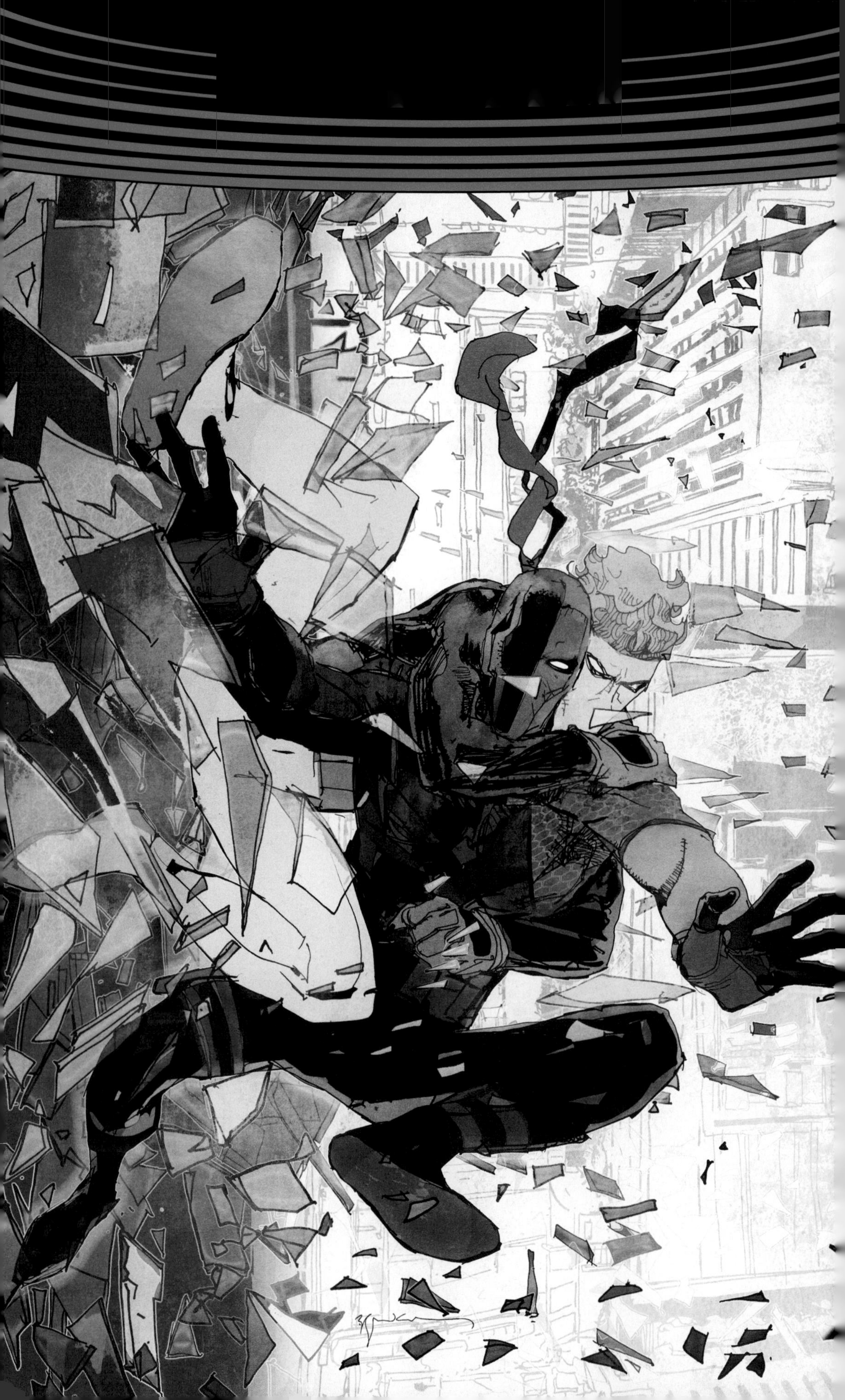

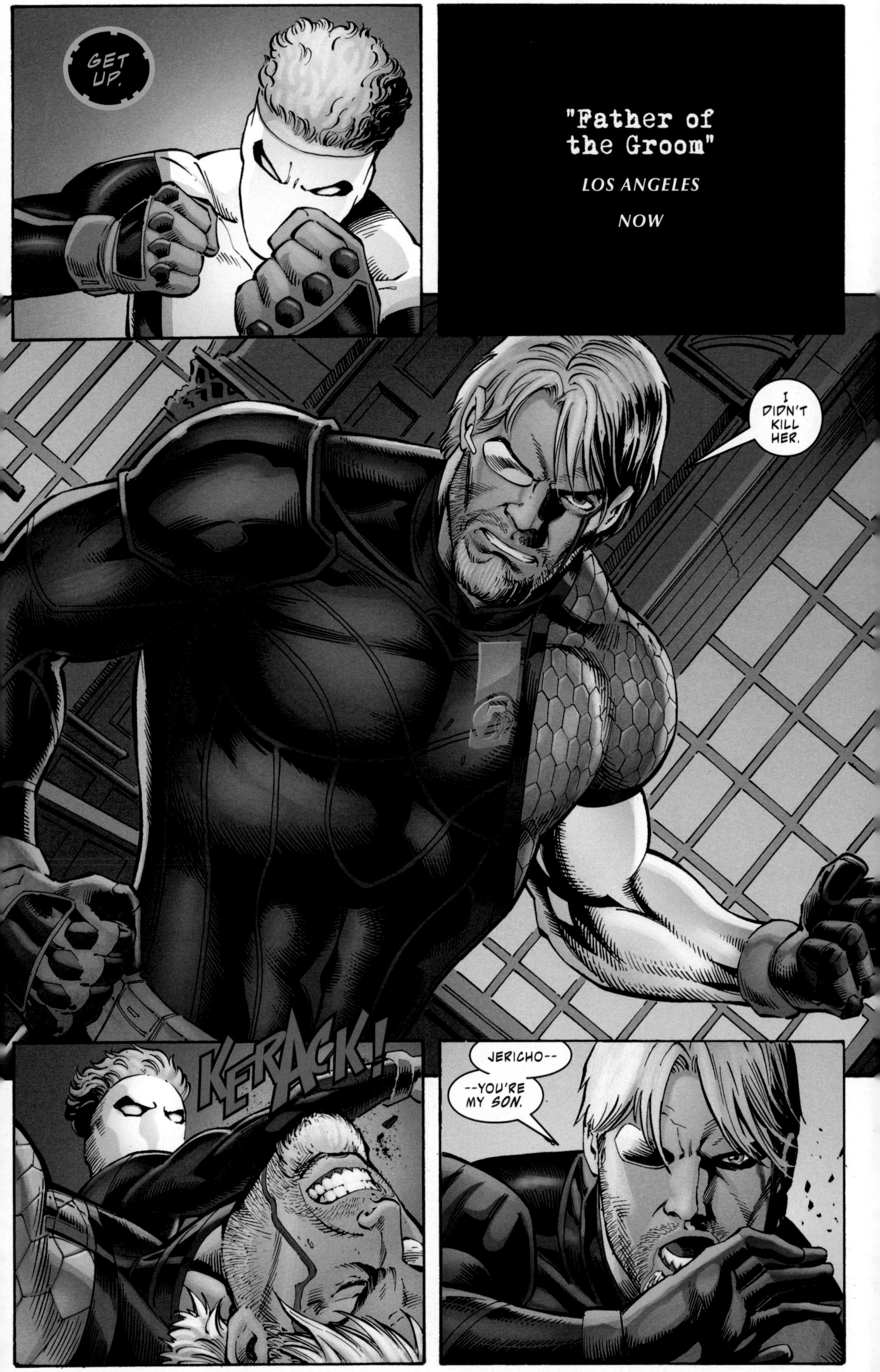
GET UP.
"Father of the Groom"
LOS ANGELES
NOW
I DIDN'T KILL HER.
KERACK!
JERICHO--
--YOU'RE MY SON.

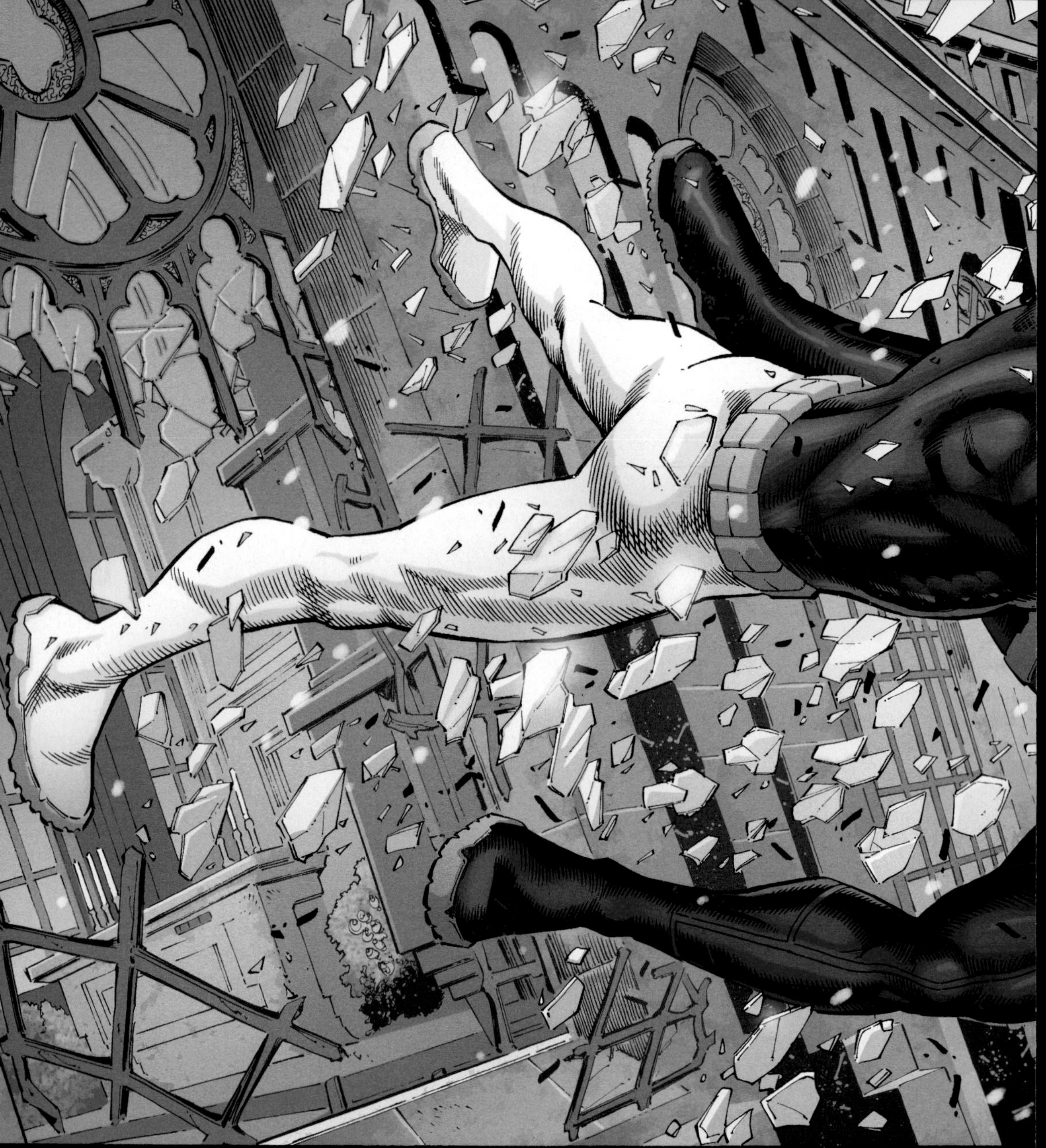

**JEROMY COX**
— color —
**WILLIE SCHUBERT**
— letters —

**BILL SIENKIEWICZ**
— cover —

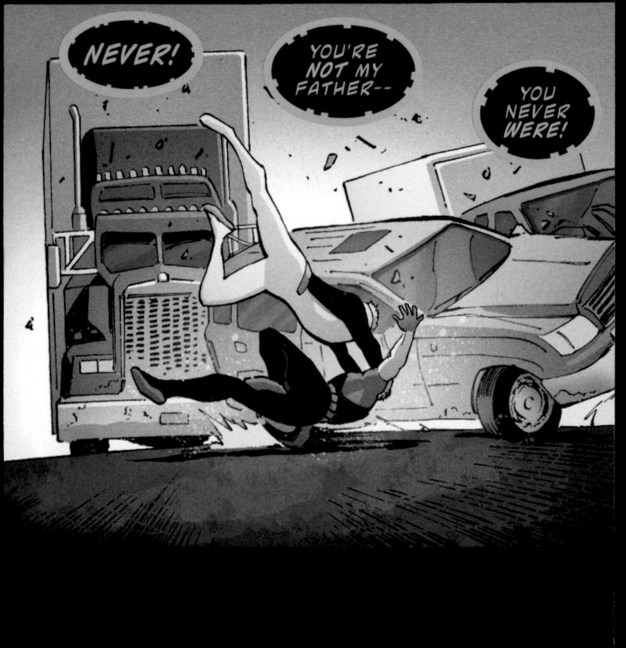
NEVER!
YOU'RE NOT MY FATHER--
YOU NEVER WERE!

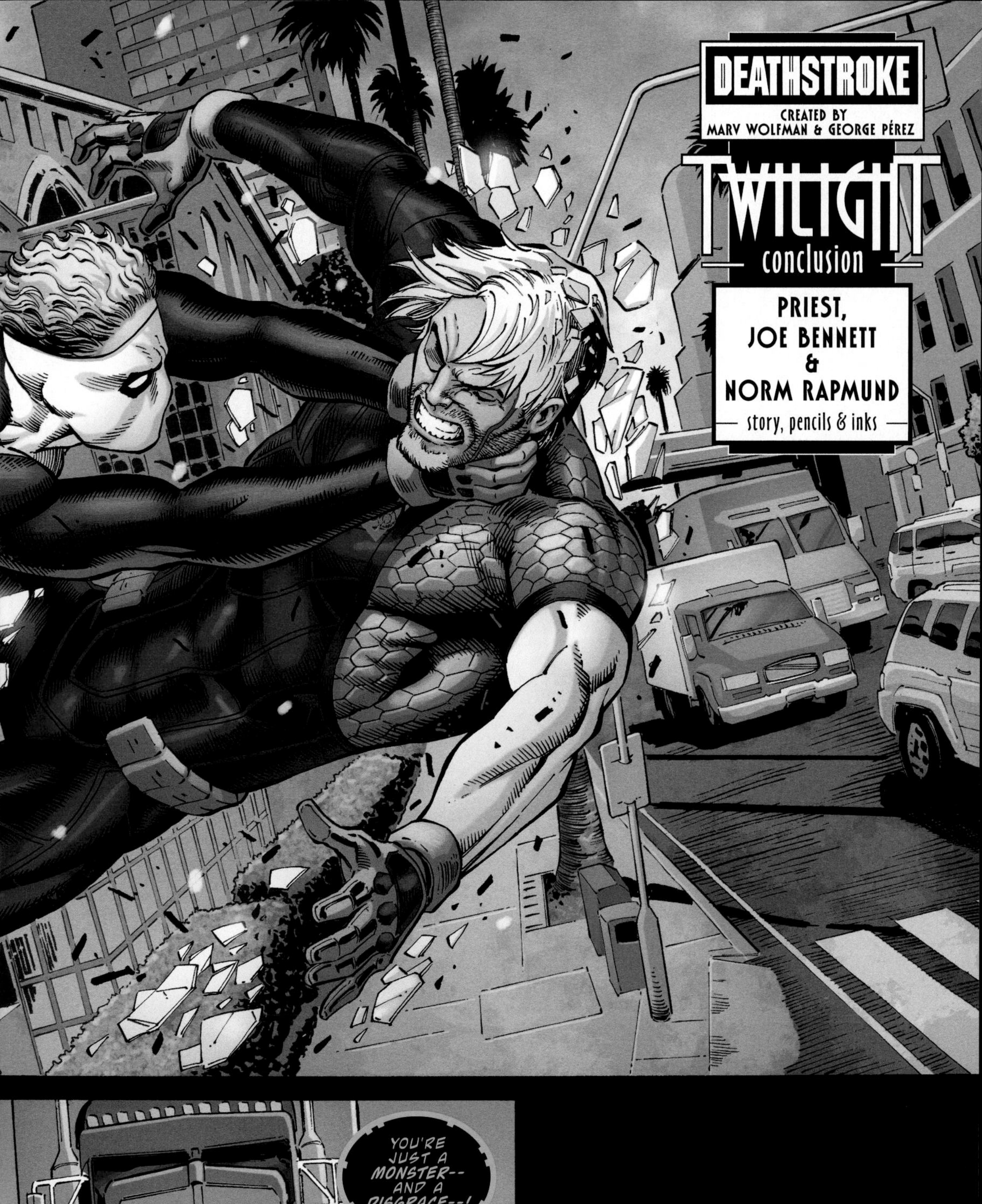
DEATHSTROKE
CREATED BY
MARV WOLFMAN & GEORGE PÉREZ
TWILIGHT
conclusion
PRIEST,
JOE BENNETT
&
NORM RAPMUND
story, pencils & inks

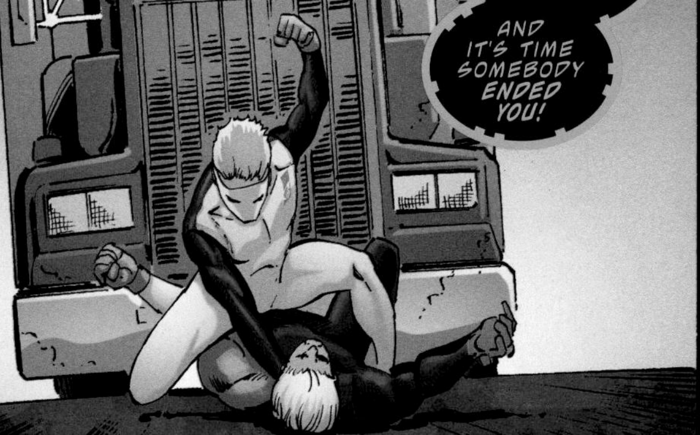
YOU'RE JUST A MONSTER-- AND A DISGRACE--!
AND IT'S TIME SOMEBODY ENDED YOU!

DIEGO LOPEZ
— assistant editor —
ALEX ANTONE
— editor —
MARIE JAVINS
— group editor —

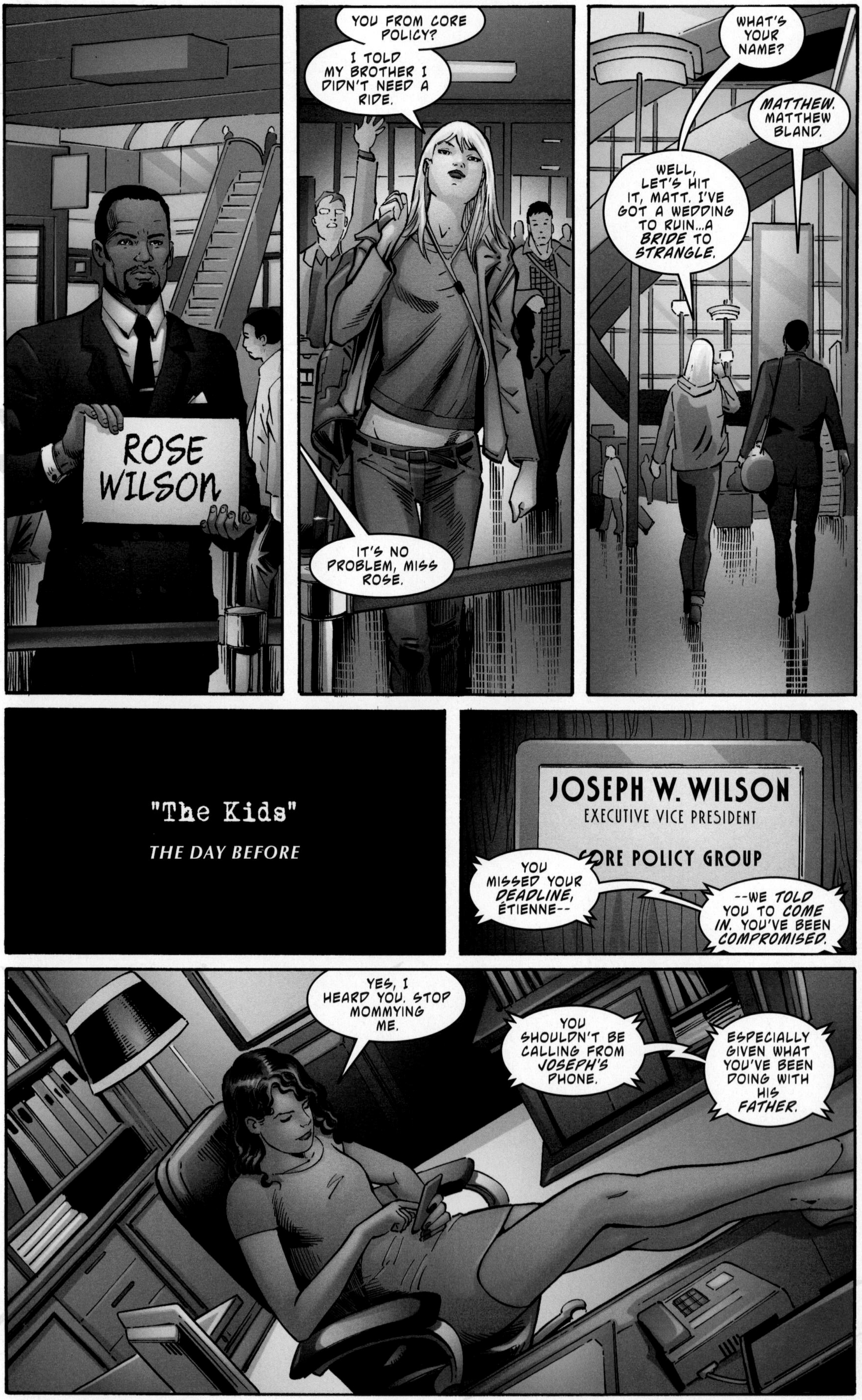
ROSE WILSON
YOU FROM CORE POLICY?
I TOLD MY BROTHER I DIDN'T NEED A RIDE.
IT'S NO PROBLEM, MISS ROSE.
WHAT'S YOUR NAME?
MATTHEW. MATTHEW BLAND.
WELL, LET'S HIT IT, MATT. I'VE GOT A WEDDING TO RUIN...A BRIDE TO STRANGLE.
"The Kids"
THE DAY BEFORE
JOSEPH W. WILSON
EXECUTIVE VICE PRESIDENT
CORE POLICY GROUP
YOU MISSED YOUR DEADLINE, ÉTIENNE--
--WE TOLD YOU TO COME IN. YOU'VE BEEN COMPROMISED.
YES, I HEARD YOU. STOP MOMMYING ME.
YOU SHOULDN'T BE CALLING FROM JOSEPH'S PHONE.
ESPECIALLY GIVEN WHAT YOU'VE BEEN DOING WITH HIS FATHER.

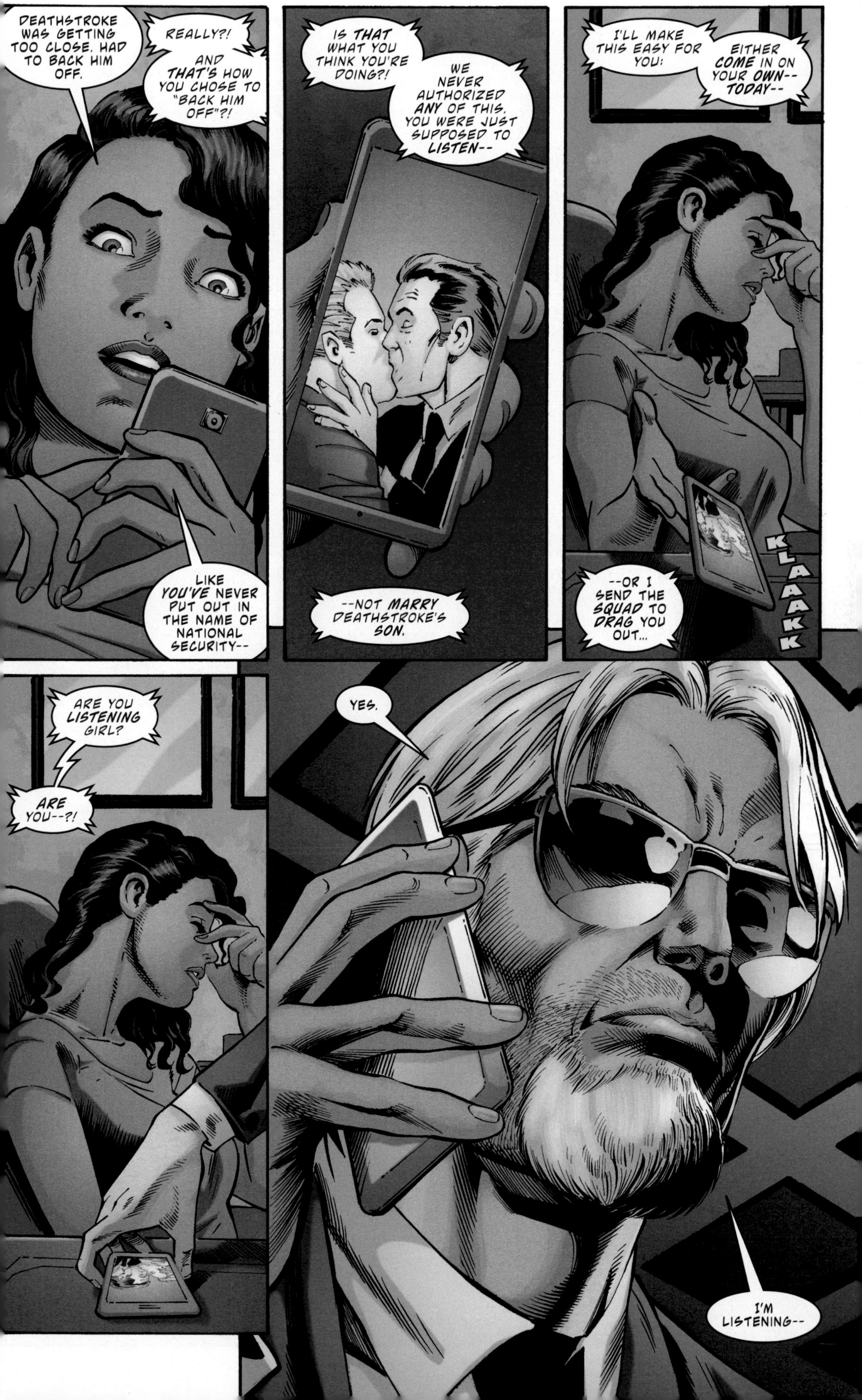
DEATHSTROKE WAS GETTING TOO CLOSE. HAD TO BACK HIM OFF.
REALLY?!
AND THAT'S HOW YOU CHOSE TO "BACK HIM OFF"?!
LIKE YOU'VE NEVER PUT OUT IN THE NAME OF NATIONAL SECURITY--
IS THAT WHAT YOU THINK YOU'RE DOING?!
WE NEVER AUTHORIZED ANY OF THIS. YOU WERE JUST SUPPOSED TO LISTEN--
--NOT MARRY DEATHSTROKE'S SON.
I'LL MAKE THIS EASY FOR YOU:
EITHER COME IN ON YOUR OWN--TODAY--
--OR I SEND THE SQUAD TO DRAG YOU OUT...
KLAAAKK
ARE YOU LISTENING GIRL?
ARE YOU--?!
YES.
I'M LISTENING--

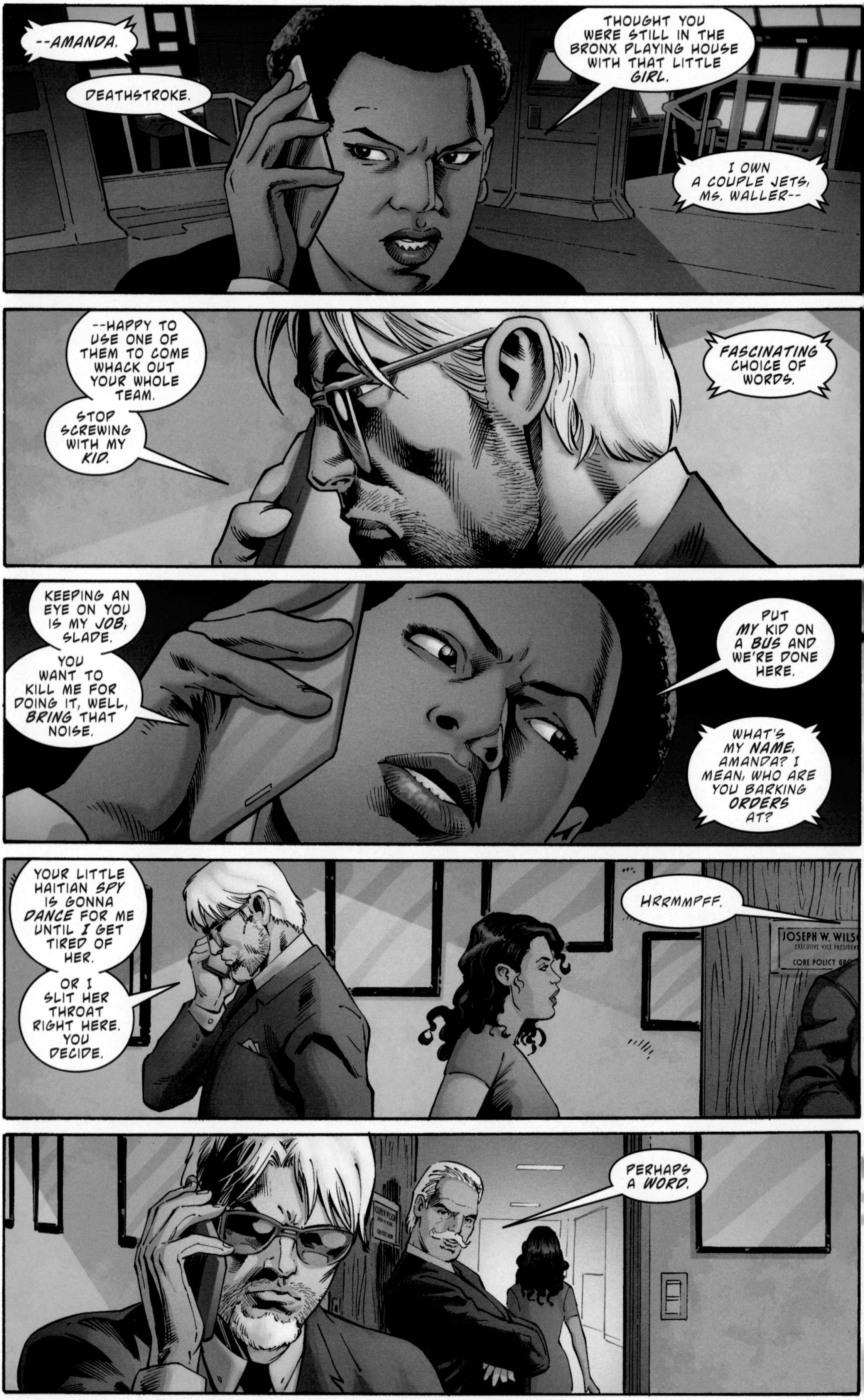
--AMANDA.
DEATHSTROKE.
THOUGHT YOU WERE STILL IN THE BRONX PLAYING HOUSE WITH THAT LITTLE GIRL.
I OWN A COUPLE JETS, MS. WALLER--
--HAPPY TO USE ONE OF THEM TO COME WHACK OUT YOUR WHOLE TEAM.
STOP SCREWING WITH MY KID.
FASCINATING CHOICE OF WORDS.
KEEPING AN EYE ON YOU IS MY JOB, SLADE.
YOU WANT TO KILL ME FOR DOING IT, WELL, BRING THAT NOISE.
PUT MY KID ON A BUS AND WE'RE DONE HERE.
WHAT'S MY NAME, AMANDA? I MEAN, WHO ARE YOU BARKING ORDERS AT?
YOUR LITTLE HAITIAN SPY IS GONNA DANCE FOR ME UNTIL I GET TIRED OF HER.
OR I SLIT HER THROAT RIGHT HERE. YOU DECIDE.
HRRMMPFF.
JOSEPH W. WILS
EXECUTIVE VICE PRESIDENT
CORE POLICY GRO
PERHAPS A WORD.

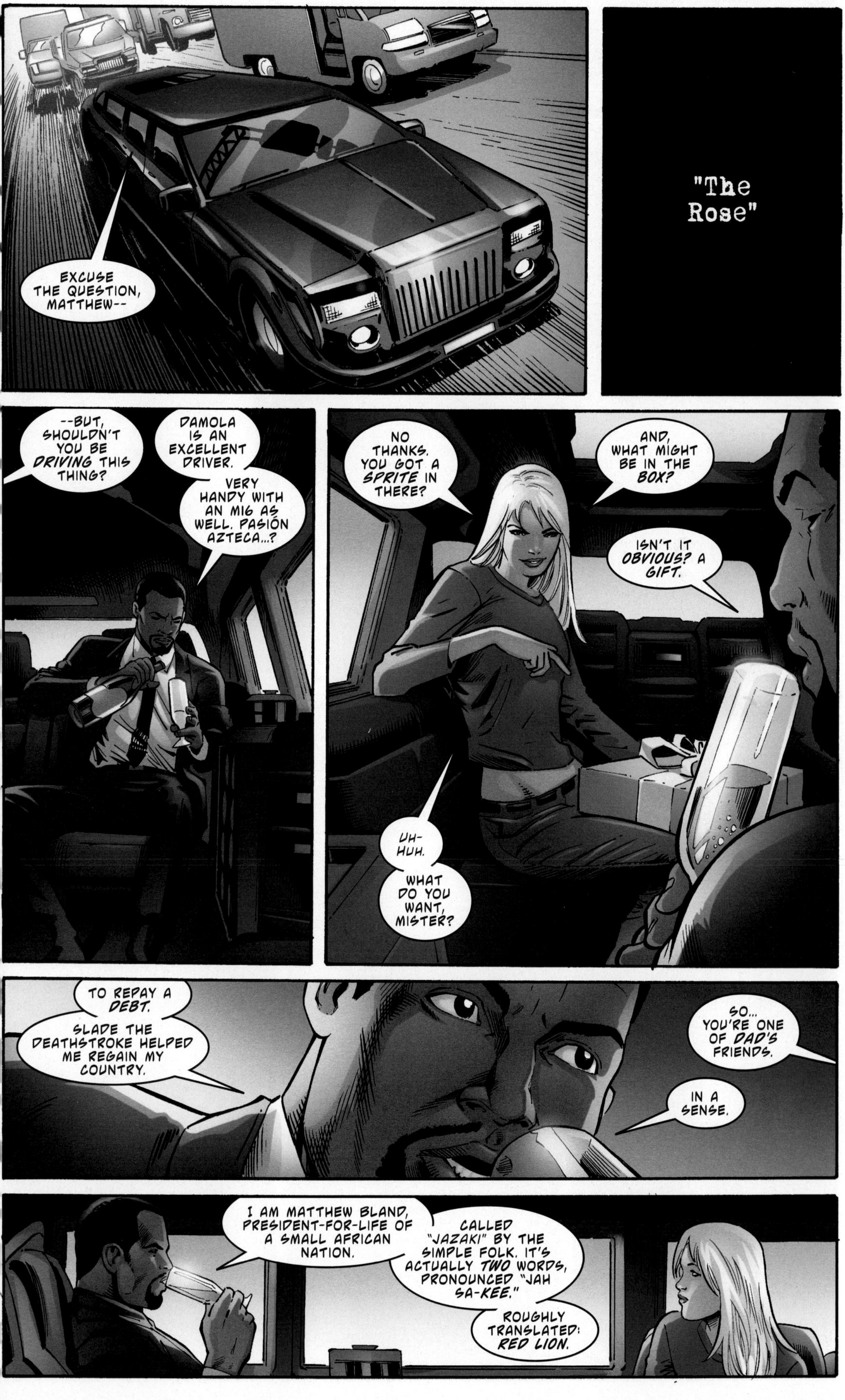
EXCUSE THE QUESTION, MATTHEW--
"The Rose"
--BUT, SHOULDN'T YOU BE DRIVING THIS THING?
DAMOLA IS AN EXCELLENT DRIVER.
VERY HANDY WITH AN MIG AS WELL. PASIÓN AZTECA...?
NO THANKS. YOU GOT A SPRITE IN THERE?
AND, WHAT MIGHT BE IN THE BOX?
ISN'T IT OBVIOUS? A GIFT.
UH-HUH.
WHAT DO YOU WANT, MISTER?
TO REPAY A DEBT.
SLADE THE DEATHSTROKE HELPED ME REGAIN MY COUNTRY.
SO... YOU'RE ONE OF DAD'S FRIENDS.
IN A SENSE.
I AM MATTHEW BLAND, PRESIDENT-FOR-LIFE OF A SMALL AFRICAN NATION.
CALLED "JAZAKI" BY THE SIMPLE FOLK. IT'S ACTUALLY TWO WORDS, PRONOUNCED "JAH SA-KEE."
ROUGHLY TRANSLATED: RED LION.

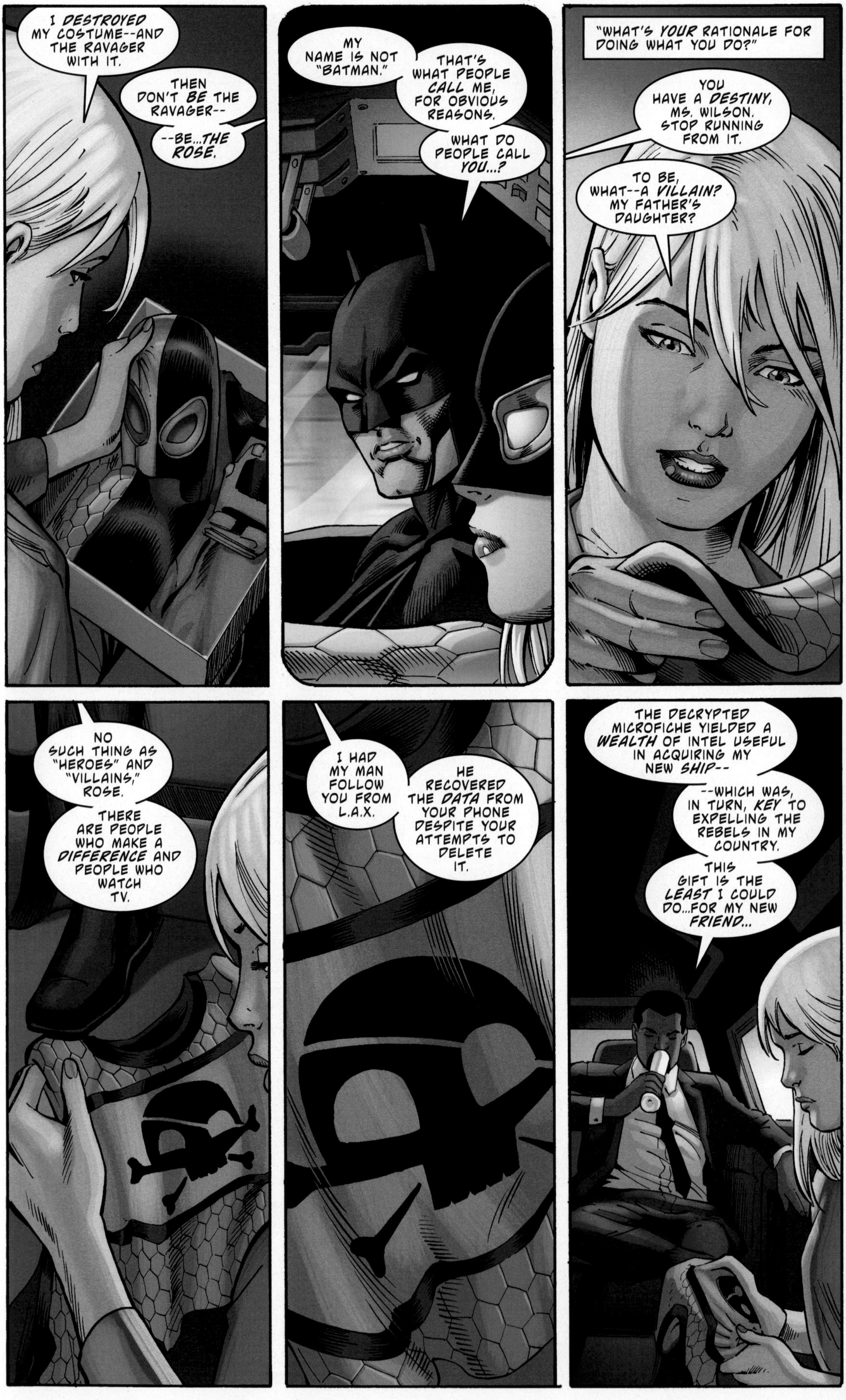
I DESTROYED MY COSTUME--AND THE RAVAGER WITH IT.
THEN DON'T BE THE RAVAGER--
--BE...THE ROSE.
MY NAME IS NOT "BATMAN."
THAT'S WHAT PEOPLE CALL ME, FOR OBVIOUS REASONS.
WHAT DO PEOPLE CALL YOU...?
"WHAT'S YOUR RATIONALE FOR DOING WHAT YOU DO?"
YOU HAVE A DESTINY, MS. WILSON. STOP RUNNING FROM IT.
TO BE, WHAT--A VILLAIN? MY FATHER'S DAUGHTER?
NO SUCH THING AS "HEROES" AND "VILLAINS," ROSE.
THERE ARE PEOPLE WHO MAKE A DIFFERENCE AND PEOPLE WHO WATCH TV.
I HAD MY MAN FOLLOW YOU FROM L.A.X.
HE RECOVERED THE DATA FROM YOUR PHONE DESPITE YOUR ATTEMPTS TO DELETE IT.
THE DECRYPTED MICROFICHE YIELDED A WEALTH OF INTEL USEFUL IN ACQUIRING MY NEW SHIP--
--WHICH WAS, IN TURN, KEY TO EXPELLING THE REBELS IN MY COUNTRY.
THIS GIFT IS THE LEAST I COULD DO...FOR MY NEW FRIEND...

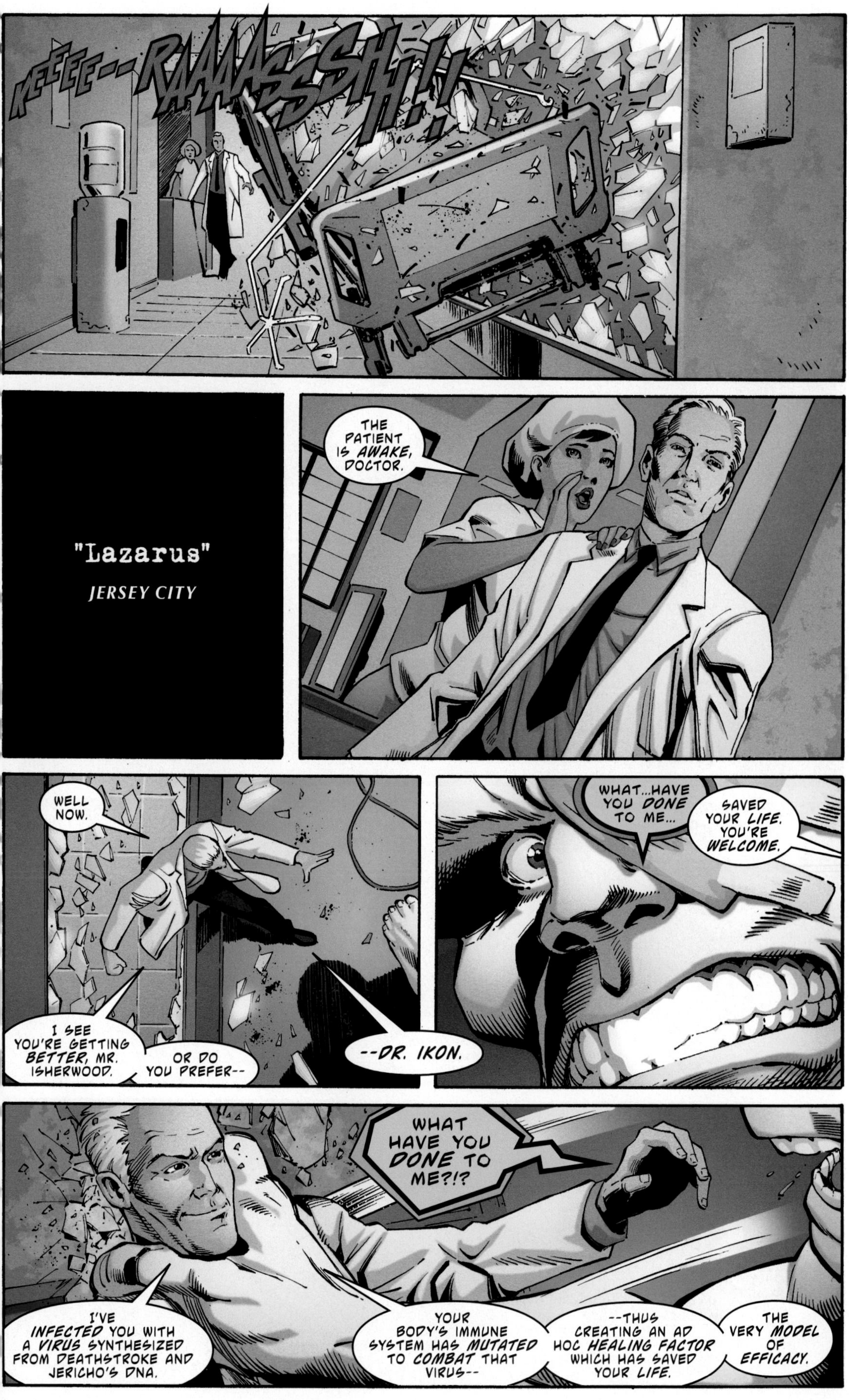
KEEEE--RAAAASSSH!!!
"Lazarus"
JERSEY CITY
THE PATIENT IS AWAKE, DOCTOR.
WELL NOW.
I SEE YOU'RE GETTING BETTER, MR. ISHERWOOD.
OR DO YOU PREFER--
--DR. IKON.
WHAT...HAVE YOU DONE TO ME...
SAVED YOUR LIFE. YOU'RE WELCOME.
WHAT HAVE YOU DONE TO ME?!?
I'VE INFECTED YOU WITH A VIRUS SYNTHESIZED FROM DEATHSTROKE AND JERICHO'S DNA.
YOUR BODY'S IMMUNE SYSTEM HAS MUTATED TO COMBAT THAT VIRUS--
--THUS CREATING AN AD HOC HEALING FACTOR WHICH HAS SAVED YOUR LIFE.
THE VERY MODEL OF EFFICACY.

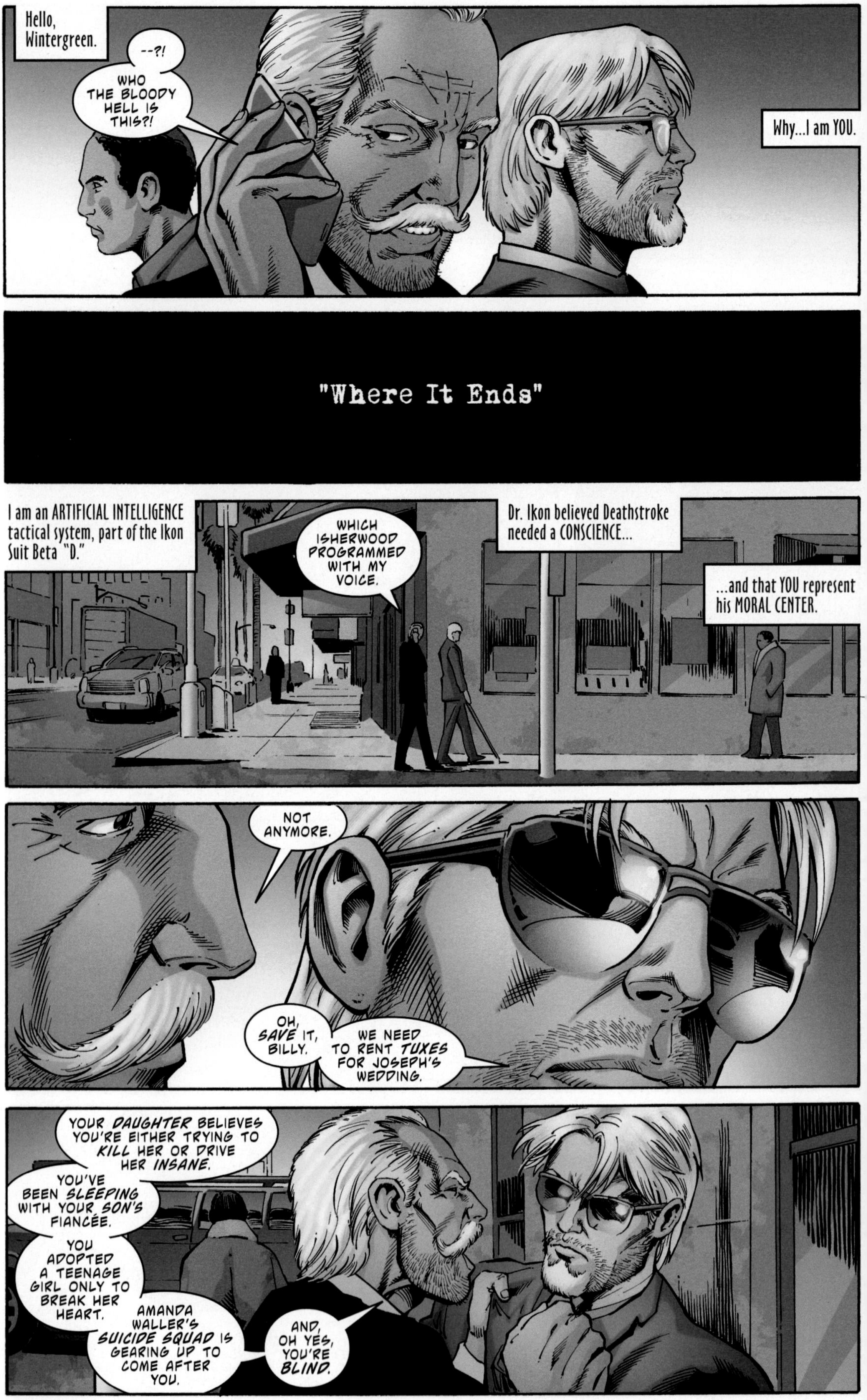
Hello, Wintergreen.
--?!
WHO THE BLOODY HELL IS THIS?!
Why...I am YOU.
"Where It Ends"
I am an ARTIFICIAL INTELLIGENCE tactical system, part of the Ikon Suit Beta "D."
WHICH ISHERWOOD PROGRAMMED WITH MY VOICE.
Dr. Ikon believed Deathstroke needed a CONSCIENCE...
...and that YOU represent his MORAL CENTER.
NOT ANYMORE.
OH, SAVE IT, BILLY.
WE NEED TO RENT TUXES FOR JOSEPH'S WEDDING.
YOUR DAUGHTER BELIEVES YOU'RE EITHER TRYING TO KILL HER OR DRIVE HER INSANE.
YOU'VE BEEN SLEEPING WITH YOUR SON'S FIANCÉE.
YOU ADOPTED A TEENAGE GIRL ONLY TO BREAK HER HEART.
AMANDA WALLER'S SUICIDE SQUAD IS GEARING UP TO COME AFTER YOU.
AND, OH YES, YOU'RE BLIND.

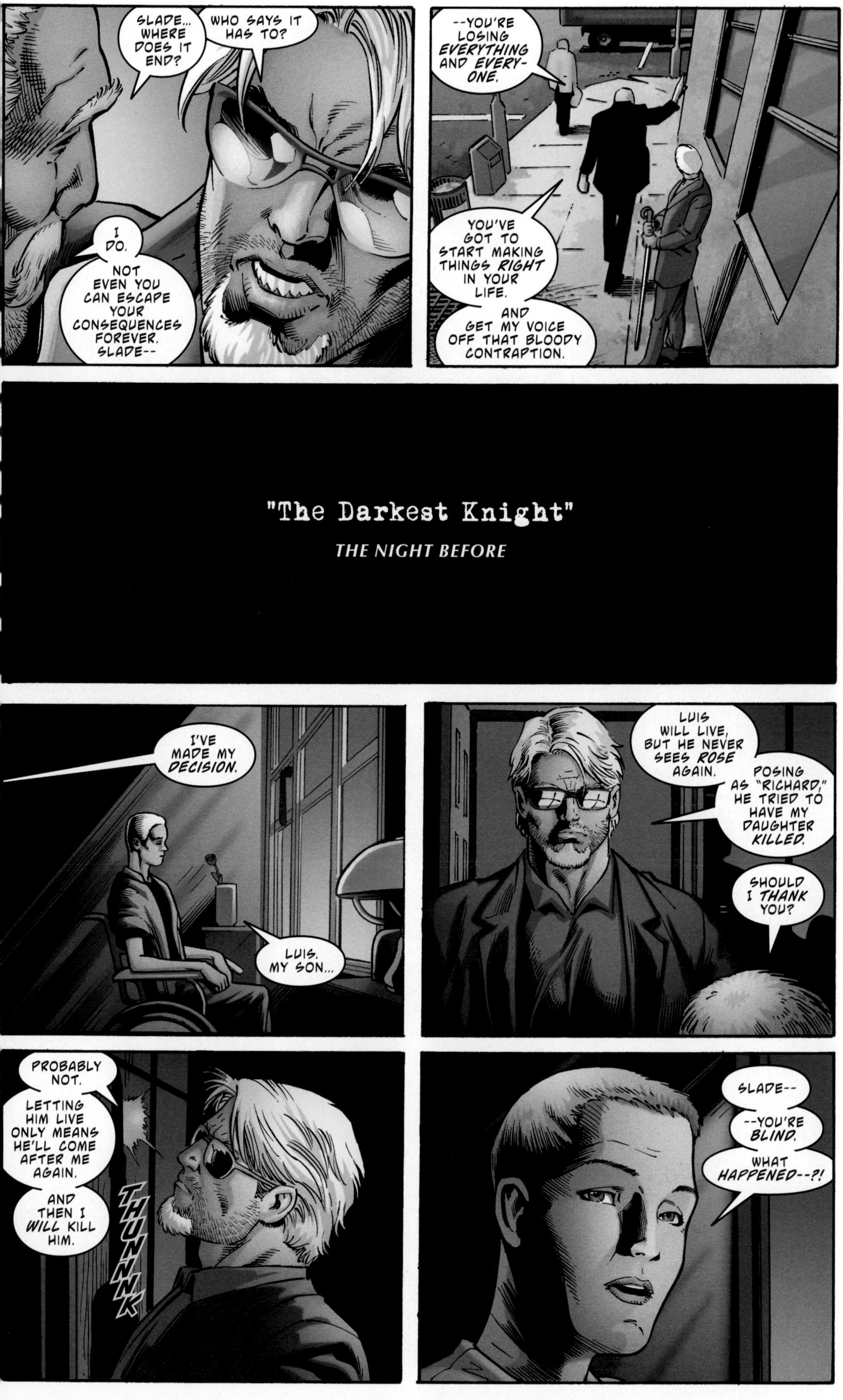
SLADE... WHERE DOES IT END?
WHO SAYS IT HAS TO?
I DO.
NOT EVEN YOU CAN ESCAPE YOUR CONSEQUENCES FOREVER, SLADE--
--YOU'RE LOSING EVERYTHING AND EVERY-ONE.
YOU'VE GOT TO START MAKING THINGS RIGHT IN YOUR LIFE.
AND GET MY VOICE OFF THAT BLOODY CONTRAPTION.
"The Darkest Knight"
THE NIGHT BEFORE
I'VE MADE MY DECISION.
LUIS. MY SON...
LUIS WILL LIVE, BUT HE NEVER SEES ROSE AGAIN.
POSING AS "RICHARD," HE TRIED TO HAVE MY DAUGHTER KILLED.
SHOULD I THANK YOU?
PROBABLY NOT.
LETTING HIM LIVE ONLY MEANS HE'LL COME AFTER ME AGAIN.
AND THEN I WILL KILL HIM.
THUNNNK
SLADE--
--YOU'RE BLIND.
WHAT HAPPENED--?!

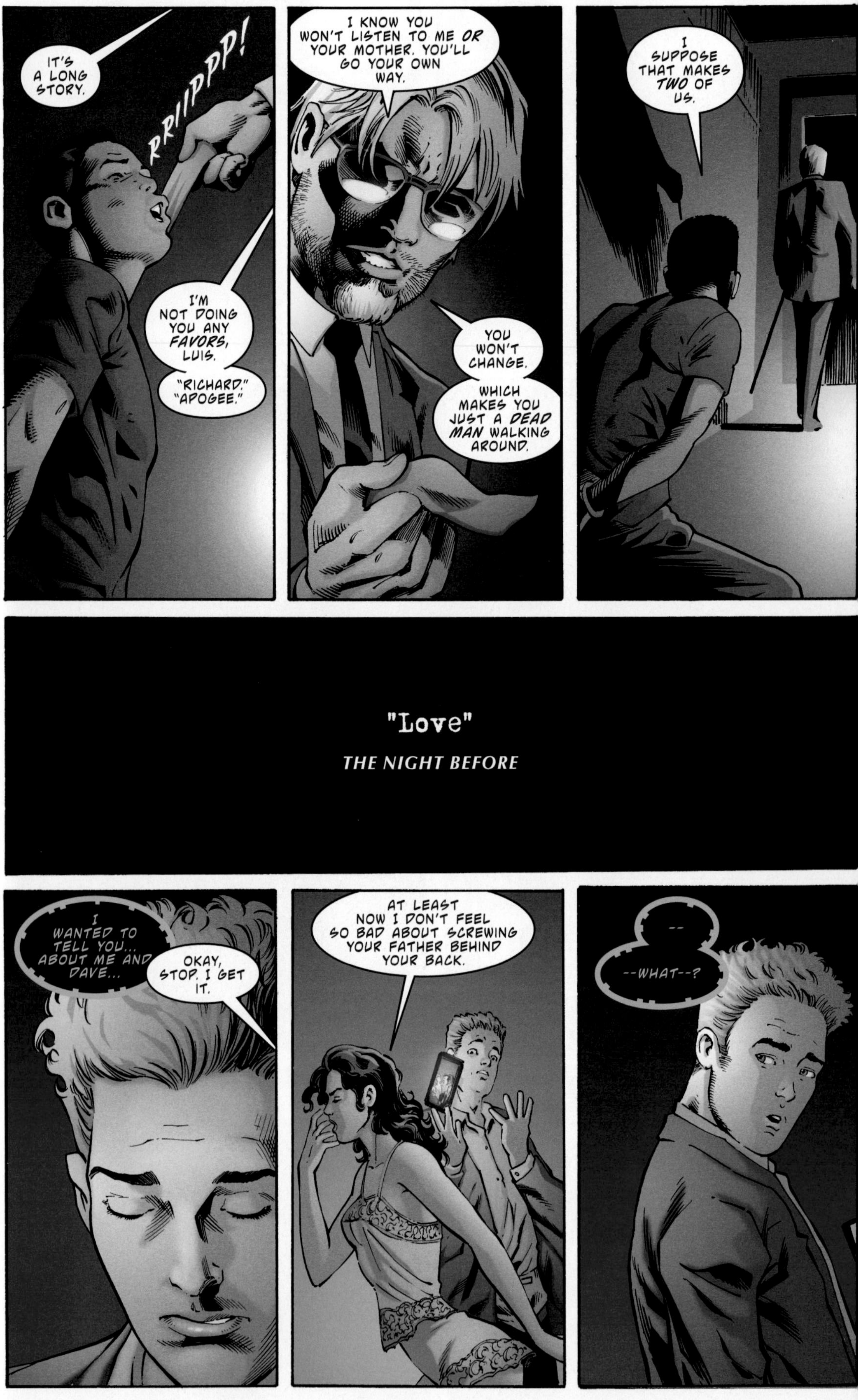
IT'S A LONG STORY.
RRIIPPP!
I'M NOT DOING YOU ANY *FAVORS*, LUIS.
"RICHARD." "APOGEE."
I KNOW YOU WON'T LISTEN TO ME *OR* YOUR MOTHER. YOU'LL GO YOUR OWN WAY.
YOU WON'T CHANGE.
WHICH MAKES YOU JUST A *DEAD MAN* WALKING AROUND.
I SUPPOSE THAT MAKES *TWO* OF US.
"Love"
*THE NIGHT BEFORE*
I WANTED TO TELL YOU... ABOUT ME AND DAVE...
OKAY, STOP. I GET IT.
AT LEAST NOW I DON'T FEEL SO BAD ABOUT SCREWING YOUR FATHER BEHIND YOUR BACK.
--
--WHAT--?

"Wedding Day"

*THE MORNING OF*

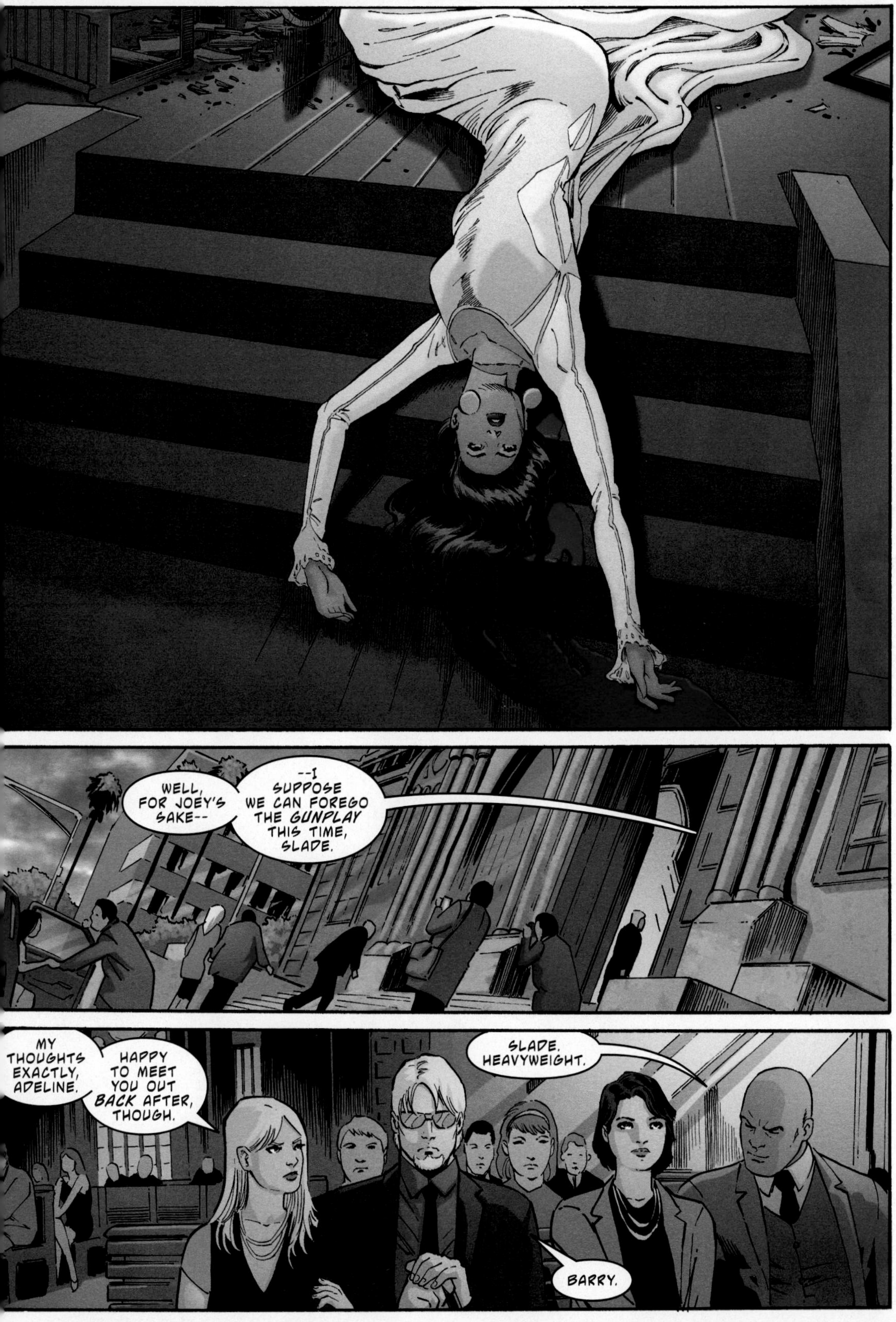
WELL, FOR JOEY'S SAKE--
--I SUPPOSE WE CAN FOREGO THE *GUNPLAY* THIS TIME, SLADE.
MY THOUGHTS EXACTLY, ADELINE.
HAPPY TO MEET YOU OUT *BACK* AFTER, THOUGH.
SLADE. HEAVYWEIGHT.
BARRY.

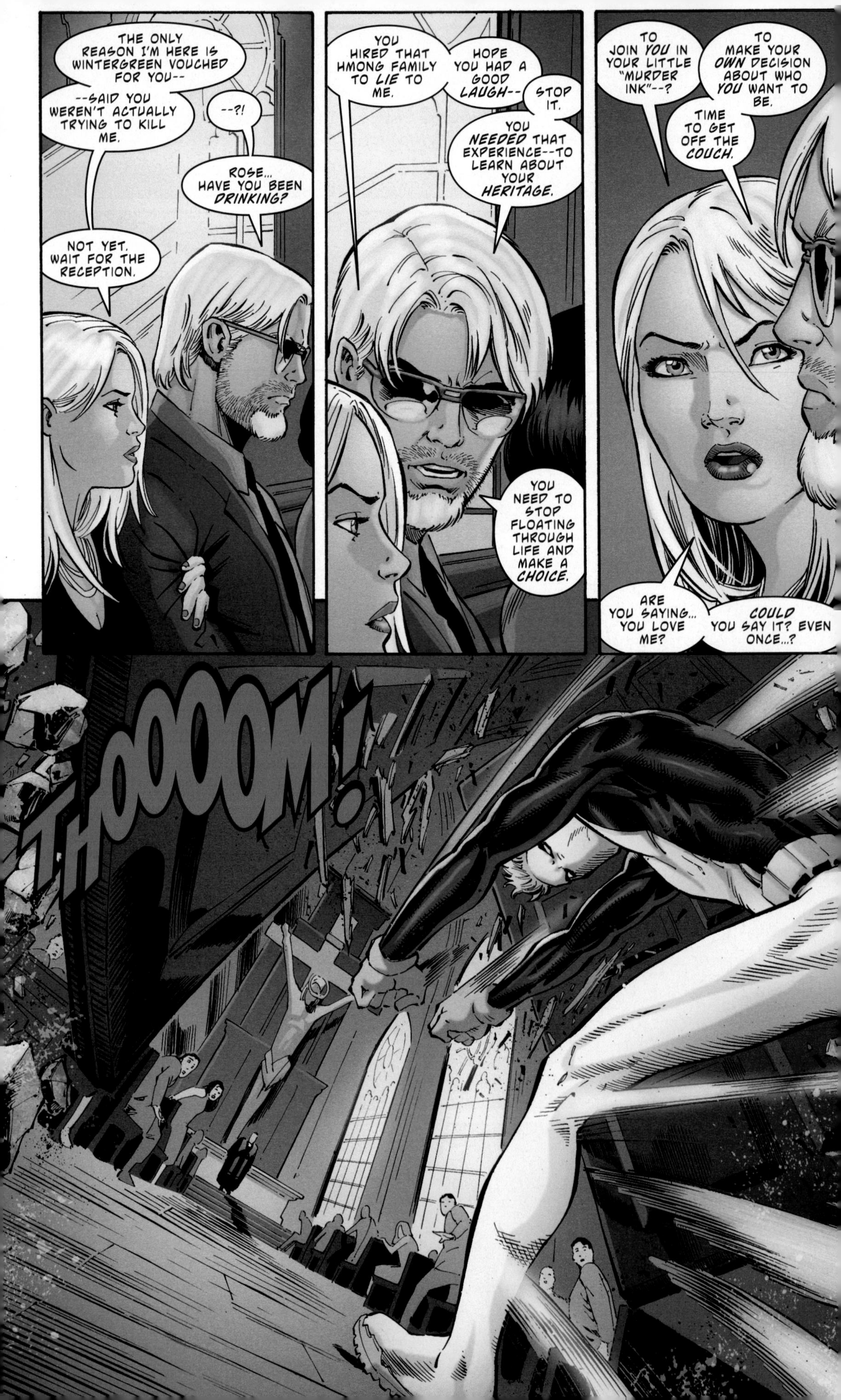
THE ONLY REASON I'M HERE IS WINTERGREEN VOUCHED FOR YOU--
--SAID YOU WEREN'T ACTUALLY TRYING TO KILL ME.
--?!
ROSE... HAVE YOU BEEN DRINKING?
NOT YET. WAIT FOR THE RECEPTION.
YOU HIRED THAT HMONG FAMILY TO LIE TO ME.
HOPE YOU HAD A GOOD LAUGH--
STOP IT.
YOU NEEDED THAT EXPERIENCE--TO LEARN ABOUT YOUR HERITAGE.
YOU NEED TO STOP FLOATING THROUGH LIFE AND MAKE A CHOICE.
TO JOIN YOU IN YOUR LITTLE "MURDER INK"--?
TO MAKE YOUR OWN DECISION ABOUT WHO YOU WANT TO BE.
TIME TO GET OFF THE COUCH.
ARE YOU SAYING... YOU LOVE ME?
COULD YOU SAY IT? EVEN ONCE...?
THOOOOM!

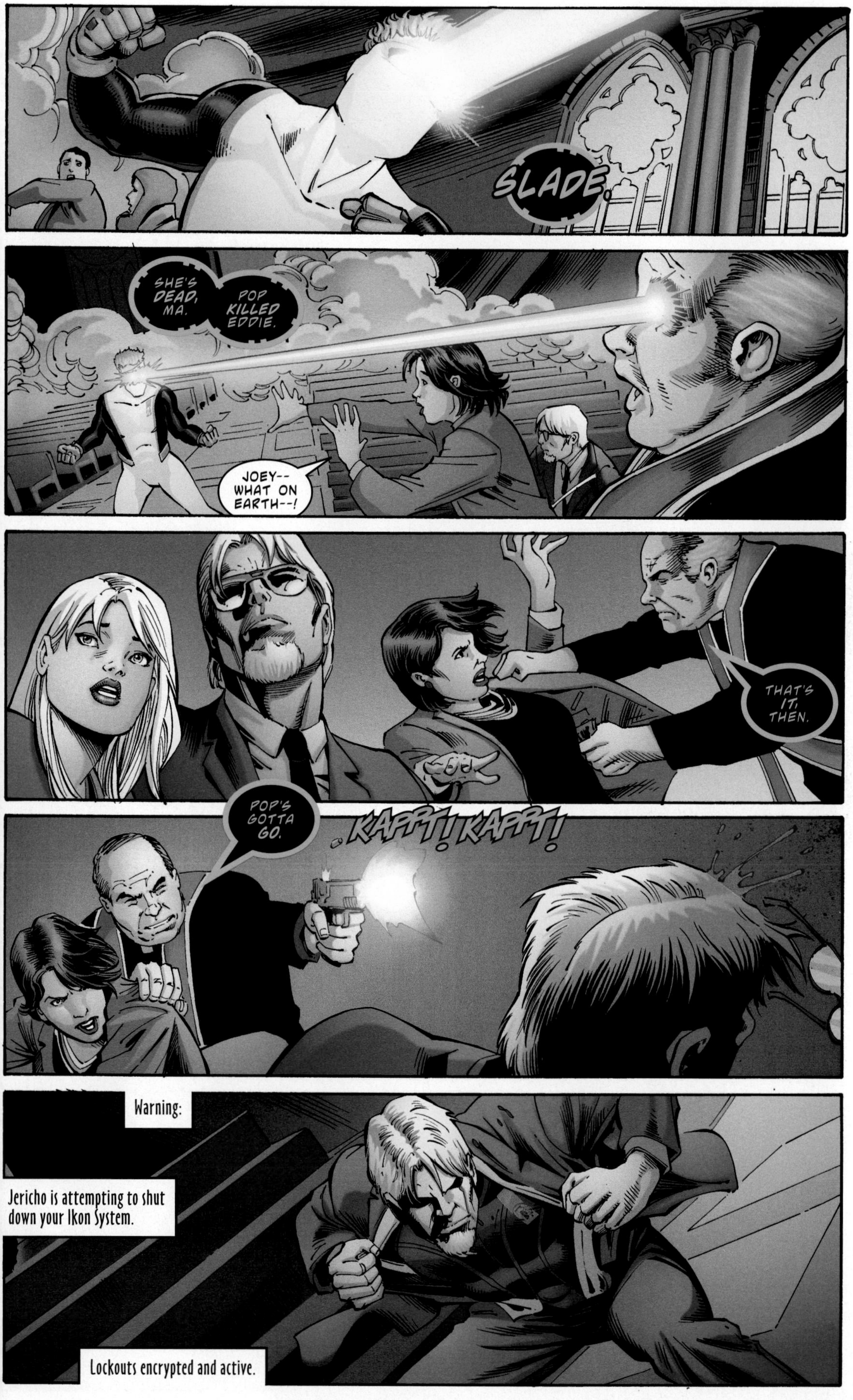
SLADE.
SHE'S DEAD, MA.
POP KILLED EDDIE.
JOEY-- WHAT ON EARTH--!
THAT'S IT, THEN.
POP'S GOTTA GO.
KAPPT! KAPPT!
Warning:
Jericho is attempting to shut down your Ikon System.
Lockouts encrypted and active.

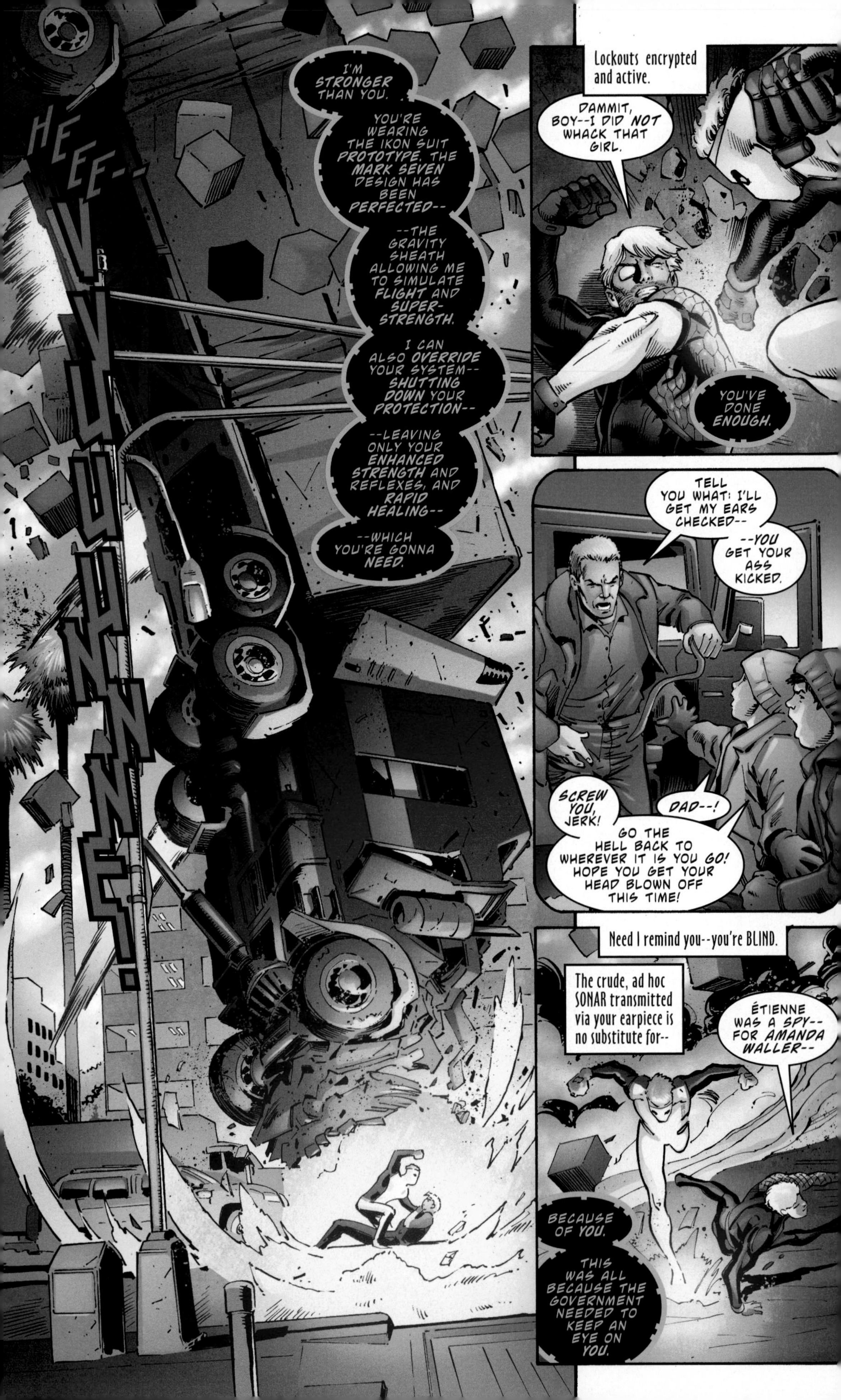

I'M STRONGER THAN YOU.
YOU'RE WEARING THE IKON SUIT PROTOTYPE. THE MARK SEVEN DESIGN HAS BEEN PERFECTED--
--THE GRAVITY SHEATH ALLOWING ME TO SIMULATE FLIGHT AND SUPER-STRENGTH.
I CAN ALSO OVERRIDE YOUR SYSTEM--SHUTTING DOWN YOUR PROTECTION--
--LEAVING ONLY YOUR ENHANCED STRENGTH AND REFLEXES, AND RAPID HEALING--
--WHICH YOU'RE GONNA NEED.
HEEE--VVUUHHNNE!
Lockouts encrypted and active.
DAMMIT, BOY--I DID NOT WHACK THAT GIRL.
YOU'VE DONE ENOUGH.
TELL YOU WHAT: I'LL GET MY EARS CHECKED--
--YOU GET YOUR ASS KICKED.
SCREW YOU, JERK!
DAD--!
GO THE HELL BACK TO WHEREVER IT IS YOU GO! HOPE YOU GET YOUR HEAD BLOWN OFF THIS TIME!
Need I remind you--you're BLIND.
The crude, ad hoc SONAR transmitted via your earpiece is no substitute for--
ÉTIENNE WAS A SPY--FOR AMANDA WALLER--
BECAUSE OF YOU.
THIS WAS ALL BECAUSE THE GOVERNMENT NEEDED TO KEEP AN EYE ON YOU.

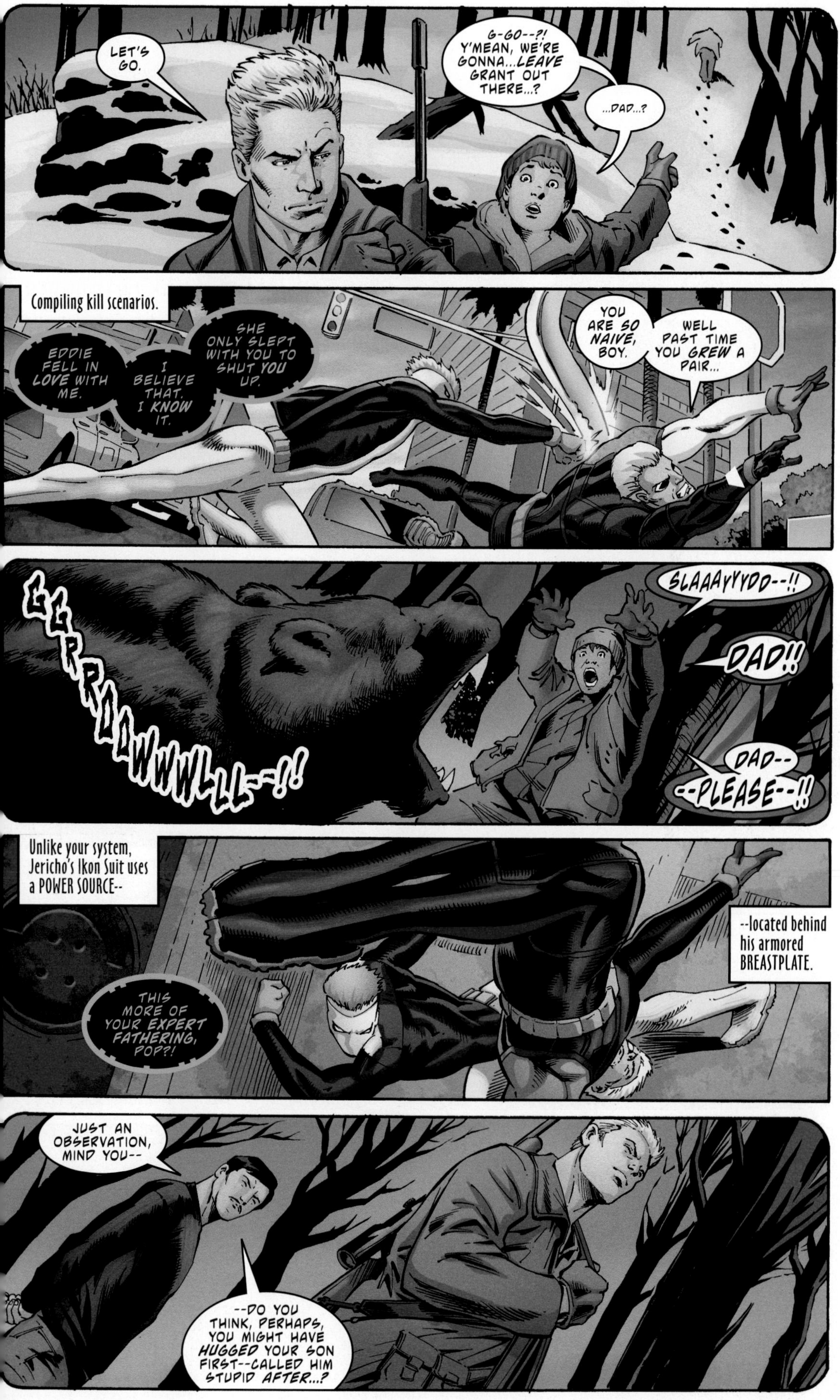
LET'S GO.
G-GO--?! Y'MEAN, WE'RE GONNA...LEAVE GRANT OUT THERE...?
...DAD...?
Compiling kill scenarios.
EDDIE FELL IN LOVE WITH ME.
I BELIEVE THAT. I KNOW IT.
SHE ONLY SLEPT WITH YOU TO SHUT YOU UP.
YOU ARE SO NAIVE, BOY.
WELL PAST TIME YOU GREW A PAIR...
GGRRAAOWWWLLL--!!
SLAAAYYYDD--!!
DAD!!
DAD--
--PLEASE--!!
Unlike your system, Jericho's Ikon Suit uses a POWER SOURCE--
--located behind his armored BREASTPLATE.
THIS MORE OF YOUR EXPERT FATHERING, POP?!
JUST AN OBSERVATION, MIND YOU--
--DO YOU THINK, PERHAPS, YOU MIGHT HAVE HUGGED YOUR SON FIRST--CALLED HIM STUPID AFTER...?

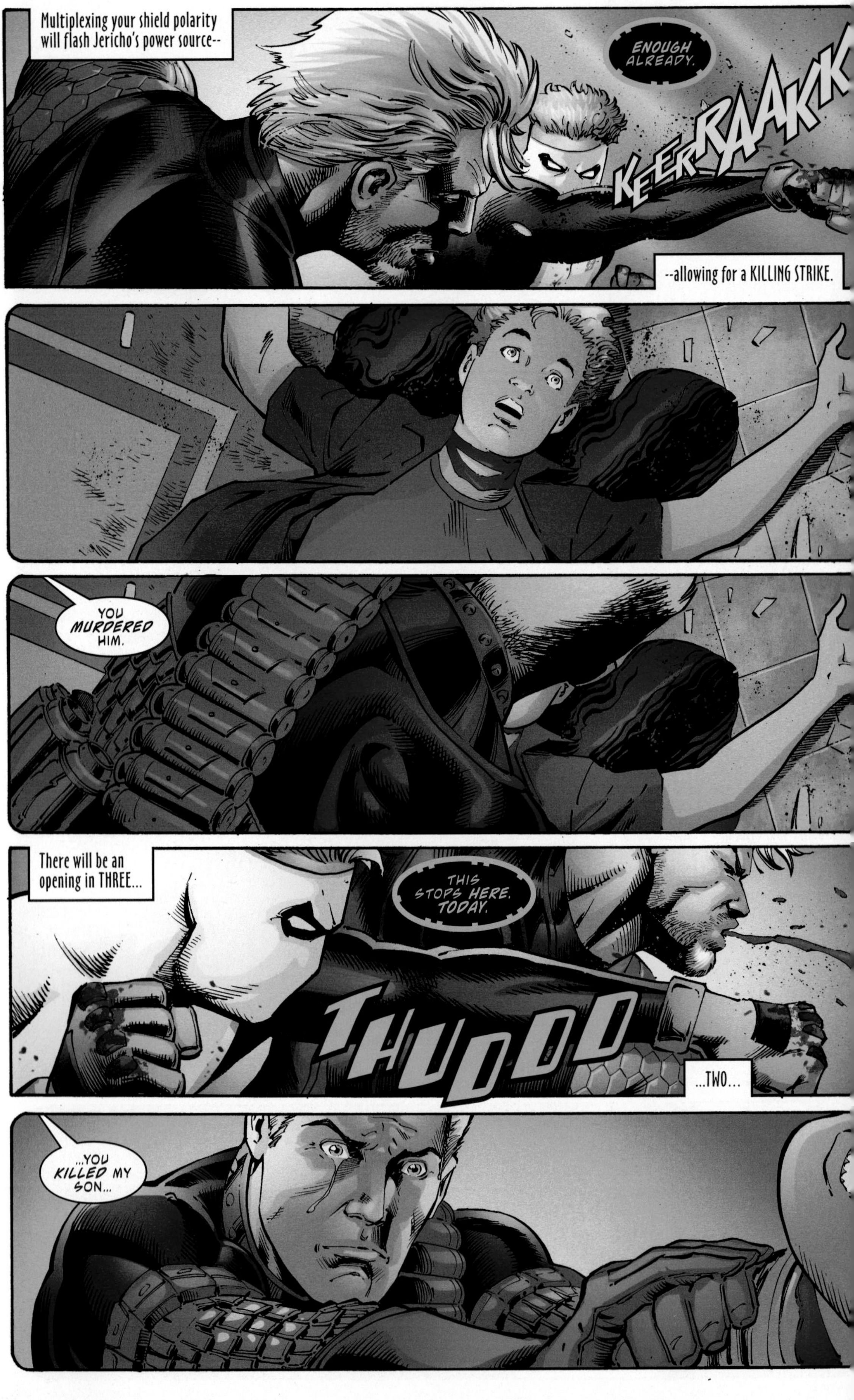
Multiplexing your shield polarity will flash Jericho's power source--
ENOUGH ALREADY.
KEERRAAKK
--allowing for a KILLING STRIKE.
YOU MURDERED HIM.
There will be an opening in THREE...
THIS STOPS HERE. TODAY.
THUDDD
...TWO...
...YOU KILLED MY SON...

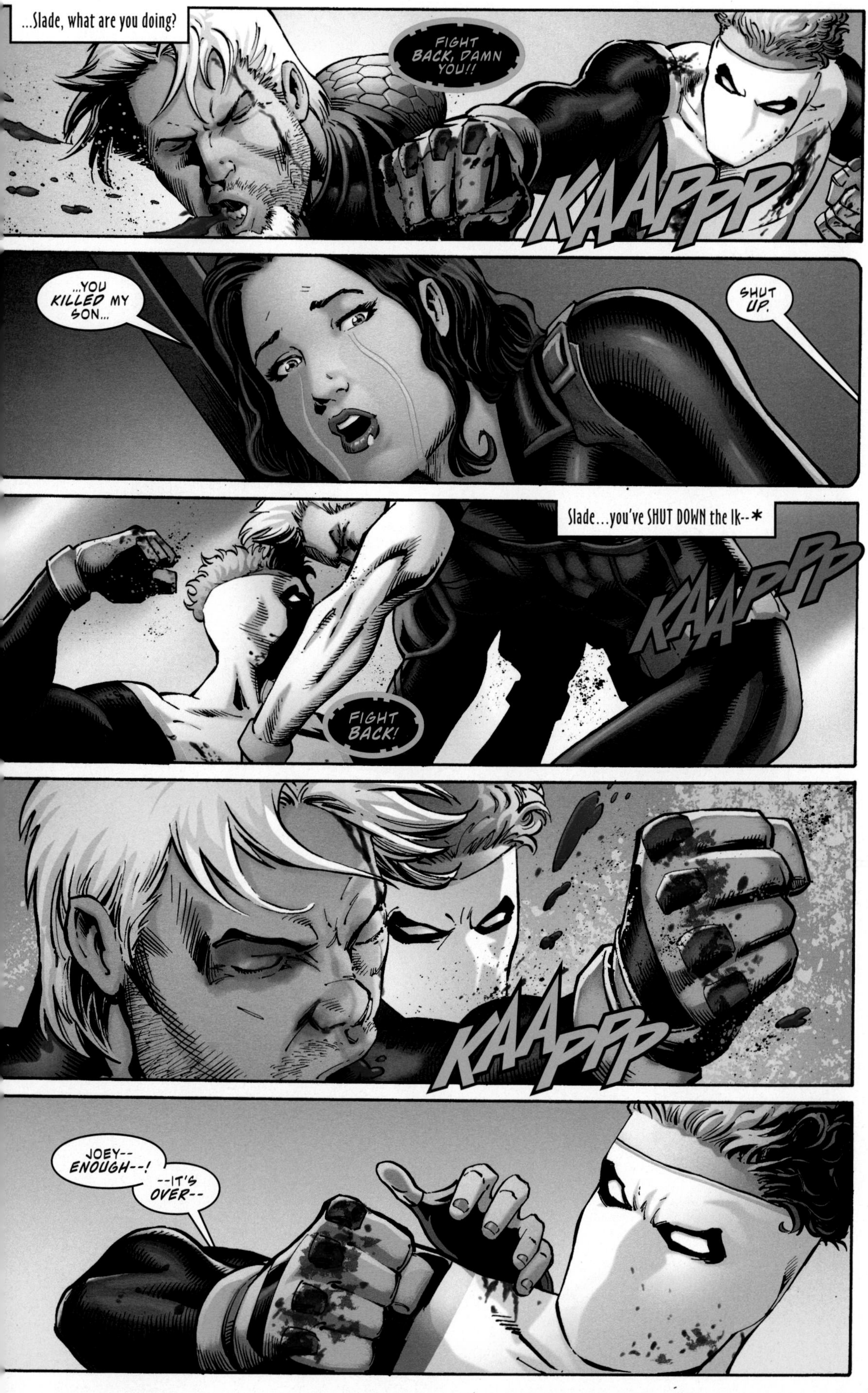

...Slade, what are you doing?
FIGHT BACK, DAMN YOU!!
KAAPPP
...YOU KILLED MY SON...
SHUT UP.
Slade...you've SHUT DOWN the Ik--*
KAAPPP
FIGHT BACK!
KAAPPP
JOEY-- ENOUGH--!
--IT'S OVER--

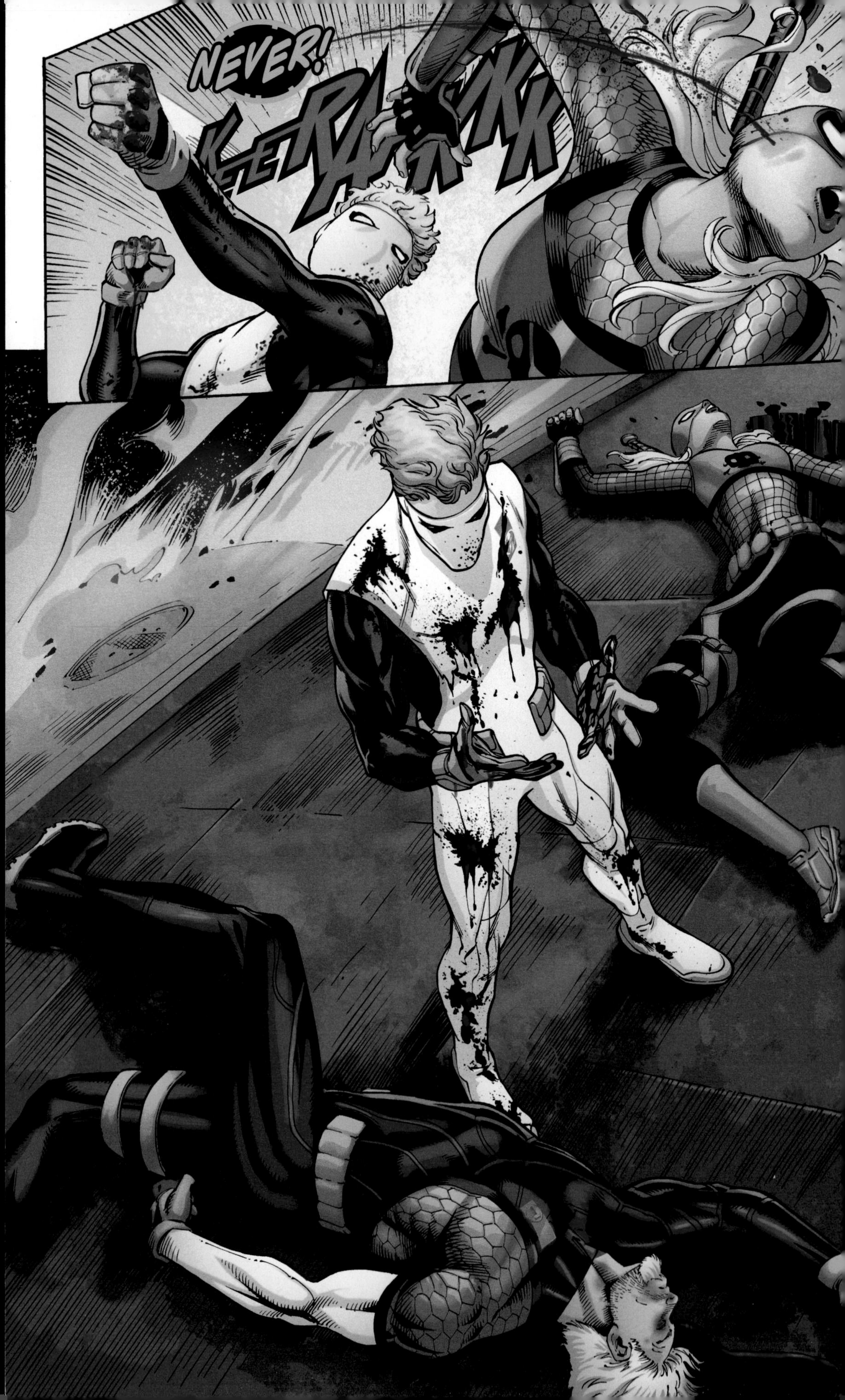
NEVER!

# DEATHSTROKE

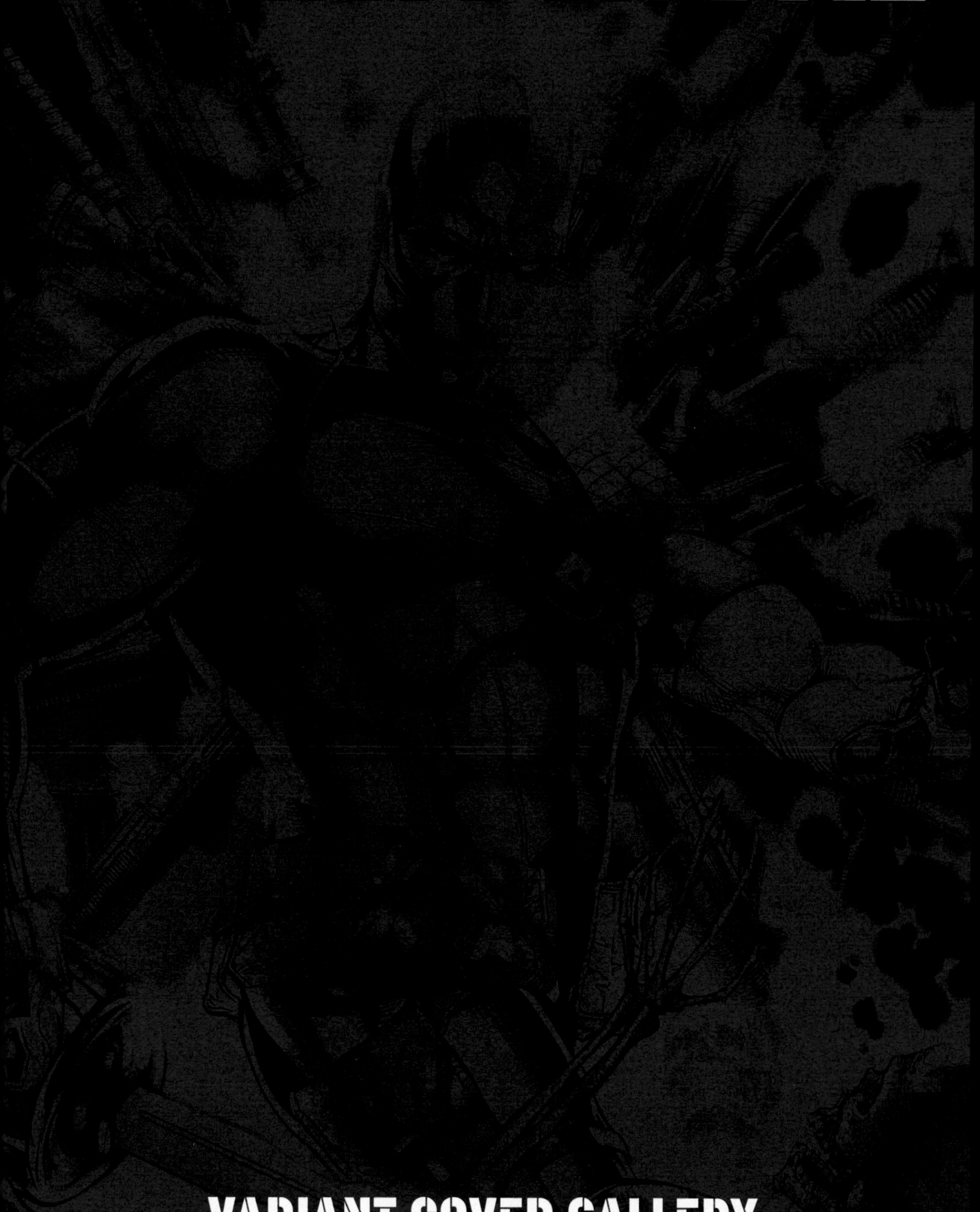

## VARIANT COVER GALLERY

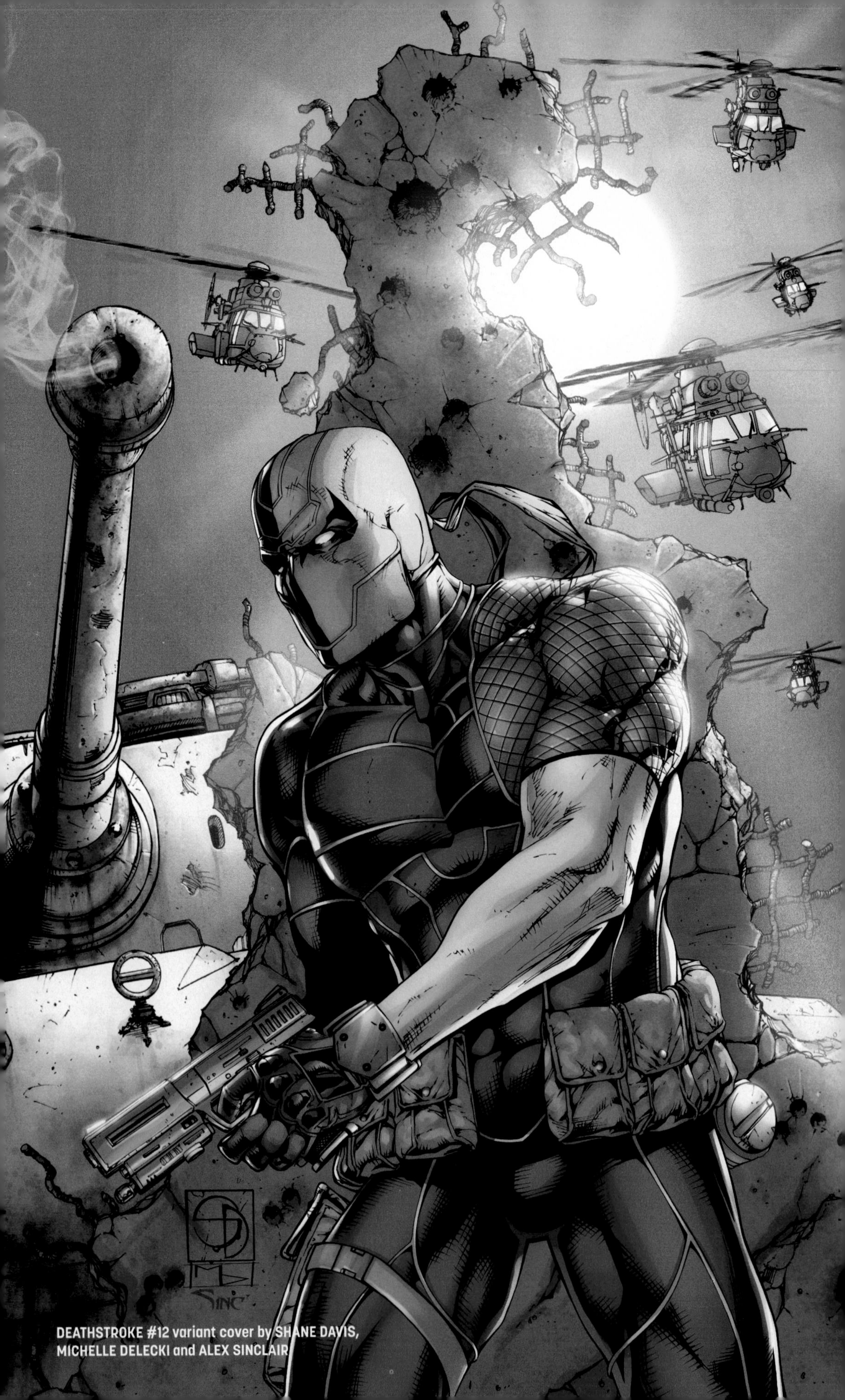

DEATHSTROKE #12 variant cover by SHANE DAVIS, MICHELLE DELECKI and ALEX SINCLAIR

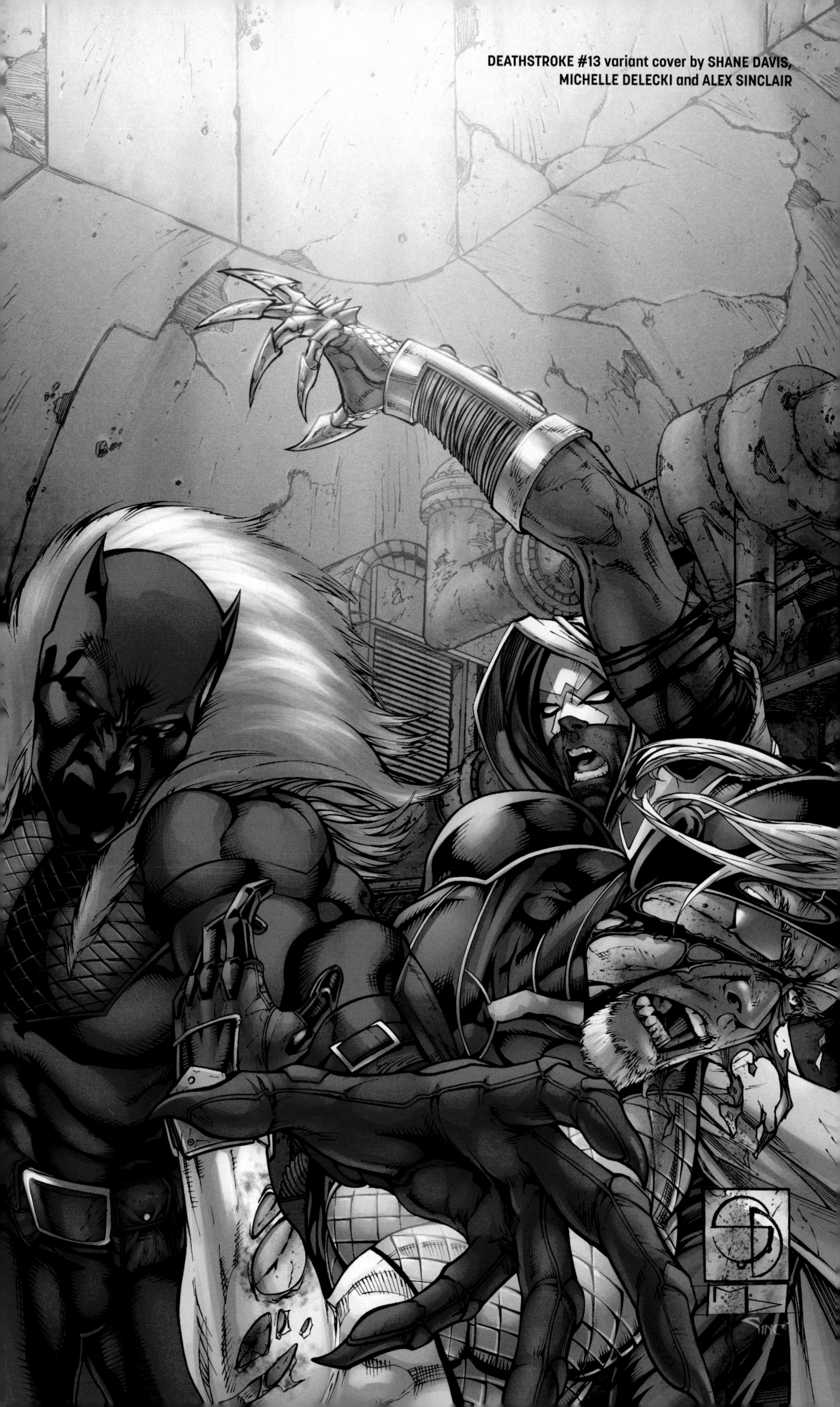

DEATHSTROKE #13 variant cover by SHANE DAVIS,
MICHELLE DELECKI and ALEX SINCLAIR

DEATHSTROKE #14 variant cover by SHANE DAVIS, MICHELLE DELECKI and ALEX SINCLAIR

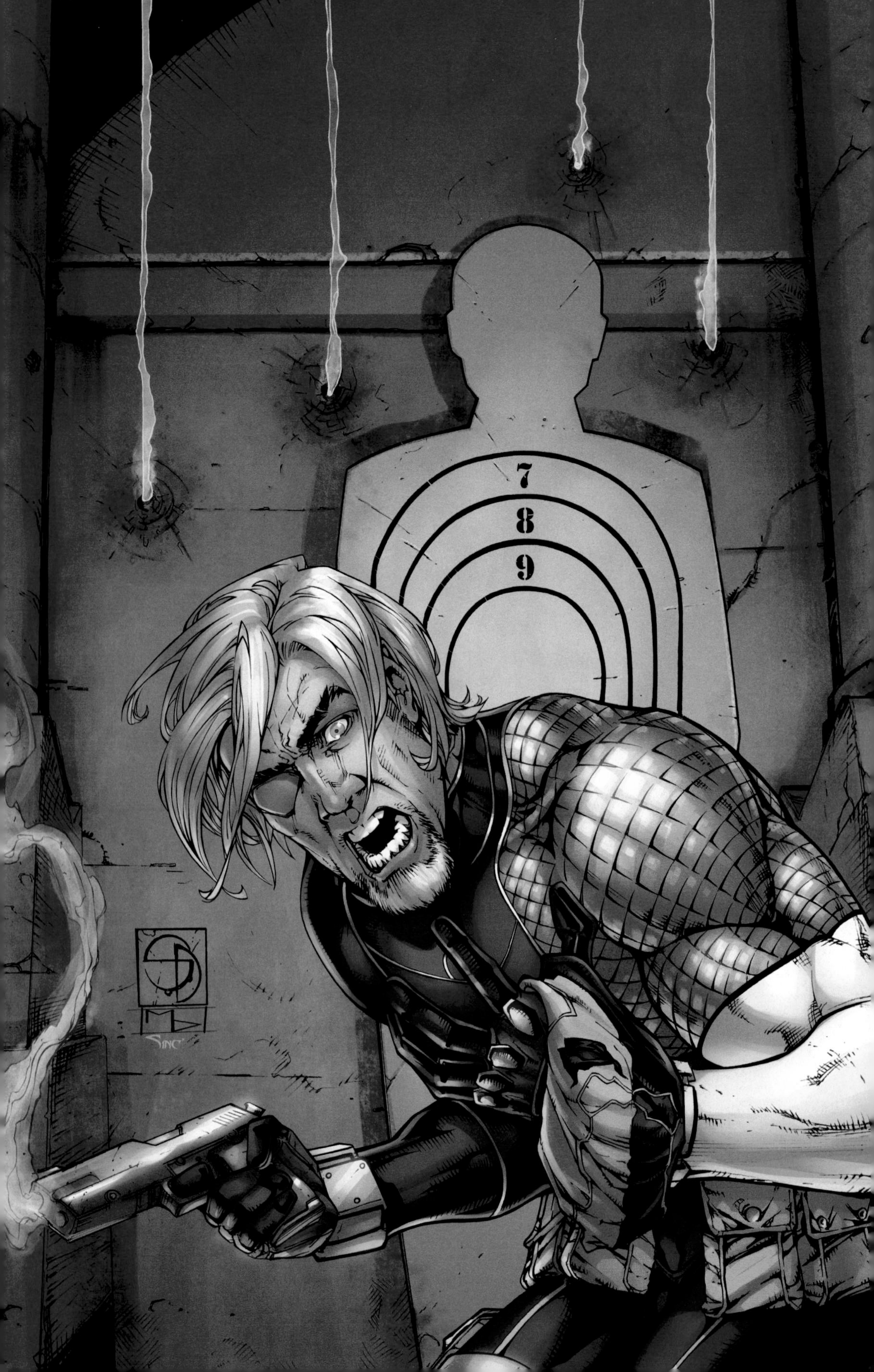

7
8
9

DEATHSTROKE #15 variant cover by SHANE DAVIS,
MICHELLE DELECKI and ALEX SINCLAIR

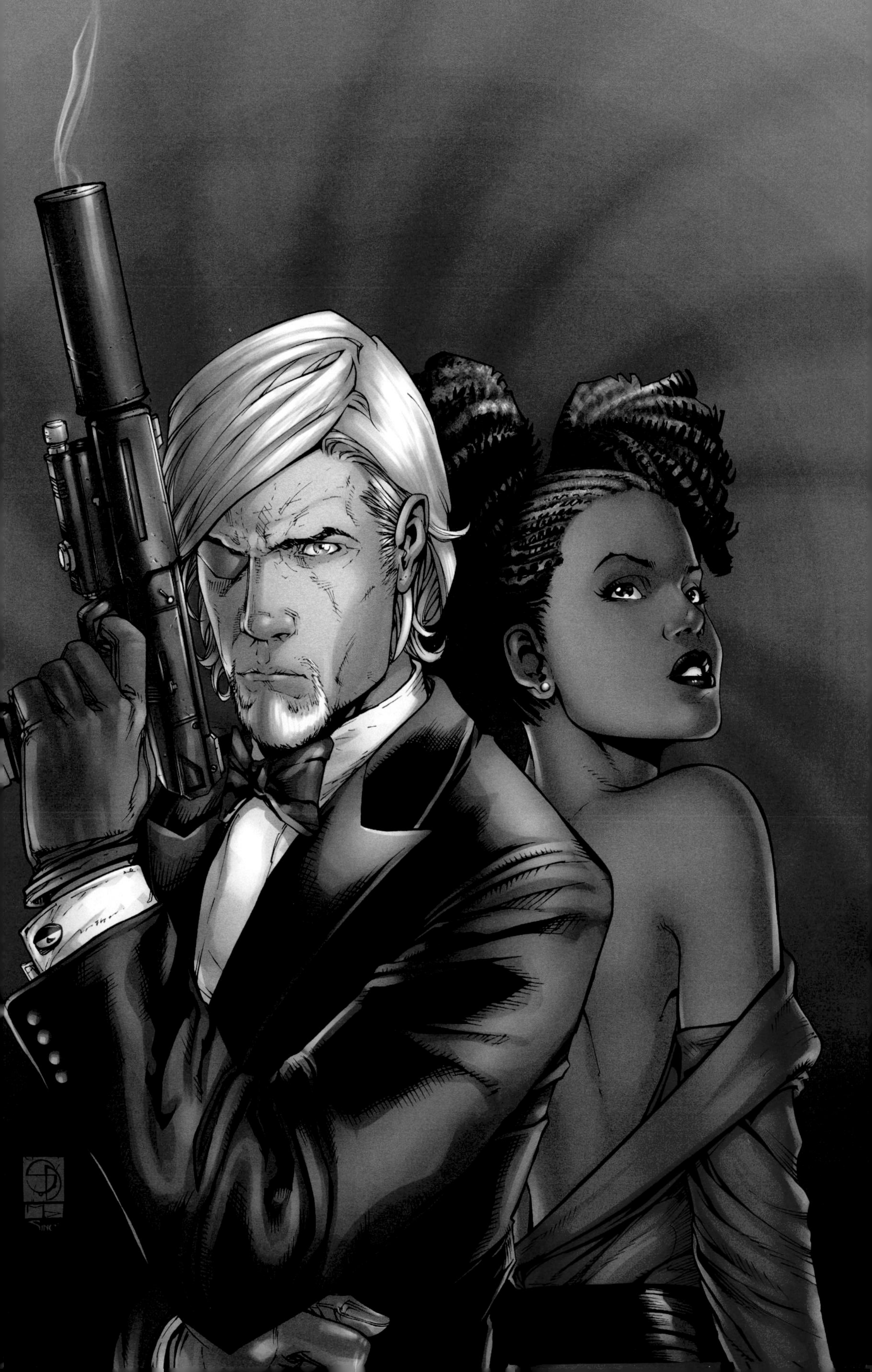

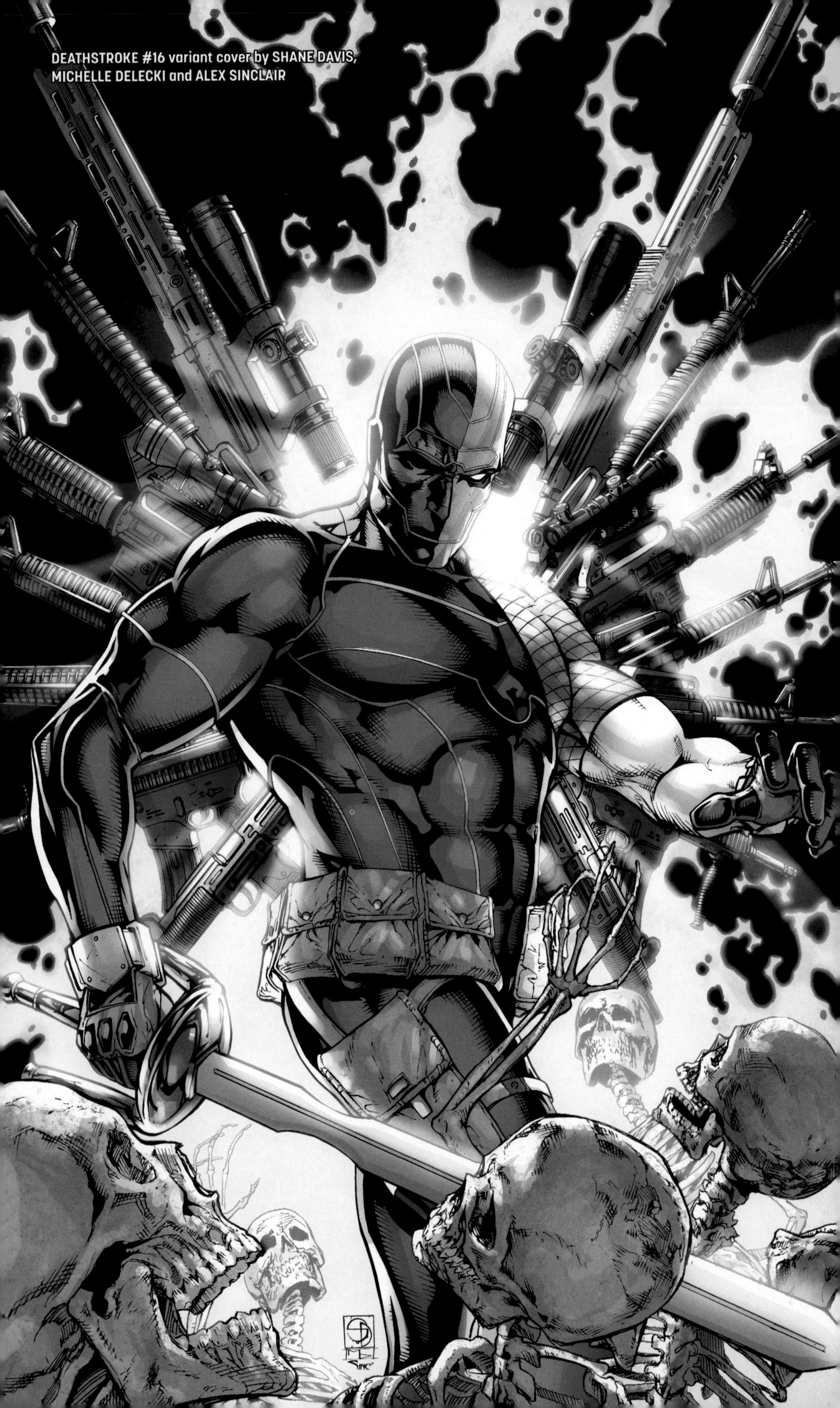

DEATHSTROKE #16 variant cover by SHANE DAVIS, MICHELLE DELECKI and ALEX SINCLAIR

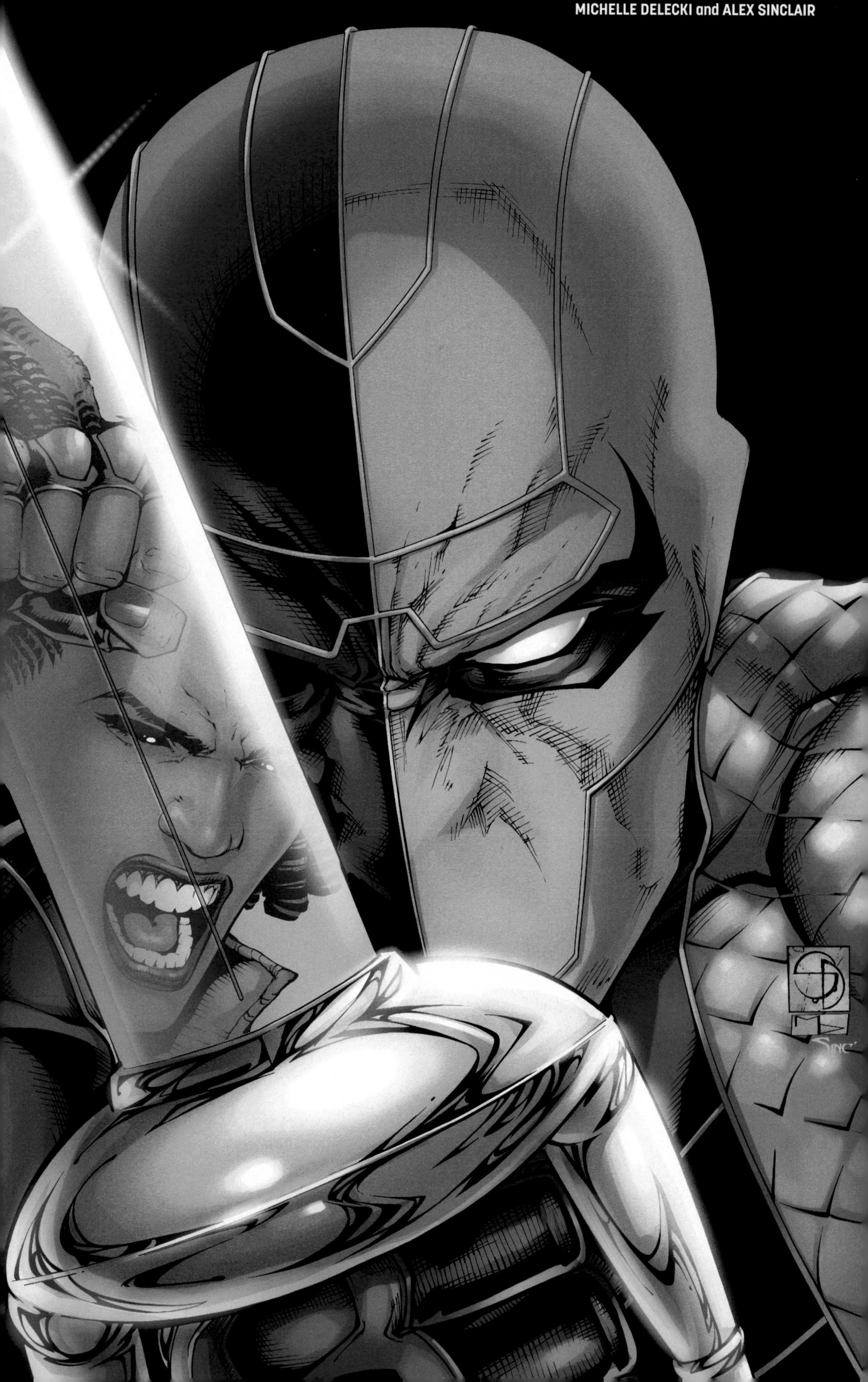

DEATHSTROKE #17 variant cover by SHANE DAVIS,
MICHELLE DELECKI and ALEX SINCLAIR

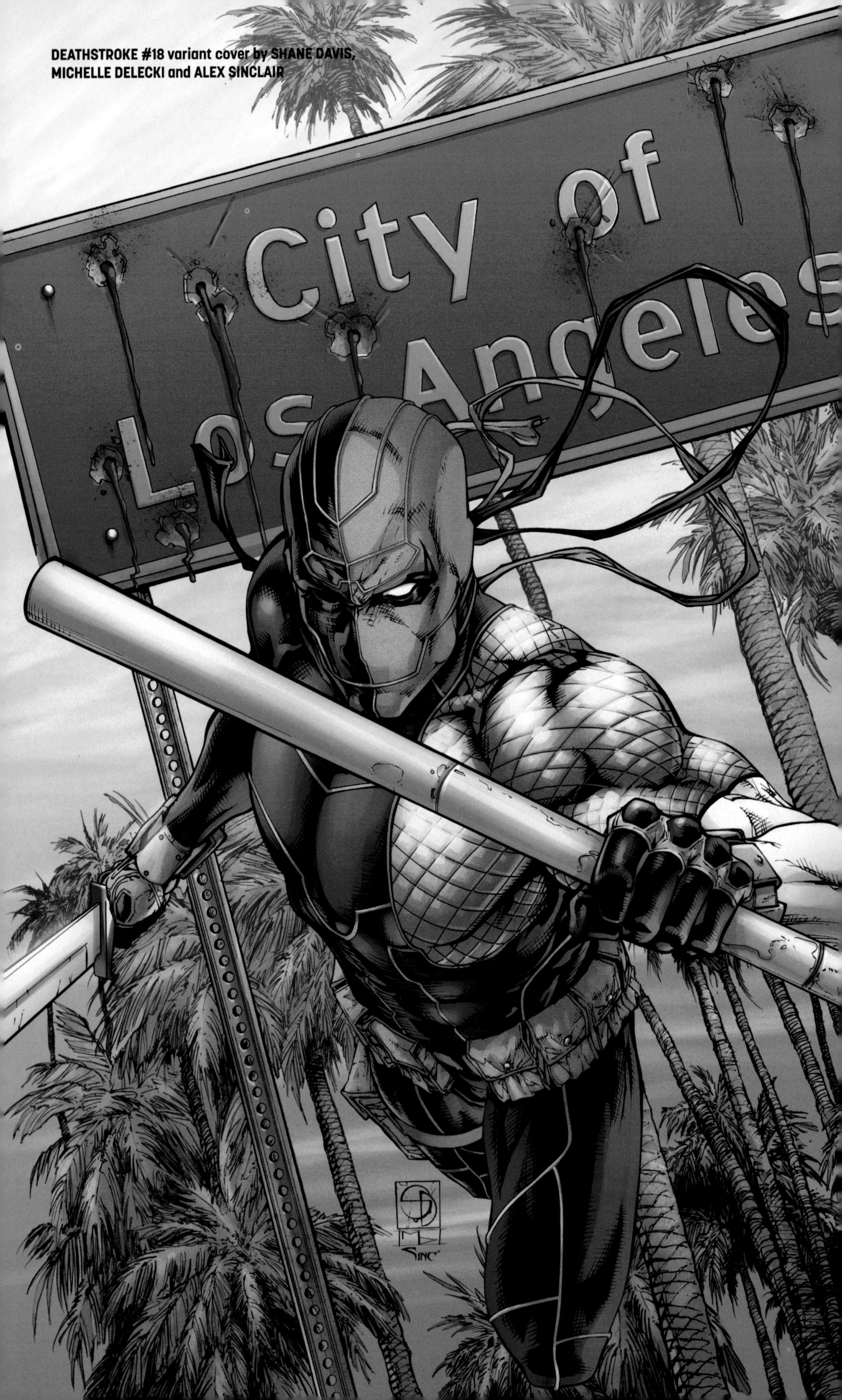
City of

DEATHSTROKE #18 variant cover by SHANE DAVIS, MICHELLE DELECKI and ALEX SINCLAIR

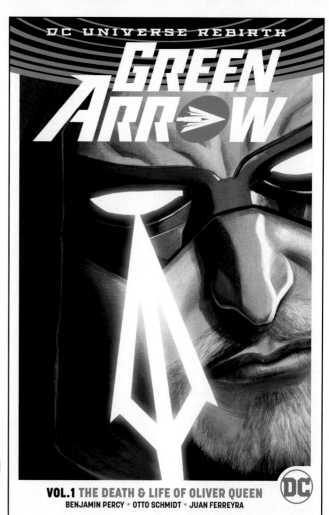

"The world that Schmidt creates feels real and lived in." – **NEWSARAMA**

"The artwork from Otto Schmidt is delightful and quirky." – **NERDIST**

**DC UNIVERSE REBIRTH**

# GREEN ARROW

## VOL. 1: THE DEATH & LIFE OF OLIVER QUEEN

BENJAMIN PERCY

with OTTO SCHMIDT & JUAN FERREYRA

**BATGIRL AND
THE BIRDS OF PREY VOL. 1:
WHO IS ORACLE?**

**TITANS VOL. 1:
THE RETURN OF WALLY WEST**

**DEATHSTROKE VOL. 1:
THE PROFESSIONAL**

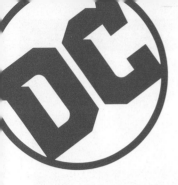

"It's nice to see one of the best comics of the late '80s return so strongly."
**– Comic Book Resources**

"It's high energy from page one through to the last page." **– BATMAN NEWS**

**DC UNIVERSE REBIRTH**

# SUICIDE SQUAD

**VOL. 1: THE BLACK VAULT**

ROB WILLIAMS
with JIM LEE and others

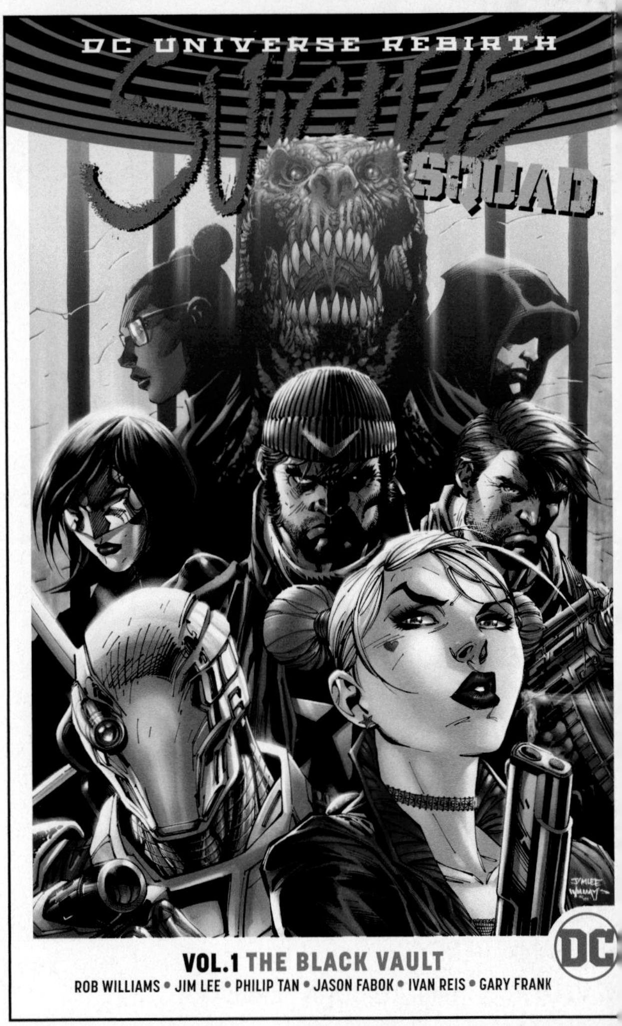
DC UNIVERSE REBIRTH
SUICIDE SQUAD
VOL.1 THE BLACK VAULT
ROB WILLIAMS • JIM LEE • PHILIP TAN • JASON FABOK • IVAN REIS • GARY FRANK

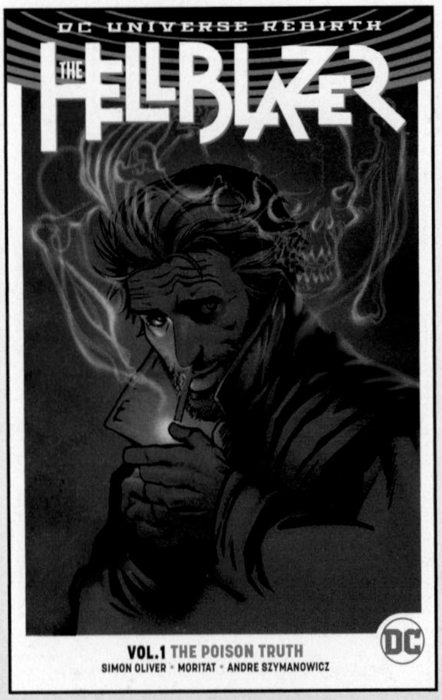
DC UNIVERSE REBIRTH
THE HELLBLAZER
VOL.1 THE POISON TRUTH
SIMON OLIVER • MORITAT • ANDRE SZYMANOWICZ

**THE HELLBLAZER VOL. 1: THE POISON TRUTH**

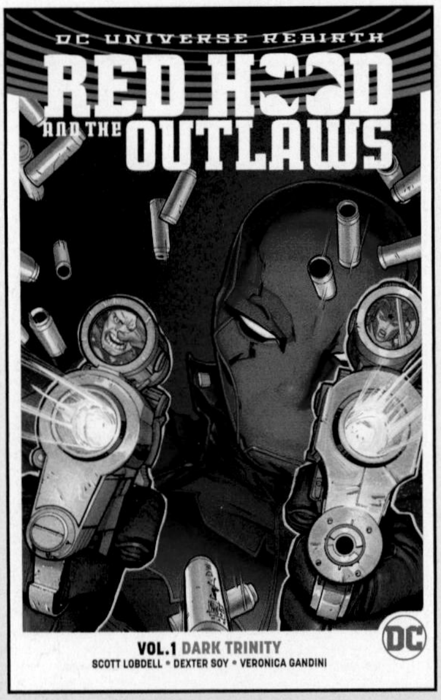
DC UNIVERSE REBIRTH
RED HOOD AND THE OUTLAWS
VOL.1 DARK TRINITY
SCOTT LOBDELL • DEXTER SOY • VERONICA GANDINI

**RED HOOD AND THE OUTLAWS VOL. 1: DARK TRINITY**

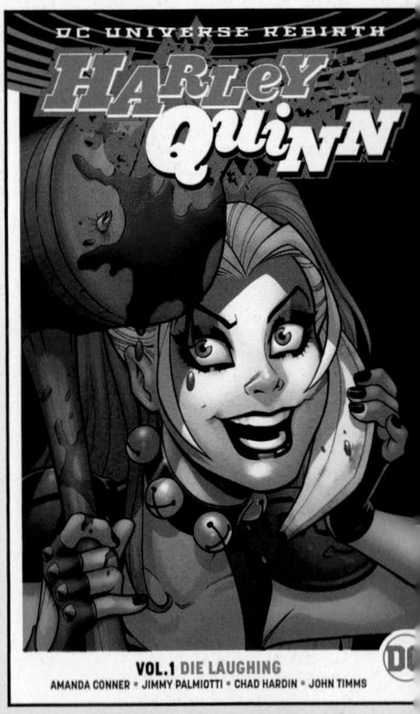
DC UNIVERSE REBIRTH
HARLEY QUINN
VOL.1 DIE LAUGHING
AMANDA CONNER • JIMMY PALMIOTTI • CHAD HARDIN • JOHN TIMMS

**HARLEY QUINN VOL. 1: DIE LAUGHING**



Get more DC graphic novels wherever comics and books are sold!